# CONVERGENCES

*Inventories of the Present*

Edward W. Said, General Editor

# THE HAUNTING OF

## OF

# *Sylvia Plath*

JACQUELINE ROSE

Harvard University Press
Cambridge, Massachusetts
1992

Library of Congress Cataloging-in-Publication Data
Rose, Jacqueline.
  The haunting of Sylvia Plath / Jacqueline Rose.
    p.   cm. — (Convergences)
  Includes bibliographical references (p.      ) and index.
  ISBN 0-674-38225-0
  1. Plath, Sylvia. 2. Poets, American—20th century—Biography.
I. Title. II. Series: Convergences.
PS3566.L27Z85   1992
811'.54—dc20                                                91-26313
[B]                                                              CIP

*for Jen White
and in memory of Allon*

# CONTENTS

Abbreviations     viii

Preface     ix

Acknowledgements     xiii

Introduction     1

1   'She'     11

2   The Body of the Writing     29

3   The Archive     65

4   No Fantasy without Protest     114

5   Sadie Peregrine     165

6   'Daddy'     205

Notes     239

Bibliography     273

Index     283

# ABBREVIATIONS

*LH* *Letters Home: Correspondence 1950–1963*, selected and edited with a commentary by Aurelia Schober Plath, London: Faber & Faber, 1975.

*Johnny Panic* *Johnny Panic and the Bible of Dreams and Other Prose Writings*, introduction by Ted Hughes, London: Faber & Faber, 1977; revised edition, 1979.

*CP* *Collected Poems*, edited by Ted Hughes, London: Faber & Faber, 1981.

*J* *The Journals of Sylvia Plath*, Frances McCullough, Editor, Ted Hughes, Consulting Editor, New York: Random House (Ballantine), 1982.

Smith The Sylvia Plath Collection, Smith College Library, Rare Book Room, Smith College, Northampton, Massachusetts.

Lilly The Sylvia Plath Collection, Lilly Library, Indiana University, Bloomington, Indiana.

*Note:* Whenever reference is made to extracts from the Smith and Lilly Collections which have been omitted from published texts, the page of the published version where the omission occurs is given in parentheses after the full reference.

# PREFACE

Interpretation of a literary work is endless. There is no one true place where it can be halted. It cannot be arrested at the point where it comes into conflict with how a writer sees their own depiction of others or of themselves. Once a piece of writing has been put into circulation, it ceases – except in the most material sense – to be the property of its author. Nor can it be controlled and limited by the views of any one individual, no matter how close to the subject they may have been, or still feel themselves to be. In writing this book, I have faced what I believe to be an attempt to exercise such control and to impose limits on what may be said about the writings of Sylvia Plath. This attempt has been made in the name of protection of privacy, of 'factual' accuracy and of the ethics of scholarship. It has been reinforced by the threat, overt and implied, of legal action. The publication of this book therefore represents an assertion of the diversity of literary interpretation and of the right of every reader of Sylvia Plath to form her or his own view of the meanings and significance of her work.

Throughout this book, my focus is on writing – its own process, the way it has been edited, presented and read. This is not a biography. I am never claiming to speak about the life, never attempting to establish the facts about the lived existence of Sylvia Plath. First, because what I am interested in is writing, in what – independently of a writer's more concretely lived reality – it can *do*; secondly, because accounts of the life – and nowhere has this been demonstrated more clearly than in relation to Plath – have to base themselves on a spurious claim to knowledge, they have to arbitrate between competing and often incompatible versions of what took place.

Working on Plath, the thing that has seized my interest

most strongly is the circulation of fantasy in her texts, how she writes of psychic processes, the way she lets us – with what strikes me as extraordinary generosity – into her mind. These things are private and intimate, although Plath also demonstrates the importance of fantasy for the widest sweep of our cultural and historical life. Fantasy should not be confused with reality – it is, like literature, one way that individuals work with and transform what their inner and outer reality can be. But given Plath's endless return to the world of the psyche, to suggest, as it has been put to me, that one should not discuss fantasy in relation to Plath's writing, because it impinges too closely on reality (hers but not only hers), is tantamount to saying that one cannot write about Sylvia Plath.

To write about Sylvia Plath is, inevitably, to raise and confront difficult ethical issues – about the legitimate scope of interpretation; about the rights of literary interpretation to discuss living as well as dead writers; about the difficulty involved in analysing textual figures when these appear to refer to real persons, both living and dead; about how or whether to use material that has been omitted from Plath's published writings, given that to do so can involve an infringement of privacy, but not to do so is to accept uncritically a version of Plath's writing that is not complete, not her own. It is a problem for a writer on Sylvia Plath that she encounters the living as figures or images in Plath's writing, as the writer whom she worked with most closely, and again as the holders of copyright in her work.

As will be seen from Chapter 3, 'The Archive', the literary estate of Sylvia Plath is under the control of Ted Hughes, who has been represented in recent years by his sister, Olwyn Hughes. As a necessary part of the process of publishing this book, they both saw a late draft of the text and made copious and detailed comments. Many of these were both useful and illuminating and have been incorporated into the text. I was happy to make a number of changes where the previously known details of an incident were incomplete, where it was a question of more fully representing their views on the editing of Plath's work, or in order to indicate where there was a disagreement between themselves and other people about the history and processes of editing involved. But my overall reading of this editing and of passages omitted from Plath's published writing, and my interpretation of one poem in particular, 'The Rabbit Catcher' in Chapter 4, have been the object of heated and unresolved dispute.

In correspondence with the Hughes's, this book was called 'evil'. Its publisher was told it would not appear. At one point an attempt was made to revoke previously granted permissions to quote from Plath's work. I was asked to remove my reading of 'The Rabbit Catcher', and when I refused, I was told by Ted Hughes that my analysis would be damaging for Plath's (now adult) children and that speculation of the kind I was seen as engaging in about Sylvia Plath's sexual identity would in some countries be 'grounds for homicide'.

It is one of the paradoxes of my interaction with the Sylvia Plath estate that, as the demands on me have become more and more restrictive and impossible to meet, so it has become more evident how distressing the situation is for all those who were, and who become, involved in Plath's work. It is understandable that people who were as close as they to Sylvia Plath should find themselves in strong disagreement with the interpretations of those who comment on her writing. This is perhaps the inevitable result of the way literary analysis can seem, to those who had a lived relation to the writer, to have a purely personal significance or biographical reference that was not intended by the critic and which will not be understood as such by the reader who is not linked to the writer's life in the same way.

It is one thing, however, to acknowledge that difficulty, quite another to acquiesce to requests, or rather demands, to mould my own readings to fit Olwyn or Ted Hughes's gloss on what Plath has to say about her life, or to fit their understanding of the meanings of her literary works. To block literary interpretation on the grounds of special, privileged, involvement or interest is to sever the link between the work and the wider meanings through which a culture responds to it and keeps it alive. In this context, what matters is not the boundary between living and dead writers, but the distinction between those writers who live through the responses they give rise to, and those who – for want of such attention – fall into oblivion or merely die.

On the points over which we have failed to agree, it appears that for Ted and Olwyn Hughes there is only one version of reality, one version – their version – of the truth. But how should one respond when one is told that a remark has been lifted out of Plath's journals on the grounds that it is not only 'damaging' but 'untrue'? In fact, I do not suggest that we can, with any certainty, believe either Plath's statement or its repudiation, but that together they confront us with a moment of indecision which in turn generates anxiety – an anxiety that can be productive if we allow it to indicate how uncertain truth can be. My suggestion throughout this book is that we should try, as I believe Plath did constantly in her writing, to stay with that anxiety and not resolve it. Nothing demonstrates more to me the futility of the too hasty resolution than the demand for singular truth which, throughout these negotiations, has been directed to me by the estate of Sylvia Plath.

In one of Ted Hughes's strongest statements about Plath, he wrote that she went straight for the 'central, unacceptable things'. In my reading, Plath regularly unsettles certainties of language, identity and sexuality, troubling the forms of cohesion on which 'civilised' culture systematically and often oppressively relies. My suggestion that this might be the case, specifically in the field of sexuality, has provoked the strongest reactions from the estate. The question then arises – who is to decide the limits of the unacceptable? Who is to decide what it is acceptable for the unacceptable to be?

What follows is one reading of the work of Sylvia Plath, one part of a story that has clearly not come to an end.

*March 1991*

# ACKNOWLEDGEMENTS

Many people have contributed to the writing of this book. My thanks to Rachel Bowlby, Neil Hertz and Cora Kaplan for reading and commenting on the whole of the manuscript with such insight. Cora Kaplan's pioneering work on women and poetry has been a constant reference point for me in thinking about Sylvia Plath. Thanks to Alan Sinfield for his detailed comments on Chapters 4 and 5, and to Sally Alexander for her continuing support and for her comments on the Introduction. Thanks to Ann Rosalind Jones for conversations about Plath over the years, and for all her help when I was working on the Plath papers at Smith College in 1988. The librarians at Smith College Library, especially Ruth Mortimer, and at the Lilly Library were immensely helpful. I am grateful to the Leverhulme Trust for a grant that allowed me to complete the writing of the book, to Sussex University for financial assistance and to Stuart Laing for all his support. Special thanks to Brian Raymond, who read the manuscript more than once with immense forbearing and provided crucial comments that I simply could not have managed without. My debt to him is inestimable. Ruthie Petrie read and commented on the manuscript for Virago; my thanks to her for all the work she did on the text. I am especially grateful to Ursula Owen – for her encouragement, her kindness, her comments on the whole text, and for turning editing into friendship. Finally, my thanks above all to John Barrell for his support, for seeing the project through from the beginning, and for bringing to it his own skill in reading poetry while always understanding what I was trying to do. The book is also for him.

# INTRODUCTION

Sylvia Plath haunts our culture. She is – for many – a shadowy figure whose presence draws on and compels. What she may be asking for is never clear, although it seems highly unlikely that she is asking for what she gets. Execrated and idolised, Plath hovers between the furthest poles of positive and negative appraisal; she hovers in the space of what is most extreme, most violent, about appraisal, valuation, about moral and literary assessment as such. Above all she stirs things up. More than any other writer, perhaps, she lays bare the forms of psychic investment which lie, barely concealed, behind the processes through which a culture – Western literary culture – evaluates and perpetuates itself.

Plath wrote a great deal about haunting and ghosts. 'All the long gone darlings,' she called them; 'they get back, though, soon, soon.' Mostly by means of festive occasions and symbolic events – wakes, weddings, childbirths or a family barbecue – but in fact 'any touch, taste, tang's fit for these outlaws to ride home on'. The traffic is two-way: the ghosts ride home, the living are hauled in: 'How they grip us through thin and thick'. Plath called this poem 'All the Dead Dears', and then wrote a short story with the same title, the only title that repeats itself in her work. Mrs Nellie Meehan sees ghosts: 'Not ghosts, exactly, Dora, but *presences*', 'They're waiting', 'They come back', she says: 'And so they gossiped gently on, calling up the names of the quick and the dead, reliving each past event as if it had no beginning and no end, but existed, vivid and irrevocable, from the beginning of time, and would continue to exist long after their own voices were stilled.'

At the end of 'All the Dead Dears', Nellie is called away by the dead Maisie Edwards, who greets her 'like a glad hostess who has waited long for a tardy guest'. In Fay Weldon's novel *Down Among the Women*, there are two characters, X and Y, who are never named. Husband and wife, they are both artists. X leaves Y for Helen. Y dies and then comes to get Helen. 'Will you join me?' Y asks. 'Wait,' Helen replies, 'I will be with you soon.' Calling her

1

characters Y and X, Weldon both resists and invites the association with Sylvia Plath and Ted Hughes. She thereby makes her characters formulaic, the abstract emblems of something about men and women artists and the power struggles between them, of something about the shared destiny of women, of something about repetition and death. More crucially, perhaps, she makes them representative of something about the constraints surrounding the story of Sylvia Plath. She may be endlessly present within the culture, but her presence also seems to open up a rent or gap in the world. The injunction to go on talking about her is matched by an equal injunction not to say too much.

The image of Plath as a ghost requires some qualification. In another of her early poems, 'The Lady and the Earthenware Head', the speaker decides to rid herself of a clay model of her head, but cannot find a place where it will be free of the molestations of birds and boys. She contemplates the ash-heap, but it could be stolen; then she drops it in a mountain lake, but it surfaces, 'lewdly beckoning', out of the water. Finally she resolves to lodge it ceremoniously in the crotch of a willow tree, from where it can survey the world beneath. But this gesture, which saves it, produces a greater crisis than would have followed had it been ill-treated or destroyed. Despite her wrung hands, tears and prayers, the head steadfastly refuses to vanish, refuses to diminish 'by one jot its basilisk look of love'. There is no getting rid of this head. The more she tries to be free of it, the more it returns. The effigy haunts the original. It loves and terrifies the very being it was intended to represent.

This poem adds a crucial dimension to the difficulty of writing about Plath — or rather, it issues a warning. What we are dealing with is, obviously enough, not Plath herself but her representations, her own writing, together with all the other utterances which have come to crowd it — joining in the conversation, as one might say. Often, as we will see, it is technically impossible to separate Plath's voice from those who speak for her ( a large part of her writing was published and, more importantly, edited after her death). Plath's writings and the surrounding voices stand in effigy for her, they speak in her name. It is this effigy that haunts the culture. This is of course true of any writer who is no longer living — in fact of any writer, whether living or not. It takes on an added significance in relation to Plath, because the editorial control and intervention have been so visible, but also because of the intensity with which writing on Plath seems to invest itself in the idea of her person. So bitter have been the quarrels about Plath, it is hardly surprising that at moments it seems as if the effigy, like the earthenware head of her poem, haunts her.

Above all things, Sylvia Plath desired fame. As she put it at one point in her *Journals*: 'it is sad only to be able to mouth other poets; I want someone to mouth me'. There is a well-known fairy story in which a man is granted three wishes, and tormented by the too literal fulfilment of casually expressed desires, he has to use his third wish to undo the baneful effects of the first two. At moments, it feels as if Plath might be in something of the same position. Certainly, with hindsight, she seems to have bitten off more than she could (be expected to) chew. As she put it herself, reviewing a biography of Byron's wife in the *New Statesman* in December 1962: 'a sudden muzz of camp followers and rhetoric had swallowed Annabella'.

It is one of the ironies of Plath's story that she should have so coveted fame, and then received it, come to represent it, so dramatically at its most deadly and perverse. For one of the things Plath surely demonstrates about our general culture is the perverse component (voyeurism and sadism) of public acclaim. If, too, this process can be called deadly, it is because Plath herself has also become a figure for death. Death in the shape of a woman, femininity as deadly – we will see how these two come together in one significant strand of critical appraisal of her work.

It has often been remarked that commentary on Plath tends to split into two antagonistic camps. There are those who pathologise Plath, freely diagnose her as schizophrenic or psychotic, read her writings as symptom or warning, something we should both admire and avoid. Diagnosis of Plath tends to make her culpable – guilt by association with the troubles of the unconscious mind. The spectre of psychic life rises up in her person as a monumental affront for which she is punished. Feminism has rightly responded to this form of criticism by stressing the representative nature of Plath's inner drama, the extent to which it focuses the inequities ( the pathology) of a patriarchal world. But in so doing, it has tended to inherit the framework of the critical language it seeks to reject. Plath becomes innocent – man and patriarchy are to blame. More important, psychic life is stripped of its own logic; it becomes the pure effect of social injustice, wholly subservient to the outside world which it

3

unfailingly reflects. Anything negative or violent in her writing is then read as a stage in a myth of self-emergence, something which Plath achieved in her poetry, if not in her life – an allegory of selfhood which settles the unconscious and ideally leaves its troubles behind.

It is, however, hardly surprising that the unconscious and its difficulty has had to be jettisoned by feminist criticism, when we see, in relation to Plath, the extent to which it has been abused. In fact, despite first appearances, those diagnoses of Plath remove the problem of the unconscious even more than the criticism that has come in reply. There is nothing like the concept of a purely individual pathology for allowing us, with immense comfort, to conjure it all away (her problem, not mine; or, talking about danger as a way of feeling safe). For me one of the central challenges presented by Plath's writing has been to find a way of looking at the most unsettling and irreducible dimensions of psychic processes which she figures in her writing without turning them against her – without, therefore, turning her into a case.

But if I do not, at any point in this book, pass judgement on the issue of Plath's pathology, it is also because I do not believe we can take writing as unproblematic evidence for the psychological condition or attributes of the one who writes. Commentaries on Plath give us the measure of this difficulty, precisely in so far as they treat the texts as the person and then disagree so strongly as to what these texts reveal. What we can do, however, is locate the mechanisms of the writing (its process), but the question remains of the relationship which holds between the writing and the life (expression, denial, compensation, to suggest just three). Writing may be a revelation of character, it may even be a form of madness, but for the one who writes, it can equally be a way of staying sane. Daniel Schreber whose memoirs were the subject of a famous case-study by Freud, had a whole delusional system going at the same time as he was a high court judge. It is a truism to say that writing something very nasty can be a way of keeping nice.

Even from inside the space of her writing, Plath offers no singular form or vision on which such a diagnosis could safely alight. From the poems to the stories, to the letters, to the journals, to the novel, what is most striking is the differences between these various utterances, each one contradicting as much as completing the others, each one no less true for the disparity which relates them and sets them apart. Plath's relentless return in so many different forms to the question of her own subjectivity appears to illustrate first of all that relationship of indirect representation which Freud set at the heart of our attempts to figure ourselves in language or speech. For Freud, the utterance can only ever be partial, scarred as it is by the division between conscious and unconscious – by the gap, but also the mutual interference, between what we choose to say and what is repeatedly excluded from the bounds of our speech.

It is that provisional, precarious nature of self-representation which appears so strikingly from the multiple forms in which Plath writes. What she presents us with, therefore is not only the difference of writing from the person who produces it, but also the division internal to language, the difference of writing from itself. It is then all the more striking that so many critics have felt it incumbent upon themselves to produce a unified version of Plath as writer and as woman, as if that particular form of fragmentation or indirect representation were something which, through the completion of their own analysis of her, they could somehow repair. The frequent diagnoses of Plath seem to me to have as at least one of their effects, if not purposes, that they have transposed into a fact of her individual pathology the no less difficult problem of the contradictory, divided and incomplete nature of representation itself.

Inside her writing, Plath confronts us with the limits of our (and her) knowledge. In this context it becomes more than a commonplace of recent literary analysis to insist in advance that there is no direct access to the writer, that the only thing available for commentary and analysis is the text. We do not know Plath (nor indeed Hughes). What we do know is what they give us in writing, and what they give us in writing is there to be read. In this book, in the analysis of those writings, I am never talking of real people, but of textual entities (Y and X) whose more than real reality, I will be arguing, goes beyond them to encircle us all. It has been objected that writing on Plath is a fantasia with no purchase on, or even interest in, the truth. This book starts from the assumption that Plath is a fantasy. But, rather than seeing this as a problem, it asks what her writing, and responses to it, might reveal about fantasy as such. Far from being an obstacle, fantasy will appear in what follows as one of the key terms through which Plath's writing, and responses to her writing, can be thought.

One of the most striking things about the story of Plath is the way that, despite all of this, it seems so effortlessly to transmute itself into soap opera. On the one hand Plath's writing vanishes into the conditions of its own utterance; on the other she, and those associated with her, seem to come out on the other side with all the compelling reality of the most familiar of family scenes. As Plath put it in relation to a saga not dissimilar to one renowned version of her own: 'Liz Taylor is getting Eddie Fisher away from Debbie Reynolds, who appears cherubic, round-faced, wronged, in pin curls and house robe – Mike Todd hardly cold. How odd these events affect one so. Why?'

The answer to her question may be hidden inside her own description – in those symmetrical images of woman as seductress and as wronged. Soap operas are one of the means of negotiating the stereotypes of the culture. They offer vicarious pleasure and invite moral judgement: sexual narrative as gossip ('so they gossiped gently on . . . as if [each event] had no beginning and no end'), morality as a form of licensed pleasure in itself. The pull of the Plath story is that it calls up a language of victimisation and blame with such force. Pathology, as I have already said, makes her guilty – her tragedy the inevitable outcome of the troubles of her mind. Patriarchy means that man, meaning Hughes or the male sex he stands for, is to blame – the woman internalises, turns against herself, the violence of the world outside. Above all, someone or something has to be responsible for those aspects of negativity and violence that Plath articulated with such stunning clarity in her work. As we watch this pattern unfold, it is clear that the question of guilt, in relation to Plath, is carrying the question of what we can bear to think about ourselves. For in neither of these readings is it acceptable that there might be a component of psychic negativity with no singular origin, which no one will take away for us, for which no one can be blamed. Thus Plath becomes a symptom – or rather, responses to her writing become a symptom – of one part of the cultural repressed (it is not her problem, it is ours).

If Plath is a ghost of our culture, therefore, it is above all because of what she leads that culture to reveal about itself. We say 'he did it'. The proposition doesn't work. But nor does the proposition that she did it all – only – to herself. And the failure of both of these propositions turns them into a question that we have to address to ourselves. Why do we want or try to make them? What form of logic is involved? And what does this process of distribution – blame/no blame, inner/outer worlds – tell us about the way we unconsciously organise, give meaning to, generate, our partici- pation in the widest processes of sexual and cultural life? It is not to deny real injustice against women to say that the image of the wronged woman can close off difficult areas of sexuality and fantasy for women, leaving a residue of subjectivity, its pleasures and dangers, unexplained. Plath wrote about wrongs both inside and outside the mind, tracking the links between them, tracing out the complex logic which binds and negotiates their often antag- onistic claims. Her writing crosses the very boundary repeatedly marked out in her name.

This residue is historical, political. Not just because the personal is political – for a long time feminism has insisted that what goes on in private is a political matter that concerns us all – but because psychic life in itself will not be relegated to the private, it will not stay in its proper place. It shows up on the side of the historical reality to which it is often opposed. Nowhere is this clearer than in Plath's own use of historical reference, where it is always the implication of psyche in history, and history in psyche, that is involved. Plath has been criticised for the way she weaves her personal mythology into historical moments and events, notably fascism and the Holocaust. She has been accused of trivialising history and aggrandising herself, of turning real horror into fantasy, of taking advantage of such horror by using it as a metaphor for the discovery and expression of herself.

I see the presence of these images in her writing as revealing something of the way fantasy operates inside historical process. Fascism is in fact one of the few historical moments which historians have generally recognised as needing psychoanalytic concepts of desire and identification in order for it to be fully understood. At this level fascism could be described as the historical annexing, or collective seizure, of unconscious drives (this does not, of course, exhaust the historical reality of fascism). In fascism, the realm of politics reveals itself as massively invested with the most private and intimate images of our fantasy life. Plath's writing presents us with those images at work, producing what I see as her own sexual iconography, as well as her own diagnosis, of one of the sub-texts of fascism. In doing so, she provides an extraordinary instance of the inseparability of history and subjectivity. Her work

7

can be seen as offering what is a unique but also representative inmixing of these terms.

There is, therefore, another truism to be made in relation to Plath, one whose implications stretch way beyond those most obviously recognisable (famous or infamous) moments of historical allusion in her writing. There is no history outside its subjective realisation, its being-for-the-subject, just as there is no subjectivity uncoloured by the history to which it belongs. The division between history and subjectivity, between external and internal reality, between the trials of the world and the trials of the mind, is a false one. The distribution of opposites which has so relentlessly attached itself to Plath is the consequence of a false premiss, a false antagonism, from the start.

Before leaving this particular history, however, we should note how it appears, and not only in Plath's own writing, as a form of haunting in itself. For when Plath alludes to fascism – and, more specifically, to the Holocaust – she is evoking that piece of collective memory which it is hardest for the culture to recall, hardest for those who did not live through it, hardest often – as their own testimony suggests – for those who did. Finding its way back into memory, it then appears like the return of the repressed – a fragment of the cultural unconscious that will not go away.

Most striking across all these instances are the forms of repetition, the constant overlapping of the most discomforting aspects of Plath's writing and her own status in the culture, or between her own status in the culture and the cultural phenomena of which she writes. Plath is a fantasy, she writes fantasy. She is a symptom, she writes the symptom. She anticipates, uncannily; she retaliates in advance. I have said that she haunts and is haunted by the culture; she writes of those most traumatic historical moments when a culture comes to haunt – can only become a phantom of – itself.

Culture, however, is neither a singular entity nor a neutral term. It has its own history, its own divisions: amongst others, the division between the literary and the non-literary, between high and low art. Plath has been made into an emblem for the flight of poetry – poetry as the expression of a transcendent selfhood, poetry as rising above the dregs of the culture which it leaves behind. The idea of a residue can refer to the unmanageable, vulgar bits and pieces of the culture as much as to those of the mind. Plath wrote fiction for magazines, expecially women's magazines, throughout her career.

Yet despite her commitment to the field of popular fiction, over and again she is discussed as if her poetry – specifically her very last poems – were the only part of her writing that should be read. The way those late poems are detached from the body of her other writing becomes a little allegory for the process whereby culture divides itself up, discriminates against one part of itself. Once again, this is a boundary that Plath transgresses: certainly she writes high poetry, but she also writes – and very often prefers to write – low prose.

There is an extraordinary collage that Plath put together in 1960. At the centre, Eisenhower sits beaming at his desk. Into his hands, Plath has inserted a run of playing cards; on the desk lie digestive tablets ('Tums') and a camera on which a cutout of a model in a swimsuit is posed. Attached to this model is the slogan 'Every Man Wants His Woman On A Pedestal'; a bomber is pointing at her abdomen; in the corner there is a small picture of Nixon making a speech. A couple sleeping with eye shields are accompanied by the caption: 'It's HIS AND HER time all over America'. In the top left-hand corner of the picture, this news item: 'America's most famous living preacher whose religious revival campaigns have reached tens of millions of people both in the US and abroad.' There are moments of prophecy in this collage – Nixon and the religious revival of the New Right. There are also clichés of sexual difference, together with a feminist association between male fantasy ('woman on a pedestal') and war. The perfect body of the woman is a target of fantasy and aggression, perfect couples look as if they are blind, the perfect political body seems to be suffering from the undigested surfeit of itself – another caption refers to Consolidated Aluminium (starting salary, fringe benefits and pension rights).

Like all collages, this collage offers itself as a set of fragments. It is also not unlike a picture puzzle or *rebus*, which is the model Freud offered for the language of dreams. It shows Plath immersed in war, consumerism, photography, and religion at the very moment she was starting to write the *Ariel* poems. It shows her incorporating the multiple instances of the very culture against which these same poems, or one vision of these poems, is so often set.

It is tempting to see this collage as an image of postmodern culture which tends to be described in terms of abandon, a superseding or crowding out of any logic, whether of society or the mind. There is also a feminist version of this image which has been

9

specifically applied to Plath – one which sees the privilege of femininity in the disordered, fragmented, shifting subjectivity which women oppose to a destructively linear world. But the specific details of Plath's collage, and of her writing more generally, are too precisely focused for that. Plath works across boundaries, psychic, political, cultural, but the contours of their opposing elements never completely lose their shape.

In this book, Plath will be seen as offering different visions of poetry and culture, of sexuality, of the body and writing, in their relation to each other. Plath is not consistent. It has been the persistent attempt to impose a consistency on her which has been so damaging – whether as diagnosis or celebration of her work. But to say that Plath is not consistent is not to say that she does not articulate something very precise about some of the most difficult points of contestation in our contemporary cultural and political life. Plath is neither one identity, nor multiple identities simply dispersing themselves. She writes at the point of tension – pleasure/danger, your fault/my fault, high/low culture – without resolution or dissipation of what produces the clash between the two.

There has been a long-running debate in recent literary criticism about whether the author, in her or his subjectivity and intention, can really be known; whether anything takes place in literary analysis other than the critical institution revealing a truth (any number of truths) about itself. I read Plath as a type of analyst of her critics and culture alike. If Plath is a ghost of the culture, one thing that will be clear in everything that follows is the extent to which she haunts me.

# 1

## 'SHE'

We have been told that there is a Plath fantasia which deforms the truth of her writing, distorts the facts of her life.[1] To begin with, at least, it might be worth taking this argument at its word. What happens if we ask, not what truth does the Plath fantasia *conceal*, but what truth does it *express*? Not about Plath herself in this first instance, but about the discourse of literary criticism. I want to start by looking at the worst of what has been done to Plath – not simply to castigate it, nor to repeat, with the ultimate desire of bypassing it, the truism that she has so endlessly been constituted as a myth. If it seems appropriate to start here, it is because no writer seems to reveal so clearly, so grotesquely, the forms of fantasy, of psychic and sexual investment, that can be involved in the constitution of literature itself.

Here are three quotations from different critics. The first is from Edward Butscher describing his attempt to write his biography of Plath in an essay called 'In Search of Sylvia'. He is referring to the friends, teachers and classmates he tracked down as 'witnesses' for the book:

> . . . 'witnesses' is appropriate as I soon came to view myself as a literary Lew Archer in pursuit of another violated little girl, another doomed Oedipal victim, who had been as contradictory as she had been gifted.[2]

The second is by Richard Howard in an essay, 'Sylvia Plath: "And I Have No Face, I Have Wanted To Efface Myself"', in Charles Newman's 1970 anthology *The Art of Sylvia Plath*:

> There is no pathos in the accents of these final poems . . . only a certain pride, the pride of an utter and ultimate surrender (like the pride of O, naked and chained in her owl mask, as she asks Sir Stephen for death).[3]

The third is from Hugh Kenner in an article called 'Sincerity Kills' from Gary Lane's 1979 collection *Sylvia Plath: New Views on the Poetry*:

11

As who should say, 'The price of absorption in pornography is an incremental deadening of the spirit, an attenuation of the already frail belief in the sanctity of personhood. I shall now show you a pornographic film.' All her life a reader had been someone to manipulate.[4]

I came across these quotations at random when I was preparing for the first time to teach Sylvia Plath. If in one sense they seem to require no commentary, it might none the less be worth trying to uncover something of their logic in order to pull them back, and our own reaction to them, from the realm of the safely outrageous or joke. Jokes they indeed are, but precisely by being so they reveal a particular economy of fantasy, one which passes from a recognition of the woman as ultimate victim, sexualised through that very recognition (the Lew Archer hunt), through the pornographic scenario of the woman's utter surrender, to arrive finally at the accusation of the woman as pornographer (the trajectory can equally work the other way round). Thus Plath becomes the ultimate manipulator (crudely, the artist of the hand job), accountable for – or even guilty of – the different sexual scenarios that these male critics have generated to meet her.

But what each of these quotations also suggests is that the drama rests in the relationship between the writer and her audience in a very specific way. It is a crisis of *address* that Plath produces in the critic, as if to accuse: 'Who is she talking to?' or 'By what right does she speak?' or 'What is it that she is doing to, or withholding from, me?' What matters, therefore, is not just the sexuality of these responses to Plath and their too easily predictable misogyny, but the way that the sexuality and the misogyny belong on the boundary between the literary text and its reader. As Shoshona Felman puts it, in her analysis of Henry James's short story 'The Turn of the Screw' and its critics, the scandal provoked by the text belongs in the realm of a 'reading effect'.[5] It resides not just inside the work but in our relationship to it – in how it gets to us, as we might say. The outrage of Plath – what, at least partly, calls up the intensity of sexual reaction – may therefore have something to do with a crisis provoked at the furthest edge of the literary, at that point where the literary work recognises, situates and delimits itself, or in this case fails in that delimitation.

This might become clearer if we go back to the quotations and note how, if they do have a logic, it is one which in each case is based on a contradiction. In Butscher's case, it is the contradiction between the image of a violated little girl and the image of an Oedipal victim, or rather between that 'Oedipal' and that 'victim'. For it was precisely the concept of the Oedipus complex in Freud's work that shattered the image of the hysteric as victim by introducing childhood fantasy into the understanding of psychic disturbance, and thus throwing into question his earlier belief that hysteria could best be understood in terms of the violation of little girls (this is Freud's famous relinquishment of the seduction theory of hysteria, which has been the object of much recent critique[6]). But that Butscher wants his little girl violated *and* Oedipal is a way of having your cake and eating it too. Let her be utterly done over and somewhere desiring it at the same time (the classic pornographic scenario).

The same contradiction is there in the Howard example, which precisely activates that scenario through the explicit reference to *The Story of O*. The *Ariel* poems are totally without pathos, expressive only of a certain pride, which may seem the more active emotion, except that this same pride is the pride of total surrender asking (the man, inevitably) for death. So the quotation makes the same move, gets into the same muddle as to where sexuality and desire can be located. What is the sexual distribution of roles? Active male, passive female, or the female active in her pursuit of the ultimate passivity (death)? Who, finally, is accountable to whom? Only in the Kenner quote is that contradiction subordinated to the idea of a self-knowing and willed manipulation. Plath disavows her intention to do it to the reader, and then does it all the more viciously all the same. If I, the critic, cannot sort out, define, control what it is that this woman is doing sexually in her writing, then it must be that she is doing it (the critical confusion) to me.

Psychoanalysis would recognise in this the mechanism of projection, to be distinguished from that of transference, which has become current in recent discussion of psychoanalysis and literature. In Henry James's story, it is not clear to the reader whether the governess is the saviour of the children in her charge, or whether she hallucinates the very evil she thinks she is protecting them against. This is the question the text holds in suspense. By trying to answer it, critics have simply repeated the drama of the governess herself, entering into the argument that the writing is having with itself. The implications of this are far-reaching. By repeating the demand of the governess that the events in which she is implicated should, in terms of their origin and destination, unequivocally make sense, these critics have acted out one of the central demands of a whole tradition of literary critical thought which rests its authority in the clarity of its own activity as well as on the aesthetic unity it looks for in the literary text.

For Shoshona Felman, this is the mechanism of transference, first restricted by Freud to the field of neurosis, where patients transfer on to the analyst during the course of treatment their unconscious fantasies and desires. In relation to literature, transference refers to the way critics read their unconscious into the text, repeating in their critical analysis the structures of meaning called up by the writing. Thus transference suggests a process of mutual implication (the critic repeats and enters into the text). In the case of projection, on the other hand, that same repetition works by exclusion – a structural incapacity, that of psychosis, to recognise your relation to something which seems to assail you from outside. The subject expels what he or she cannot bear to acknowledge as his or her own reality, only to have it return even larger, and more grotesquely, than reality itself (this is, of course, also the subject of 'The Turn of the Screw' – do the ghosts belong inside or outside the mind?).

Melanie Klein describes one form of this mechanism as 'projective identification', the model or prototype of later aggressivity, a mechanism which aims to protect the ego but which – in an ironic twist – finally weakens it because what has been evicted is intimately bound up with the 'power, potency, strength, knowledge and many other desired qualities upon which the ego relies'.[7] Apply this concept of projection to literary analysis, and what you would expect to discover is a criticism once again caught up in the writing, but this time in the form of deadly struggle *against* it. In the course of this struggle, the text itself must be evicted by the critic. Above all, what must be got rid of is any trace of the critic's own relationship to, or implication in, the writing as such.

Would it be going too far to suggest that Plath has generated a form of 'psychotic' criticism? And not only because of the speed with which critics have rushed to apply the labels 'psychotic' and 'schizophrenic' to her work? (Anne Stevenson's biography – the most recent – is saying nothing new in this context, it simply rejoins the very point of origin of the Plath myth.)[8] It is more that the stakes seem to be so raised in response to Plath's writing: from the question posed by James's story as to whether the governess hallucinates (desires) sexuality or is defending the children against it (an issue of sexual innocence or guilt), to the issue of a sexuality conceived of as so violent that it can only be repudiated – the question the critic then repeatedly asks being whether he (never mind Plath) can survive. Thus Plath puts the whole enterprise of criticism – 'its power, potency, strength, knowledge' – at risk.

This is David Holbrook's epigraph to his book *Sylvia Plath: Poetry and Existence*, published in 1976, one of the first full-length studies of Plath.[9] The quotation comes from George MacDonald's *Lilith*, written in 1895, which belongs, along with Rider Haggard's *She*, to that genre of late-nineteenth-century imperialist texts in which the Christian conquest of other worlds takes the form of an encounter with a deadly female principle:

> The strife of thought, accusing and excusing, began afresh, and gathered fierceness. The soul of Lilith lay naked to the torture of pure interpenetrating inward light. She began to moan and sigh deep sighs, then murmur as if holding colloquy with a dividual self: her queendom was no longer whole; it was divided against herself. One moment she would exult as over her worst enemy, and weep; the next she would writhe as if in the embrace of a fiend whom her soul hated and laugh like a demon. At length she began what seemed a tale about herself, in language so strange, and in forms so shadowy, that I could but here and there understand a little . . .
>
> Gradually my soul grew aware of an invisible darkness, a something more terrible than aught that had yet made itself felt. A horrible Nothingness, a Negation positive infolded her; the border of its being that was yet no being, touched me and for one ghastly instant I seemed alone with Death Absolute! It was not the absence of everything I felt, but the presence of Nothing. The princess dashed herself from the settle to the floor with an exceeding great and bitter cry. It was the recoil of Being from Annihilation . . .[10]

Note how this evokes its own pornographic scenario: 'She began to moan and sigh deep sighs.' Note too how it is beginning to take on the form of diagnosis: 'a dividual self' (a self dangerous because divided, as opposed to a self which does not threaten because it is integrated and whole). In his introduction, Holbrook reports that his book was circulated in manuscript form among analysts working on schizophrenia, and that it was already being used in clinical work (a literary interpretation of Plath thus acquires the status of a clinical case).[11] This idea of a 'dividual self' also carries its own aesthetic values. We will see at various points the extent to which the opposing idea of authenticity, integrity, psychic and aesthetic wholeness has appeared as the standard against which Plath has been measured. Speaking in the name of that wholeness, criticism thus establishes its own sanity through the distance it strikes from her work.

Above all – and nowhere more transparently than here – it is the critic's implication, or possible identification with this drama which must at all costs be denied. Accordingly, Holbrook's quotation from *Lilith* cuts these lines from right out of the middle of the passage as it appears in the original text: 'Yet the language seemed the primeval shape of one I knew well, and the forms to belong to dreams which had once been mine, but refused to be recalled.'[12] It is a staggering instance of projection on the part of Holbrook – in fact with the missing part back in, the passage from the novel can be read as a description or analysis of projection in itself. The spectator in the novel acknowledges the relation between his own unconscious and the horror ('dreams which had once been mine'); acknowledges too the resistance to acknowledgement itself ('refused to be recalled'). Holbrook then acts out this resistance by taking out the moment of recognition, thereby propelling the horror outside and away from himself.

Already, in this quotation, the pornographic scenario can also be read as a fantasy of literary criticism: 'naked to the torture of pure interpenetrating inward light'. Somewhere the opposition 'woman' versus the 'logos' is at stake. The critic takes up the position of witness to a form of the terrible, to the terrible as form. As witness, he cannot be the source of the terror which displays itself to him (or at least not in Holbrook's version), but he is no less threatened by it – he is perhaps even more threatened – for all that. If the violence of Plath presents itself (to reuse Felman's expression) as the violence of a reading-effect, then in this case the experience of reading operates like the sight of the Medusa, a full-frontal assault. The witness survives this display of evil by the woman, in the Lilith story at least, only in so far as he stands squarely in the place of God.

16

If all this seems extravagant, untypical, in the order of excess, compare the basic trope or rhetorical figure of this passage with the first lines of the epigraph to Anne Stevenson's biography, *Bitter Fame*: 'There was a tremendous power in the burning look of her dark eyes; she came "conquering and to conquer"' (the quotation from Dostoyevsky's *The Devils* continues more kindly, but it unquestionably starts in the same place).[13] Similarly, Stephen Spender, in his essay on Plath, 'Warnings from the Grave', describes her as a 'priestess cultivating her hysteria', a hysteria which seems to refer outwards to history (the prophetess), but finally refers only to femininity itself: 'her femininity is that her hysteria comes completely out of herself'.[14] He is comparing her with Owen, whose poetry, he argues, comes out of the concrete experience of the war. From prophecy back into the hysterical body of femininity, Spender's move is strikingly similar to the reversal at the centre of D.M. Thomas's *The White Hotel*, in which the woman seems to have foreknowledge of the impending Holocaust but in fact, through her sexuality, she *is* it.[15] Spender's diagnosis offers the perfect image of male literary critical chauvinism – a point made by Mary Ellman in her book *Thinking About Women*, in 1969.[16] Ellman rightly objects to the removal of the woman from history, this turning-in-on-herself of all historical and literary process. I would go further, and suggest that it is basic to this fantasmatic scenario that the woman becomes the horror of which she speaks.

Holbrook may be ridiculous, exaggerated and excessive, but at the same time he is supremely representative of the sexual imaginary precipitated by Plath's work. His reading merely inflates a dynamic which repeats itself across a range of responses to her writing. From the Oedipal little victim, to the hysteric, to O, to Lilith, we watch the standard figures of femininity transmuting themselves one into the other along the axis of a violence whose logic seems finally to be that of sexual difference itself. According to this logic, it is the fact of femininity which appals. Sexuality is horrifying because of the gap which it wrenches open in the order of things. The specific scenarios of victimisation, pornography and apocalypse merely embody as visual dramatisation the lapse from certainty which occurred when sexuality first ushered evil into the world. There is one account of Freud which states that the boy child *recognises* that moment in the body of the woman, but there is a better one which says that he *projects* it *on to* her, endlessly staging

17

and restaging an accusation against her for a difference of which, by definition, she cannot be the single source.[17] According to the writer Julia Kristeva, it is this structure of projection that can be recognised as the mechanism at the basis of the writings of Céline in their monstrous depiction of the woman as both source and destroyer of life.[18] Plath, however, is herself the producer of words. The problem she poses as a woman does not belong only to the images inside the text, but hurtles back to the origins of writing. Femininity becomes accountable for what went wrong in the beginning – but also, as we will see, for the end of the world.

Taking Holbrook as merely symptomatic, we can then expect to find, alongside this degraded and abused image of femininity, the idealisation to which it is almost invariably attached. This idealised femininity is set up as the principle whose task it is to hold the original evil in check. There is a famous article by the psychoanalyst D.W. Winnicott, 'Creativity and its Origins', which starts by describing the instability of sexual identity and ends with a mythical image of femininity and masculinity which he more or less lifts out of Robert Graves.[19] A whole school of psychoanalytic literary criticism has been founded on the celebration of the female principle of pure being that surfaces in this mystified ending to Winnicott's text.[20] It is this 'female-element-being quality' to which Holbrook appeals. The schizoid woman, he writes, tries to 'unite the disparate elements of her identity', but all she can find is 'two death-male-elements, neither male with a female component, nor female with a male component'.[21] This is the 'secret of the schizoid woman, who has within her an impulse to annihilate the male – the animus which becomes malevolent because it cannot find itself "female-element-being" quality' (this is the kind of thing that gives psychoanalysis a bad name).[22] The worst evil in woman is a masculinity untempered by an essentially female modification. Maleness becomes evil in the woman, who then seeks to annihilate men.

I think what Holbrook believes he is doing in this reading of Plath is describing the failure of her femininity. What I think he is actually doing, however, is projecting on to Plath a familiar fantasy of femininity which makes it accountable for the destruction or salvation (one or the other) of mankind. Similarly, Ruskin argued in the nineteenth century that women's sphere was not political, historical – 'The man, in his rough work in the open world, must encounter all peril and trial' – but that she was none the less responsible for all evil in the outside world: 'There is not a war in the world, no, nor an injustice, but you women are answerable for it.'[23]

It has to be acknowledged, however, that it is not only male critics who have turned on Plath in relation to femininity in this way. In her essay on Plath, 'The Death Throes of Romanticism', Joyce Carol Oates writes on 'Magi' from *Crossing the Water*: 'its vision is exclusively Plath's and, in a horrifying way, very female', although later in the same article she suggests that, if there is any horror of femininity, it is Plath's own: 'a woman who despises herself as a woman obviously cannot feel sympathy with any other woman'.[24]

Holbrook's account of Plath's femininity also has another significance. We can recognise in it a classic description of/projection on to the feminist. The lines about the 'two death-male-elements' ends with a parenthesis: '(And this apparently makes her ideal for Women's Liberation!)'.[25] Repeatedly he juxtaposes his image of Plath's failed femininity with feminism: 'One can see how Sylvia Plath appeals to the women's liberators... Sylvia Plath could scarcely find anything within her that was feminine at all ... she is sadly pseudo-male, like many of her cultists.'[26] It is the all too familiar stereotype of the feminist as failed woman and then (the one as a consequence of the other) as destroyer of men. If Holbrook is important here, it may also be because his writing on Plath reveals so starkly the economy of sexual fantasy which underpins one form of attack on feminism by the Right.

The sexual issue is therefore a political issue in the fullest sense of the term. This account of Plath is weighted with the responsibility for the global survival of culture in our time. We are living at a moment of 'extremism, violence, gross indecency', when we are 'being urged to cultivate our psychoses and endorse decadence and moral inversion'.[27] What Plath has to say about 'male and female and other subjects' is 'grossly distorted and false'.[28] Holbrook's image of true femininity reveals itself as part of a pedagogic project in which literature occupies the privileged place: 'culture is primary in human existence', 'the reading of literature refines the emotions and helps to civilise us'.[29] Plath must not be taught in schools or, if she is, she must be taught only in order to establish the essential falseness of her vision. She seems to occupy roughly the place of the homosexual in relation to the recent legislation of Clause 28 – homosexuality can be acknowledged in schools, but only if it is condemned (the term 'moral inversion' appears no fewer than four times in the introduction to Holbrook's book alone).[30] If we fail in this task, then 'what values can we invoke to condemn those who blow up children with terrorist bombs or harm their consciousness with cruel exploitation?'[31]

This account of the civilising and humanising mission of culture has come to be associated in the twentieth century with the work of F.R. Leavis, who articulated it most clearly in the 1930s and then again after the war. It has become a commonplace of recent Marxist literary criticism to point to its elitism, its assumption and creation of cultural privilege, its anti-democratic politics, and its defence of a tradition of Englishness founded in an imperialism which was still – and continued for some time (many would say continues) to be – in place. The role of culture was to transcend all materialism – meaning socialism on the one hand, the rise of a consumerist and commodity culture on the other. The authority and influence of this school (Leavis and the journal *Scrutiny*, which he founded in 1932) rested, to a great extent, on the way it succeeded in elevating this vested political account of culture to a realm outside all historical time.[32]

To this extent, Holbrook is merely continuing an established tradition whose reactionary implications at the level of our cultural life were starting to be unravelled at about the same time as he was writing his book on Plath. What is distinctive about this later version, however, is the place it assigns to feminism and the woman writer. It is as if the argument 'for' culture was being forced to acknowledge its investment in something that can be called the symbolic order, meaning the implicit rules which govern our language and sexuality, and the forms of fantasy, especially in the sexual field, on which such ordering relies. Sexuality – or, more precisely, a dread of femininity – reveals itself as one of the sub-texts of Holbrook's vision of culture. That vision may be transcendent and mythic in its terms, but it is rooted in a specific historical configuration in which 'feminism' (and/or 'failed femininity') and the 'survival of the culture' are pitted against each other from remarkably similar positions to those occupied by 'socialism' (and/or 'consumerism') versus the 'literary' in the *Scrutiny* battles of the decades before. In this new battle, I would argue, Sylvia Plath comes to occupy a crucial place, one in which the question of cultural survival is sexualised and the woman writer who might be said to have made survival the stake of her own writing becomes somehow accountable for those who blow up children with terrorist bombs.

If it is tempting to dismiss this reading as pathological, it might be worth turning from Holbrook, who wants Plath out of the educational system, to A. Alvarez, the critic in England who did most in the early stages for the promotion of her work (he could almost be described as her impresario). Alvarez places Plath, along with Robert Lowell, at the forefront of a new movement of poetry which he calls 'Extremism'. He sets this movement against what he sees as the middle-class, welfare-state gentility of Britain after the war. Plath and Anne Sexton were the only women poets included in Alvarez's 1966 revised edition of his anthology, *The New Poetry*, first published, as part of his definition of this type of writing, in 1962.[33]

At first glance Alvarez seems to be writing from a position diametrically opposed to everything we have seen so far. If psychoanalysis appears in his discourse, it is as much part of a collective as individual diagnosis, which means it is not being used to hold the psychically disturbing at bay: 'it is hard to live in an age of psychoanalysis and feel oneself wholly detached from the dominant public savagery'.[34] Certainly he never turns against Plath the violence that he reads in her poetry, and he was attacked by Holbrook for promoting her work.[35] And yet despite that immediate difference of assessment, what is most striking is the remarkable similarity of the language in which, at key moments, this defence of Plath is expressed. Perhaps more than any other critic, it is Alvarez who most clearly demonstrates the extent to which Plath becomes part of – is almost produced as a literary object in response to – a battle about the limits and survival of culture.

Again, this is criticism in the apocalyptic mode. For Alvarez, true – read 'high' – culture has been destroyed. Extremist poetry stands as the last bastion against a general cultural mediocrity. Along with B movies, television and spectator sports, a pseudo avant-garde panders to the middle classes. Relegated to a 'subdivision of the entertainments industry', the arts have become, in Saul Bellow's words: 'something to goose the new middle class with'.[36] Compare Holbrook: 'Does not a great deal of our commercial and avant-garde culture . . . rape us, even at the heart of our being?'[37] Alvarez

21

constantly demands that the artist speak of the worst of social evils, but it is clear that his apocalyptic vision rests at least as much with this notion of cultural degeneration as it does with the forms of contemporary political horror (the 'dominant public savagery') to which he repeatedly refers: '[The Extremist style] may, after all, have less to do with the prognosis of a nuclear holocaust than with the relatively simple understanding of the fact that the traditional basis of the arts has been smashed.'[38] In this context, Plath herself becomes the very image of poetic vision concealed inside, or wrestling with, the crude trappings of a commodity culture:

> She was a tall, spindly girl with waist-length sandy hair, which she usually wore in a bun, and that curious, advertisement-trained transatlantic air of anxious pleasantness. But this was a nervous social manner; under it, she was ruthless about her perceptions, wary and very individual [the opening lines of the article published by Alvarez in *The Review* at the time of Plath's death].[39]

The Extremist artist stands for the due intensity of highbrow art in an increasingly commercialised world. Plath's intensity is what ensures that the world (that she) is not *cheap*: 'there is always the delicate question of how common common sense should be'.[40]

For this image of culture, the philosophy is Social Darwinism. A last survivor, the Extremist artist emerges as the 'creatively fittest' through a process of natural selection: 'Art always depends on a principle of natural selection . . . Extremism, however, is based on a form of psychic Darwinism that is far beyond the most stringent usual demands of talent' (the remark immediately follows a reference to Plath).[41] Similarly, Holbrook appeals to a 'philosophical biology' with its 'primary realities of the evolutionary process'.[42] Extremism then appears as the culmination of a Leavisite aesthetic: art as the ascendancy over (the aesthetic-cum-political containment of) the many by the few.

Paradoxically, the only art that can survive in this world is that which knows the present impossibility of art: 'They survive morally by becoming, in one way or another, an imitation of death in which they share.'[43] Alvarez insisted that he was not offering Plath as the 'sacrificial victim offering herself up for the sake of her art', but it is clear that suicide (her suicide) represents the truest state, and measure, of the art: 'In following this black thread [suicide], I have arrived at a theory which, for me, in some way, explains what the arts are about now' (preface to *The Savage God*, Alvarez's study of literature and suicide).[44] Plath is the prologue, Alvarez's own failed suicide attempt the epilogue, of this book: 'I want the book to start, as it ends, with a detailed case-history.'[45] For all the denials, that 'case-history' indicates the pathologising of art, or the romanticising of art as pathology. Alvarez had to add a qualifying note to the essay he had written on Plath at the time of her death: 'I was *not* in any sense meaning to imply that breakdown or suicide is a validation of what I now call Extremist poetry.'[46] The comment seems to imply that the very concept of Extremism emerged only after (in response to?) Plath's death. Thus Plath engenders a literary movement constituted in the very image of her death. Either the woman destroys the culture, or her self-immolation is the precondition for culture to survive.[47]

If, therefore, Holbrook identifies Plath with the inversion and degeneracy of cultural value, Alvarez lays on her the weight of reparation for the same collapse of the moral and cultural world. She is either beneath or above culture: 'beneath' as in 'hidden behind' or 'accountable for', 'beneath' as in 'low'; 'above' as in 'superiority' or 'higher forms', 'above' as 'transcendence'. The second may be the more favourable judgement, but it effectively removes the writer from historical and cultural time. Alvarez was undoubtedly the critic who, in the earliest stages, allowed Plath to take off. Rereading Plath's beginnings as a cultural icon today gives us a unique opportunity to watch the cultural politics of this still influential vision of cultural ascendancy. As we will see, however, Plath herself took pleasure in the multifarious forms of the culture, both high and low, crossing over the limit which she has so repeatedly been used to enforce.

It could be argued that Alvarez's writing on Plath is remarkable for how little attention it pays to the fact that she was a woman. As Alan Sinfield has pointed out, this can be seen as a form of political denial in itself.[48] Sexual difference has to be ignored in order to secure that universalism, or transcendence, of aesthetic terms: 'She steers clear of feminine charm, deliciousness, gentility, supersensitivity and the act of being a poetess. She simply writes good poetry.'[49] But this does not mean that his account of the end of culture has nothing sexual at stake. Note that link between gentility and feminine charm. Plath's access, or condition of entry, to the highest form of culture is that she leaves her femininity *behind*. In his article 'Literature of the Holocaust', Alvarez asks, alluding to Matthew Arnold: 'How do *people* measure up to it as *men* [*sic*]?'[50] On the subject of Lowell: 'A poem succeeds or fails by virtue of the balance and subtlety of the man himself.'[51] By virtue of his manhood – the traditional aesthetic qualities of balance and subtlety migrate and find their last refuge in the image of masculinity itself. Sandra Gilbert and Susan Gubar have commented on the pervasiveness of this masculist image of writing, but it is not restricted to male critics alone.[52] Joyce Carol Oates opens her essay on Plath: 'Tragedy is not a woman, however gifted, dragging her shadow around in a circle . . . tragedy is cultural, mysteriously enlarging the individual.'[53] The association of woman/shadow/circle is a conventional one (it is taken from Plath's poem 'A Life'[54]). But which body, and which part of that body, mysteriously enlarges itself? Compare too Oates's critique of lyric poetry for not coming up to size: 'How quickly these six-inch masterpieces betray their creators!'[55] I think this has to be an (intended) joke.

Alvarez and Holbrook finally have in common this sexualisation of the cultural stakes. A decadent culture is onanistic and impotent. In the first issue of *The Review*, in a discussion with Donald Davie, Alvarez compared aestheticism to masturbation on the ground of their shared relinquishment of the realities of life.[56] Compare Holbrook: 'our essential cultural experiences [gramophone, television set, wireless or cinema] are not celebrative, they are, rather, onanistic'.[57] He then spends a great deal of time on the line 'Masturbating a glitter' from Plath's poem 'Death and Co.', arguing that it establishes her psychosis via a reference to a case-study of a German boy who shot a prostitute and, apparently surrounded by shining objects, used to masturbate a lot.[58] It is easy, however, to follow this logic: the weakening of the culture, the dissipation of sexual energy, a kind of premature sexual-cum-nuclear waste (the sexual and political terrors are closely linked).

The dispute over Plath is therefore aesthetic as well as sexual and cultural-political in scope. If she is hysterical prophetess for Spender, it is at least partly because her poems are lacking in form: 'they don't have "form". From poem to poem they have little principle of beginning or ending, but seem fragments, not so much of one long poem, as of an outpouring which could not stop with the lapsing of the poet's hysteria' (Plath's poetry is the 'emotional-mystical' extension and continuation of hysteria).[59] But we should not expect Alvarez's praise of Plath to involve in any way a validation of this image of a writing, part hysteric, part onanistic, spilling out of itself. Despite his argument for extremity and his critique of literary convention, Alvarez speaks finally in the name of a very traditional aesthetic, visible in his rejection of the avant-garde, in his ideal of a language transparent to the world and to the man ('the poems since *Life Studies* have gained a kind of transparency: you see through them to see the man as he is'), in that image of the unity, identity and coherence of the poetic which counters the holocaust of culture.[60] Extremism is not a challenge to form but the final securing of its possibility, the art of an identity which asserts itself against the odds. For Alvarez, the task of the artist, faced with the failure of 'all our traditions and beliefs', is to secure 'his own identity' from scratch.[61] This identity, forged – self-engendered – by the writer, is thus proposed by Alvarez as a solution to a 'post-modern' predicament which many today would see as a challenge to the category, and the pretensions, of singular identity as such.

Plath is not therefore, being sponsored, as an artist of the irrational. Extremism never means letting up the essential artistic control: 'Like Coleridge's Imagination', it reconciles 'a more than usual state of emotion with a more than usual order' (a type of D.H. Lawrence and T.S. Eliot combined).[62] This is extremism in the rationalist mode, a mode that Alvarez opposes to fascism, although today we might see those very terms of supreme control, identity and aesthetic heroism as just as likely to be part of fascism itself – 'marshalled . . . and ordered', to use Alvarez's own expression from his 1963 essay on Plath.[63] Kristeva's account of Céline as a fascist writer suggests that what is involved is not irrationalism but a highly regulated fantasy world subject to a super-competent ego that controls and distributes, according to a rigid sexual economy, the worst of its terms. Already it is clear, however, that – in relation to Plath (although not only in relation to her) – we need a conception of writing as neither marshalled nor fragmented, neither surplus order nor a hysterical body pouring out of itself.

The main point of this first chapter has been to show how Sylvia Plath is constituted as a literary object on the battleground of cultural survival. Through the intensity of their investment in her, and beyond any immediate differences of appraisal, she becomes for Holbrook and Alvarez (and not only for them) an object of desire.

Alvarez makes little of Plath as a woman, but his account of the last months of her life in *The Savage God* follows the conventions of the narrative/sexual pursuit. Plath has become – the point has been made before – the Marilyn Monroe of the literati: with this difference – that it is not only the survival of manhood (the manhood which survives by fetishising the woman) but the very capacity of culture to symbolise its own lineage and perpetuity which is at stake. This is not the first time the concept of culture has been invested with the future of civilisation. Doesn't the very definition of the classic rest on the question of whether a text will *survive*? Only this time, we can clearly see that the cultural object is not simply the refuge from a larger terror, but also embodies it. For good or for evil, Plath has come to symbolise that terror for a literary discourse which, according to the most traditional valorisation of its own high social function, is still asking literature to carry the privileged weight of the future of man. In these terms, Sylvia Plath is either the apotheosis or the apocalypse (or both together) of art.

A difficult aesthetic question remains. For some time now, feminist criticism has seemed to be divided between a reading of women writers which bemoans the lack of – or attempts to retrieve for them – a consistent and articulate 'I', and one which celebrates linguistic fragmentation, the disintegration of body and sexual identity, in the name of a form of writing which has come to be known as *'écriture féminine'*.[64] The first is expressed most clearly by Sandra Gilbert and Susan Gubar:

> For all literary artists, of course, self-definition necessarily precedes self-assertion: the creative 'I AM' cannot be uttered if the 'I' knows not what it is. But for the female artist the essential process of self-definition is complicated by all those partriarchal definitions that intervene between herself and herself.[65]

The second can be related to a number of French feminist writers, amongst them Hélène Cixous:

> If there is a 'propriety of woman', it is paradoxically her capacity to depropriate unselfishly, body without end, without appendage, without principal 'parts' ... This doesn't mean that she's an undifferentiated magma, but that she doesn't lord it over her body or her desire ... Her libido is cosmic, just as her

unconscious is worldwide. Her writing can only keep going, without ever inscribing or discerning contours.[66]

We can recognise the awkward proximity of these conceptions to Alvarez's consistency of representation on the one hand, and, on the other, to Spender's disintegration of writing as a femininity spilling out of itself.[67] In fact, these early responses to Plath provide an early version of a still unresolved drama about femininity and writing. As we read them, we can watch unfold the stark alternative between, on the one hand, a masculist aesthetic and on the other, a form of writing connoted feminine only to the extent that it is projected on to the underside of language and speech.

But there is also, I would argue, a strange proximity between these two accounts of women's writing, in the way that they each situate the woman inside an exclusively personal struggle to express either the self or the non-self. Both seem to remove the woman writer from historical process, the first through the image of a sustained lineage of women writers across all historical differences (cultural perpetuity for women), the second by dissolving the very possibility for women of any purchase on historical time. And both seem attached to the same valorisation of high culture, whether in its coherent 'realist' or its fragmented 'modernist' mode (it has been pointed out that the argument between them inherits the terms of the realist/modern dispute[68]). We should also ask – since this will be such a central issue in relation to Plath – what image of sexual relations these different accounts of women's writing seem to imply – a battle of the sexes, meaning a battle between unequivocally gendered and sexually differentiated egos,[69] or a disintegration into a body without identity, shape or purpose, where no difference, and no battle, can take place.

And what, finally, is this image of the body in language? When feminism takes up, and valorises for women, the much-denigrated image of a hysterical outpouring of the body, it has often found itself doing so, understandably, at the cost of idealising the body itself. According to this argument, writing castigated as hysterical is writing where the passage of the body through language is too insistently present; it is writing in which a body, normally ordered by the proprieties of language and sexual identity, gets too close. Fragmented and disorderly, this writing refuses to submit to the aesthetic norms of integration and wholeness against which it is

27

diagnosed and judged. Its body can be called feminine to the precise degree that it flouts the rigidity (the masculinity) of the requisite forms of literary cohesion and control.

In a classic feminist move, this argument inverts a traditional devalorisation of women. But in the very process of this inversion, what is most discomforting about the body disappears. The body must be positive, it must figure as pure (aesthetic and moral) value if its low-grade ideological colouring is to be removed. Thus uplifted, this body often seems remote from sex and substance, strangely incorporeal, suspended in pure fluidity or cosmic time. Ironically, then, this celebration of the woman's body in language seems partly to share with the criticism it answers the image of a body that repels. No writer more than Plath has been more clearly hystericised by the worst of a male literary tradition. No writer more than Plath, as we will now see, demonstrates the limits of responding to that tradition, and its barely concealed repulsion, by cleaning up the woman writer, thereby re-repressing one part of what that tradition so fiercely, and with such ceaseless misogyny, expels.

# 2

# THE BODY OF THE WRITING

The edge cannot eat the center.
(Roethke, 'The Shape of the Fire', in *The Lost Son and Other Poems*)

What is the body of Plath's writing? That is, what is the body that Plath writes? For if there is a body *of* her writing — an archive edited, glossed and cut — there is no less, and no less crucially, a body *in* her writing, a body whose relationship to writing and representation Plath's texts repeatedly comment on and speak. For Plath, words plunge into the body, and writing is a sexual act. The editors of the *Journals* take out Plath's 'nasty bits' and 'intimacies' ('Some of the more devastating comments are missing . . . and there are a few other cuts — of intimacies — that have the effect of diminishing Plath's eroticism, which was quite strong'[1]), but they leave in — fail to notice? — those passages where what is 'nasty' and what is 'intimate' reveal their proximity in relation to the act of writing itself:

> . . . until I make something tight and riding over the limits of sweet sestinas and sonnets, away from the reflection of myself in Richard's eyes and the inevitable narrow bed, too small for a smashing act of love, until then, they can ignore me and make up pretty jokes.

> Wicked, my hand halted, each night at writing. I fell away into sleep, book unwritten in. Woke today at noon, coming drugged to the surface, after a lost weekend. All the deep rooted yawns. Plunged to the depths of my fatigue, and now: bushels of words. I skim the surface of my brain, writing. Prose now, working over the kernel chapter of my novel, to crouch it and clench it together in a story [ . . . ] I can do it if I sweat enough.[2]

With what might be seen as startling vulgarity, Plath in these passages names writing as sex, as height or as depth: riding tight over the limits, or crouching, clenching, working over the kernel, plunging into bushels of words. But if sex and writing come together here in the act, the encounter between them is represented no less in terms of desire, as something prohibited or deferred. Writing finds itself in the space of the body only to be immediately arrested there – whether by 'inevitable' constriction ('the inevitable narrow bed') or by an act which can only be referred to as 'wicked', which cannot in fact be named because it is the ultimate taboo. Note too how that 'tight and riding over' of the first example can also be read as a masculine identification – woman on top as the position connoted to the male (compare Lowell's later 'He stalls above me like an elephant'[3]). The desire to be more than 'the reflection of myself in Richard's eyes' seems therefore also to carry a desire to *be* Richard, or at least to occupy his sexual place. Riding like a man, plunging into the bushel of herself, Plath thus symbolises writing in terms which seem to straddle the difference between Sandra Gilbert and Susan Gubar, on the one hand, and on the other, the French feminist Luce Irigaray (writing as male potency, writing as the most intimate relation of the body of the woman to itself).[4] In doing so, she also situates the sexuality of her writing on either edge of what might pass more recognisably as sex (the 'intimacies' which the editors remove). To call these two passages transgressive is simply to point to the fact that where writing appears as sexuality, that sexuality immediately goes over its own limits. Paradoxically, sex is removed as 'intimacy' only to speak more loudly here in a form which the general culture would be just as inclined – possibly more inclined – to consider as 'nasty bits'.

It would be misleading, however, to represent this relation between the body and writing exclusively in terms of sex, even if qualified by the notions of transgression or taboo. For while those notions suggest something in excess of normative sexuality, they none the less have that same sexuality as their final reference point – transgression only taking its meaning from the very norm which it ostensibly leaves behind. As these passages show, Plath's writing runs across this sexual space, but it also works a different axis, better described perhaps as vertical to both sexuality and writing, in so far as it opens up or exposes the preconditions of sexuality and writing as such. In this space writing rejoins the orality out of which language was itself first produced – here words are tongued and mouthed, or else they vanish and thin: 'I feel stifled, weak, pallid, mealy-mouthed' . . . 'It is sad only to be able to mouth other poets. I want someone to mouth me' . . . 'All I have ever read thins and vanishes' . . . 'rereading the thin, thinning nucleus of my poetry book'.[5] In this space language is at once corporeal and precarious, like the phenomenal world whose reality is no less at risk: 'The horror is the sudden folding up and away of the physical world . . . That same horror which comes when the paraphernalia of existence whooshes away.'[6] If language fails, there is no bulwark against what is at moments experienced as the complete loss of, at others as an unmanageable saturation by, life: 'Words, words, to stop the deluge through the thumbhole in the dike'.[7]

In this precarious interchange between language and the world, Plath seems almost to be dramatising the origins of language. In that last quotation, it is not clear what floods through the dike, what it is that words are being required so urgently to stall. But the image perfectly embodies the idea of something indispensable because it acts as a substitute for what is missing or out of place. Words here are a stopgap, a stand-in for something absent but not named. As one psychoanalytic account would put it, the mouth fills with words because what is really desired – a primordial if mythic presence – is definitely out of reach. According to this narrative, it is language which gives to the child its first unwelcome sense of being separate in the world, opening up a rent which it endlessly – Sisyphus-like – struggles to repair.[8] Irremediable gap into which words pour: 'Words, words, to stop the deluge through the thumbhole in the dike'.

In her commentary on the process of writing, Plath constantly underscores this physicality of language – origin but also endlessly repeated condition for the production of speech. At one crude or basic level, not to be able to write is to be physically sick. No less basic (no less crude), language and orality run back into each other, their connection made literal – writing as biting, sucking, vampire-like, on the substance of life: 'I maunch on chagrins' . . . 'Faces and violence. Bites and wry words. Try these.'[9] The proximity between them can, however, be too closely felt:

I could not go up to the door and knock and say: Let me come in and suck your life and sorrow from you as a leech sucks blood; let me gorge myself on your sensations, ideas and dreams; let me crawl inside your guts and cranium and let me live like a tapeworm for a while, draining your life substance into myself . . . no.[10]

At one level, that 'I could not' and that 'no' cry out to be read as the classic sign of negation, described by Freud as the process whereby the patient in an analytic setting allows something repressed to be spoken on condition of denying it at the same time (if the patient, invited to associate to the content of a dream, starts by insisting 'It's not my mother', the analyst can fairly ask from where, therefore, the idea of the mother has suddenly come). Accordingly Plath, in this passage, acknowledges the oral passion of her writing only by insisting that it is not what she desires ('I could not . . . no'). But even more important in this context is the link Freud proposes between the act of negation and orality itself. Thus Freud makes negation, in his famous paper of that title, the foundation of judgement, linking it to the process through which the child first recognises, takes in and ejects, the objects of its world, incorporating what gives it pleasure, casting into the outside world what gives it pain:

> Expressed in the language of the oldest – the oral – instinctual impulses, the judgement is: 'I would like to eat this', or 'I would like to spit this out'; and put more generally, 'I should like to take this into myself and to keep that out'.[11]

Taking the world in, the child devours it; recognising it as a distinct reality, the child spits it out – a self-defeating operation whose perverse logic will first be analysed in detail by Melanie Klein.[12] Eventually words will come to substitute for this mechanism, but they will always wear the colour of the oral process they both inherit and replace. As Freud himself puts it when describing the only ever partial disappearance of repressed ideas: '[they] are rather like the *shades in the Odyssey which awaken to a certain degree of life as soon as they have drunk blood*' (the lines are heavily underlined in Plath's own copy of *The Basic Writings of Sigmund Freud*).[13] By placing this process at the basis of human logic, Freud gives a new meaning to the old adage: 'out of the mouths of babes and sucklings'.

In relation to that passage by Plath, we can say that it describes writing as orality twice over, both in its form (the act of negation) and in its content (the vampirism it describes), even as it attempts to save the writer, and her victims, from the worse ravages of its effects. In a predictable reversal, writing can be represented as the opposite of vampirism, possible only on condition that the body vanishes and thins: 'The great vampire cook extracts the nourishment and I grow fat on the corruption of matter. I must be lean and write and make words beside this to live in.'[14] Reading Freud's 'Mourning and Melancholia', Plath picks out 'the "vampire" metaphor Freud uses, "draining the ego": that is exactly the feeling I have getting in the way of my writing'.[15]

In this figuring of writing, Plath runs back and forth across the passage of the body into words. In so doing, she identifies within writing a violence which belongs inside the body, in the most fundamental mechanisms through which a body comes to identify and recognise itself as such. The child experiences as murderous the process through which it draws in and expels fragments of the surrounding world. In this way, introjection and projection can be seen as the origins not just of thinking, but of guilt.[16]

There is of course a sense in which to write, to create worlds in language, is necessarily to work at this interface where language is embodied and where the body transmutes itself, or is figured, through words. To say this, however, is not to idealise literary writing as a lyrical return to some true bodily state. Projection and introjection give the dimensions of this body, and fear is its associated affect. In her book *Powers of Horror*, Julia Kristeva describes this as the realm of what she calls abjection. Abjection is a primordial fear situated at the point where the subject first splits from the body of the mother, finding at once in that body and in the terrifying gap that opens up between them the only space for the constitution of its own identity, the only distance which will allow it to become a user of words.

Into this gap, the phobic object inserts itself – strictly a stopgap, because it fills out a more fundamental and horrifying void. For Kristeva, all writing then becomes counter-phobic: an attempt to control, through the process of language, the very same fear that was there at the beginning of speech. Kristeva has often been associated with writers such as Hélène Cixous and Luce Irigaray, with their more lyrical celebration of the woman's body as writing. For Kristeva, however, this body is without gender, and in this account at least, it figures as the most lowly (most abject) of corporeal substance, reduced to an oral fragment of itself. The body appears at the origin of language, not as idealisation, therefore, but as that which places both the subject and language most fundamentally at risk. Abjection belongs at the boundary of language, vanishing point and point of emergence for the subject, and it reappears when a threatened loss of meaning carnalises itself as an object which pulls and threatens from the outside:

> . . . one can fairly assume that *any* verbalising activity, whether or not it names a phobic object, is an attempt to introject what has been incorporated. In this sense, verbalisation is from the outset confronted with that 'ab-ject' which is the phobic object. Learning to speak is like trying to make one's own an oral 'object' which slips away, and whose necessarily deformed hallucination threatens us from the outside.[17]

Writing then becomes 'a "savoir-faire" with phobia . . . any exercise of speech, in so far as it belongs to writing, is a language of fear'.[18] The writer uses words to ward off an anxiety which at some level is precipitated by nothing less than language itself: 'the writer: a phobic who succeeds at metaphorisation so that, instead of dying of fear, she or he is resuscitated through signs'.[19]

A great deal has been written about Plath and fear, but it usually either takes the form of diagnosis or is analysed as the logical reaction on her part to the cruelty and harshness of the world. This second reading is important, and I will return to it at a number of points in the course of this book. But what I want to suggest here is that by reading that fear as either symptom or legitimate response, we give it either too little of a logic or too much. Instead of which, Plath seems to me – and at least as much as the (male) literary writers discussed in her book by Julia Kristeva – to be laying out something which could be called a psychic economy of writing – that is, the unconscious and normally covered-over conditions or substrata of speech. In this context the idea of symptom (aberration) or of rationale (given by the world outside) are equally misplaced or equally appropriate in relation to Plath. If there is a symptom, it is not merely that of an individual pathology; and if there is a rationale, it does not belong exclusively to the external world. What if Plath gives the rationale of the symptom in relation to writing, by representing what is symptomatic in the production of speech?

Plath is not alone among women writers of this period to write along the edge of language where words fill with an orality they have only partly subsumed, where to speak is to mouth or to tongue – a substitution both metaphoric and literal in so far as it lays bare the grossness latent to, and productive of, the physical act of speech. In Anne Sexton's first short story, 'Dancing the Jig', the narrator's desire to dance fuses with the memory of her early attempts to eat and to speak, watching her mother, tasting the sound of her voice: 'I can taste the sound of her voice . . . Her words slip out between bites; they run out as if her food was spilling back out between her lips', 'I am starting to talk myself. The words are running out of my mouth and she is catching them and hurling them back at me . . . my lips move on words and meat.'[20] The dance is as much repetition as freedom. It pitches her into the memory of that first identification which gave to her (took from her, hurled at her) the body of words. In this story, to dance is itself to devour: 'I think I have eaten the music. It runs through me as if I had swallowed it whole.'[21]

In the famous circle constituted by Plath, Sexton and Lowell, eating, sucking, provide a set of figures through which they come to represent themselves: Lowell (borrowing from Lévi-Strauss) describing poetry as 'raw' and 'cooked' when he accepts the National Book Award for *Life Studies*; Sexton later describing her meetings with Plath as talking, sucking on, death: 'We talked death with burned up intensity . . . Sucking on it!' – orality as part of public discourse (if not quite table talk), orality as part of the most intimate (and deadly) of private speech.[22]

In Plath's writing, that connection between the body and language knows no limit – not in the sense that it captures some aesthetic process of a physicality without bounds, but because it touches on the limit, crossing over the boundary between inside and outside, where what is incorporated is ejected, where food transforms itself into refuse or waste: 'I am a conglomerate garbage heap of loose ends', 'one taste, one touch, one vision from the ruck of the day's garbage'.[23] In this space, writing attaches itself to the frontiers of the body, where the limits between inside and outside are most precarious and can break down. To quote Kristeva: 'it is as if the skin, fragile container, no longer guaranteed the integrity of the "proper", but, flayed or transparent, invisible or distended, gives way before the casting out of its contents'.[24] Plath writes: 'I go

35

plodding on, afraid that the blank hell in back of my eyes will break through, spewing forth like a dark pestilence, afraid that the disease which eats away the pith of my body with merciless impersonality will break forth.'[25] In fact, the editors of the *Journals* and of the *Letters Home* take out much of Plath's body in this further sense: 'nasty bits' meaning not what might be judged ethically distasteful (the meaning aimed at or intended by the term) but the body at its most abject in the more familiar sense – in Plath's case the sinusitis which runs through her writing and which meant, when it afflicted her, that she could barely breathe (the references are present in the published writings, but it is their repetitive insistence that has been reduced).

Even more striking, perhaps, is the way the writing spills across different parts of the body, confusing the different narratives they tell. Like this example which frames and gives added significance to a quotation already discussed: 'I want to rush into print any old tripe. Words, words, to stop the deluge through the thumbhole in the dike. This be my secret place . . . I must bridge the gap between adolescent glitter and mature glow.'[26] Writing is tripe or refuse (deluge of shit?), but writing is precisely what stops the rot. And this is her secret place (bushel and kernel of herself?) – the link to the meaning of private pleasure is confirmed by what one is tempted to call the tongue-in-cheek moralism of the injunction to bridge another gap (thumb another dike) between 'adolescent glitter and mature glow'. It is worth noting in passing that the implied hierarchy here between adolescence and maturity and their associated sexual pleasures for women is also worthy of some of the worst things Freud said about female sexuality (relinquishment of clitoral masturbation for women as the measure of the female norm).[27] Equally, and still along the lines of the same basic paradigm, the body can be threatened by the undigested surfeit of itself: 'If I can digest changes, in my novel. Not swell tumid with inarticu-lateness.'[28] Failure to digest swells up the body and jams the possibility of speech. Naming inarticulateness as 'tumid', the passage hands failure to write over to another sexual narrative ('tight and riding over') in which a masculine body swells with nothing other than the measure of itself. Across the range of these examples, writing is, and is the counter to, morbidity or potential death.

If, therefore, this process is deadly, it goes way beyond the biographical reference to which that idea in relation to Plath (and

Sexton) is normally confined. Writing is violence, not because it talks about violence – offers it as the subject matter of the text – but because writing brings with it the violence internal to the physical substratum of speech. To call Plath's writing a 'murderous art', and then lock into a debate about whether she could survive her own representation of violence inside the text, is to overlook the way Plath locates this same violence in the 'before' of writing, in the precondition of enunciation whose psychic dynamic she repeatedly writes out in her text: 'I can slice into the depths of people' . . . 'What inner decision, what inner murder or prison break must I commit if I want to speak from my true deep voice in writing?' . . . 'Where are my small incidents, the blood poured from the shoes?'[29] To say this is not to ignore the extent to which violence appears progressively in her writing as theme. It is, however, to give to the violence of her writing both less and more of a crucial place. Violence belongs here to the act of symbolisation itself, and cannot be understood with exclusive reference to the content of the stories she tells or the narrative of her life. By belonging to the act of symbolisation, it resists diagnosis as much as the apportioning of blame. No one can be held accountable, for this is a negativity without ownership, without property rights or rights in the person, arising as it does at that most precarious point where identity first constitutes itself in speech.

One of the most graphic accounts of this process, this site, is given by Allon White in 'Too Close to the Bone: Fragments of an Autobiography', when he describes how he identifies with his dead sister, taking her into himself and, with her, the guilt of a death for which he could in no sense be blamed:

> I can hardly begin to approach this level of my being. Here Be Monsters. Nothing can be held steady enough for language in this place, things flicker and slide, shapes loom and melt away. There is none of that elegiac lyricism of drowning and summer afternoons here – gentle *kaddish* for the dead. Here it burns and hurts. It is violent, spasmodic, monstrous. There is no wholeness. I am not *myself* here.[30]

To discuss Plath in this way is to suggest that, at this level at least, she can be defined in Kristeva's terms as a writer of abjection, a writer for whom the limits of the body and of symbolisation are constantly worked over or put at risk. This is not, however, to reinstate a new form of that most familiar of literary valorisations, a new type of 'humanist' criticism which would substitute the emergent for the developing self. This is an instance where it is not possible to talk in terms of a self; if there is a narrative of emergence here, therefore, it is best understood as the narrative which that other account of literary selfhood, in its stress on an affirmed individuality of personhood, constantly has to repress.

If this abjection is not guilty, in the sense of being available for diagnosis-cum-moral-judgement, it none the less takes up, or even turns on, the issue of guilt. The passage from the *Journals* in which Plath writes of the 'dark hell' at the back of the eyes, the disease at the 'pith of her body', continues: 'I can begin to see the compulsion for admitting original sin, for adoring Hitler, for taking opium.'[31] Negativity transmutes itself into the more recognisable fantasies of our collective social, political and religious life, where it reappears as pleasure – culpable *as* pleasure, culpable in each of these examples because of the specific cultural form that it takes. If these fantasies are culpable, therefore, in this passage it is crucially because they are carrying the weight of a guilt that belongs to the inner life, a guilt much less easy to identify because it resides at that point where the body constitutes itself in words. Thus Plath appears to be tracking the passage, or rather tracing one possible sequence, between negativity in the inner and outer world – which is not to give priority to one of these over the other: we will see how Plath constantly articulates the interdependence between the two. Note the proximity between these two passages, the first from Plath's *Journals*, the second from Dostoyevsky's *The Devils*, quoted by Kristeva:

One night, late, we walked out and saw the lurid orange glow of a fire down below the high school. I dragged Ted to it, hoping for houses in a holocaust . . . The fire was oddly satisfying. I longed for an incident, an accident. What unleashed desire there must be in one for general carnage . . . Nothing happens. I walk the razor edge of jeopardy . . .[32]

. . . the horror and a certain sense of personal danger, combined with the well-known exhilarating effect of a fire at night, produce in the spectator (not, of course, in one whose house has burnt down) a certain shock to the brain and, as it were, a challenge to his own destructive instincts, which, alas, lie buried in the soul of even the meekest and most domesticated official of the lowest grade. This grim sensation is almost always delightful.[33]

If Plath has been condemned for this, she has of course also been sacralised. Like all oppositions, the two responses are intimately linked – both denigration and adulation have their place inside what it is that Plath herself describes. Although Kristeva discusses no women writers in her book, her account of what happens to the writer of abjection comes uncannily close to, and can act as a caution against, one predominant strand of critical response to Plath:

> It is only after her or his death, possibly, that the writer of abjection will escape his lot as waste, cast-off or abject. Then either she or he will sink into oblivion, or accede to the rank of an incommensurable ideal . . . In the last analysis, death protects us from that abjection which contemporary literature claims to expend by speaking it. A protection which settles its accounts with abjection but perhaps equally with the awkward, incandescent stake of literature itself, cut off from its specificity by being promoted to the status of the sacred.[34]

The writer of abjection dies into oblivion or idealisation. Either way death becomes the protection, and not only for the writer, against abjection itself. The death of the (woman) writer – a death so clearly sacralised in the case of Plath – thus comes to participate in an act of repression which, for Kristeva, cuts literature off from the very processes which makes of it literature as such.

It is important to stress this trap of the sacred, the way in which abjection lends itself to mystification (the lowest transposing itself into the most high) in order to make clear that to discuss Plath in terms of abjection is not to place her in a sacrosanct zone, where literary language is allowed its relation to the body only so that it can more surely take flight (leaving the dregs of the body as well as of culture behind). This would be to allow for that aspect of her writing only on condition that it transcend itself or finally wipe itself out. It would also be to ignore the commentary, centrally and repeatedly offered by Plath's writings, on the political implications of the psychic mechanisms she describes. In fact Plath walks the edge, not only between the body and language but also, as the passages above suggest, the edge – occupied by body and language together – between public and private space.

To turn now to one – central – example. 'Poem for a Birthday' is in one sense the most 'intimate' of Plath's poetic works, but Plath gives us the more public, institutional face of its narrative, both inside the poem and in 'Johnny Panic and the Bible of Dreams', the short story she writes at the same time; and both are given a further political dimension by the other texts which surround them and on which she draws.[35] In this context, intertextuality has a meaning in addition to that of the discursive context to which it usually refers (the surrounding texts of the culture, the discourses informing any piece of writing – which, whether consciously or unconsciously, it necessarily evokes). Intertextuality here indicates the spill and spread of negativity which runs back and forth across the space of poetic language, institution and contemporary political life.

'Poem for a Birthday' is usually described as a transitional poem – transitional in relation to the development of Plath's poetry, either as breakthrough: 'The end of her first phase of development' . . . 'Suddenly she found herself free to let herself drop, rather than inch over bridges of concepts',[36] or as the undeveloped forerunner of what was to come later with *Ariel*: 'interestingly transitional works'.[37] Transitional also in relation to England and America, since Knopf, the American publishers of *The Colossus*, the collection in which Plath included it, asked for the poem to be removed because of its too obvious derivation from Theodore Roethke. Two parts of the poem were finally included which, it seems, Plath herself insisted on. But in her letters to her mother she represents Knopf's selection as miraculously coinciding with her own: 'By a miracle of intuition, I guessed (unintentionally) the exact ten they would have left out' (they also asked for the removal of another five of the poems).[38] That 'by a miracle' strangely repeats her own account of how 'Poem for a Birthday' came to be written: 'Miraculously I wrote seven poems in my Poem for a Birthday sequence.'[39] In her *Journals*, however, at the time of writing the poems, she reads the difference between England and America in other terms, precisely as difference – that is, in terms of the cultural distinction between them: 'I feel we must find a publisher here, yet the macabre is so outside our tradition.'[40] England, as she puts it several months

40

earlier, looks 'small and digestible from here'.[41] Leaving America for England, Plath notes already here that her 'Poem for a Birthday' may not find its place in the country of her birth.

'Poem for a Birthday' has also found itself at the interface of competing interpretations of Plath, or rather at the interface between denigration and sacralisation of her writing. Holbrook uses 'Poem for a Birthday' (he calls his chapter 'Poem for a False Birth') as the basis for his definitive judgement on, and diagnosis of, Plath.[42] Judith Kroll, after (or with) Hughes, reads the sequence as one of the clearest signs of Plath's emergent mythology of self-transcendence, a mythology which she traces through the whole of Plath's work.[43] Immediately it seems that something troubling is being located in this sequence of poems by its readers on condition that it either destroys or sublates itself (the trouble is either evidence of Plath's self-destructiveness, or it is what the poem triumphantly leaves behind). The aesthetic-cum-psychic-cum-moral stakes here are considerable. In response to a text which presents itself in fragments comes the judgement that this is the poem 'where the self, shattered in 1953, suddenly finds itself whole'.[44]

That question of 'wholeness' is crucial. Margaret Dickie Uroff writes at the end of her analysis: 'the poems as a whole and as a series lack the force of their parts'.[45] Anne Stevenson says of 'Witch Burning': 'the shape-shifting proceeds at such a pace that the poem scarcely makes sense'.[46] Kroll writes: 'sometimes not only she, but the poem itself seems confused', and situates the poems on a path 'towards absoluteness', towards the later poems, 'where typically, mythological structures are completely appropriated into the poetic vision, and the speaker does not stand apart from the poem, but, rather, discloses her mythic character'.[47] She praises 'The Stones', the last section of the poem, in terms which underline the link between psychic and aesthetic integrity:

Unlike the other poems, the imagery in 'The Stones' successfully embodies complex themes, without straining the sense of how the poem legitimately may develop. Many of the images in the earlier poems crowded one another, making conflicting claims; in 'The Stones', the imagery, even when grotesque, is unitary and coherent, reflecting the coherence of the speaker, who has understood and ordered her experience.[48]

These are of course the recognisable, and perhaps now too easily targeted, claims of a traditional aesthetic – control of experience, poetic language as coherent, legitimate and unified, as opposed to a language and experience that are crowded and conflictual in their demands. The issue is clearly one of aesthetic and psychic (and bodily) mastery – what is grotesque is acceptable on condition that it does not 'strain' the sense.

Wholeness is at issue in another sense in the cutting of all but two of the poem's five sections ('The Stones' is one of the two that remain), which breaks up the poem in the name of wholeness – Plath's poetic integrity without derivation. A fragment without poetic lineage is therefore seen to possess more, or a superior, unity to the unity given to it by its place in the body of the text. Anticipating those readings which see Plath's poem – and indeed much of her work – in terms of a myth of self-emergence, Knopf ask, in their original objection to the poem, that Plath should engender *herself*. According to Hughes, however, the poem was originally conceived as a 'deliberate Roethke pastiche, something light and throwaway to begin with, but might lead to something else' ('pastiche', the key concept of postmodernism, appears already here in opposition to the concept of the 'whole self' of Hughes's later account).[49] In relation to Roethke however, Plath, seems to situate herself differently: 'Roethke's influence, yet mine'.[50] Less negation than fetishism ('Yes, but'), her comment offers writing as necessary division – between herself and the male writer, between influence and autonomy, between taking in and giving out words.

POEM FOR A BIRTHDAY

1. WHO

The month of flowering's finished. The fruit's in,
Eaten or rotten. I am all mouth.
October's the month for storage.

This shed's fusty as a mummy's stomach:
Old tools, handles and rusky tusks.
I am at home here among the dead heads.

Let me sit in a flowerpot,
The spiders won't notice.
My heart is a stopped geranium.

If only the wind would leave my lungs alone.
Dogbody noses the petals. They bloom upside down.
They rattle like hydrangea bushes.

Moldering heads console me,
Nailed to the rafters yesterday:
Inmates who don't hibernate.

Cabbageheads: wormy purple, silver-glaze,
A dressing of mule ears, mothy pelts, but green-hearted,
Their veins white as porkfat.

O the beauty of usage!
The orange pumpkins have no eyes.
These halls are full of women who think they are birds.

This is a dull school.
I am a root, a stone, an owl pellet,
Without dreams of any sort.

Mother, you are the one mouth
I would be a tongue to. Mother of otherness
Eat me. Wastebasket gaper, shadow of doorways.

I said: I must remember this, being small.
There were such enormous flowers,
Purple and red mouths, utterly lovely.

The hoops of blackberry stems made me cry.
Now they light me up like an electric bulb.
For weeks I can remember nothing at all.

## 2. DARK HOUSE

This is a dark house, very big.
I made it myself,
Cell by cell from a quiet corner,
Chewing at the gray paper,
Oozing the glue drops,
Whistling, wiggling my ears,
Thinking of something else.

It has so many cellars,
Such eelish delvings!
I am round as an owl,

I see by my own light.
Any day I may litter puppies
Or mother a horse. My belly moves.
I must make more maps.

These marrowy tunnels!
Moley-handed, I eat my way.
All-mouth licks up the bushes
And the pots of meat.
He lives in an old well,
A stony hole. He's to blame.
He's a fat sort.

Pebble smells, turnipy chambers.
Small nostrils are breathing.
Little humble loves!
Footlings, boneless as noses,
It is warm and tolerable
In the bowel of the root.
Here's a cuddly mother.

### 3. MAENAD

Once I was ordinary:
Sat by my father's bean tree
Eating the fingers of wisdom.
The birds made milk.
When it thundered I hid under a flat stone.

The mother of mouths didn't love me.
The old man shrank to a doll.
O I am too big to go backward:
Birdmilk is feathers,
The bean leaves are dumb as hands.

This month is fit for little.
The dead ripen in the grapeleaves.
A red tongue is among us.
Mother, keep out of my barnyard,
I am becoming another.

Dog-head, devourer:
Feed me the berries of dark.

The lids won't shut. Time
Unwinds from the great umbilicus of the sun
Its endless glitter.

I must swallow it all.

Lady, who are these others in the moon's vat –
Sleepdrunk, their limbs at odds?
In this light the blood is black.
Tell me my name.

### 4. THE BEAST

He was bullman earlier,
King of the dish, my lucky animal.
Breathing was easy in his airy holding.
The sun sat in his armpit.
Nothing went moldy. The little invisibles
Waited on him hand and foot.
The blue sisters sent me to another school.
Monkey lived under the dunce cap.
He kept blowing me kisses.
I hardly knew him.

He won't be got rid of:
Mumblepaws, teary and sorry,
Fido Littlesoul, the bowel's familiar.
A dustbin's enough for him.
The dark's his bone.
Call him any name, he'll come to it.

Mud-sump, happy sty-face.
I've married a cupboard of rubbish.
I bed in a fish puddle.
Down here the sky is always falling.
Hogwallow's at the window.
The star bugs won't save me this month.
I housekeep in Time's gut-end
Among emmets and mollusks,
Duchess of Nothing,
Hairtusk's bride.

## 5. FLUTE NOTES FROM A REEDY POND

Now coldness comes sifting down, layer after layer
To our bower at the lily root.
Overhead the old umbrellas of summer
Wither like pithless hands. There is little shelter.

Hourly the eye of the sky enlarges its blank
Dominion. The stars are no nearer.
Already frog-mouth and fish-mouth drink
The liquor of indolence, and all things sink

Into a soft caul of forgetfulness.
The fugitive colors die.
Caddis worms drowse in their silk cases,
The lamp-headed nymphs are nodding to sleep like statues.

Puppets, loosed from the strings of the puppet-master,
Wear masks of horn to bed.
This is not death, it is something safer.
The wingy myths won't tug at us any more:

The moults are tongueless that sang from above the water
Of golgotha at the tip of a reed,
And how a god flimsy as a baby's finger
Shall unhusk himself and steer into the air.

## 6. WITCH BURNING

In the marketplace they are piling the dry sticks.
A thicket of shadows is a poor coat. I inhabit
The wax image of myself, a doll's body.
Sickness begins here: I am a dartboard for witches.
Only the devil can eat the devil out.
In the month of red leaves I climb to a bed of fire.

It is easy to blame the dark: the mouth of a door,
The cellar's belly. They've blown my sparkler out.
A black-sharded lady keeps me in a parrot cage.
What large eyes the dead have!
I am intimate with a hairy spirit.
Smoke wheels from the beak of this empty jar.

If I am a little one, I can do no harm.
If I don't move about, I'll knock nothing over. So I said,
Sitting under a potlid, tiny and inert as a rice grain.
They are turning the burners up, ring after ring.
We are full of starch, my small white fellows. We grow.
It hurts at first. The red tongues will teach the truth.

Mother of beetles, only unclench your hand:
I'll fly through the candle's mouth like a singeless moth.
Give me back my shape. I am ready to construe the days
I coupled with dust in the shadow of a stone.
My ankles brighten. Brightness ascends my thighs.
I am lost, I am lost, in the robes of all this light.

## 7. THE STONES

This is the city where men are mended.
I lie on a great anvil.
The flat blue sky-circle

Flew off like the hat of a doll
When I flew out of the light. I entered
The stomach of indifference, the wordless cupboard.

The mother of pestles diminished me.
I became a still pebble.
The stones of the belly were peaceable,

The head-stone quiet, jostled by nothing.
Only the mouth-hole piped out,
Importunate cricket

In a quarry of silences.
The people of the city heard it.
They hunted the stones, taciturn and separate,

The mouth-hole crying their locations.
Drunk as a foetus
I suck at the pap of darkness.

The food tubes embrace me. Sponges kiss my lichens away.
The jewelmaster drives his chisel to pry
Open one stone eye.

This is the after-hell: I see the light.
A wind unstoppers the chamber
Of the ear, old worrier.

Water mollifies the flint lip,
And daylight lays its sameness on the wall.
The grafters are cheerful,

Heating the pincers, hoisting the delicate hammers.
A current agitates the wires
Volt upon volt. Catgut stitches my fissures.

A workman walks by carrying a pink torso.
The storerooms are full of hearts.
This is the city of spare parts.

My swaddled legs and arms smell sweet as rubber.
Here they can doctor heads, or any limb.
On Fridays the little children come

To trade their hooks for hands.
Dead men leave eyes for others.
Love is the uniform of my bald nurse.

Love is the bone and the sinew of my curse.
The vase, reconstructed, houses
The elusive rose.

Ten fingers shape a bowl for shadows.
My mendings itch. There is nothing to do.
I shall be as good as new.

We can read the poem as seven poems, or we can read it as one. Like Plath's later verse play, 'Three Women', 'Poem for a Birthday' demands to be read as a unity and as divided at one and the same time.[51] In the later poem, the divisions correspond to the three women's voices, each with their own story. In fact, on the night of the first broadcast, two of the three readers were unable to take part and the voices were not 'differentiated as clearly as they should have been'.[52] In this instance, chance decided an issue of poetic language which later revealed its unmistakable ideological dimension. Thus, when the BBC published the script in 1968, the voices were distinguished as 'Secretary', 'Girl' and 'Wife' — a blatantly normative interpretation, since the label 'Wife' is given to the woman who keeps her baby, whereas in fact only the woman who miscarries has, and goes home to, a husband in the text.[53] Plath herself had removed the names of the women from an early draft of the poem, differentiating them solely as first, second and third voice.[54] The differences between them are then confounded further by semantic and syntactic repetitions throughout the verse.

The same tension between narrative and repetition (legitimate development and confusion, to use Kroll's terms) appears in 'Poem for a Birthday' – the poem divides itself up into units, and then repeats and recalls itself across the space of those divisions. The tension can, however, just as well be stated in reverse, since the poem seems to offer a continuous narrative in relation to which those same divisions – which create moments of discreteness and unity inside the poem – act as breaks. At one level, as in 'Three Women', the tension between division and unity is what the poem is speaking about. The ambiguity of the title – birthday of the speaker and new birth – also resides internally to the act of gestation. In 'Poem for a Birthday' the speaker engenders something which is a part of, and other to, herself.

At the crudest level, the narrative of the seven sections can be described in terms of location, as a passage through spaces designated inside and outside. 'Who' and 'Dark House' situate the speaker inside (shed and dark house); 'Maenad' and 'The Beast' start at least by going back into memory; 'Flute Notes from a Reedy Pond' sinks down; 'Witch Burning' ascends; 'The Stones' signals the passage out. This is the story of the poem as sequence, legitimate development, self-emergence – a story whose parts could be situated as 'inside', 'inside', 'back', 'back', 'down', 'up' and 'out'. According to this narrative, by the time we get to the last section the speaker is produced, and produces herself, as 'good as new'. Commentators have remarked on the ambiguity of that last line of the poem which suggests, on the other hand, that this might be a false or cosmetic borning – transcendence, not as self-recovery, but as amnesia. This is not the only poem by Plath to offer such a caution. We will see later (Chapter 6) how in other poems she presents this problem of amnesia in terms of its specifically, and potentially lethal, political effects.

If, despite that first level of narrative, the idea of sequential development does not work for this poem, however, it is also because the poem operates by means of repetitions, bits and pieces constantly reappearing, as if the poem were constructing the memory of itself. In this context, memory has two meanings – the personal recollection of a subject (something a subject retrieves as part of an ongoing narrative of her or his life), but equally, and in tension with that first meaning, something which works against subjectivity as narrative by constantly returning on itself. The concept of repetition in Freudian thinking shares a similar ambiguity – it can mean going back to the beginning in order to retrieve the mythic narrative of an individual history, or repetition as insistence without content, something which Freud called the death drive because it precipitates the subject to the end of her- or himself.[55] Seen in this way, the changing locations of the poem are less easily read in terms of an identifiable progression because of the forms of repetition, at the level of language, with which that progression is constantly overlaid; location becomes not sequence (the discrete and distinguishable moments of a one-track journey) but question, reiterated but given as unanswerable by definition because of the syntactic and semantic instabilities of the text. Reading the poem, one gets a sense of something constantly running ahead of itself, as if meaning was not anticipated but arises – shakily and not always in a form that can be identified *as* meaning – through the course of the writing itself.

That instability is established from the beginning by the relation between the frame and the body of the verse. The title 'Poem for a Birthday' is followed by '1. Who', a question which is also not a question – it has no question mark, it does not ask 'whose' – that is, 'whose birthday' – but 'who'. That 'who' is both relative and interrogative, suspended without a referent in the text. Likewise the 'I' of the first stanza is disembodied – 'I am all mouth' – or else is *only* a body, mouth without other appendages – that is, without subjectivity other than the orifice of itself. Shrunk to such an orifice, the speaker makes her home in the shed surrounded by the objects of nature and its transformations (fruit, old tools, handles, rusky tusks, dead flowers and cabbageheads) and then transmutes herself further, sinking or disappearing (root, stone and owl pellet) into the earth.

This is the minimalism of Roethke. In a famous paper on poetics, Roman Jakobson describes the way poetic language exploits the two organisational principles of ordinary language – selection from a set of grammatically or semantically substitutable elements and their combination into the contiguous or co-present elements of a linguistic chain. Poetic language draws the discarded alternatives up into the utterance, placing alongside each other units linked by rhyme or reason, units we normally have to choose between, but which we associate automatically in the mind.[56] This would be a way of describing Roethke's minimalism, where the metaphoric equation – human = nature – is precipitated from the axis of substitution into that of contiguity to provide the components of the poem's narrative space; or, going back along the same axis, where the components of the natural world are ingested into the body of poetic speech. In Roethke's 'The Lost Son', however, the speaker retains a greater separateness from the elements into which he sinks: 'At Woodlawn, I heard the dead cry' . . . 'Voices come out of the silence/Say something' . . . 'At the wood's mouth,/By the cave's door/I listened to something/I had heard before' . . . 'The way to the boiler was dark . . . Once I stayed all night.'[57] The 'I' situates itself as observer – uninvited guest, so to speak, at the ceremony of nature's beginnings. It is a relationship of proximity which seems to sit on the edge of a menacing identification, the identity between the speaker and what he watches suggested but hesitant and uncertain.

There are, however, moments in 'The Lost Son' when the speaker seems to slide more directly into – become? – the creatures of the bog: 'I feel the slime of a wet nest./Beware Mother Mildew./Nibble again, fish nerves.' At moments like this it is not easy to situate the subject of the line; it is not clear whether Mother Mildew or fish nerves are the agent of the verb 'nibble', nor whose are the fish nerves. The same syntactic ambiguity affects the personal narrative which, as with Plath, accompanies the descent into the natural world: 'Rub me in father and mother'. Are the father and mother addressees of the verb, invoked and exhorted to intimacy by their child, are they the agents of this mingling with nature, do they rub him in; or are they the indirect objects of the verb, the body into which the speaker is rubbed, in which case does going down into nature mean a descent into the bodily pre-beginnings of himself? In Roethke's poem it is impossible to disambiguate moments like this, to separate out their linguistic or physical components. Nor is it possible to establish a hierarchy, or relationship of priority, between them. The psychic can be read as the contiguous and accompanying narrative *for*, as much as the psychic condition *of*, the subject's drama in the natural world, even though the title of the poem sets up the psychic as frame, if not cause. In fact the distinction between psyche and nature is a false one, since what is being figured in this writing is that permeability of boundaries, described by Kristeva in terms of abjection, which allow objects to pass back and forth across inner and outer space.

When Roethke seems to place, or name, this realm as abjection, he does so, however, at a distance (the distance proper to naming, we could say) which sets it at bay and turns it into an object of nostalgia: 'I want the old rage, the lash of primordial milk'. Or else it becomes the realm from which, by the intervention of the father, he is saved: 'Scurry of warm over small plants./Ordnung! Ordnung!/Papa is coming' (we can recognise in these alternatives the familiar stereotypes of male identity). In response to this call in the name of the father, all nature returns to its place (this is in one sense the meaning of the 'lost' son).

What Plath then seems to do is to open this realm back up into the space of incorporation – the site of that first metaphoric substitution between language and the body, where what is at issue is the taking in and casting out of both objects and of words. Everything which surrounds the speaker in the first part of 'Who' either eats or is eaten – note those first lines, where the clash between the syntactic and line break means that 'Eaten or rotten' can refer either to the 'I' or to fruit (The fruit's in,/Eaten or rotten. I am all mouth'). But in 'Poem for a Birthday', this drama is represented by Plath as inherent to the production of speech. To be minimal, to shrink into the objects of the natural world, means for Plath to go over in language the mechanisms through which the world and its objects come to be – a direct confrontation with what Kristeva terms the 'desirable and terrifying, nourishing and murderous, fascinating and abject inside'.[58] It is a type of grotesque embodiment, or defamiliarisation, of that familiar and clichéd set of poetic equivalencies between mother/body/earth: 'Mother, you are the one mouth/ I would be a tongue to. Mother of otherness/Eat me.' In these lines the alternatives seem to be entering into, tonguing the mother, speaking – by implication – her words; or identifying the mother as the site of difference, something which is no less coveted by the speaker, even though – because – this is an otherness which devours.

What passion of language is being represented here – what impossible turning in of the body and language on themselves?

Either a speech which means disappearing into the mouth of the mother, or severance, which might equally, or more safely, be seen as the precondition of body and language, but which means that the subject is no less totally effaced. It is in this space that the speaker transmutes herself, shrinks into, the objects of the natural world. We can call this abjection, therefore, provided we note that abjection does not belong only on the inside but resides at the point where inside and outside are differentiated, where the most elementary distinctions – animal, mineral, vegetable – are constituted but also threaten to break down.

One of the reasons why the poem is so difficult to read is that this instability works at the level of the most fundamental physical identity of the speaker. We simply never know from where, or rather what body, she is speaking. The 'I' enters into its objects, confounds the limit or distinction between them. Again we can compare this with those moments in Roethke where he seems to enter into the body of something which he still, at another level, observes, or where he more certainly puts himself at a controlling distance to what he describes.

Roethke asks:

> The shape of a rat?
> It's bigger than that.
> It's less than a leg
> And more than a nose,
> Just under the water
> It usually goes.

He makes the question of 'which animal?' a game, the game played by the child which works simultaneously as learning and as a way of transforming knowledge back into jest. The speaker in 'Poem for a Birthday' plays, we could say, a related or similar game ('whom, or what am I?'). The poem is a type of hide-and-seek twice over – the speaker hides: 'Let me sit in a flowerpot' . . . 'When it thundered I hid under a flat stone' . . . 'If I am a little one, I can do no harm'; but she also conceals herself in another sense, since we never know with any certainty what she is. Flower then root, stone, owl pellet in 'Who'; something which seems to be a wasp 'chewing' its nest out of 'gray paper' (the substance the wasp chews and then regurgitates out of itself) but which also whistles and wiggles its ears in 'Dark House'; maggot (bean eater) in 'Maenad': 'Sat by my father's bean tree/Eating the fingers of wisdom'; tape worm or some form of internal parasite in 'The Beast' ('the bowel's familiar' that house-keeps in 'Time's gut-end'); caddis worm and water insect in 'Flute Notes from a Reedy Pond'; rice beetle and moth in 'Witch Burning'. Some of these have a mythological significance – according to Robert Graves's *The White Goddess*, which Plath is known to have read, for the Pythagorean mystics bean eating was taboo: 'to eat beans was to eat one's parents' heads'.[59]

Sometimes the speaker seems to be these insects, sometimes they people the world in which she moves. They also mutate themselves (caddis worm into water nymph, mite into moth). The identity of the speaker therefore mutates itself into things which in turn mutate. But these identities are always fragile, bits and pieces of attributes, fragments of the only partly recognisable creatures they evoke – which is another reason why it makes no sense to read them as a one-way passage from the caterpillar into butterfly which takes flight. Transformation is always liable to go back on itself. Bodies go forward and wind back into the origins of themselves.

Likewise, the image of orality which runs through 'Poem for a Birthday' participates in a related form of inversion. It recurs across the seven sections of the poem and can in some sense be seen as its refrain: 'I eat my way/All-mouth licks up the bushes/And the pots of meat.' ('Dark House'); 'mother of mouths' . . . 'A red tongue is among us.' . . . 'Dog-head, devourer:/Feed me the berries of dark.' . . . 'I must swallow it all.' ('Maenad'); 'King of the dish' ('The Beast'); 'The moults are tongueless' ('Flute Notes from a Reedy Pond'); 'Only the devil can eat the devil out.' ('Witch Burning'); 'The mouth-hole crying their locations' ('The Stones'). The importance of the image, however, resides not just in that reiterated content but in the problem of agency it places at the centre of the poem, as if two questions were being put at once and in the form of their most intimate relation – who is speaking, and where does the subject of the utterance reside, is she inside or outside the words she speaks? Take that example from 'Dark House' where, as the agent of the verb 'to eat', the 'I' seems to be in apposition to 'All-mouth', who is then separated, gendered as different, targeted as an object of blame ('He's to blame'). Or the lines from 'Maenad', where the speaker asks to be fed by the devourer 'Dog-head, devourer:/Feed me', and then describes herself as the ultimate devourer (devourer of the ultimate), the one who must (desire or forcing?) swallow the 'endless glitter' that 'Time/ Unwinds from the great umbilicus of the sun'. Everything converges on the body of the speaker, requiring, even where it seems to come at her, that she take it all in. That image of time, running its great body into hers, is reminiscent – a type of version for the woman – of a famous image from the case of Daniel Schreber. First persecuted by and then imagining himself the object of special, divine, attention, he received into himself the rays of a paternal godhead.[60]

Once again, moments like this and their recurrence make it difficult to read the poem only in terms of its own progress, as a sequence which passes logically from its beginning to its end. In the last section, all of this seems to belong in the past: 'I entered/The stomach of indifference, the wordless cupboard.//The mother of pestles diminished me', only to have it repeat itself, to be rediscovered, in the body of the very transformation she undergoes: 'The food tubes embrace me. Sponges kiss my lichens away' – strange transformation where one creature latches on to the body and removes, by means of embracing, another substance that cleaves.

This is not, however, the whole story. It is equally important to notice how Plath offers another level of narrative in the text. If we go back to 'Who', then at the point where the shed becomes 'These halls . . . full of women who think they are birds', she is also situating the transmutations recorded by the poem in a different sense by identifying them as fantasy or hallucination. This allows the reader to recognise the location of the poem, at least partially, as the institution (the 'madhouse') which diagnoses – wipes out – mutation, or metaphor, as such. Situated in this way, these mutations take on another meaning. In this context their very fluidity, or availability, can threaten the speaker, since if she is minimal (insect?) and the other inmates are birds, she must transform herself again, along the lines of an infinite regress, if she is not to be eaten. This is one of the meanings of 'root', 'stone' and 'owl pellet', which bury her further into the earth, or make her inedible or indigestible – the owl pellet being the undigested remnant thrown up by carnivorous birds (one could of course say that this means she has been all the more totally consumed). Shrinking appears here as a form of evasive action – the central character in Plath's 1955 short story 'Tongues of Stone' (which can be read as a draft for the mental hospital episode in *The Bell Jar*) stares at the buzzing black flies 'as if by concentrating she could shrink herself into the compass of a fly's body and become an organic part of the natural world'.[61]

Crucially, therefore, the poem disperses the agency or source of negativity across the text; like the body of the speaker, it can appear almost anywhere. The threat is internal, structural, in relation to the process of abjection, but it also finds its embodiment in more than one aspect of the outside world – in the fantasies of the inmates, as well as in the institution which threatens the memory of what takes place. Thus at the one point in 'Who' where the speaker directly speaks or identifies her own statement, it is precisely an instruction to remember which she once issued to herself: 'I said: I must remember this, being small' (remember being small, or being small as the reason why she must remember). The institution endangers in so far as it puts memory (the memory of abjection) at risk: 'For weeks I can remember nothing at all.' The first section of the poem therefore presents something which could be called an inner psychic battle, but it also represents a battle over that first battle's right to representation. What the madhouse threatens is the subject's symbolic capacity, her being in language, whose frightening, but no less necessary, preconditions are represented by the poem as the (minimal) preconditions of (minimal) life.

If we turn for a moment to 'Johnny Panic and the Bible of Dreams', we can recognise something of the same story. A secretary in a Boston psychiatric hospital keeps her own private record, her bible and treasure-house, of the patients' dreams (the motto of this bible is 'Perfect fear casteth out all else').[62] The dreams come out of a great lake – 'the sewage farm of ages, transparence aside' – which forms the only content of her own dream.[63] She records dreams, but she also invents them, until she is caught and, like the speaker at the end of 'Who', is given electrotherapy: 'The crown of wire is placed on my head, the wafer of forgetfulness on my tongue.'[64] In this story, however, memory and dreaming are saved in an apocalyptic moment by Johnny Panic, in whose name she had collected the dreams. In both this story and 'Poem for a Birthday', which were written at the same time, the psychic process – dreaming or abjection – is doubled over by the issue of its symbolisation. It is not just the experience but its ability to be represented that is at stake. This is important if we are to avoid one predominant attempt to identify an enemy in relation to Plath (electrotherapy, and through it, the oppressive mental institution, as what drives her mad). For it is clear from these two pieces of writing that the damage of electrotherapy is not just what it does *to* the speaker, something negative it forces upon her, but equally what it takes *away* – a negativity which she identifies no less firmly as something internal to herself.

Twice in her *Journals*, Plath cites passages from writers about this relation between inner and outer worlds. From Oesterrich's *Possession: Demoniacal and Other*: 'Although the patient appeared possessed, his malady was not possession but the emotion of remorse. This was true of so many possessed persons, the devil being for them merely the incarnation of their regrets, remorse, terror and vices'; from Defoe's *Journal of the Plague Year*:

it was the opinion of others that it [the plague] could be distinguished by the party's breathing upon a piece of glass, where, the breath condensing, there might living creatures be seen by a microscope of strange, monstrous and frightful shapes. [Plath glosses: '"The chaemeras" of the sick mind also']65

Julia Kristeva writes:

If it is true that the abject at once solicits and pulverises the subject, one can understand why it is experienced at its strongest when, weary of the vain attempt to recognise oneself on the outside, the subject finds the impossible within: when the subject finds that the impossible constitutes her or his very *being*, discovering that it is only as abject that the subject *is* other, that she or he *is* none other than abject.66

For Kristeva, abjection is the only grounds for self-differentiation, the only process through which the subject, in its painful distinction from the other, comes to be. It seems to me crucial to recognise this process as it is represented by Plath; to recognise too what it is that she is representing in relation to recognition as such ('weary of the vain attempt to recognise oneself on the outside'). If Plath is laying out the conditions of symbolisation, then it becomes as impossible to pathologise her as it is to insist that everything negative in her writing is the fault of others, that negativity can always be located, in an unequivocal act of accusation, on the outside. As Shoshana Felman puts it in relation to madness:

> To state that madness has well and truly become a commonplace is to say that madness stands in our contemporary world for the radical ambiguity of the inside and the outside, an ambiguity which escapes human subjects who speak only by misrecognising it [ . . . ] A discourse that speaks of madness can henceforth no longer know whether it is inside or outside, internal or external to the madness of which it speaks.[67]

If we corporealise that inside/outside dichotomy, then what Felman is describing here almost as a problem of ethics – by what right do you call someone mad? – can be seen as a drama played out and repeated (remouthed) in the most fundamental processes of speech. But if we add Felman's quote to the concept of abjection, we can also see the link – the link Plath represents here – between that drama and its more concretely social dimension; between subjectivity and the institutions in which it finds its cultural, historical destiny.

The more precise relation that Plath articulates between these two dimensions will be discussed in more detail later in this book. But note already how the representation of agency – the confused location of who or what does what to whom – in this poem troubles, even as it figures, one sexual political schema through which Plath is often read. There is something personified in the form of the male gender which the speaker accuses in the poem: 'All-mouth' ('He's to blame') or 'The Beast' ('He won't be got rid of' . . . 'I've married a cupboard of rubbish'). But perhaps in no other poem by Plath is it quite so clear that this male thing cannot have the status of a cause, or unique target of blame. Thing rather than identifiable person, it shifts, together with the accusation laid against it, like everything else in the poem. We can watch where else it alights – mother, surgeon, inmate, black-sharded lady – provided we also stress that all these entities are subject to the same hesitancy of definition as the speaker. It is often not clear quite who or what they are. External agency is unstable as well as shifting from place to place. One of the meanings of the poem's transformations is therefore that blame belongs to no one and to everyone because it is something which is passed around: 'It is easy to blame the dark: the mouth of a door,/The cellar's belly' (abjection not to blame but the place from which the problem of blame can be spoken). It might be worth stressing, therefore, that to read the poem in terms of abjection does not involve some personalised accusation against the mother (there is absolutely no point in trying to decide whether Plath's mother or husband is at fault).

This is not to say, as we will see, that there are not things about which Plath strongly protests. Rather, it is to stress that what she represents in 'Poem for a Birthday' is an irreducible instance, point of emergence of the body and language which, precisely as such a point of emergence, can only ever partially be given face. As if Plath were offering a warning, or replying in advance to those readers of her poetry who will battle it out over whom she really hated, or who is the real target of her rage.

Before leaving the poem, it might be worth asking, therefore, what is it about 'The Stones' and 'Flute Notes from a Reedy Pond' that, so to speak, passes; what is it that lets them through – on Plath's own insistence, it would seem, but agreed by Knopf? What is it about them that makes them more acceptable – less obviously derivative seems to be the judgement from Knopf; less conflictual, more aesthetically coherent, as Kroll's commentary – on 'The Stones', at least – seems to imply. For the criticism that Plath is derivative seems to be absolutely pointless in a context where the engendering of language, the relation of body to body which underlies and gives it shape, is what is being represented inside the text. In fact the poem could be said to stage the pre-Oedipal version of the anxiety of influence – the question being not what she took from Roethke but what it is about taking and giving, in relation to language, that she uses him to explore. It would seem, then, that the more manageable parts of the poem will be the parts where this drama is less obviously rooted in the problem of linguistic and poetic identity, is more under control (the criticism about derivation and the one about aesthetic coherence – both arguments about a lack of the proper forms of distinction – being somewhere one and the same).

If we look at 'Flute Notes from a Reedy Pond', what is striking is the sudden note of elegy it introduces into the poem: 'Now coldness comes sifting down, layer after layer/ To our bower at the lily root', together with the greater relative length of the syntactic units, which seem to glide towards the completion of themselves: 'Overhead the old umbrellas of summer/ Wither like pithless hands.' Whatever negativity the poem represents at the level of its content feels held up – given sustenance – by the comforting lyricism of its syntactic frame: 'Already frog-mouth and fish-mouth drink/ The liquor of indolence, and all things sink// Into a soft caul of forgetfulness.' There is no shifting, unsettled poetic 'I' in this part of the poem; it is in fact the only one in the sequence to use the first person plural: 'our bower', 'The wingy myths won't tug at us any more' – a collective destiny in which, for a moment at least, things seem to have returned to their proper place. In this sense this part of the poem is in fact much closer to moments in Roethke than the rest.

'This is not death, it is something safer' – in his autobiography, Allon White gives a perfect account of this realm: 'There is none of that elegiac lyricism of drowning and summer afternoons here – gentle *kaddish* for the dead', contrasting it with that other, more violent, domain of monsters where all form and language slide away.[68] The same contrast is there, of course, in 'Poem for a Birthday', which presents 'Flute Notes' not as an independent unit, but rather as a moment of suspension, framed on either side by 'The Beast' and 'Witch Burning', which precede and follow it in the text. 'Flute Notes' seems to embody that pure objectless state of being – oceanic feeling, as Freud once called it – which is so often idealised, but whose idyll, as one analyst has put it, is totally deceptive because it is the ultimate omnipotent fantasy, possible only because everything has been consumed into the self.[69]

Even inside the poem, this state is presented as possible only on condition of wiping out memory, that memory which 'Poem for a Birthday' represents elsewhere as the stake of battle, as what it is fighting to preserve. It is ironic, therefore, that this part of the poem should have been given an autonomous identity, like the god that unhusks himself into the air in the last lines – lines which in context seem to offer a critique of transcendence at least as much as its celebration. In fact to read these lines in terms of transcendence, as the birth of a god child which is also the rebirth of the poetic self, could be seen as a misreading, since the stanza together with the preceding line presents this moment in quotation marks, so to speak, as the end of myth ('the wingy myths won't tug at us any more') and as a song that is no longer sung: 'The *moults are tongueless that sang from above the water*/Of golgotha at the tip of a reed,/And how a god flimsy as a baby's finger/ Shall unhusk himself and steer into the air' (my emphasis). The question remains open as to whether the song is no longer sung because what it once sung of is impossible, or because it has been fulfilled.

If 'Flute Notes' presents the elegiac side, or counter to, abjection, then 'The Stones' can be read as its narrative mastery or control. Abjection, of course, is not a content or object – where there is elegy or coherent narrative, it is in some sense meaningless to talk about its 'presence' in the text. But 'The Stones' is clearly that part of 'Poem for a Birthday' which lends itself most easily to a narrative interpretation, even if the resolution ('I shall be as good as new') is ambiguous and, as with 'Flute Notes', can be read as the criticism of itself – even if, as we have already seen, the process of transformation which is intended to remake the 'I' of the poem, to set it off from its most treacherous moorings, takes on their very shape.

This is the poem which creates the past tense of what has gone before: 'I entered/The stomach of indifference, the wordless cupboard', where the 'I' is stable – emptied of any possible identification with insects, it stands as the purely empty category of itself. This is, as the poem itself puts it, the poem of the 'after hell', the poem of reversion to identity and sameness: 'daylight lays its sameness on the wall'. It is also the poem that represents the coming into being of femininity in terms of one of the most traditional poetic epithets or clichés of itself: 'The vase, reconstructed, houses/The elusive rose.'[70] It is also – the two may be related – the poem in which electrotheraphy takes its course: 'A current agitates the wires/Volt upon volt.' If we place this poem in context, then it offers resolution as wipe-out – that is, resolution as the severance of the subject from the preconditions of herself.

Is this the 'wholeness' of which Hughes – amongst others – speaks? Less personally, more pertinently, what is it that Plath, at the level of poetic representation and language, is being asked to relinquish? As we will see, far from being purely a question of personal or moral accountability (the most familiar version of a battle between the sexes), the encounter between Plath and Hughes takes place in this territory over the function and purpose of poetic language, over the poetic and fully gendered distinction between abjection and transcendence, or, more precisely, between the different and antagonistic images of femininity which can attach to each.

A final point about Plath's sources for this poem. 'All-mouth' who eats up the bushes ('Dark House') and 'the city where men are mended' ('The Stones') are lifted, as Judith Kroll and others have noted, from two stories in the collection of native African folktales collected and published in 1952 by the famous enthnographer Paul Radin (Hughes comments, in his 'Notes on the Chronological Order of Sylvia Plath's Poems', that she was reading Radin at the time).[71] 'Mantis and the All-Devourer' tells the story of the Man who eats bushes, sheep and his own children, and is finally cut open by his grandchildren, whereupon everybody inside him, together with the community he threatened, is freed.[72] In 'The City Where Men are Mended', one of the girls in the town is trapped inside a tree when she refuses to barter with the devil, is then devoured by a hyena, and is finally taken by her mother to the city where men are mended, where she is repaired. The mother's journey is a type of ordeal in which she must turn away three times from food she comes across on her way. Her rival, who then kills her own, ugly daughter in the hope that mending her will make her beautiful, fails the ordeal and is left with a monstrosity, a daughter of bits and pieces who has been only partly restored.[73]

Some of the images in these stories, like the red tongue of 'All-mouth', are directly picked up by 'Poem for a Birthday' ('A red tongue is among us'). They can also be read as prototypes of its narrative and some of its meanings. The stories represent the same relation between engendering and devouring, or devouring and language, that we have seen in Plath's text. For example, Mantis invites 'All-mouth' to the home, against the admonitions of 'All-mouth's' own daughter, and risks being devoured by him because only then will he be able to speak: 'Then I can talk, for I do not talk now.'[74] In this case the devourer is a paternal figure, father and grandfather to the other characters in the story. It is a gender division which Plath herself crosses over in other poems: in 'The Colossus', the world arises out of the dead father's tongue: 'The sun rises under the pallor of your tongue'. In 'The City Where Men are Mended', the mother is accountable for the remaking or undoing of the daughter, who is literally dismembered and refigured in the text. If 'All-mouth' threatens to devour his offspring, here the mother can re-engender her daughter only if she herself refuses to eat. As we will see, this drama about the origins of body and language is represented by Plath at different moments of her writing in relation to both maternal and paternal speech.

Following Lévi-Strauss, therefore, these African folktales could be read as mythic narratives of which Plath's poem is the modern and Westernised variant (this is not the same as representing them as the primitive underside of her work).[75] On the other hand, to see them like this is to extract them from the context and frame in which Radin himself presents them, where the question of how to read these stories, with all its political ramifications, is explicitly at stake. Radin publishes these stories as part of an argument about language, meaning and culture. They have been selected precisely for their literary qualities, to save the concept of the folktale from some of the connotations of 'myth'. Equally, he is concerned to rescue their violence from the concept of the 'primitive' by reading it in terms of the 'force and brutal conquest' to which Africa has been subjected, thereby placing it firmly in political and historical context: 'Assuredly we have the right to infer that it is largely because these people are living in an insecure and semi-chaotic world, with its loss of values and inward moral demoralisation, that cruelty and murder loom so large in many of their tales.'[76] In one of the stories the link to imperialism is explicit – the giant who devours and introduces death into the world has the hair of the white man.[77]

We can therefore see how the inside/outside dichotomy so central to Plath's poem reappears here in a different, more recognisably political, form. Seen in this light, 'Poem for a Birthday' is surrounded by a debate about origins in relation to violence as 'primitive' or politically – that is, externally – imposed (in this context Radin's introduction acts as a crucial caution against ethnocentrism). That dichotomy then reappears in the difference between the two sources of Plath's poem, between Roethke and Radin, between violence in the toolshed and violence which belongs to a more recognisably political outside. Although Plath seems to empty this second meaning out of the African folktales she partly draws on for 'Poem for a Birthday', it would not be true to say that it does not form part of her concerns. In a section – one of many which speaks of politics – omitted from the published *Journals*, she writes:

. . . while America dies like the Great Roman Empire died, while the legions fail and the barbarians overrun our tender, steak-juicy, butter creamy, million dollar stupendous land, somewhere there will be the people that never mattered much in our scheme of things anyway. In India, perhaps, or Africa, they will rise.[78]

Why are passages like this cut?[79] A number of further questions arise: what are the politics of Sylvia Plath; what are the sexual politics, both inside her writing, and in relation to the editing, framing and interpreting of her work; what is the archive, the body of her writing as we might call it in another, and perhaps more basic, sense? All these questions are related, but I will start at least by considering them apart.

# THE ARCHIVE

> Is he the archive of their accusations?
> Or their ghostly purpose, their pining vengeance?
> Or their unforgiven prisoner?
> (Ted Hughes, 'Crow's Nerve Fails')

I hope each of us owns the facts of her or his own life.
(Ted Hughes, 'Sylvia Plath: the facts of her life and the desecration
of her grave', *The Independent*, 20 April 1989)

In April 1989, a controversy broke out in the pages of the *Guardian*
and *The Independent* about the grave and the memory of Sylvia
Plath. The immediate precipitating cause was the absence of the
headstone at Plath's grave in Heptonstall in Yorkshire. Over a
period of years the grave had been defaced four times – on each
occasion the letters of the last name had been prised off the
inscription 'Sylvia Plath Hughes'. This time the stone had not yet
been replaced. Plath's grave remained unmarked, and her memory –
it was argued in a series of letters in the *Guardian* and in a feature
article in *The Independent* by Ronald Hayman – neglected.[1] For
Hughes the need to repair the headstone, together with the successive assaults, was sufficient explanation for the delay ('like me [the
mason] probably feels there is no hurry').[2] In fact the gravestone
was soon to be replaced, but for most of the commentators the
failure by the Hughes family to replace it immediately could be read
as the sign of the same abuse of Plath that had prompted the
original defacement – that is, the control by Ted Hughes of Sylvia
Plath's legacy and her work.

Sylvia Plath died intestate and her literary estate passed to her
husband, from whom she was at the time separated, with the result
that Hughes has been responsible for the posthumous publication
of a large part of Plath's writing. In his article in *The Independent*,
Hayman pointed out that on one occasion this has involved, as
Hughes himself has acknowledged, the destruction of a portion of

her work: 'He was legally within his rights when he destroyed the last volume of her journals. "I didn't want her children to have to read it," he said.'[3] Central to the controversy was the question of whether Plath had signed divorce papers or not. The first letter to the *Guardian* had suggested that she had done so, and that Plath and Hughes were therefore effectively divorced, which would mean that Hughes's control over the estate was morally illegitimate.[4]

Not surprisingly, when Hughes uncharacteristically broke his silence to reply to these various critiques (in the form of a long letter to the *Guardian* and an article in *The Independent*), he devoted a central and repeated part of his reply to refuting this suggestion – there were, he insisted, no divorce proceedings under way.[5] For Hughes, it was a piece of wilful misinformation characteristic of the extraordinary 'Fantasia' that surrounds Sylvia Plath. Typically, he argued, 'morally strident demands for more truth' in relation to Plath were accompanied by the 'swallowing of a blatant historical untruth'.[6] The issue was not therefore the availability, or not, of the truth, but something provoked by Plath in the relationship to truth as such: 'the truth simply tends to produce more lies . . . The Fantasia about Sylvia Plath is more needed than the facts.'[7] What Hughes was arguing was that Sylvia Plath seems to precipitate a perversion of our relationship to knowledge. Against this perversion – this 'Fantasia' – Hughes was speaking for the 'facts'.

The question of the 'facts', of who controls them and for whom, was, however, what was at issue. Indeed, it could be argued that it was precisely Hughes's claim to speak for the 'facts' in relation to Plath that was being contested by the defacement of Plath's grave, as well as by the other accusations on the subject of her writing which have accompanied it. Hughes acknowledges in a parenthesis that his own relationship to Plath makes his claim to speak for the facts problematic ('this is a complication, I realise, but there it is, it can't be helped'), although one of his objections is that where he has offered a correction to a distortion, it tends to be treated merely as a 'variant hypothesis'.[8] What seems to be at stake in this dispute, therefore, is not just the question of the facts, but that of interpretation. For it is in so far as a fact never comes independently of its context and enunciation (who is offering the facts and why) that it is liable to be interpreted, to become a hypothesis, or an unrecognisable variant of itself. In a later letter to the *Observer* on the publication of Anne Stevenson's biography, Hughes insists on the distinction. He had advised Stevenson and her informants 'to stick to observed fact, and to make clear at every point that opinion is opinion', to 'avoid interpreting my feelings and actions for me, and to beware how they interpreted Sylvia's'.[9] Observe without interpretation, stick to fact.

One of the most striking things about the correspondence was the way the various participants found themselves rapidly drawn into a discussion about language or interpretation. The signatories of the first letter to the *Guardian* also argued in a subsequent letter in reply to Hughes that they had been misread: 'It is true that any piece of writing is open to interpretation by its readers, but we find it hard to understand how our letter could have given an impression so very far from our purpose.'[10] By a strange twist, the correspondence started to repeat the problem at the heart of the controversy as it demonstrated the ease with which language can be turned against its intention. To say that 'nobody owns fact' is simply to underline the extent to which this process is an unavoidable facet of language itself. It was in response to this statement in the article in *The Independent* that Hughes commented 'I hope each of us owns the facts of her or his own life.'[11]

Nothing demonstrates more clearly, however, the problematic nature of such a statement – of that 'own' and that 'owns' – than the legacy of Sylvia Plath. Clearly Plath does not own the facts of her own life, not just because she is no longer here to speak for herself but because even in relation to one's 'own' life (especially in relation to it) there can be no simple ownership of the facts. For that potential for misreading which lies between speech and its reception also resides internally to subjectivity itself. As Hughes himself puts it: 'I know she told many different people many different things, and different things at different times.'[12] We can note too the ambiguity of the word 'own' itself in this context – own as possession, own as to acknowledge, to admit to, or confess ('to own *to* something'). Confession, with all that it implies by way of redeeming honesty, would not of course exist as a concept were it not that we constantly use language to deceive others as well as ourselves.

In this context, where what is centrally at issue is Hughes's ownership of Plath, the ambiguity of his own statement, which leads in exactly the opposite direction to the one intended, is striking – as much as claiming an objective relation to knowledge in relation to Plath, Hughes could be seen as culpabilising, or accusing, himself. As we will see, it is the survivors of Plath, the inheritors of her legacy, who have turned this story into a case of what psychoanalysts Nicolas Abraham and Maria Torok term 'transgenerational haunting', by repeatedly conducting themselves *as if* they were the perpetrators of a crime.[13] For no crime need have been committed, no sense of criminality need exist on the part of the protagonists (acting in this instance in their own terms from the highest of motives), for a saga such as this one to convey – all on its own and albeit perversely – an irreducible aura of guilt.

In fact, it is not through any simple imputation of guilt that we can best make sense of this story. One of the things I will be arguing here is that the logic of blame which seems to attach itself so relentlessly to the story of Sylvia Plath needs once and for all to be left behind. For if at one level the editing of Plath certainly invites such a logic, it also provides a startling demonstration of its self-defeating futility. The story to be told here will therefore be a contradictory one – an account of what, at the most immediate and obvious level, has been done to Plath's work in her name, but also a story of ambiguity – of an uncertainty which unsettles the very form of judgement on which that first account appears to rely.

If the dispute in the *Guardian* and *The Independent* suggests that this uncertainty is a difficulty inherent to language and subjectivity, it is equally the difficulty on which poetic language thrives. One of the things to which Hughes objected in the article in *The Independent* was its *literal* reading of one of Plath's late poems, 'Letter in November' ('In the classroom, his literal reading of that poem would be laughable. One wonders if it is any better in *The Independent*').[14] In this context, therefore, literal interpretation is a joke. Later in his reply, he takes issue with the article's reading of Plath's first collection of poems, *The Colossus*, and produces his own reading of the gender relations in that text and in the whole of Plath's subsequent work. This makes it clear that the issue of sexual difference and sexual politics is one of the things at stake in the fight over the ownership and meaning of Plath's work. The language appealed to is that of the courtroom (the verifiable facts), but the scenario unfolding here is more akin to a family saga (we will see later how the two come together) – a family saga into which everyone, regardless of whether they belong inside it, seems to be drawn. As the writer in *The Independent* put it: 'her readers feel personally involved, almost as if she were a member of the family'.[15] Far from simply establishing the facts and drawing up a barrier between inside and outside (Hughes's repeated and understandable request for privacy), the effect of the Plath legacy has been to reveal what is most troubling and uncertain about language, what is most intimate, familial, sexual about our relationship to knowledge itself.

Furthermore, this disturbance of language and knowledge strikes at the most fundamental, if fragile, insignia of our symbolic identities – memory, grave and name. In direct proportion to the insistence on the facts, this fragility exposes itself in relation to the literary remains and legacy of Sylvia Plath. One of the strange things about the controversy over the gravestone is that despite the uncertainty and contested ambiguity of the poet's name – Sylvia Plath Hughes, Sylvia Plath, Sylvia Hughes – it is none the less in her name that each of the participants to the dispute claims, unhesitatingly, to be speaking.

The unintended effect of all this is that it is impossible to read Plath independently of the frame, the surrounding discourses, through which her writing is presented. Linguistics makes a crucial distinction between the frame and content of the utterance, between what the utterance speaks of and the place of enunciation from which it is spoken. And it argues that discourses which seem to speak directly and without any intervening framework have simply deployed the appropriate rhetorical devices through which their own status as language can the more effectively be effaced (the literary tradition of 'realist' writing would be the most obvious instance of this).[16]

Plath is celebrated, and condemned, as the high priestess of direct psychic speech, for the speed and seeming lack of inhibition with which she goes for what Hughes once described as the 'central, unacceptable things'.[17] We saw in the last chapter how those 'things' are intimately bound up with the representation of language in her writing, how they do not come independently of, but refer at the most basic level to, the processes of language out of which they can be seen to emerge. What can be seen from looking at the archive of her writing is a distinct but related point. In direct proportion to the extent that Plath writes of psychic conflict and subjectivity in the body of her writing, as *theme*, so the content of that writing is duplicated, can be rediscovered at its most intense and problematic, in the frame that surrounds and most literally, most physically, constitutes her work – frame meaning here not her own enunciation but the editing, publication and presentation of her writing. Only if this is ignored can Plath be accused – as if she were the sole and cursed progenitor – of what she most troublingly represents in the body of her texts.

Who speaks for Plath? What is the body of her writing? What is her name? How should she be remembered? Should there be a more permanent literary memorial to her work? If the controversy over Plath is important, beyond the forms of vicarious interest which it gives rise to and to which Hughes takes exception, it is because it makes so transparent the lack of innocence with which any of these questions can be answered – the lack of innocence, indeed, with which they can be broached. What follows, then, is one attempt (there have been and will be others) to respond to some of these questions, a reading – of necessity speculative – of the editing of Plath's work.

Most immediately, most visibly, the first two of these questions lead unavoidably to Hughes – to that editing, controlling and censoring presence which one encounters, of necessity, as soon as one even attempts to approach the body of Plath's work. At this level, Hughes's role has been unequivocal precisely to the extent that he has commented on it himself. Thus, to take the more striking examples, the destruction of the last journal ('In those days I regarded forgetfulness as an essential part of survival')[18], or the reordering of the *Ariel* poems published two years after Plath's death:

> The *Ariel* eventually published in 1965 was a somewhat different volume from the one she had planned. It incorporated most of the dozen or so poems she had gone on to write in 1963, though she herself, recognising the different inspiration of these new pieces, regarded them as the beginning of a third book. It omitted some of the more personally aggressive poems from 1962, and might have omitted one or two more had she not already published them herself in magazines – so that by 1965 they were widely known.[19]

Both of these moments have received ample commentary – outrage at the destruction of a piece of Plath's writing; anger at what seems to be a fairly straightforward violation of the poet's own intention, her own sense of the appropriate contents and order of her work. Now clearly the factors determining such a selection after the death of the poet will be multiple and complex (according to Olwyn Hughes, the desire to secure Plath's reputation from what might have been read as 'appalling vindictiveness', and the fact that those later poems – as well as a poem like 'Daddy', which Hughes would have liked to omit – had already appeared).[20] But that the 'more aggressive poems' removed from *Ariel* were in large part the ones whose aggression has since been interpreted as directed at Hughes (notably 'The Rabbit Catcher', 'The Detective', 'The Courage of Shutting-Up', 'A Secret', 'The Jailor', 'Stopped Dead', 'Amnesiac', 'Purdah') has laid him open to the charge that the whole process has been in the service of self-interest, where 'interest' means unequivocally the interest of the man. Why, for example, is 'Daddy' in, but 'The Jailor' out, given that they were *both* published in *Encounter* in 1963? ('Stopped Dead', 'Amnesiac' and 'Purdah' also appeared in the same year).[21] Ironically, by omitting these poems on the grounds that their reference is too personal, Hughes is engaging in the very form of literal interpretation of which he is so contemptuous in reply to Hayman in *The Independent*. He might of course argue that it was precisely because their meaning would be literalised that they had to be removed. Either way it is clear how feminism will interpret this – Hughes silencing Plath, the man silencing the woman, substituting his interests for her voice.

As Marjorie Perloff has pointed out in her article 'The Two Ariels: The (Re)making Of The Sylvia Plath Canon', there is another implication.[22] For Plath ordered her own version of *Ariel* to start with the poem 'Morning Song' and to end with the last poem from the Bee sequence, 'Wintering', which would have opened the collection on the word 'love', ended it on the word 'spring'. This was to have been a collection in which that famous Plath 'aggression' would have been surrounded by a positive frame. The effect of Hughes's editing of *Ariel* was therefore, paradoxically to remove the aggression but to increase it at the same time. On this basis, Perloff can argue, as other readers of Plath will argue, that what was suppressed by this editing is nothing less than the 'rebirth of an isolate [female] self'.[23] According to this reading, therefore, Hughes not only silenced Plath's legitimate anger, he also – in an act which explains that anger and justifies its repetition – deprived feminism of a positive identity and selfhood.

In all of this, *Ariel* is not the only text by Plath to be affected. As we saw in the last chapter, the published *Journals* take out the 'intimacies' and 'nasty bits'.[24] Here the purpose seems to be the selective protection of people Plath knew (by no means exclusively Hughes) as well as, in a gesture of unmistakable moralism, the (sexual) protection of Plath from herself. Taken together, the editing of *Ariel* and the *Journals* leaves a strange disembodied corpus of writing – minus one form of aggression and – one could argue – its symbolic reparation in *Ariel*, minus, in the *Journals*, one form of Plath's anger and sex. As if what is removed are the two furthest reaches of psychic life, or rather what could be judged as the good (uplifting) and the bad (nasty and low), the best and the worst of Sylvia Plath. Which is not of course to suggest that there is nothing of this left in the published texts, that moments of the highest and lowest intensity do not remain to be read. It is the logic of the editing (as stated, for example, in this opening note to the *Journals*) and the fact of the cutting which are at stake.

The problem is then compounded by the way the process of editing, specifically in relation to the *Journals*, strikes at the corpus of the writing in the most vulgar, physical sense. In the published text, cuts are marked with ellipses and 'omission' signs: McCullough uses the latter to indicate cuts requested by the Estate, ellipses indicate some of her cuts, others are unmarked. Scholars who go to Smith College to read the unedited version are presented with a text part original, part publisher's typescript (replying to the charge of censorship, the Estate has pointed to the availability of this material), with the latter at various points literally cut to pieces – pages with sections cut out in the middle, other lines made illegible by heavy black ink, sections ringed in red and marked 'cut'.[25] Faced with this, it is not difficult to see how this editing could be regarded as violation – '*corps morcelé*' – body in bits and pieces: 'made to do violence on', as Plath puts it in one of her early poems, 'Strumpet Song'.[26]

Not only in this instance, however, has the question of censorship been something of a distraction, diverting attention from what are no less important but far more subtle pieces of editing by Hughes. In the introduction to the *Collected Poems*, he explains why he has grouped everything prior to 1956 at the back of the book under the heading 'Juvenilia': 'A logical division occurs, conveniently, at the end of 1955, just after the end of her twenty-third year.'[27] Plath herself, in a letter to her brother in July 1958, says that she has discarded everything she wrote from before two years ago, although discarding of past writing was something which she repeated over and again, and in relation to different moments, throughout her career. As Hughes himself puts it in his essay on the chronology of her poems with reference to 'Poem for a Birthday': 'two years later, she dismissed everything prior to THE STONES as Juvenilia'.[28]

In his notes to the *Collected Poems*, Hughes explains that 1956 was the year in which Plath started to write the poems of her first published collection.[29] But look at those first poems in the *Collected Poems* in the context of the *Journals*, and we then find that the second poem can be dated as 20 February, the third as March, in the days shortly before and after her first meeting on 26 February with Hughes.[30] It is the start of her relationship with Hughes which marks this particular break in her writing (there had indeed been a pause since a previous productive period in early 1955).[31] The effect of this division is, therefore, that Hughes structures, punctuates, her writing definitively with himself (a move symmetrical to that earlier attempt to remove himself from what comes at the end). The effect is to make his presence seem more and more conspicuous, either as too little or too much.

Even more important is the way he presents all Plath's work in terms of a constant teleological reference to *Ariel*, with the result that everything else she produced is more or less offered as *waste*. Introducing the collection of her prose fiction, *Johnny Panic and the Bible of Dreams*, he writes: 'Reading this collection, it should be remembered that her reputation rests on the poems of the last six months', thereby dismissing the collection in the act of publishing it, while also dividing the stories up unhesitatingly into 'The more successful short stories and prose pieces'; and 'Other stories' (the first category does not refer only to successful publication, as it includes the unpublished 'Snow Blitz').[32] And in the Foreword to the *Journals*: '*Ariel* and the later poems give us the voice of that [real] self . . . All her other writings, except these journals, are the waste products of its gestation.'[33] Let's already note how close, aesthetically, that notion of the emergent real self is to the feminist reading of Plath in terms of an isolate selfhood that Hughes has also been seen as suppressing.

What starts to emerge is that the editing of Plath's work engages not only issues of sexual politics and power, but also concepts of writing and poetic language – not only what physically *can*, but also what aesthetically *should*, and *how* it should, be read. As we will see, the two issues are finally inseparable. But we might also ask here what it means for Hughes to talk in this context of Plath's 'real' self (which he recognised, he says, one day from three lines she recited as she went out of the door[34]). Who defines a 'real' self, which can surely have meaning only as *self*-definition, as a self-defining of self? Isn't this one of the clearest instances, therefore, of Plath owning nothing of herself? If might also indicate the vacuity, the internal impossibility, of the concept as such. What Hughes's editing reveals, or lays bare, is, however, only a general property of editing – a so-called neutral activity weighed down by the heaviest of psychosexual, aesthetic, and ethical investment.

Hughes is not, however, the only person involved in this process of editing, censoring, attempting to direct the interpretation of, and response to, Plath's work. Even where he has final responsibility for the editing, it seems clear that he is sometimes speaking for others, that he already stands as a multiple presence in the work.[35] But the situation becomes even more complex, more difficult, when we add to this scenario Aurelia Plath, Plath's mother, and Hughes's sister, Olwyn Hughes. The latter was placed by Hughes in control of literary permissions for the Estate; her publishing venture, Rainbow Press, also issued two limited and exclusive editions of Plath's poetry before the publication of the *Collected Poems* in 1981.[36] Aurelia Plath edited Plath's famous collection of letters from Plath to her, *Letters Home*, although as she has explained in response to criticisms of the omissions in that collection, she had to get permission for their publication from Ted Hughes (since the letters were written by Plath, Aurelia Plath had physical control but the literary copyright goes to the writer of the letters – that is the Estate: copyright in the published collection was subsequently given to Aurelia Plath).[37] From their correspondence, it would seem that Aurelia Plath consulted a lawyer over the publication of the letters from her daughter when Hughes demanded a large number of cuts of extracts explicitly alluding to him, to which he had not at first taken exception. These cuts were finally made.[38]

If this looks at first glance like another case of censorship by Hughes, the presence of these two women, however, makes the sexual narrative of the story inevitably more complex. To the man–woman (husband–wife) power relation is added the relation between brother and sister, between mother and daughter, and then between each of these protagonists in turn. Aurelia Plath published the *Letters Home* as a corrective to what she describes as the 'raging adolescent voice' of *The Bell Jar*, the novel by Plath first published under the pseudonym Victoria Lucas in January 1962;[39] the collection was put together after the novel was published in 1971 in America in Plath's own name, a publication Aurelia Plath wanted to prevent on the grounds that this was a voice in which Plath had not wanted to recognise herself.[40]

The mother therefore intervenes to correct the daughter's fictionalised self-narrative. Note how this mirrors and complements Hughes's gesture of self-protection in relation to *Ariel* – the husband subtracts from Plath's writing, the mother adds (Hughes will then respond with a further addition in turn). For Aurelia Plath, however, there is no question but that the image of the mother in the novel refers, cruelly, unjustly, to herself. It is as if the signing of the text with the name Sylvia Plath removed the novel from the realm of fiction, assigned it a status as 'truth', and thus made it available for adjudication (a process which will reach its climax in the legal suit brought against *The Bell Jar* in 1988).

Aurelia Plath recognises that Plath has transformed memory in the service of art, but she none the less judges the text false. We have seen this concept of misrepresentation, or falsity, before – except that this time it is Sylvia Plath's own writing, rather than commentary about Sylvia Plath, that is accused of wilful distortion of the facts: 'manipulation of events' and 'violation of actual circumstances'.[41]

The charge of falseness then spreads across the whole of Plath's work – the remembrance written by Aurelia Plath in 1985 as her final statement consists largely in showing how Sylvia Plath's 1957 poem 'The Disquieting Muses' distorts the facts of both of their lives: 'cruel and false caricatures, misleading though artistically more convincing than the truth would be'.[42] For Plath, on the other hand, this is not a process that can be measured (how far, how fairly did she distort?); distortion – dismemberment – belongs, without apology, to the process of writing: characters 'netted' from the life who 'manage to turn up, dismembered or otherwise, in stories' (author's note to one of her earliest publications in *Mademoiselle*).[43]

What is most striking (and disquieting) about this is the way that charge of falseness circulates between all the protagonists concerned. As we will see, this is not the only time this charge is levelled at Plath – the biography which has had the greatest co-operation from the Estate's literary agent, Anne Stevenson's, makes falseness, distortion, perversion, the key characteristic of Plath herself.[44] It is as if the refusal of the various protagonists to recognise falseness, uncertainty, multiplicity of often incompatible points of view, as a property of language and psyche, leads them all to engage in a battle to locate it somewhere, thereby turning it into an exclusively ethical problem, on condition that it does not implicate – contaminate – any of the protagonists themselves.

In this context, to own the facts of one's own life is not self-evidence, it is *war* – a war in which husbands and wives, mothers and daughters battle over the possession of – or rather, the constitution of what will pass *as* – the truth. To call this war is not, however, to deny the complexity of motives, the more simple forms of self-protection, or indeed the psychic pain which for each of these protagonists is no doubt involved – the irreducible pain, for example, for a mother, for an estranged husband, of Sylvia Plath's death. It may be to suggest, however, that the greater the pain attaching to such a drama, the higher the emotional stakes, the more fiercely such a battle is liable to be fought.

Six years after the publication of the *Letters Home* – roughly the same number of years as pass between the American publication of *The Bell Jar* and the letters – Ted Hughes publishes the *Journals*. In 1977, in the Introduction to *Johnny Panic and the Bible of Dreams*, he had stated: 'How much of it ought to be published is not easy to decide' (he included 'a few of the more harmless pieces – by no means the best').[45] When the *Journals* are published in 1982, everything else, apart from *Ariel*, is characterised as 'waste'. In a longer essay, 'Sylvia Plath and her Journals', written as an alternative to his introduction to the *Journals*, Hughes made it clear that this publication comes at least partly in response to the *Letters Home*, as 'ballast' against the 'wild unknown quantity' with which the fact of her death 'multiplies every one of her statements', an effect 'hardly steadied by the account she gave of herself in her letters to her mother'.[46] Note again that appeal to the privileged reality of this text: 'offered in the hope of providing some ballast for our idea of the reality behind the poems'. (Note too the lack of reference to anything other than the poetic writing of Plath.)

76

Before looking at these two publications in more detail, before commenting on the way this battle carries over into the editing of these texts, it is therefore worth making an obvious but easily forgotten point – that what is most problematic about them may not be the omissions, the editorial commentary and control, but the fact that these pieces of writing – neither of which was ever intended for publication – were ever published at all. As Hughes himself puts it in the same article, but not in the published Foreword: 'The motive in publishing these journals will be questioned. The argument against is still strong.'[47] What price, we might ask, that demand for privacy which Hughes has on more than one occasion made in relation to others (his and Plath's children, Plath's mother, former acquaintances of Plath) and himself? For while it could be argued that these people are living and most closely affected by Plath's writing, whereas Plath is now dead, the problem still remains as to how such lines of protection should, or can, be drawn (the issue precisely being the rights of those who are no longer in a position to decide or speak for themselves).

It is a question which rebounds, of necessity, on to anyone who tries to write about Plath's work. What position can such a writer occupy? Retriever of Plath's voice against the censorship of her family, or participator, extender, repeater of the same violation, the same intrusion into forms of writing, one of which was unequivocally addressed to herself alone? The writer on Plath immediately finds herself in the position that she can 'judge' the Estate and its associates, establish her case against them, only by participating in the same 'crime'. I say 'judge', but the precarious nature of these documents is just one of the instances where the issue of judgement, so dramatically called up at one level by this editing, starts to come undone. The problem can be put another way: What is the status of these manuscripts? Are they personal or cultural property? Or is the problem precisely that they are hybrids which sit on the boundary, or expose the delicacy, the artificiality, of the boundary, between the two?

And yet, as with all forms of censorship, the problem resides not only in what gets removed from these publications, but as much – and sometimes as clearly – in what remains. Thus Hughes himself advises Aurelia Plath to cut the original version of the letters drastically on the grounds that it was in danger of producing the opposite effect from the one desired – not the positive relationship between mother and daughter, not the positive image that the daughter offers to the mother, but a desperate attempt to reassure the mother and conceal from her a more difficult relationship and truth.[48] Precisely in so far as the letters are presented as closeness, total communication, full speech ('Honestly, I appreciate your rational understanding of me so much. In return, I have always felt I can be completely honest with you'[49]), so they can start to tip over into their opposite, suggesting something negative all the more potent to the extent that it cannot be spoken. The effect will be false, Hughes suggests, to the precise extent that the letters offer themselves as whole (as opposed to partial) truth. In this exchange between Hughes and Aurelia Plath, language is acknowledged in its capacity to dupe, to deceive, to work – sometimes deliberately, sometimes unintentionally – against itself. The cuts were made, but the effect of the letters, commented on by numerous critics, was for the most part the very one Hughes had warned against.[50]

For this reason it becomes at one level both crucial and yet also strangely irrelevant to discover from the unedited correspondence just how much, by way of difficulty (personal, political, physical), Aurelia Plath takes out of the letters she publishes, since the omission of difficulty, especially between herself and her daughter, is so glaringly declared by the contents of the published letters themselves. Going from the published to the unedited letters, the impression is constantly of something one *already* knows – as if the published text was operating rather like the contents of a psycho-analytic setting, where what is presented to consciousness bears the most intimate relation to the unconscious thoughts it is most concerned to disguise. As it says on the inside jacket of the first hardback edition of the letters: 'there is much to be read between the lines'.

These unpublished letters cannot be fully quoted or paraphrased. The picture they give is, however, constant. For what is removed by Aurelia Plath from these letters is anything at the level of psychic and political life that might jar – signs of hostility towards her mother, demands for autonomy and separation, which slip through Plath's almost seamless assertions of what is positive, in her life and in their relationship; references to her constant physical ailments (specifically sinusitis) which are so much more recurrent and debilitating than is allowed to appear in the published text; and political sympathies, whole letters, together with many of Plath's

allusions to Communism.[51] With regard to Plath's illness, on more
than one occasion it seems to be diluted from acute, physical reality
spoken by Plath into the mother's report – as if, therefore, the text
was somehow disembodying itself, or as if illness, or Sylvia Plath's
relation to her illness, should not express *itself*: 'Sylvia suffered
another deep-seated sinus infection at The Belmont' . . . 'I've told
you the grimmer side of the week [she'd been ill].'[52] (Commentary
on Plath has then glossed over her illness in turn).[53]

What body, what psyche, is being constituted here? One in which
anger, illness and left-wing politics are all equally marked as flaw.
Beyond the immediate gesture of protection (clearly visible in
relation to Plath's illness) we can recognise here that familiar link
between the political and the physical, the demand that they should
both, together, be integrated, coherent and clean.[54] Predictable in
retrospect, or if we read between the lines, these specific cuts have
none the less been decisive in their effects. For that removal of the
worst of the body from Plath's own account of herself has played a
crucial part in creating the image of Plath as someone whose misery
simply feeds off itself (on one occasion, for example, the removal of
physical illness leaves a moment of self-recrimination disembodied
and without explanation[55]), just as the taking out of many of the
political allusions from the letters as well as from the early journals
has laid her open to the often repeated charge that politics appears
only opportunistically, as a form of self-aggrandisement, at the very
end of her life and work.

In relation to Aurelia Plath herself, it is of course a self-defeating
operation because what is left simply accentuates the limits of
communication with the mother, limits which appear all the more
insuperable to the extent that they succeed in drawing a line around
what can, and what cannot, appear in the text. Thus editing
designed to establish a positive image of the relationship between
Plath and her mother reads instead as repetition of, or participation
in, the psychic defences or barriers of Sylvia Plath herself: 'wrote a
letter to mother which gave her the gay side'.[56] As Plath expressed it
in her *Journals* with reference to the letters written during her stay
in Cambridge in 1956:

One reason I could keep up such a satisfactory letter-relationship
with her while in England was we could both verbalise our
desired image of ourselves in relation to each other: interest and

sincere love, and never feel the emotional currents at war with those verbally expressed feelings [57]

(letter-writing in itself as one of the ultimate forms of misrecognition). If, however, the difficulty between mother and daughter is removed where it appears as *difference* or antagonism, it then surfaces in the published letters all the more clearly as *sameness* or identification, in the form of a constant blurring of boundaries between them. Struggle does not always involve distinct and antagonistic interests or a clash of wills. The problem can equally arise, not when protagonists are at odds with each other, but rather when they are too nearly identified, when communication becomes dangerous or fails in its purpose because the participants come too close. Mother as trusted confidante, mother as lover and soulmate:

> I will settle for nothing less than a great *soul* . . . what possible knight could overcome this image? This dynamic holy *soul* which we share [the reference is to Richard Sassoon] . . . I hope you understand that all this is very private, and I am sharing it with you as I would the deepest secrets of my *soul* [my emphasis].[58]

What Plath seeks in, already enjoys with, her lover is a sharing of souls. Communicating that desire to the mother is to enact it – to situate the mother in, or declare as already occupied, that very place. The overvaluation of the sexual object which has so often been commented on with reference to Plath's relationship with Hughes reveals here a more ambiguous destination. It is in this same letter that Plath sends to her mother the poem 'Pursuit', which she wrote after her first meeting with Hughes: 'I am hypnotised by this poem and wonder if the simple, seductive beauty of the words will come across to you if you read it slowly and deliberately aloud.'[59] If Hughes is the referent of the poem, her mother appears therefore to be the addressee. It is an ambiguity which continues after Plath's death – in a much later letter to her mother, Hughes comments on the fact that Plath returned his early letters to her to Aurelia Plath, rather than to him.[60]

At the very least, this process of exchange troubles the available identifications – the distinctions, for example, between mother and lover, between Aurelia Plath and Ted Hughes, a difference which will be so heavily underscored (disagreements settled finally only by a formal agreement between them) when they come to fight for the ownership of Plath in relation to the body of this very text. Not to mention that appeal for privacy, once again, and so explicitly in this example, disregarded by the fact of publication itself ('I hope you understand that this is very private, and I am sharing it with you as I would the deepest secrets of my soul'). It is an ironic situation where the more the letters assert the exclusive, inviolable intimacy of the mother–daughter relationship, the more that same intimacy, by the very fact of publication, is undermined.

If this identification, this proximity, is sexual, it is also literary. For isn't it the case that, in this battle for the ownership of Plath, what is being contested between these participants, what in fact identifies them all so closely, is writing itself? As Aurelia Plath put it in an interview conducted in 1976, she had herself wanted to be a writer but did not feel she could expose her children to the uncertainty of a writer's life.[61] And in her long introduction to *Letters Home*, she stresses the literary heritage she passed on to her daughter.[62] In an unpublished letter to Hughes she describes this exchange as going backwards and forwards across generations – her mother reading, feeding her own hunger for literature, from her daughter's books, the same books that Aurelia Plath will in turn pass on to her daughter.[63] One of the strangest set of elisions in the correspondence occurs in a letter in which Sylvia Plath is encouraging her mother to write: 'articles about your teaching job ... for one of the women's magazines. I'd love to edit for you', which takes out the suggestion that she should try the *True Confessions* market again, the implication being that she has done so before.[64] In a corresponding passage from the same period in the *Journals* (also cut) Plath states that she has discarded her 'supercilious attitude' to this very form of writing: 'it takes a good tight plot and a slick ease that are not picked up overnight like a cheap whore'.[65] Plath's attraction to and involvement with such writing appears at various points throughout the published *Journals* and the *Letters Home*. But this moment of cutting none the less suggests that a specific image of Plath as writer is being privileged (high versus low culture), an image – with all its crucial cultural and political implications, especially in relation to the woman writer – which, as we will see in Chapter 5, Plath does not, in any straightforward way, share.

Compare the same downgrading of the popular, the vulgar, by Hughes in his Foreword to the *Journals*:

Nearly all her earlier writings (and definitively all the prose she wrote for publication) suffered from her ambition to see her work published in particular magazines . . . This campaign of wilful ambitions produced everything in her work that seems artificial.[66]

Note too the moral judgement ('wilful'), as well as that charge of falsity again ('artificial'). The published *Journals* then remove her experiments with popular fictional forms, especially from the early journals, but leave in tracts of stream-of-consciousness writing after her breakdown (writing as high art, as the most intimate inner drama of herself). There is, therefore, a set of decisions being taken here as to whether, and to what extent, Plath can be allowed to be *low* – low as in nasty, low as in the degradation of culture. It is at the very least equivocal which, in the view of her editors, is the greatest offence.

But what that moment of symmetrical editing also removes is one of the key signs of an identification between mother and daughter at the level of the production of words. Even before that flood of communication which will eventually produce *Letters Home* (as Plath puts it in one unpublished postcard, she *cannot stop* writing to her mother[67]), it is language and writing itself that the mother and daughter most intimately share: 'We were critical of our verbal and written expression, for we shared a love of words and considered them as a tool used to achieve precise expression, a necessity for accuracy in describing our emotions, as well as for mutual understanding.'[68] Words as (precision) tools, accuracy in describing emotions, the necessity of mutual understanding – it is hard not to read in this passage, alongside the shared love of language, or rather, as its necessary but disavowed portion, the most oppressive of injunctions to full speech (the obligation to communicate as much as the free exchange of words). This could help to explain the moment in the *Journals* when Plath describes her own writing as an always inadequate gift offered to her mother, as well as the ease with which that same writing can turn into a weapon against her (*The Bell Jar*, to which the publication of the *Letters Home* by Aurelia Plath comes as the reply).

What we then discover from the unedited correspondence is that this is an issue which has ramifications which go beyond the

82

personal drama played out by the protagonists to touch on the most fundamental aspects of the way our culture institutionally encodes the relationship between language and psychic life – the question we saw represented both in 'Poem for a Birthday' and in 'Johnny Panic and the Bible of Dreams'. Omitted from the *Letters Home* is a lengthy correspondence with Olive Higgins Prouty, writer of popular fiction and Plath's benefactor, which dates from the time of Plath's breakdown in 1953, on the subject of the form of treatment Plath received (three edited letters are included in the text). In each case, it is a difficulty about the treatment that is removed – about the insulin, the shock therapy, the doctor, the hospital, the payment. There is no sign in the published commentary, for example, of Prouty's suspicions about insulin treatment (Aurelia Plath comments: 'Sylvia received insulin treatment and after several weeks showed definite signs of improvement').[69] There is no mention of the controversies surrounding Dr Erich Lindemann from Massachusetts General Hospital in Boston, one of the doctors who treated Plath, whose ideas, Prouty suggests, were not wholly welcome at McLean (the hospital where Plath was treated) – he is described in a 1987 textbook on American psychiatry as part of a movement away from Social Darwinism in psychiatry to a greater attention to the 'social, economic and political environment . . . the social and legal matrix in which illness or instability occurred'.[70] Aurelia Plath mentions the shock treatment Plath received and her subsequent improvement, but not the fact that they had been on the point of withdrawing Plath from the hospital and were persuaded not to on the grounds that the treatments were about to begin.[71] McLean also offered to pay all Plath's expenses after 1 January because she was such an interesting case.[72] It is at McLean too that Plath starts to see Ruth Beutscher (who is mentioned in the published text) who gives her the psychotheraphy that she will return to in Boston in 1959.

The only problem to appear in the published letters is Prouty's complaint at the lack of occupational therapy and outdoor exercise at the hospital.[73] She herself exhorts Plath to take up work on the loom – one of a number of forms of traditionally female activity which, according to another textbook, were introduced into the hospital for women in 1910: 'basketry, leather work, lacemaking, weaving and other forms of industry'.[74]

What is remarkable about all this is that an episode presented in the letters as breakdown and recovery – that is, as sequence (compare the last chapter) – appears from the full correspondence as the fiercest of controversies about what constitutes illness and how it should be treated. What goes missing first of all is the gravity of Plath's illness (we can recognise here that same gesture of protection which suppresses or effaces what is most difficult – for the reader but, one feels, also for Plath). But once again the question of language is crucial, the question of the limits of what can be communicated to the mother, of what she should and should not know. For Prouty, the priority is that communication should be total – Aurelia Plath should know everything that passes between herself and the doctors, as well as between herself and Sylvia Plath (according to her notes for a talk at Wellesley College in 1976, Dr Lindemann, on the other hand, warned Aurelia Plath against too much proximity, too close an identification with her daughter).[75] The extent to which Prouty involves herself in the medical aspect of the case leads her at one point to suggest herself that further intervention on her part would be unethical.[76] But this involvement (remarkable in itself) is matched only by the extent to which she insists that she and Aurelia Plath must express everything freely to each other, that they must know exactly (her word) what is going on in each other's minds.[77]

All of this in a context where we learn that Plath's mail was being censored and that a letter sent from her to Prouty had gone to Aurelia Plath instead. It is a crisis which once more reveals the potential for mix-up that underlies communication as such (reveals precisely as fantasy the ideal of communication without mishap, supplement or reserve). Prouty responds by insisting that everything she writes to Plath, and vice versa, should be freely available to her mother: then, in the same letter, she objects to Plath's therapy with Ruth Beutscher on the grounds that it brings this chain of full communication to a halt.[78] Beutscher's therapy is dangerous, she explicitly argues, because of the hostility towards the mother it promotes, but the content of the treatment is less important in this context than the fact that it arrests the circulation of words, cutting the daughter's communication with the mother – cutting language off, therefore, from its true destination (and, we might say, source). But in so far as it circulates, language can, by definition, always fail to reach its mark or alight in the wrong place. The mix-up of correspondence affecting Hughes's letters to Plath, and here Plath's to Prouty, provides a graphic illustration of this.

Psychotherapeutic treatment (as opposed to insulin or electro-therapy) makes this its starting premiss, offering a space where the problem of origin and destination in relation to language, the subject's division *in* language, can be spoken. Division (the coexistence of contradictory thoughts or feelings) needs to be distinguished from cancellation (one thought or feeling completely wiping another out). Cancellation is, however, the term Aurelia Plath uses when she allows, with a pain that must also be respected, the publication of those journal extracts, taken from Plath's 1959 return to therapy with Beutscher, in which Plath expresses her hostility towards her mother with such force. Aurelia Plath comments: 'I have no doubt that many readers will accept whatever negative thoughts she reveals here as the whole and absolute truth, despite their *cancellation* on other, more positive pages.'[79] Compare this with her introduction to the final letters: 'I must ask the reader to remember the circumstances in which they were written and to remember also that they represent *one side of an extremely complex situation*'[80] (my emphasis in both cases).

Qualifying Plath's representation of Hughes, Aurelia Plath allows for a multiplicity of coexisting points of view, but she wipes out – cancels – the negative in relation to herself. At the same time, the first statement is prefaced with an editorial comment on the therapy which represents it as a liberation from symbiosis and the precondition for 'Poem for a Birthday', described as Plath's 'first major work'.[81] Partly protecting the mother (seeking her permission to publish these extracts, allowing her a voice), partly locating the problem in her (or in her daughter's tendency to 'fuse' with her mother), this moment of editing is the only point where difference is allowed to surface in the text, graphically figured by the presence of the two statements on the same page.

Throughout this process, it is clearly Sylvia Plath, her illness, her language, who is the object of exchange – suspended in 1953 somewhere between speech and basket-weaving, somewhere ironically between the two activities allowed to women in the best and worst moments of Freud (he was the first to listen to the hysteric's discourse, but in an infamous passage he suggests that women's weaving is a symbolic attempt to hide the deficiency of their genitals by matting their pubic hair).[82] Exchange here also takes on its most material significance – the money passed from Prouty to the hospital, their offer of free treatment, the fact that Aurelia Plath once joked that a nervous breakdown was the one illness the family could not afford.[83] In fact, money and its significance, as much as the problem of language, could be seen as the repressed content of the entire drama played out in relation to Plath's work. The despair of Plath's last letters focuses as much on money as on the issue of alleged desertion by Hughes. Many of her accusations against Hughes on this subject of money are taken out,[84] but enough is left for Aurelia Plath to comment against her daughter:

> Actually, this emphasis on her lack of funds may have been an exaggeration intended to convey her sense of urgency. Ted Hughes says that he borrowed money when he left and between September and early February gave her over £900.[85]

By the time we get to Anne Stevenson's biography, that 'Hughes says' has become 'It is recorded', point of view has been transformed into fact: 'Financially, too, she was well off. *It is recorded* that between October and her death four months later, Hughes gave Sylvia about £900' (my emphasis).[86] We can add to this those exclusive, expensive publications of Plath's poetry before the *Collected Poems* appeared in 1981: the 1968 Turret edition of *Three Women* (180 copies at £10.50), the 1971 Rainbow Press Editions of *Crystal Gazer* (400 copies ranging from £120 to £21) and of *Lyonesse* (400 copies from £110 to £12.50).[87] Money can also be seen as the sub-text of the archive itself. For by selling the manuscripts to the Smith and Lilly libraries, it is the Estate and its associates (Hughes and Aurelia Plath) who have released them out of their control. Not to mention the dispute over whether monies were withheld for the editing of the *Journals* as a result of disagreement over the final text.[88]

It is in the last letters, too, that Plath makes her often-quoted comment to her mother about the necessity of acknowledging and writing about what is destructive in the world:

> Don't talk to me about the world needing cheerful stuff! What the person out of Belsen – physical or psychological – wants is nobody saying the birdies still go tweet-tweet, but the full knowledge that somebody else has been there and knows the *worst*.[89]

Aurelia Plath leaves this in, but she has taken out most of its prehistory at that point where it touches on the relationship with herself. In view of this, I think we should be very cautious about attempting to read Plath's writing in terms of a positive emergence of selfhood, of turning what may be better thought of in terms of the unbearable coexistence of opposites into a narrative progression from suffering into self-discovery or flight. Are we not at risk in doing this of putting ourselves, putting feminism, in the place of the idealised and idealising mother who can bear to see nothing bad in her daughter? Isn't it as a direct consequence of this that all guilt then has to be located in the person of the man, in this case Ted Hughes? And doesn't that risk blinding us, too, to the no less real political horrors which Plath pleads with her mother here to see (Marjorie Perloff's reading of the *Ariel* canon is scathing, as are so many critics, about the references to politics in Plath's later work[90])?

Aurelia Plath's editing finally leads back to Ted Hughes because, at a number of points in the correspondence, it is his presence we start to feel behind hers. What appears to be removed at his own injunction is the most intensely positive as well as the most negative representations of him by Plath: moments at the beginning of their relationship, for example, when her idealisation sets him up, and by implication herself, as superhuman (spiritual beings naked before the sun and the future breeders of a new race),[91] as well as those moments where she expresses her fear of his destructiveness as she sees it, his reputation – in her terms – as seducer, breaker and blaster of women and things.[92] The omitted sections of the letters make clear, however, that these positive and negative images are not opposites but coexist in the most intimate relation – the 'horror' (her word) of being with Hughes arises directly out of what she most values in him: 'the might of his arm is to be wondered at' . . . 'his iron will to beat the world across'.[93]

What Plath offers here is an account of psychic fantasy, specifically the link between horror and the ideal (a fantasy scenario which – from her letters to Sassoon, for example – can be seen as going way beyond Hughes).[94] By taking these extracts out, Hughes once again ironically leaves himself vulnerable to a more straightforwardly ethical judgement – especially to the charge, made over and over again in the last letters, that Plath has reason (the reasonable response to injustice or unreasonable behaviour) to be angry, hostile, and frightened of him. This is not, of course, to suggest that her accusations are *without* reason, but merely to point

87

to the way that the editing of her work substitutes for a complex logic of psychic and moral causality, a much more reductive logic which rests on a straightforward apportioning of blame. To that extent, it invites the very feminist polemic against which the Estate and its associates most vehemently protest.

It is in these terms too that I think we can best make sense of the editing of the first encounter between Plath and Hughes, a passage from the *Journals* which has become famous because it was cut between the galleys sent out to reviewers and the final publication of the text. The cut removed Hughes's snatching of Plath's earrings and hairband, but left in her biting of him – left, therefore, a violence for which she appears as the sole and self-generating source.[95] A recent letter from Frances McCullough suggests that the Estate originally wanted the whole episode (bite included) removed. This is Olwyn Hughes's telegram to McCullough: 'WITH RAPE AND BITE OUT TED EDITOR STOP IF INTRUDED QUOTE CONSULTANT EDITOR UNQUOTE ONLY REGARDS OLWYN.'[96] (according to McCullough, 'rape' here refers to a remark of Plath's about American virginity and rape, which was the other passage she insisted on retaining.)

By the time the text is published, however, this logic seems to have shifted or gone into reverse. The bite remains, but it is Hughes's own moment of aggression which is taken out. But if we place Hughes's gesture back in the passage, we are left not with his culpability, as the editing itself seems to imply, but rather with an act of exchange, in which violence passes back and forth between them, as well as with a question, equally lost by this moment of editing, of what is seen by Plath most troublingly in Hughes that she desires. What starts to emerge from these oscillations at the level of the editing is that it is the act of exchange itself which is the greatest threat (I return to this in the next chapter).

Also removed is Plath's reference to their first night together – a 'holocaust' night, as she puts it in her journal, which leaves her bruised.[97] The brief allusion in no way answers the question it raises as to where that violence originates, of what pleasure was at stake, the pleasure – it could be argued – in the very language Plath deploys (it is the censorship which turns this moment into an indictment of Hughes). The problem is only posed all the more sharply by the coexistence of the intensely positive moments which the editors also remove – the idealisations, but equally those instances where she credits Hughes, simply and appreciatively, with being the sole support of her life.[98] It would be wrong to suggest, therefore, that intimacy or privacy is never what is being cherished or preserved.

In the published *Journals*, however, the horror which attaches to the beginning of the relationship is explicit:

> Something very terrifying too has happened to me, which started two months ago and which needed not to have happened [did not need to happen, needed not to happen] . . . I am living now in a kind of present hell and god knows what ceremonies of life or love can patch the havoc wrought.[99]

The line 'What ceremony of words can patch the havoc' is the last line of the poem which opens the *Collected Poems* of 1981.[100] The section which included this passage in the *Journals* is then followed by this editorial comment: 'Sylvia and Ted Hughes were married on June 16, 1956. After the wedding they went off for a honeymoon summer in the little fishing village of Benidorm in Spain.'[101]

But if this raises the question of censorship – censorship *of* Plath – it no less dramatically raises the question of the censorship that Plath carries out in relation to herself. Put the poem and the journal entry together, plus the letters which she is writing to Aurelia Plath at the same time, and you get an extraordinary instance of intertextuality, one which offers a striking demonstration of the forms of denial, suppression and connection that can link different utterances or texts. To take just one moment – the beginning of the relationship with Hughes. First the censored passages of the letters, the idealisations and the anxiety about Hughes, alongside Plath's insistent reassurances to her mother – Plath partly expressing, partly denying her own fear. Then the horror felt by Plath which is so much more fully stated in the journals, and which then appears like the hidden content, or suppressed psychic truth, of the letters home. Then the way the affirmation and denial of her fear converge on what can only be described as the proto-fascist fantasy of the letters: the image of the couple as godhead that rises above all anxiety, all horror, all human limitation, as the future bearers of a divine race (Plath's attempts to reassure betray themselves by their very excess). And finally the status of all this as the starting point – the initiation –

of the Plath *œuvre* as it presents itself to us today: the poem 'Conversation Among the Ruins', which opens the *Collected Poems* of 1981:

> Through portico of my elegant house you stalk
> With your wild furies, [ . . . ]
>    rending the net
> Of all decorum which holds the whirlwind back.
>    [ . . . ] I sit
> Composed in Grecian tunic, and psyche-knot,
> Rooted to your black look, the play turned tragic . . .

Follow this through and we can watch the personal battle transforming itself, not just into poetry but into a battle over the meaning and possibility of poetry, of culture, as such – Dionysus versus Apollo, wild furies versus Grecian tunic and psyche-knot. It is the start of a tragic play to which words will, and will not, the poem suggests, be adequate: 'What ceremony of words can patch the havoc'. That ceremony, that inadequacy, can then be taken, amongst its other meanings, as the figure for the always inadequate, the always partial, nature of representation in relation to subjectivity itself (no one, true, voice of Plath behind the ordering and censoring of her writing).

If we go back to the *Journals*, then once again it seems that, as with the letters, what is finally most important is not what gets taken out, but what remains, what is passed over – or, alternatively, what is felt to require commentary by the editors of the text. If we read across the distinct versions of Plath's writing, what emerges is the uncertain logic of difference ('she told different people many different things, and different things at different times').[102] In the editing, however, the issue seems to be that of singular accountability or blame. In her editor's note, Frances McCullough explains: 'There are a couple of longer notes where it seemed important to place the material in some sort of perspective.'[103] The following quotation is taken from the second one (the first introduced the therapy of 1959);[104] it prefaces an episode where Plath, suspecting Hughes of infidelity, directs her anger with particular intensity at him:

> About this time, and for months afterward, Plath began to feel an upsurge of rage, an emotion she rarely allowed herself. In the

passage that follows it is a rage against her husband in which a small incident takes on enormous proportions, and is quickly transferred to some girls in a public park. As Plath notes eight months later (December 27), the real source is her father, though it would be several years before she could make the connection in any deep way.[105]

Like the other commentary from 1959, it does not matter in a sense where the ill is located provided it never comes to rest on Hughes (in that instance, he was seen as the displaced recipient of the too-close relationship to the mother). But even more striking across the range of all this editing is the division or parcelling out of psychic qualities that is repeatedly involved. If Aurelia Plath had sought to remove any traces of what is most negative, especially in relation to herself, the editing of the *Journals* can be seen here going back in the opposite direction, preserving, underscoring, what is negative (a number of simple passages where Plath expresses her ability to cope and be happy are also cut);[106] and then locating it, away from Hughes, as firmly as possible in the inner drama which Plath conducts in relation to herself. What strange splitting is being enacted here, what strange inflation of the positive or negative aspects of psychic life? What demand that Plath take entire and exclusive responsibility for – that she embody – what is wholly 'good' or wholly 'bad'? Strange repetition (or anticipation) in which the editors (the protectors) of Plath's legacy enact the same mechanisms of projection which we saw in the first chapter in the worst of critical responses to Plath.

Those moments of editorial commentary read like Samuel Richardson's footnotes to *Clarissa*, which became more and more anxious, more and more directive of the reader's opinions, as he realised that his audience were not judging his characters in the way he had planned (in this case they were not condemning Lovelace the villain).[107] Richardson's footnotes started as reminders, but as he panicked increasingly so they started, as here, to allude forwards to what had not yet happened in the book. In relation to Plath, what is ruled out by the commentary is that the episode may be *overdetermined*, that Plath's later recognition does not necessarily 'cancel' the earlier causality, or that the later explanation, far from being definitive, might in turn be affected by its own form of uncertainty. As Plath herself asks in the passage from 27 December to which the editors refer: 'Is this a plausible interpretation?'.[108] Compare, however, the commentary to this episode ('not Hughes, but her father') with the reading of Plath's psychic life and writing offered by Hughes in *The Independent*, where he argues that it is not the father, in fact hardly ever men, but women who were almost exclusively the real targets of her rage:

> . . . the hostile elements tend [in *The Colossus*] to be female – a tendency which strengthened greatly in her later poems. Male figures excited her rage, in her later poems, chiefly when they exposed her to those she feared and hated who (the evidence is distasteful but it cannot be denied, it makes up a considerable part of her work) were almost exclusively women.[109]

It is as if Plath's anger, following the laws of the unconscious, is subject to infinite displacement, where displacement signifies uncertainty of location, but is being read by those who edit and present her writing according to its other, more familiar meaning: 'anyone, provided it is not me'. In this fight, Plath herself also plays her part. She writes: 'Irony: in almost two years [I've been] turned from a crazy perfectionist and promiscuous human-being-lover, to a misanthrope, and . . . a nasty, catty and malicious misanthrope.'[110] The published text includes this but omits its continuation: 'How he praised this in me.'[111] What power, we might ask, do these cuts assign to her language (the same power ironically assigned to Plath whenever it is argued that everything is her fault), what crediting of her utterance do they involve? – an idea of language in which saying makes it so, and a belief that everything Plath states will be read without reserve. For surely what this line suggests is not that Hughes *is* necessarily the source and encourager of her malice, but precisely that one of the things going on between them might be a battle as to where negativity resides, whom it belongs to – the very battle over the location of the cause which the editing of her work so desperately finds itself repeating.

Nowhere is this made clearer than in the publication of Anne Stevenson's biography of Plath, and the part played in that publication by Olwyn Hughes, the final protagonist in the story.[112] It is also with reference to this publication that the vexed and contested relation between the 'factual' and the 'distorted', between 'objectivity' and 'perversion', has reached a type of extreme. Olwyn Hughes herself has situated the biography firmly within this framework, at that point where it reverts back on to the Estate: 'The myth of the Plath estate is fast becoming as unpleasant and artificial as the Plath myth itself. It seems that the same group of hacks, self-publicists and extreme feminists are busy with both.'[113] The reference is to a review of Linda Wagner-Martin's biography, but also to the successive manuscripts of the biography itself: 'invention of a low order or dramatised scraps of fifth-hand gossip' typical of the 'great fashion for sensationalised debunkings in the American unauthorised literary-biography industry' with their 'outlandish speculations . . . presented as facts' and 'shockingly low standards of research'.[114] In this context, there are 'facts' and there is 'point of view'. For 'point of view' read 'feminist': 'in Wagner-Martin's biography, this was crudely feminist'.[115]

Compare this language – these scraps, gossip, debunkings – with the 'wealth' of the new material that Olwyn Hughes, acting as Stevenson's literary agent, made available for her biography, selling the biography to Penguin and Houghton Mifflin on the understanding, as she herself puts it, that Stevenson incorporate this material into her book – the only meaning of the now notorious statement by Anne Stevenson that she was made to rewrite her biography five times (this material coming in right up to completion of the manuscript).[116] Anne Stevenson then credits Olwyn Hughes with effective dual authorship, as well as attributing to her a large part of the readings of the late poems in a prefatory note to the book.[117]

All of this is worth noting only because of the extraordinary nature of this partly authorised biography. Now something of a 'cause célèbre' in the genre of abusive biography, it shows the coercive nature of biography as a form of writing, the fantasy of omnipotence which supports it.[118] The biography sets itself to correct a specific image of Plath, one which presents her – in the words of a source cited as criticising this image in the Preface – as the 'pathetic victim of Ted Hughes's heartless mistreatment'.[119] But it is impossible to read the counter-image that it offers as anything other than a systematic assault on Plath: her 'blindness', her 'perversity', her 'self-destruction' – crucially, her constant distortion of the truth.[120] For, in a strange process of doubling, this account of Plath constantly refers to – situates its accusation of

Plath inside – the fact of enunciation, the process of utterance through which knowledge is produced as such. If Plath is 'cursed' ('She was indeed cursed'[121]) it is not just because of the psychic drama which the book attributes solely to her inner world ('The hell Sylvia Plath experienced was an inner hell'[122]) but also, and far more, because of the perverse nature of her relation to the truth: 'her peculiarly hallucinatory imagination' . . . 'her self-justifying interpretation' . . . 'self-justifying and unforgiving' . . . 'whatever "facts" she invented'.[123] It is of course the very charge made against her commentators, as we saw at the start of the chapter, by Ted Hughes. But nowhere is it ever suggested by Stevenson that what she offers as the much-needed correction to Plath's self-representation (the three personal testimonies, for example, published as Appendices to the book) is not objectivity but equally self-interested, self-justifying point of view.[124] That a whole range of new primary material was made available for this biography is not in question here. What is at issue is its own principles of selection, its own partiality of representation, its self-presentation as singular truth against the distorted vision of Plath (Plath's own vision and the vision of those who have differently – more sympathetically – presented her).

Note how the charge of distortion affects not only the decisive points of Plath's relationship with Hughes: 'what she supposed was Ted's weakness and perfidy' . . . 'Ted had "deserted her"' . . . 'she claimed to have lost 20 pounds over the summer' . . . 'Sylvia's alleged poverty';[125] it also spreads across to the assessment of her writing: 'her blindness and incompleteness of the imagination' . . . 'her false metaphysic' . . . and, with reference to her difficulty in writing: 'she could exaggerate, distort, caricature, remodel and interpret, but she could not easily invent'.[126] Thus Plath's 'falseness' is situated at the origins both of her writing and of her failure to write.

The question of this biography's truth, of its own frame of utterance, becomes all the more glaring as a result of its own truth-relation, the fact that it situates its accusations of Plath so firmly along the axis of a true/false divide. Inevitably, that insistence on Plath's falsity leads back to the conditions of enunciation of the biography itself, to the place from where it is itself being spoken. In whose interests is this book being written – or rather, in whom does its own truth-claim finally reside? In Olwyn Hughes herself, who, according to her own account, researched, checked, got in material, wrote up and rewrote parts of the book (work which, it is suggested in one article, is seen to justify her share of the royalty which it puts at 40 per cent and 30 per cent respectively on the British and American editions of the book)?[127] Or Peter Davison, the consulting editor (the American edition has on the title page 'A Peter Davison book'), who also knew Plath and is quoted on their first sexual encounter: 'she hardly waited to be asked to slip into my new bed'.[128] What this is meant to establish about Plath is not clear (or rather, it is only too clear). Compare this remark from Stevenson about Plath in Cambridge: 'Mrs. Sylvia Hughes was indeed quite a different person from the garish, sexually rapacious man-chaser of her first terms'.[129]

What 'sensationalised debunking', what 'scraps', what 'low order gossip' is this? Peter Davison could in fact be fairly described as the final arbiter or hidden author of the book. In a discussion of the book, screened on 'The Late Show' on BBC television on 17 October 1989, Anne Stevenson explained how he had undertaken to mediate and decide between the competing and incompatible views of the poems that she and Olwyn Hughes produced: 'Without Peter Davison, I don't think there would have been a book.'

But the fact that this biography is written so clearly as a vindication of Hughes does not allow us to conclude that Olwyn Hughes speaks for him, that his interests or desires coincide in any simple way with her own (Olwyn Hughes: 'and why should not this "vindication" take place if that is what serious research ends up with?').[130] We assume this, in fact, only by producing the very identification between them which appears, not as pre-given fact or reality, but rather as the *symptom* of the text. Hughes himself has in fact dissociated himself from the book: 'I do not approve of the book and dissociate myself from any responsibility for the opinions and conclusions contained in it.'[131] In a letter to *The Independent*, Hughes objects that this remark has been taken out of context, since it originally continued: 'just as I dissociate myself from the distorting and damaging fantasies' of so much else that is written about Plath.[132] But that 'just as' makes it appear that Hughes is saying, albeit indirectly, that distorting and damaging fantasy is what he also reads in Stevenson's book.

In this context, a point about the book's own relationship to the archive and its own sources. On several occasions Olwyn Hughes is herself quoted, countering or correcting the impression conveyed by Plath in a letter to her mother or a comment to a friend, remembering and quoting verbatim on one occasion a line from the journal that was destroyed.[133] But at no point does Stevenson ever address the question of the editing of Plath's writing, not even when she cites without comment edited extracts from the published journals and correspondence whose unedited version one can only assume she has read.[134] Once again, even without recourse to the unpublished material, one can ask what principles of selection are at stake. Take this passage, for example: 'Yet Sylvia also desired power: "The vampire is there, too. The old, primal hate. That desire to go round castrating the arrogant ones who become such children in moments of passion".'[135] In the *Journals* these lines come immediately after these:

> I imagine Richard here, being with me, and my growing big with his child. I ask for less and less. I would face him, and say simply: I am sad that you are not strong, and do not swim and sail and ski, but you have a strong soul, and I will believe in you and make you invincible on this earth.[136]

Once more Plath presents herself in terms of an ambivalence which her commentators attempt to reduce to one or other of its two extremes.

This is not to enter into the discussion of whether or not Plath was a nice person, whether or not she was a victim. It would be ridiculous to respond to this drama with an inverse repetition which gave to everyone *except* Plath the status of cause. The question has to be put as to what it is on Plath's part that makes all these protagonists engage in such retaliatory actions, what it is that makes them feel they are the objects, somewhere, of Plath's own assault. And rather than locate that factor in the ethics of day-to-day behaviour (the stories and gossip with which this biography is packed), couldn't we see it at least partly in terms of Plath's death – suicide as an act of violence, as Freud put it, which is always aimed at more than one person?[137] This would give another meaning to Hughes's comment that Plath's death multiplies all her statements with a quantity that is wild and unknown. Hughes is of course referring to the aberrations of commentators, but the concept rebounds here most dramatically back on to the Estate. Death would then appear as the content of that 'pass the parcel' in relation to negativity (who's to blame?) in which they all engage, the necessary surplus to the whole process – death without measure, death as precisely what cannot be placed in the scales.

But what this biography finally makes so clear is once again the impossibility of objectivity, the limits of knowledge as such. It is, so to speak, the wild culmination or caricature of everything in relation to the archive we have seen. The more it asks for judgement, the more it assigns the reader to a position in which the conditions of such judgement definitively fall apart. One of the strangest effects of reading this book, especially if you have read the unedited letters and journals, is that it precisely becomes impossible to know whom to believe. To take just one example – Plath's insistence, repeated over and again in her last letters, that she has been deserted by Hughes.[138] In the biography this is presented as a travesty, a piece of self-victimisation designed to conceal the fact that Plath, against Hughes's wishes, insisted on the separation herself (Plath is reported as boasting to three friends that she threw Hughes out).[139] In her intervention into the *Guardian* correspondence over the gravestone, Olwyn Hughes presents this view as fact: 'after insisting in October 1962 that she and Ted Hughes should separate'.[140]

It is of course impossible to know which of these versions is true (they are not, of course, necessarily incompatible); nor does the fact that the more damaging statements in relation to Hughes have been taken out of the published letters settle the question either way. But if you have read those letters – read, indeed, the anger they express, read Plath saying that she wishes to be associated with Hughes no longer, even in name – then you are put in an impossible position.[141] Either you believe her, see her as the aggrieved party, her voice put down in the interests of the one guilty of her distress; or you accept the view of the biography, discredit her utterance and disbelieve what you have read. If the only sane position is finally to conclude that you do not know, then we should none the less note that this form of sanity is a position which can also drive you mad. And madness, we find, is in fact the condition or wager that Hughes lays down for anyone trying to write about Sylvia Plath. Writing on Linda Wagner-Martin, he stated: 'She's so insensitive that she's evidently escaped the usual effects of undertaking this particular job – i.e. mental breakdown, neurotic collapse, domestic catastrophe – which in the past has saved us from several travesties of this kind being completed.'[142]

Like the child caught up in a hideous divorce case between its parents, the writing of the life of Sylvia Plath, both by herself and by those who knew her, forces you – and makes it impossible for you – to take sides. Whom to believe, how to know, what is the truth of the case? Behind the self-interest of the protagonists lies a drama about the limits and failure of knowledge and self-knowing. We can settle it, like indeed the proceedings of a divorce case, but only by entering into the false and damaging forms of certainty for which those settlements are so renowned.

We should perhaps ask in passing what might be involved in such a biography for Anne Stevenson herself, who wrote an earlier article on Plath in one of the first collections of feminist literary criticism.[143] In that piece Plath represented the woman of the 1950s trapped in a limiting domesticity. She represented, in fact, nothing less than the prototype for the woman writer that Stevenson is herself – the article was precisely called 'Writing as a Woman'. The question Stevenson put in this article (although it appeared as much in the form of oscillation as question) was: Who is accountable for those limitations, the imposing limits of the culture or her own? Her own hesitancy seemed to be expressive of the need for, and the final inadequacy of, a certain logic of blame. Seen in this context, the biography appears as an attempted resolution of a problem she herself had identified as at once political and personal for women. It is as if the more nuanced position of that article, its careful suspension of any one-sided accusation against either the outside world or herself, could simply not be sustained. In an interview in the *Observer*, Stevenson said that she wrote the biography in order to find an 'answer' to Plath.[144] In a poem, 'Letter to Sylvia Plath', she makes more explicit the type of exorcism that was involved (expulsion of the bad in the form of Plath, as we have repeatedly seen it here):

> Dear Sylvia, we must close our book.
> Three springs you've perched like a black rook
> between sweet weather and my mind.
> At last I have to seem unkind
> and exorcise my awkward awe.
> My shoulder doesn't like your claw.[145]

All of this might help to explain the self-complacent, and terrifying, normality from which Stevenson claims to speak (and write).

Commenting during the 'Late Show' discussion on the way Plath magnified her world in her writing, Stevenson stated: 'most of us don't do this' (most of us, without distortion or conflict, register the self-evident truth of our world).

Out of this resolution, Plath emerges as the aggressor. Feminism is relegated to the status of 'simplified ideology'; feminists who situate her alongside Adrienne Rich, for example, misunderstand her 'with a degree of perversity equal to her own'.[146] Gone is any trace of the idea that Plath might none the less have something to say of relevance to feminism (compare 'hacks, self-publicists and extreme feminists' above). Thus not for the first time Plath finds herself caught up in a rejection of feminism, a caricature of feminism, and of herself as 'perverse'. In this context, hostility to feminism seems to be the only point of unity between Plath's supporters and her detractors. In the 'Late Show' discussion, the irrelevance of feminism to an understanding of Plath was the one thing on which Stevenson and Alvarez (criticising the biography) could agree.

There is of course another way of telling this story: that this defensive onslaught on Plath comes in response to a feminism which has been happy, precisely, to represent itself specifically in relation to Plath as 'perverse'. Thus Robin Morgan wrote (and rewrote under legal pressure from her publishers) her poem 'The Arraignment', which accuses Ted Hughes of murder and ends with an imagined scene of his dismemberment.[147] In the commentary which accompanied the two versions when they were finally published together, Morgan refers no fewer than three times to her poetry as her 'tool': 'As a feminist artist, my poetry is one of my strongest tools or weapons – perhaps, in the long run, my only one'; she finally rewrites the poem because a purer refusal to do so would leave her unable to 'disseminate' [sic] her tools.[148] The radical feminist thus identifies her writing with an image of the very organ in which she locates what is most violent about male power (compare too Aurelia Plath's account of words as 'tools' above). To say that Anne Stevenson's biography comes partially in response to this is not to legitimate it in any way. Rather it is to point to the passage of violence, even at – especially at – the point of the greatest claims to objectivity, back and forth across the body of Plath's work. In this battle, words themselves function as weapons, exposing a violence in language which all the protagonists seem to be furiously attempting to locate somewhere else – whether in Plath's 'cursed' inner drama, according to Stevenson, or in the 'patriarchal violence' represented for Morgan by Hughes.

It might finally be, however, that the importance of Plath resides in the way she brings together two accounts of causality which so often tend to be opposed – one which locates difficulty in the outer, the other which locates it exclusively in the inner, world. For it is possible, as well as necessary, to recognise in relation to Plath the forms of protest and frustration to which she gives voice with reference to domesticity, mothering, childcare, financial independence and writing, as well as her feeling, at the end, of personal betrayal by Hughes (that anxiety about money in the last letters reads, not like self-justification, but more like a living out of Virginia Woolf's *A Room of One's Own);*[149] while simultaneously acknowledging the relative autonomy of psychic life, its own violence and its own laws to which, as we saw in the last chapter, Plath gives voice. Instead of which, commentaries on Plath divide into two antagonistic forms of explanation – Plath as the victim of a hostile male world, Plath as asking for everything she gets (crudely the opposition between Linda Wagner-Martin's and Anne Stevenson's biographies, between Robin Morgan and Olwyn Hughes). It is, however, the necessary overlap, and no less necessary disintrication, of these two levels – of real injustice and unapportionable blame – which (and not only in relation to Plath) is so difficult and important.

In Anne Stevenson's case, it becomes clear that in some sense it is psychic life itself, in all its complexity, that is under attack. Her book is constructed according to a set of binaries: the violence of Plath's writing is solipsistic and internal, that of Hughes's is expansive, referring outwards to the natural world; hers is a matter of pure psyche, his belongs to the wider span of our cultural and political life (we will come back to this in the next chapter); Plath is responsible for everything that happens to her, Hughes is wholly without blame.[150] Inner and outer, psyche and politics, blame and no blame. If we line up these rhyming oppositions, then what we get is the guilt of the psyche, the conviction, which seems latent to this biography, that the psyche *is* blame – the 'rubbish of the subconscious', to use Stevenson's expression at one point in the book, beautifully echoing and rejoining that other opposition between 'scraps' and 'wealth' used by Olwyn Hughes.[151] For Stevenson, 'pathology is not excusable', to use the words of one reviewer of the book.[152] Although this in itself assumes that we are dealing with pathology, something which no one is now in a position to prove or disprove, without – as this biography makes so glaringly clear – revealing their own investment in the question, without revealing their own investment in the category of pathology as such. But it is surely only because Plath is a woman that images of violence, *even if* inner and psychic, are read not as vision or insight, but as perversity or illegitimate rage?

Once again the feeling starts to emerge that beyond that repeated protection of self-interest (of which this biography is merely the most glaring instance) it is the problem of uncertainty, in relation to both language and psychic processes, that is playing itself out most fundamentally in relation to Plath's work. When the published *Journals*, for example, correct 'Poem on birthday' to 'Poem on [her] birthday', or 'I am experiencing a grief reaction for Mother's love' to 'I am experiencing a grief reaction for [the loss of] Mother's love', it suggests that it is ambiguity (which birthday? – hers, her future child's, the poem's itself?) and ambivalence (mourning for a love experienced as *at once* too little and too much) that is constantly failing to be read in her writing.[153]

All this brings us back full circle to the question of language and writing in relation to Plath; to the sense that the closest, most intimate of links binds the issue of moral accountability to that of language and psyche, and then each of these to that of aesthetic judgement in turn. If we return to Aurelia Plath and Ted Hughes, then we can see most simply how their different positions generate their own, very specific, interpretations of Plath's work. For Aurelia Plath, subservience to the market is accountable for what is most disturbing in Plath's writing: 'Sylvia discovered that her exuberant, joyous outbursts in both poetry and prose brought rejection slips, while the story or poem with pathetic twist was found more acceptable.'[154] Compare Plath in 1956: 'They are obviously in the market for a new lyrical woman. And they are *happy* poems.'[155] On the publication of *The Colossus*, Aurelia Plath comments: 'The haunting memories of emotional terror voiced in some of the poems were in direct contrast to the strong, affirmative voice she gave forth in her letters and conversations with her family' (note how this reads all terror as memory, places it definitively in the past tense); and on the late poems: 'magnificently structured poems, renouncing the subservient female role, yet holding to the triumphant note of maternal creativity in her scorn of "barrenness"'.[156]

In a talk to Wellesley College in 1976, she cites three extracts from Plath's verse play 'Three Women', all of which are taken from the voice of the woman who wants and keeps her child, without any allusion to the other two women, the one who miscarries and the one who rejects her infant, the context without which the voice of the first woman makes little sense.[157] Against terror, towards a resurgent, maternal femininity, Aurelia Plath leads the poems back to the mother – back, by implication, to herself. The Editor's Note to the *Journals* proposes a different relation between the poetry and the life, one which leads the writing up and away from the biographical reference it is simultaneously seen to evoke:

> The interrelation [between her life and the germs of her work] is especially important in a writer whose work was so completely centred on her biographical details, though it's important to understand that the autobiography does not work in Plath as it does in the 'confessional writers', but rather in a mythological sense – as can be seen most clearly in Judith Kroll's critical study *Chapters in a Mythology*.[158]

Compare Hughes on the late poems in his earlier article on the *Journals*: 'raising her new self out of the ruins of her mythical father' (the reference is to 'The Stones') . . . 'A Jungian might call the whole phase a classic case of the chemical individuation of the self.'[159] Note too how, in the later discussion of *Ariel*, this form of reading is accompanied by only passing allusion to what was concretely taking place in her life: 'According to the appointed coincidence of such things, after July her outer circumstances intensified her inner battle to the limit' (outer circumstances as adjunct but never *cause*).[160] Ironically, by appearing as a form of self-protection, such a reading invites the very biographical reduction it is trying to avoid. Ironic, too, that the spectre of self-interest makes it almost impossible to recognise in Hughes's comments what is clearly at one level his own strong affirmation of Plath.

But something more complex, more important, finally seems to be going on in relation to language and meaning in this mythic interpretation by Hughes. What starts to become clear is that his concept of an emergent true self carries a very specific psychic weight. It is, for him, the end of contradiction and simultaneously the creation of pure, unadulterated speech: 'A real self, as we know, is a rare thing. The direct speech of a real self is rarer still ... Most of us are never more than bundles of contradictory and complementary selves.'[161] Real self, direct speech – what all this inevitably gravitates towards is nothing less than the concept of the absolute, indisputable, fact: 'This is the *objectivity* of her subjective mode' ... 'the succession of images in "The Stones" ... has to be given *the status of fact*'[162] (my emphasis):

> Surveyed as a whole, with attention to the order of composition, I think the unity of her opus is clear. Once the unity shows itself, the logic and inevitability of the language, which controls and contains such conflagrations and collisions within itself, becomes more obviously what it is – direct, and even plain, speech.[163]

But this notion of language as unique, direct and singular, I would argue, scarcely applies to Plath, even though in relation to the poetry she did on occasions evoke it herself. A very different conception of writing, for example, can be called up from the *Journals*, which are described in that opening editorial note as a 'treasure house of thousands of loose ends'.[164] We are much closer here to that image of language put forward in 'Mourning and Melancholia', the only work by Freud directly cited in Plath's *Journals*, where he talks of ambivalence, of the multiplication of meanings which can attach to any one object or sign – of significance, to use his own expression, reinforced by 'a thousand links'.[165] For Freud, the unconscious means that there can be no definitive resolution of subjectivity, only 'suspense on the quicksands of ambivalence', to take a line from 'Love is a Parallax', one of Plath's early poems; or the ability to 'smooth differences into the acceptance of paradox', as she puts it in one of her letters home.[166]

None of this, of course, is to dispute Hughes's right to his reading of Plath's work. Rather, the problem is the way that reading naturalises itself into the process of editing, where it appears as a transcendent aesthetic judgement, thus taking on the character of the poetry to which it is meant to apply. On the other hand, it is only more recent critical approaches to literature that have criticised the celebration of a writer's unity, seeing it as a form of resistance to the complexities and difficulties of language and subjectivity which such unity (such celebration) resolves or denies.

At issue in our reading of the Plath archive – as well as at issue between Plath and Hughes – there are therefore different conceptions of language which carry very different images of psychic life. They correspond, as we will see in the next chapter, to the disagreement between Freud and Jung, both of whom Hughes and Plath draw on and to whom, in different ways, they both refer. But at the most obvious level, to try to construct a single, consistent image of Plath becomes meaningless, not just because of the vested interests that so often appear to be at stake in the various attempts to do so that we have seen, but far more because the multiplicity of representations that Plath offers of herself make such an effort so futile. As Plath writes herself across her journals, letters, novel, short stories and poetry, her different voices enter into an only ever partial dialogue with each other which it is impossible to bring to a close. To which of these voices are we going to assign an absolute authority – the voice of *The Bell Jar*, which she publishes under a pseudonym; the voice of the *Letters Home*, in which she communicated another, but incompatible, truth; the voice of the *Journals* which seems, so cruelly at moments, to give to those letters the lie; the voice of her poems, which can be read as the upflight of a transcendent femininity away from the men who constrain it, or as the expression of a hostility towards women (and not only for Hughes) – a hostility that can be seen as one of the undersides of that very transcendence for women which it has served repeatedly, historically, to undermine (the impasse at the heart of one celebratory image of feminism)? Above all, these differences of writing and interpretation should act as a crucial caution against one conception of censorship – the idea that behind it can be uncovered the single, unadulterated truth. Plath may be censored but, as we have seen, she also censors, transforms and endlessly rewrites herself.

In relation to Hughes himself, the disparity between the various accounts which Plath offers of herself, the fought-out relation between these accounts, makes it clear that the question of what can and can't be spoken, what can and can't be heard, does not apply only to him – he gives an inflated and patriarchal version of a difficulty in language in excess, by definition, of the concrete power which he undoubtedly exerts. In this context, the idea of 'bundles of contradictory and complementary selves', to which he refers so dismissively, can in fact serve as a warning, since it alone allows for complex and contradictory motivations on his part – self-protection as well as validation of Plath, control of her as well as her release; allows us to avoid the trap of judging as the expression of monolithic self-interest his own editing of, and commentary on, the writing of Sylvia Plath.

At the start of this chapter, I commented on the strange relation played out in this narrative between different registers of know-ledge, between the concept of evidence proper to the courtroom and literary language, between the idea of objectivity and the most personally and fiercely invested of family scenes. Like all family sagas, the story of Sylvia Plath seems to have the power to draw everybody who approaches into its orbit, to make you feel that somehow you belong (this is not quite voyeurism whose pleasure rests on exclusion, on a position that remains firmly outside). The Plath story at once involves you and asks for judgement. It asks you to apportion blame, to parcel out innocence and guilt.

In different ways, all the protagonists appeal to a legalistic conception of truth, something incontrovertible which could be established beyond all reasonable doubt (this is the concept of evidence proper to criminal proceedings as compared to the civil courts, where judgement rests on the 'balance of probabilities'). In each case, they set this truth against the fantasia, perversions, distortions, to which Plath's commentators, or Plath herself, subject the true facts – according to their own perceptions – of the case. At several points, as we have seen it is the relationship to truth itself, rather than the more easily recognisable matter of moral accounta-bility, which appears to be up for judgement, or on trial. In the case of Hughes, the concept of the indisputable fact appears at different moments as the measure of objective reality and of the highest aesthetic form (we will see in Chapter 5, however, that at one – crucial – point in relation to Plath's writing, it is her attachment to the 'blunt fact' which he criticises, as the limitation or prison of her prose).

Such a conception of truth is, I have argued, undermined in direct proportion to the intensity with which the various participants lay claim to it. It is in any case especially vulnerable when it is the register of fiction to which it is meant to apply. One could in fact argue that the more the protagonists attempt to draw representations of and by Plath into the realm of ascertainable truth or falsehood, the more they have the opposite effect – it is the factual which finds itself marked irretrievably by the category of fiction. The question then arises as to what might happen when this confrontation actually takes place in a court of law. What happens when the law is asked to judge the effect of a work of fiction, when the legal conception of evidence finds itself up against a literary conception of truth?

The case in question was brought against the film version of *The Bell Jar* in the USA. Hughes alludes to it in his article in *The Independent* and again in his article in the *Observer*, arguing that it demonstrates the lack, rather than excess, of control that the estate exerts over Plath's work.[167] The plaintiff, Jane Anderson, brought the case against the film for its portrayal of her as a character, Joan Gilling, a friend of the narrator, Esther Greenwood, who makes a lesbian advance towards Esther and commits suicide near the end of the book. Anderson stated that while she had 'instantly recognised herself' as the character in the novel, the homosexual implications of her portrayal escaped her until they were drawn to her attention by Edward Butscher's 1976 biography of Plath.[168] Hughes mentions none of this explicitly, simply noting that they had considered taking Butscher to court for violation of copyright but decided not to do so. He then argues that he was charged at the trial with not exerting adequate control over what Butscher had written: 'The charge against me, basically, was that I had failed to protect her [Anderson] from Mr. Butscher's theorising about a piece of writing about Sylvia Plath.'[169] In the *Observer* article, Hughes offers this as one of the reasons behind the editorial cuts he has carried out on Plath's work – the risk of 'sitting in the libel courts, taking responsibility for the real consequences of words'.[170] As this case shows, Hughes can indeed find himself accountable for what appears in Plath's work. The problem is compounded by his dual position as custodian of her writing and as one of the central figures appearing, directly or indirectly, in her texts. Who, one might ask, is one of the most abused figures in Plath's censored writing, if not Hughes himself? Imagine then this scenario (*reductio ad absurdum* of this whole story) – Hughes, as the most aggrieved party, accusing Hughes, as representative of the Estate. The issue which emerges at the Anderson trial, however, is rather different – not the issue of who controls the facts, but what constitutes a fact in relation to the domain of literary fictions.

Anderson's charge was defamation, invasion of privacy, and intentional infliction of emotional damage on the grounds that the film company continued to distribute the film after she had lodged her case. She sued for six million dollars, but settled, in an out-of-court agreement (a 'consent judgement'), for a hundred and fifty thousand and an acknowledgement that she had been 'unintentionally defamed'. Hughes had sold the film rights, but he paid no part of the settlement since the case had been brought against the film and not the book, no doubt at least partly due to the amount of time that had elapsed since the book's publication (Anderson withdrew any additional charges against the Estate). If the distinction between literature and the cinema was clear enough in this instance, it has occasionally, in relation to *The Bell Jar*, found itself blurred. The blurb on the back of the first American edition of the novel described its account of mental breakdown as 'completely real and even rational, as probable and inaccessible [*sic*] an experience as going to the movies'.[171] It is interesting too that if the film was on trial (the lawyer opening for Anderson said that the case would demonstrate Hollywood at its 'most exploitative' and 'worst'), it was the one juror who admitted to reading books (Richard Wright's *Native Son*) who was discharged.[172]

The novel was, however, central to the case to the extent that a crucial issue was whether *The Bell Jar* was a literal (in the guise of fiction) or a wholly fictional representation of the facts in Plath's life. Hughes stated under oath that the novel was fiction ('"based on my experience as a writer and on my knowledge of Sylvia Plath, I can state without reservation that *The Bell Jar* is fiction"'), although he also said that his aim in laying down conditions for the film had been the protection of Aurelia Plath (from the correspondence she appears to have been distraught at the announcement of the film, which she also appears to have first heard of through the press).[173] The novel is therefore fiction, but it is real enough for individuals who might recognise themselves in it to need subsequent protection. If this inconsistency seems to make the case for Anderson, it none the less touches on an ambiguity which lay at the heart of the whole case: how to determine the truth-quotient of a form of writing which hovers between autobiographical reference and fiction, which displays the logic of both empirical and unconscious truth?[174] Thus Hughes and others argued that the character of Joan Gilling in the novel was a composite, made up of a number of real individuals condensed into a single form[175] (for Freud, condensation was one of the chief properties of unconscious thought). The character was therefore both real (several times over) and distorted – that is, it was both real and unreal. This in fact evokes an ambiguity inherent to autobiography, which constitutes, as much as it transforms, the reality to which it is presumed to refer. As Esther Greenwood herself puts it in *The Bell Jar*: 'I wondered if I had made Joan up'.[176]

In relation to Plath, we can also ask what could be the truth of autobiography given the different and contradictory types of writing in which she represented herself? For the lawyers commenting on the case, the issue was that of balancing the constitutional right to individual freedom against the rights of the individual not to be maligned, or the clash between fiction and libel: 'fiction is entitled to a special measure of constitutional protection'.[177] But what we will see in addition to this is that at every level of the case there is a tension which strikes at the heart of what constitutes fiction, what constitutes reference itself.

It is a tension that reappears right at the centre of Anderson's complaint. Anderson's case rested, necessarily, on a double claim – that she both recognisably was, and wasn't, the character portrayed in the novel and in the film. She *was* in so far as it was – unmistakably, she argued – a representation of herself; she was *not* in so far as it defamed her – she was not and had never been homosexual, and clearly had not hanged herself. The more Anderson established that this was an untrue representation, the more it could be asserted that her case was groundless in so far as she had so convincingly established the fictional nature of the text.

At one level this is the logic proper to the law of defamation – a character must first be recognisable in order for defamation to be claimed. But in US law, this relationship between belief and disbelief is complex. For a charge of defamation to be successfully brought in the United States, the plaintiff must establish that he or she will be identified and that the defamatory description is such that a 'reasonable reader would believe that it could apply to an actual person'.[178] If the representation is too outrageous, therefore, the case fails (like the case of Ms Wyoming against *Penthouse*, which was lost on the grounds that the activities represented were so extreme that 'no reasonable reader would have believed it to be a description of the plaintiff's actual conduct').[179] For the plaintiff, therefore, the depiction must be true enough to be believable, untrue and defamatory enough to cause the original outrage and give a right to sue, but not so outrageous that it appears impossible or necessarily untrue. What we see here is the law breaking up the concept of truth, revealing in this set of legal discriminations (reference, fairness, credibility) the fundamental non-unity of the term. But what we also see is the non-commensurability between these careful distinctions and the far less certain, more amorphous, category of truth as it operates in the realm of literary fictions. If the final verdict suggests, as one commentator put it, that 'reality won in principle',[180] nothing was technically decided, no precedent has been established, because there was no written judgement in the case.

There is, however, a straightforward sense in which the trial was self-defeating. Anderson had brought the case to clear herself of the imputation of lesbianism, which was for her the most damaging charge – she argued that if it were believed it would irrevocably damage her self-image and her career (as a psychiatrist she was particularly concerned that her college-age patients might see the film).[181] Yet by bringing the case to trial, she served to broadcast the possibility of her lesbianism to the whole world. Thus the trial was the expression of, and inadvertently served to reinforce, the very homophobia against which the charge of libel was intended to protect her – 'I am not now a homosexual and I have never been a homosexual' was the last statement issued by Anderson in relation to the case.[182] Compare this with the case brought against the film *Woodstock* by a Canadian hairdresser who argued that a shot which showed him disappearing with a woman into the bushes had ruined his career, which depended on his clients thinking he was in fact gay.

Clearly, therefore, there was a crucial issue of sexual politics at stake, one which touches on what is for many feminists the hidden other scene of the heterosexual imperative played out so dramatically between Plath and Hughes. In this context it is worth noting that, unlike the better-known case of the film of *The Color Purple* (based on Alice Walker's book), the film of *The Bell Jar* accentuates, rather than plays down, the lesbianism in the original text (another

109

reason, probably, why Anderson sues the film and not the novel).[183] This might have something to do with the fact that the aim with *The Color Purple* was to make a wholly popular text in which the general (read 'heterosexual') humanity of the characters would neutralise what might otherwise be the alienating black identity of the film; whereas in the case of *The Bell Jar*, the market or chief reference point was assumed to be literary (sexual transgression as permissible in the high culture to which Plath is once again confined). Alternatively, the film might have been trying to have it both ways – a vicarious glimpse at the sleazy underface of high art.

If we go back to the *Bell Jar* trial, then we see that it is not only in relation to homosexuality or the charge of defamation, but also in relation to the charge of invasion of privacy that the trial started to turn on itself since, in order to establish the former, the most intimate details of Anderson's life had to be brought into the court. Evidence that the plaintiff had engaged in homosexual practices was introduced and then ruled out of order, but the court did hear the testimony of her psychiatrist, as well as details from the records of Anderson's stay at McLean in 1953.[184] Anderson herself went and consulted those records, discovering for the first time that the hospital had considered her to be schizophrenic.[185] She also went back into therapy as a result of the film.[186] Anderson therefore finds herself turning to, re-enacting, the very history whose pastness she was trying to affirm ('"I have made bordering on a heroic effort to get my life together" after "very serious problems" at the age of 21 and 22').[187] On that boundary between literal truth and fiction, we therefore discover two different orders of time – the time of verifiable history, of what belongs unequivocally in the past, and the psychic time of trauma, where things do not go forward but repeat. Anderson stated that as a result of seeing the film she had started to have flashbacks, like the veterans of the Vietnam War.[188]

The political implications of all this are far-reaching – not just in relation to sexual politics, but also in relation to politics in its more familiar sense. For if the boundary between fiction and reality is uncertain, it can be crossed in both directions. Fiction has its effects on, can intervene into, concrete political life. The point was made by one commentator on the case who alluded to Lincoln's famous comment to Harriet Beecher Stowe that her novel *Uncle Tom's Cabin* had started the Civil War (the fact that it was a black writer, Richard Wright, who was mentioned by the juror excluded from the trial might also be read as indicating the unfinished nature of this history of racial division).[189]

Nor is the liberal defence of fiction – the issue for so many commentators on the trial – without its more insidious implications in this context. According to a Yale Law School professor referred to in the same article, one of the goals of freedom of expression is to maintain the necessary balance between – to forestall – 'social stultification and revolution'[190] – to maintain, one might argue, that illusion of freedom and democracy, across race and class divisions, on which Plath herself had commented as a student at Smith. Answering a question in a Government class on the conviction of the leaders of the Communist Party (Dennis v. United States 1951) – did it clash with the first and fifth amendments of the Constitution? – she wrote:

> . . . if American ideals of democracy are not secure enough, vital enough, to stand up against propaganda, they deserve to fall under Communist domination. What we need is a remedy for our seeming hypocrisy (e.g. Civil Rights legislation) so that none of our minorities will feel the *need* to support another ideology [exercise from class on Government at Smith].[191]

Not far behind *The Bell Jar* suit we find again the politics which, at various points of editing and in so much critical commentary, have been reduced or downgraded in Plath's work.


To return, finally, to the controversy over the gravestone. For isn't it the case that it is the gravestone which raises at its most unbearable the question of fictionality which we have seen played out throughout this narrative? Isn't a gravestone something which is by definition inadequate to the presence, no longer present, which it attempts to hold on to and evoke? And this regardless of whether the attachment of the survivors to the memory of the dead could be described as too little or too much. In Plath's own poem on her father's grave, 'Electra on Azalea Path', the speaker starts by reproaching the grave for its inadequacy ('cramped necropolis'), but the poem rapidly moves into a much more uncertain territory where love itself is the greatest danger, as much the cause as the remainder of death: 'I brought my love to bear, and then you died'.[192] Nor does the fact of its intensity preserve mourning from the domain of fiction: As the speaker grieves, she writes herself into a drama – 'I borrow the stilts from an old tragedy' – not wholly remote from the one we have seen:

> *The day your slack sail drank my sister's breath*
> *The flat sea purpled like that evil cloth*
> *My mother unrolled at your last homecoming.*

[Plath's emphasis]

The daughter (Electra) reproaches the father (Agamemnon) for having been willing to sacrifice her sister (Iphigenia). Death brings back the accusation of history instead of bringing it to a close.

And what could be a correct naming of Sylvia Plath in the context of that drama, of placing and identity, enacted between her survivors, but in which she also plays her part (the pun on the name of her mother in that poem's title is just one example of this)? For feminism, the name of the husband is one of the strongest insignia of patriarchal power. But even though Plath herself states in a suppressed part of one of her last letters that the name of Hughes is a name she wishes to shed, the question still remains as to what it means, beyond the point of her death, to act on such a statement on her behalf. What unreserved, unqualified certainty does such an act have to assume; and what drama does it perpetuate at the very moment that it claims to resolve it or bring it to a close? Like Catherine Heathcliff, whose name Lockwood discovers three times over in the hallucinatory opening to *Wuthering Heights* – Catherine Earnshaw, Catherine Heathcliff, Catherine Linton – Plath appears as the ghostly presence in her own story. The more we try to settle the question of her name, the more it is that story that we find ourselves inevitably repeating.[193]

Running through the various texts of Plath's writing – letters, journals, poetry – there is one line that appears as a refrain. It is the first line of a German song that Plath recalls from her childhood, one that her mother used to play and sing to her: '*Ich weiss nicht was soll es bedeuten . . .*' ['I do not know what it means'].[194] It can be read twice over as the expression of an irreducible hesitancy in language – the foreignness of the German, the incomprehension voiced by the content of the words, the whole line appearing in Plath's writing as the relic of a cultural memory which she endlessly fails to retrieve. This line can serve as a frame for the whole story I have described. From a drama enacted in terms of rights of possession we come back to the furthest vanishing point of language in relation to naming and – wild, unknown quantity – to death. In his famous essay on epitaphs, Wordsworth wrote:

> Language, if it do not uphold, and feed, and leave in quiet like the power of gravitation or the air we breathe, is a counter-spirit, unremittingly and noiselessly at work, to subvert, to lay waste, to vitiate and to dissolve.[195]

Today we might be more inclined than Wordsworth to read this as a characteristic intrinsic to language as such. It is, however, the irony and significance of this story that it reveals language so dramatically in its capacity to lay waste, vitiate and dissolve – at once as a property of discourse and as a conflict in which the most familiar (ancient) of sexual and political dramas plays itself out.

# NO FANTASY WITHOUT PROTEST

Two early poems by Plath written in 1957, both published for the first time in the *Collected Poems* of 1981, speak of the problem of poetic representation in explicitly sexual, gendered terms. In the first, 'On the Difficulty of Conjuring Up a Dryad', the speaker complains of the stubborn presence, or referentiality, of the world which refuses to transform itself into poetic shape ('My tree stays tree').[1] The tree – 'scrupulous', 'obdurate' – will not transfigure itself, will not 'concoct a Daphne'. The 'honest earth' spurns such transfiguration – 'such fiction' – 'as nymphs'. Thus feminising poetic vision (Daphne, nymphs), the speaker simultaneously downgrades it – 'counterfeit', 'fiction', 'cant', 'wiles', 'hoodwink' – and then imagines somewhere else:

> some moon-eyed,
> Star-lucky sleight-of-hand man watches
> My jilting lady squander coin, gold leaf stock ditches,
> And the opulent air go studded with seed.

In the second poem, 'On the Plethora of Dryads', the speaker stares down an apple tree in a desperate attempt to discover a quintessential beauty visible, according to the ravings of a 'white saint', 'only to a paragon heart'.[2] Again inspiration fails in the sense of 'visionary lightnings', but a different form of vision, this time wedded to the facticity of the tree of whose obduracy the first poem had complained ('each particular quirk' . . . 'every pock and stain'), surfeits the senses, provokes a 'wanton fit' and snares her in its 'miraculous art'. To be inspired here is to be playful, lascivious or lewd ('wanton'), a sexual state which takes its cue, is transferred, from what it is that provokes the inspiration itself:

> I must watch sluttish dryads twitch
> Their multifarious silks in the holy grove
> Until no chaste tree but suffers blotch
> Under flux of those seductive
> Reds, greens, blues.

This is not the first time (and it will not be the last) that Plath sexualises the act of writing or poetic vision in this way. In an even earlier poem, 'Metamorphoses of the Moon', included in the 'Juvenilia' section at the back of the Collected Poems, the speaker describes a series of acts of poetic hubris, attempts to wrench meaning from the secrets of the world, each one figured as a specifically male violation (pilot, parachutist and prince).[3] Such forcing, however, is inevitably punished by disappointment; 'exquisite truth' reveals itself as 'artifice', for which the image, once again, is that of the seductive and dissembling woman: 'some common parlor fake:/a craft with paint and powder that can make/cleopatra from a slut'.

In each of these instances, poetic writing, inspiration, higher knowledge, rely on a transforming vision which is a snare. Each time the poet fails in that vision – because she is inadequate to it, or because she passes alongside it to somewhere else, or because she seems to judge, to take her distance, from those who seek it. But if this starts to look like an allegory for women's position outside poetic language, or at least outside one significant tradition of conceiving the poetic imagination, that reading immediately finds itself stalled by the sexual connotations which attach to it. For this speaker seems to write herself into the place of a man, lured, failed, or deceived by ladies who jilt, by sluts who surfeit the senses or (and) pass themselves off as Cleopatra. Lure or tease, come-on or brush-off, what is signified here as the source of poetic vision – its attraction and its dangers – seems to be nothing other than femininity itself.

The very awkwardness of these moments can, I think, serve as a useful way into thinking about the sexual politics, the play of gender, sexuality and power in the writing of Sylvia Plath. At one level we can read them as Plath marking, inflating and parodying the literary tradition which, if it excludes women, also offers them the most elevated of places in relation to poetry, as Muse. Plath could be seen here as exposing or foregrounding the denigrated femininity on which that more inspired vision of women (and poetry) so often relies. Or else, if that feels like reading into this early writing too much political consciousness, then these moments can be read as symptomatic of the way women internalise under patriarchy, take into themselves and embody, some of patriarchy's worst sexual images and tropes. But however we deal with that problem of intentionality, whether we choose to assign to Plath a political, specifically feminist, consciousness, or lament in her the iron grip of patriarchy even on (especially on) the inner vision of women, I would suggest that we cannot understand these moments without reference to the concept of fantasy.

Commenting on the moment in 'On the Plethora of Dryads' when the speaker talks of 'Starving my fantasy down/To discover that metaphysical Tree', Margaret Uroff writes of the word 'fantasy': 'a curious word choice in this context since what she is talking about is the imagination'.[4] The opposition seems, however, to be clear – between fantasy in its specific, older meaning as concrete impression (*OED*: 'an image implanted on the mind by an object of sense' – compare the later line: 'But before I might blind sense') and imagination as inspiration; between sense and metaphysics, metaphysics being that which precisely requires the senses to be blinded and starved. But the word fantasy also takes on an added significance in this context, one which can perhaps throw some light on the sexual narrative of these poems, on the low-grade feminisation of poetic vision and on the fact that the speaker seems, at least partially, to take up the place of the man. For Plath may be situating herself here on another boundary, another distinction, between imagination and fantasy: between the coercive, intense singularity of the first and the instability proper to the second – that is, its fundamental ambivalence of sexual identity and place.

Early in Plath's *Journals* she writes: 'I am at odds. I dislike being a girl, because as such I must come to realize that I cannot be a man . . . I am part man, and I notice women's breasts and thighs with the calculation of a man choosing a mistress.'[5] Later in the same year she writes: 'Being born a woman is my awful tragedy. From the moment I was conceived I was doomed to sprout breasts and ovaries rather than penis and scrotum; to have my whole circle of action, thought and feeling rigidly circumscribed by my inescapable femininity.'[6] In her Introduction to *Letters Home*, Aurelia Plath includes this as one of a number of passages underlined by Sylvia Plath in her copy of John Langdon-Davies's *A Short History of Women*: 'men and women are purely relative terms, and long before the tendencies of our times work to their logical conclusions, men and women, as we know them, will have ceased to exist; and human nature will have forgotten the "he and she"'.[7]

For Plath, to be a woman is to be rigidly, tragically, circumscribed

– in that first passage she is objecting to a statement from her boyfriend's mother: 'Girls look for infinite security; boys look for a mate. Both look for different things', which seems to leave her with no freedom other than that of 'choosing or refusing' a mate.[8] Plath protests at this familiar platitude passed (as challenge? as injunction?) from mother to son to son's potential future wife, even as she feels herself sliding into her dictated place: 'it is as I feared: I am becoming accustomed and adjusted to that idea'.[9] But in the process of objecting she recognises in herself, not just the desire for the man's freedom – the voluntarism of independence and a greater assertion of will – but an involuntary slippage, an identification with his sexual pleasure or fantasy, which makes of the woman the surveyed and calculated object of her own desire. Trapped in her woman's body, Plath none the less discovers in herself a 'part man'. This is what she calls 'the artist and the analytical attitude toward the female body', for she is 'more a woman'.[10] Being a woman is therefore a supplement, something which comes after, a residue after protest, after a contradictory and contrary self-situating in the realm of sex.

By naming this moment of masculine identification as the attitude of the artist (the 'artist and the analytical attitude') Plath sets up a link between sexual fantasy and writing in a way that raises a different set of issues about the relationship between the body and writing from those discussed in Chapter 2. Writing seems to belong here in a space surrounded on either side by sexist platitude and (proto-)feminist revolt. Weighed down by the first, she moves into the protest of the second, only to find herself circling back to, rejoining, the masculine sexual sub-text of the very ideology to which she objects. According to one feminist account of women's writing, women can write only by identifying with the male sexual organ (the male 'part') in which our literary tradition, in barely disguised metaphor, has located its genealogy and worth.[11] Plath seems to take that account at the letter, laying bare its seamy sexual underface in which she takes her reluctant pleasure. For if we have come to acknowledge that writing may involve for the woman an enforced male identification, condition of entry for women into a tradition which has only partially allowed them a place, we have perhaps asked ourselves less what type of strange, perverse, semi-licensed pleasures such an identification might release. In this instance, that licence, that pleasure, shows the woman rediscovering herself as pure stereotype, as the reduced, reified and fragmented bits and pieces of sex. The passage underlined by Plath from Langdon-Davies's *Short History of Women* seems to be arguing that only the dissolution of sexual difference, only the dismantling of the 'he and she', will – 'long before the tendencies of our times work to their logical conclusion' – bring this situation to an end.

The passage in which Plath bemoans her woman's body ('doomed to sprout breasts and ovaries') continues:

> Yes, my consuming desire to mingle with road crews, sailors and soldiers, barroom regulars – to be part of a scene, anonymous, listening, recording – all is spoiled by the fact I am a girl, a female always in danger of assault and battery. My consuming interest in men and their lives is often misconstrued as a desire to seduce them, or as an invitation to intimacy. Yes, God, I want to talk to everyone I can as deeply as I can.[12]

Being a woman limits Plath's writing because it deprives her of an anonymity which would allow her to watch, listen to and record, but also join in, the conversation of men. What she wants is not a room of one's own, the now classic feminist demand of the woman writer, but the road, field and tavern, the expansion of a world crucially located outside: 'I want to be able to sleep in an open field, to travel west, to walk freely at night'.[13] In that world, writing is man-talk, something which she describes elsewhere as 'Plot' – people 'growing: banging into each other and into circumstances', 'big, blasting dangerous' love.[14] Banging, blasting, dangerous – Plath's image of writing takes up, acts out in fantasy, the assault and battery of which she sees herself as victim in that first quote. Note too that conventional link between violence and masculinity as rough trade (road crews, sailors, soldiers and barroom regulars). First she links violence to the female vulnerability that prevents her from writing, then she makes of violence the very image for the form of writing that she most strongly desires.

This form of writing is opposed by Plath to another one which she explicitly genders as female. It is characterised – 'overweighted' – by 'heavy descriptive passages and a kaleidoscope of similes' which can be traced to the 'emotions and senses' with which she predominantly experiences her 'woman's world'.[15] Femininity is surfeit ('plethora') and it snuffs out true form. Rejecting this form of writing, Plath passes judgement on a language which, under the name of *écriture*, has become for many feminists the true female aesthetic, counter to that other image of writing which requires the woman to become part – *the* part – of a man. She writes:

> That stubborn state where time present [is] made up only of temporary physical reality, sensual perceptions, and spasmodic streams-of-consciousness . . . but this state of mind is born of a renunciation of complexities. It is a negation of sorts. A return to the womb, Freud might have called it. Overwhelmed by lack of time, race of time, speed of time, I retreat into non-thought – merely into Epicurean sensual observations and desires.[16]

Seen in this context, the starving, blinding, of sense that Plath presented in her early poem as the precondition of poetic vision is given a further meaning in relation to gender. Sense is feminine, and poetry requires it to be displaced by a controlling, metaphysical vision. That image of inspiration as recalcitrant, seductive or sluttish is the logical consequence of an age-old scenario which represents true writing as the control of the (female) body, of matter, by (male) form.

On more than one occasion Plath stated that her real desire was to write not poetry, but prose. Her comment – 'For me, writing verse is an evasion of the real job of writing' – is quoted on the back of *Johnny Panic and the Bible of Dreams* (although the blurb also states that this 'ambition' was superseded by 'the demands of her real vision').[17] Poetry was an 'excuse' and 'escape', with prose the ultimate release ('Oh, to break out into prose'), if only Plath could get to it, past the 'glass-dam fancy-façade of numb dumb wordage', past her own fear, and into the clarity of plot: 'Prose writing has become a phobia to me: my mind shuts and I clench. I can't, or won't, come clear with a plot.'[18] If we place this in the context of that earlier description of plot – 'people growing: banging into each other and into circumstances' – then it would seem that Plath's yearning for prose is not only part of a distinction between forms of culture (high art versus storytelling) but also belongs to her persistent sexualisation of aesthetic vision. Prose, as we will see, belongs to, or is aimed at, a world of women, but what is being offered is a form of language that is proper to – can be identified with or stand in for – men.

This distinction between male and female writing does not always map on to different literary forms with such ease. As we have already seen, the idea of a controlling, or abusing, male vision is also central to the way Plath describes the genesis of poetry. Nor is she always, or unfailingly dismissive of that stream-of-consciousness writing which, in the passage of sensuous perception, and with obvious reference to Virginia Woolf, she describes as 'non-thought' ('too disparate' is another criticism that she makes of Woolf).[19] In one passage in her *Journals*, she describes herself as a female Stephen Dedalus, word-artist and heroine of just that form of writing, which she appropriates, and remoulds, into an unmistakably feminist shape: 'But I must be a word-artist. The heroine. Like Stephen Dedalus walking by the sea: ooo-ee-ooo-siss. Hissing their petticoats.'[20] Inadvertently or deliberately, Plath substitutes 'hissing' for 'hising' in Joyce's text (the slip is hers, not the editors'; it is in the original), turning the classic image of women lifting their underskirts, proffering their body to a male gaze, into an image – no image, in fact, but the onomatopoeic rendering – of women registering their protest, a protest all the more forceful for belonging outside articulated discourse in a realm where bodies (teeth and tongue) pass directly into sound.

To talk of Plath's identification with a writing connoted as masculine is not therefore to deny the force of these other moments in her work. Nor, as we will see, is it to remove from her those forms of insight where she accuses the very masculinity which she invokes. We will see that the accusation and invocation, the anger and the desire, are not incompatible, as is so often suggested, but belong together and give to Plath's representation of masculinity its particular strength. It is to suggest, however, that it is not possible to read Plath's relation to the literature that comes before her as one of oppression by a predominantly male tradition, and then – as the anticipated and required consequence of that first reading – of liberation into a female aesthetic which she at once creates and, through the discovered links with women writers before her, finds in herself.[21] Plath's desire to be a writer occupies a space in which feminism has most recently been willing to identify some of the most troubling fantasies of women, fantasies which come to meet, to join in, the very scenarios against which women so forcefully protest.[22] To say this is not, however, to depoliticise Plath – she precisely gives the political measure or stake of fantasy, as we will see. But those who argue, with barely disguised triumph, that to acknowledge such fantasy in Plath – to acknowledge the complex and difficult relation between fantasy and political intention – is to establish her irrelevance for feminism are way off the mark.

It is in this context that I want to return to that notorious moment in Plath's *Journals* where she gives an account of her first meeting with Ted Hughes – notorious because of the extraordinary piece of editing which cut the text between the galleys sent to the reviewers and publication. This is the passage as it appears in the published text:

> . . . and I was stamping and he was stamping on the floor, and then he kissed me bang smash on the mouth [omission] . . . And when he kissed my neck I bit him long and hard on the cheek, and when we came out of the room, blood was running down his face. [Omission.] And I screamed in myself, thinking: oh, to give myself crashing, fighting, to you. The one man since I've lived who could blast Richard.[23]

This is the unedited text, quoted by Nancy Milford in her original review:

> . . . and I was stamping and he was stamping on the floor, and then he kissed me bang smash on the mouth [and ripped my hairband off, my lovely red hairband scarf which has weathered sun and much love, and whose like I shall never find again, and my favourite silver earrings: hah, I shall keep, he barked.] And when he kissed my neck I bit him long and hard on the cheek, and when we came out of the room, blood was running down his face. [His poem 'I did it, I.' Such violence, and I can see how women lie down for artists. The one man in the room who was as big as his poems, huge, with hulk and dynamic chunks of words; his poems are strong and blasting like a high wind in steel girders.] And I screamed in myself, thinking: oh, to give myself crashing, fighting, to you.[24]

Milford comments: 'What has been deleted is his actions: he kisses and he rips, he takes and he keeps. Those are not small details. What we are left with instead is a text bared to her reaction. This seems to me a disservice to both of them.'[25] Anne Stevenson, with dull predictability, turns the account against Plath (true in its general configuration, but the yelling and stamping is a 'drama of the Plathian interior' and the whole account 'ridiculously exaggerated', according to Hughes).[26] Sandra Gilbert and Susan Gubar, on the other hand, place this episode, or its fictionalised rendering by Plath, at the opening of their three-volume account of women's modern writing as the emblem for the battle of the sexes which they see as characterising modernism (if women take pleasure in that ritual, it is in so far as they are 'accepting the inevitability of victimisation').[27]

These readings are crucially, politically, different, but each seems to remove the episode from the domain of writing. Either the episode is description, its status as reference again paradoxically reinforced by the cuts: 'so that's what really happened' – one can't help but react on reading what was taken out (the same idea of reference is latent to the charge of exaggeration – literature should ideally refer, without any transforming activity on the part of language, to what it describes); or it is no less suspended above the order of language in the realm of trans-historical truth (the battle of the sexes as a 'metastory' – story of stories – for modernism).[28]

Writing is, however, at the heart of this story, not just in the sense that the episode *is* writing – remembered, rewritten, recast (as Plath puts it in a separate entry two years after the episode with Hughes: 'no incident – such as biting, is more than melodrama, unless prose lifts it'[29]); but in the sense that it is *on* writing – on its pleasure and its violence – that the passage so explicitly turns. For while that first cut can be read only, as Milford argues, as a suppression of his activity (he kisses, rips, takes and keeps), an activity which her bite comes to meet, this reading cannot account for the second: 'His poem "I did it, I." Such violence, and I can see how women lie down for artists. The one man in the room who was as big as his poems, huge, with hulk and dynamic chunks of words; his poems are strong and blasting like a high wind in steel girders.'

The violence of the first moment (her bite for his theft) is therefore echoed in the second, where what she desires, what is exchanged between them, is 'huge', 'hulk and dynamic chunks of words'. Or to put it another way, that first exchange of violence leads directly to the second and is inseparable from it: 'Such violence, and I can see how women lie down for artists.' The 'violence' in this line runs backwards and forwards across the text, back to the physical and then forward to the verbal encounter. In fact each of the different versions can be read in terms of where, precisely, they locate it: in her (the published text), in him (the first cut restored), but then, if we read forward into the second omission, inside the poetic activity – 'strong and blasting like a high wind in steel girders' – which he embodies and which draws her on ('I can see how women lie down for artists'). The first cut takes out his agency, but the second, by omitting her participation in this passion of writing, no less effectively removes hers. If she then lifts, writes up (exaggerates), the moment in her journals, this is surely the whole point.

In the paragraph which follows this episode in the *Journals*, it is precisely as writer that Plath situates herself: 'And now I sit here, demure and tired in brown, slightly sick at heart. I shall go on. I shall write a detailed description of shock treatment, tight, blasting short descriptions with not one smudge of coy sentimentality.'[30] Plath associates sexual and medical violence, links the personal and the institutional, the private and the public in a way that has become one of the hallmarks of the feminist analysis of power. It is an association upheld at one and the same time by the strongest accusation and protest against male violence ('There will be no hurry, because I am too desperately vengeful now'[31]) and – again – by a vision of writing ('blasting like a high wind in strong girders', 'tight, blasting . . . descriptions') constructed in its very image. Shortly afterwards she writes: 'I lust for him, and in my mind I am ripped to bits by the words he welds and wields.'[32] Or compare this: 'Love turns. Lust turns, into the death urge. My love is gone, gone, and I would be raped.'[33]

Once again, too, the link between masculinity and writing has a disparaged femininity as its antithesis and support – 'not one smudge of coy sentimentality'. Compare 'no chaste tree but suffers blotch/Under flux of those seductive/Reds, greens, blues', the last lines of 'On the Plethora of Dryads' discussed above. Femininity, whether coy or seductive, mars the face of the earth. It should be clear already here, however, that in the case of Sylvia Plath, protest and participation, fantasy and analysis, do not rule (or 'cancel') each other out.

One of the most graphic illustrations of this is provided for me by one line cut from the *Journals* where Plath is describing a male embrace from a sexual encounter that long precedes the meeting with Hughes: 'twisting me rebelling to him hurting good'.[34] First his force ('twisting') and her protest ('rebelling'), then their immediate confusion ('rebelling *to* him'), an unexpected (and illegitimate) syntactic move in which rebellion comes to join, physically turns to, the embrace it resists; and finally 'hurting good', which makes pain into an object (*the* object) of (her) desire. Agency slides sexually across this sentence. It passes from man ('twisting') to woman ('rebelling'), the two protagonists first separated and then brought back together by the syntax, and then lights on that 'hurting', whose agency can, in US syntax, belong to either or both. Instead of trying to legislate between these meanings, we should perhaps, like Plath herself, try to produce a logic, or syntax, which can articulate their awkward relation.

If we go back to the passage from the *Journals* once more, it is perhaps worth locating the quoted line which opens that second omitted passage: 'His poem "I did it, I." Such violence . . .' It comes from the last line of Hughes's poem 'Law in the Country of the Cats', which was eventually published in his first collection of poems, *The Hawk in the Rain*.[35] The words, also in quotes in the poem – '"Let Justice be done. I did it, I"' – are the declaration of a murderer who bursts into a police station after murdering another man in the street. In this poem by Hughes that single 'violent incredible action' is the only possible outcome of an encounter between two men who hate each other 'at first meeting', who meet and find themselves discussing '"universal brotherhood",/"Love of humanity and each fellow-man",/Or "the growing likelihood of perpetual peace"'. That 'I did it, I' is therefore the reply to, the announcement that destroys, the platitude of brotherhood. This is the poem which frames or punctuates the first encounter between Plath and Hughes. Citing its last words at him, handing them back to him, proclaiming them (and by implication their act) as her own ('I did it, I'), Plath takes up her place within – requests admission to – the law of the country of the cats.

Not that this is in any sense Plath's sole or exhaustive demand. That rite of entry needs to be set alongside the very different picture we get from Plath's letters to her mother at the start of the relationship which shortly follows, where Plath writes of a destructiveness as she sees it in Hughes – in his past, in his relations to 'things and people' – which she says she will repair (these moments are cut).[36] The fantasy appears in one of her short stories, 'The Wishing Box', in which Harold tells his future wife, Agnes, about his dream of a red fox running through the kitchen 'grievously burned, its fur charred black, bleeding from several wounds', and then dreams again shortly after their marriage that it reappears 'miraculously healed, with flourishing fur, to present Harold with a bottle of permanent black Quink'.[37] Vengeance, repair, participation – we can read this as confusion (psychic or political) or as a register of positions which Plath occupies, sometimes alternatively and sometimes together; the contours of the sexual drama which she explores.

There is, however, a crucial issue about fantasy here. For in the dispute that rages around Plath there is one position that rests her relevance for feminism on what it takes to be the real and representative violence, psychic if not physical, of Hughes. Robin Morgan's poem 'The Arraignment' is the most obvious case, but the issue is one which exceeds Plath as a more general issue for feminism. To discuss that image of Hughes as violent in terms of Plath's fantasy, to discuss it precisely *as* image, would be seen by this feminism as nothing short of betrayal. But to say that this violence has its place in Plath's fantasy life in no way legislates for the reality, or otherwise, of what it is that she describes. To say even that somewhere she desires it does not mean that it cannot also be something which she sees as coming at her, abusing her, from a world outside (the passage on medical and sexual violence situates violence precisely in such a concrete domain). Like the governess in Henry James's 'The Turn of the Screw', who first desires and then discovers, or imagines, a male intruder on the estate, Plath confronts us with the rules of attraction, coincidence and mismatch between desire and event. Critics of James's story who have tried, with increasing desperation, to settle the matter have merely found themselves re-enacting the dilemma of the governess herself (see Chaper 1).

In this context there is an important point to be made. We are in fact in no position to know what happened, concretely, between Plath and Hughes. All we have is the texts of its endless rewriting ('endless' because of the way commentary finds itself drawn into, repeating, their drama). Nowhere in this book do I say – indeed, I cannot say – anything about the actual behaviour, in objective terms, of Hughes to Plath or of Plath to Hughes. But if we look again at that poem by Hughes, what it does show is that if violence is part of her poetic world, it is no less surely central to his. The point has been often made, and cannot be dealt with by insisting – in a gesture of distribution between inside and outside which does not settle, but simply mimics, the problem I am discussing here –

125

that hers is purely inner; his resides, away from him, in the outer world. It is a tension that can be read internally to the poem itself, between the distancing, citing and diagnosis of violence, and the tender lyricism of the language in which the action is bathed: 'Then one man letting his brains gently to the gutter'; and then again in the way that this action – violent, incredible – is offered up by the poem as both murder and sex: 'As each looks into the gulf in the eye of the other,/ Then a flash of violent incredible action'. Sex as murder becomes another meaning of Plath shouting, according to that famous entry in her *Journals*, 'I did it, I' at Hughes.

What we can do, therefore, is notice what passes between them symbolically, in the poems and missives, poems *as* missives (and missiles) which they exchange. In that exchange – bite, theft, words – it is precisely that distinction between real outside and imaginary inside (fantasy in its common sense of something unreal) that is confused. According to her own narrative, Hughes gives something to Plath which she comes halfway – the whole way ('she goes the whole way', as in the 1950s refrain for the girl who has sex) – to meet. Substance of the intercourse between them, it appears not only as weapon but also as gift, as well as wound in need of repair (the idea of battle – the battle between the sexes – tends to rule out these two last meanings of gift and reparation as much as it has to sidestep the question of women's pleasure).

In a series of letters written by Hughes to Plath at the time of their first separation in October 1956, he sends her the outlines of a set of short stories for her to write.[38] As Hughes explains, these stories were assignments of the kind which, at various points in their relationship, would be requested by Plath to help her with blocks in her writing (a number of Plath's poems and magazine stories started with lists of suggestions by Hughes). They include: stories of male violence, like the story of a man from the city wanted for murder who courts, in a drama of genuine reciprocity, a woman living alone in the woods; or the story of a battered wife on the brink of suicide who is saved by her love of her cat; or the poem about Bluebeard (Plath wrote her own poem on this story in her early poetry[39]); stories in which femininity seems to be the threat or thing accused, like the story of the elfin-girl who places herself physically in the way of a man's lovers by clinging to his neck, or the story of a young girl who callously goes out and joins her adolescent friends after discovering the body of her grandmother murdered while she prepared herself for the dance (this one is about the vicious world of male and female adolescence alike); stories about a danger which the man and woman share, like the story of a couple who set up a country idyll only to find the faithlessness they had associated with city life erupting in their midst.

This is not the only time Hughes finds himself anticipating in fiction what is later to come – that last story reads like a narrative of Plath's and Hughes's move from London to Devon and its crisis in 1962 (Hughes comments on this form of anticipation in relation to another episode in a letter to Aurelia Plath[40]). Far more important, however, is the act of sending these stories to Plath. Offerings for her writing, they could also be seen as a warning, but equally as a proffering up, a laying down of arms symbolically, at her feet. 'Take this' – we can read these letters as saying in both senses of the term. And she does – telling her mother that she will repair this side of him as she sees it (that she will teach him 'care') at the same time as she sends her one of its strongest testimonies – the poem 'Soliloquy for a Misanthrope' – which she praises as a 'virile' 'banging' poem when she includes it in a letter to her mother shortly after meeting Hughes in 1956.[41]

But we cannot assume, any more than we can in relation to Plath herself, that because this is what Hughes writes about, this is also what he *does*. In fact beyond – or far in excess of – the unanswerable question of what really happened, the drama between Plath and Hughes, in the form in which they write it, can be read as one of the most stunning illustrations of the brute reality, the lived effectivity, of fantasy life.

As we will see, the meaning of femininity, as much as that of masculinity, is clearly one of the things being negotiated, in their writing, between Plath and Hughes. But it is already worth stating here that it is not only something in him which, in the exchange between them, presents itself as in need of repair. For if we put back the body reduced and cleaned up by the editing of Plath's work – a body that could be racked by headaches and sinusitis, spilling, therefore, over the appropriate boundaries of itself – then it emerges that one of the things Plath offers, represents herself as offering, to Hughes is an image of that abjection which was the focus of Chapter 2. If this body has been diminished, it has none the less been allowed expression in the published *Journals* far more than in *Letters Home*: 'I am a conglomerate garbage heap of loose ends' (her image of herself and him as ideal bodies and master breeders can then be read as the reverse of the same coin).[42]

Situated precisely at the body's extremity, and far less easy to locate in terms of gender difference than the violence associated with the man, abjection has none the less come to be linked with femininity, with the realm of the mother where subjectivity and the body do not yet exist in any recognisable, bearable shape. Much has been written about the horrors of this realm – the powers of horror, to use Kristeva's term – specifically on the way that horror comes to be projected on to the woman, who then appears as both its embodiment and its cause.[43] Horror at the root, as Hughes himself puts it in his poem 'To Paint a Water Lily' – 'Whatever horror nudge her root' – one of a number of poems in which his image, his fantasy, of that realm is explored [44] (I will return to this).

At the simplest level, the *Journals* represent Hughes unmistakably, and over and over again, as taking care of Plath – this is, of course, no less than the negative moments, her representation, her image, of him. More complex, more troubling, their writing (her journals, her poetry and his) allows us to read – offers as one of its potential meanings – a different form of exchange, where what they seem to be handing over to each other at a symbolic level are the most familiar, socially sanctioned, and dramatic stereotypes of masculinity and femininity as such. 'Don Juan' or 'Bluebeard' meets 'abjection' – the stereotypes are killing – each offering to make the other good. At the point where the texts seem to invite us in, to vanish into their most intimate reality, what we discover is the most generalised of fantasy and/or cliché. But what could be the outcome of such a contract if what she fears in him, she also desires; if what he seeks to repair in her, he most fears? If this appears from inside the texts to be their ambivalence (this can only be speculation) it is, far more importantly, an ambivalence that is structured into the commonest form of the stereotype itself.

To say this is not of course to say that Plath *is* abject, to turn her into the image of one part of what she represents of herself, but merely to note how this is an element that is written into the exchange, whether as her fantasy or his. It has never been part of feminism's argument that because an image of femininity can be identified as male fantasy, it is any the less intensely lived by women. Conversely, the fact that the woman discovers something as a component of her own self-imagining does not mean that it cannot also be the object, or even product, of the wildest male projection, repulsion or desire. Who owns what? Who gives what to whom?

It should be clear, however, that to say there is something negative, or even violent, which Plath represents herself as offering is not to close down the question of violence in relation to Hughes (in how she writes of him, in how he writes of himself), any more than to recognise violence in his own writing is to wipe clear her own psychic slate. One does not become pure as the other falls into the dirt (that crazy pass the parcel acted out by so many writers on Sylvia Plath). But if that alternative is a false one, then so is another which often seems to accompany it – between the idea of Plath as the victim of patriarchy (source of all her ills) and the idea of her self-generating (blameworthy) psychic distress; between the reality of an oppressive social world and the no less real dimension of inner fantasy life. For, as we have already seen, criticism has acknowledged the force of the latter in Plath's writing only to turn it against her. Plath becomes accountable not just for her own psychic drama, not just for everything that happened in her life (the second as the assumed consequence of the first), but for the fact, and trouble, of the psyche itself (Holbrook, Stevenson).

In response to this, a feminist criticism, rightly stressing the counter-pressure, no less determinant, of ideology and institution, has tended to sidestep the issue of psychic reality. As if, inadvertently, it had taken up the accusation and internalised the judgement which makes psychic life pathological, *unless* it can be attributed unequivocally to the world outside. Hence Plath's writing as either pure projection, or ideological effect.[45] In fact such an alternative represents an impasse of sexual political analysis which Plath does much to dislodge or to expose. Why, we might ask – Plath herself seems to ask – should we choose? why should she?


So far I have discussed these problems in terms of sex and subjectivity. In the case of Plath, however, they touch on some of the most fundamental aspects of poetic language and form. Again and again in her poems – and not by any means only in texts of sexual drama – Plath's writing unsettles poetic syntax in such a way as to disturb any simple location of agency or causality, as well as those forms of accusation and/or gendering which, in the later texts, become their increasingly persistent accompaniment. In these moments in her poetry, the relation between inner and outer life is figured not as sexual drama but as an encounter with natural forces. The poems in which these moments occur tend to be separated out from those which represent issues of gender and power, but they are crucially related in terms of the subjective position they assign to the speaker, the way they constitute her interaction with an outer world that sometimes threatens, that sometimes she takes into herself, that sometimes she appears to solicit or else to turn away from and avoid. It is as if they prefigure, in the relationship to nature they explore, the issue of internal and external reality which appears in the later poems, and even more in the commentaries on them, as the issue of who is doing what to whom, where does the misery come from, in what – in which sex, in man or woman – does it find its origins and cause. Poems like 'Full Fathom Five' (1958), 'Lorelei' (1958), 'The Burnt-Out Spa' (1959), or 'Wuthering Heights' (1961), which stage the poet's confrontation with the spirits of the deep (water or earth) or the heights, force a question on the reader about the relationship – of dread and/or of pull – that the speaker entertains with forces which are always ambiguously situated in terms of outside and inside.[46] As if Plath, in these poems, was already laying down that fundamental ambiguity of location, ambiguity as to what she desires – of whether she desires – which finds its so much more sexually explicit, but no less ambiguous, representation elsewhere.

According to one reading, these poems can be understood in terms of a progression. The poet is threatened and lured by the spirits of the natural world, refuses their entreaties and then succumbs. Nature is hostile to her but grips her in its alien power until gradually, tentatively, she discovers the beginnings of an identity – unmistakably female – which will reach its apotheosis in Plath's final work.[47] 'Full Fathom Five' and 'Lorelei' are the first stages of this poetic journey – in the last lines of both poems the speaker asks for passage into the water which the rest of the poem represents as an object of danger or fear: 'Father, this thick air is murderous./I would breathe water' ('Full Fathom Five'); 'Stone, stone, ferry me down there' (Lorelei). In negative anticipation of this ending, the first lines of 'Lorelei' state: 'It is no night to drown in'.

This reading, in which the speaker is presented as passive towards the forces she confronts, comes in answer to another, no less teleological, which sees these poems as the expression of a pure death-wish (Plath herself uses this phrase in relation to 'Lorelei'), as part of a cycle tending, hurtling – the emphasis here is all on Plath's activity – towards its inexorable end.[48] Active or passive? The question arises, however, as to what, at the level of meaning and identity, these readings have first to stabilise and secure. The following lines come from 'Full Fathom Five', first published in *The Colossus*:

> All obscurity
> Starts with a danger:
>
> Your dangers are many. I
> Cannot look much but your form suffers
> Some strange injury
>
> And seems to die: so vapors
> Ravel to clearness on the dawn sea.

Who or what threatens, who is doing what to whom? The danger in these lines seems to reside as much in the process of giving something indefinable a shape as in the confrontation between identities and elements – between father and daughter, between water and air. If it is hard to make out the shape of the danger, it is because the problem of making shape and its dangers seems to be what the poem describes. Obscurity is the starting point of danger: 'All obscurity/Starts with a danger', but we can read the line as meaning either that obscurity is sparked off, precipitated, by danger, or that danger is obscurity's effect. That ambivalence (that obscurity) is then carried over into the next lines, which represent as uncertain, and never firmly establish, whether danger resides in the speaker or in the addressee. 'Your dangers are many' – is that 'you' threatened by danger or is danger something which 'you' multiply, contain? Suspended at the end of the line, the 'I' that follows seems, momentarily, to pass danger on to the speaker, but this is only partially confirmed by the continuation of the sentence, which makes her as much the pained onlooker as the bearer of a deadly look (innocent bystander and evil eye).

By comparing this whole process to that moment when mist clears and dawn breaks over the sea, the lines seem to suggest that it is the passage from obscurity to light that is the real threat. The problem of danger in this poem is thus intimately bound into a basic

131

question about the way forms come to be identified and take shape. It is as if the drama of seduction and violence played out between the speaker and the old man of the sea is almost a second stage to an even more deadly and primordial encounter in which meaning is stolen from the deep. Winding itself back to the origins of meaning and of time, 'old myth of origins/ Unimaginable', the poem suggests that to 'fathom', to imagine the unimaginable, to give shape to it, is violence (the poetic act of calling this spirit up). But this violence precipitates (is provoked by?) another, the violence of unfathomability itself – insufferable inscrutability which makes men lose their heads: 'Inscrutable,// Below shoulders not once/Seen by any man who kept his head'. How can we read the last lines of the poem – 'Father, this air is murderous/ I would breathe water' – as the speaker relenting or giving in to danger, when the danger belongs both outside and inside herself, in water and in air, as well as in the activity – the poetic activity – which gives to the elements their shape?

Rather than read a poem like this in terms of whether this world is hostile to her or benign, I think we should notice how that question is inseparable from an interrogation, or destabilising, of certain aspects of poetic language and form. What Plath seems to be doing is introducing a fundamental reversibility of agency that confounds active and passive and then dramatises, through that confounding, the question of who is agent, who is victim, who (or what) suffers and who (or what) kills? There seems to be no point in trying to establish which of these comes first – whether the linguistic generates the sexual drama, finding in that drama its most appropriate vehicle, or whether the sexual drama causes or leads straight into any instability of poetic form.

Along the lines of the former, the Yale critic Paul de Man would read these moments as figures for the irreducible tropological and specular component of language (it is the uncertain dimension of language, the way it turns on and vanishes into its own process, which those concrete images of loss and anxiety stand in for or represent).[49] Along the lines of the latter, a more familiar psychologism would see the destabilising of the syntax as the direct, unmediated expression of the upheavals of Plath's psyche and her life. What is striking, however, is the way the syntactic oppositions run into the ground rules of interaction with an object world. The syntax is uncertain, and we cannot establish unequivocally whether the objects of the surrounding world are hostile or benign. Once again (cf. Chapter 2) Plath's writing confounds the distinction between linguistic and psychic law. It seems unlikely that such a writer will present the battle of the sexes in terms of a one-directional, man-to-woman, relation of cause and effect.

These ambiguities seem to me typical in Plath's poems about encounters with the natural world. They establish the speaker's interaction with that world, not as passive, but along lines better understood in terms of a reciprocating activity or even desire (we can recognise here the outlines of a potentially sexual encounter).[50] In these poems, the problem is not just something from which she is in danger but something which she is in danger of responding *to*. 'Wuthering Heights' is another instance: 'If I pay the roots of the heather/Too close attention, they will invite me/To whiten my bones among them.' Is nature hostile here? Does it only persecute, as it seems to in much of the rest of the poem, or does it also desire her? As Plath puts it in 'Blackberrying', another poem written in the same year: 'they must love me'.[51]

In this moment, the speaker appears more as the potentially reciprocating partner in the exchange. If she pays them attention, they will invite her to join them. Her look is the necessary precondition for nature's ability to draw her in, like the slots in the pupils of the surrounding sheep – 'they take me in'. The problem here seems to be less that of alienation and separation, more that of proximity and identification. Poised on the verge of entry, the speaker is at risk from her own desire to get too close. In this set of potentially reversible relations, the speaker can be frightened of nature, but nature can also be frightened of itself – 'Darkness terrifies it' (the grass that beats its head distractedly in the last verse).

In 'The Burnt-Out Spa', the form of uncertainty resides more in the shifting of the poetic 'I' and its gendering. The speaker explores the carcass of an old spa which is signified as male ('his carcass') and then discovers in its depths 'one/ Blue and improbable person' clearly identified as female – 'O she is gracious and austere' – before turning away. For Uroff this is the 'first tentative evolution' of the female identity which will reach its apotheosis in *Ariel*. If Plath repudiates this figure in this poem, it is only after 'she has established its meaning for her'. The poem is therefore a type of allegory for a femininity on the verge of flight – Plath rejects the

133

depths to which, in the earlier poems, she surrenders, but not before she has found in them the shape of the femininity which will finally, and triumphantly, allow her to do so. It is impossible not to register here how the question of feminine (this will also come out as feminist) identity is inseparably linked to that of poetic interpretation, how such a conception of identity relies on a no less specific conception of poetic language and form. Where, for example, do we situate in this allegory – the poem itself and the evolution of Plath it is taken to represent – the moment when she compares her exploration of this burnt-out carcass to a doctor or archaeologist, picking and prying amongst entrails:

> I pick and pry like a doctor or
> Archaeologist among
> Iron entrails, enamel bowls,
> The coils and pipes that made him run.

The image of the doctor shows Plath entering into a role and identity (the medical profession) which elsewhere in her writing, and on more than one occasion, she represents in terms of the worst of male institutional and sexual power.

This moment in 'The Burnt-Out Spa' links the poem to 'The Surgeon at 2 a.m.' as much as it does to say, 'Lady Lazarus' or 'Fever 103°', two poems in which Plath's transcendent femininity is most often located.[52] It is a first-person poem which speaks, with no possibility of distance, from the place of a surgeon who is presented, in loving and graphic detail, as up to his elbows in blood: 'I am up to my elbows in it.' The poem offers this detail while appearing both to celebrate the surgeon's quasi-mystical art and to parody its metaphysical pretension. Pleasure and diagnosis – the positions that this poem takes up and offers to the reader mimic the ambivalent self-situating of the surgeon himself. More simply, more sympathetically, Plath herself describes this poem in her 1962 essay 'Context' as the 'night thoughts of a tired surgeon'.[53]

'The Surgeon at 2 a.m.' is only one of a number of Plath's poems in which she takes up a male persona ('Suicide Off Egg Rock', 'The Hanging Man', 'Insomniac', 'Leaving Early', 'Paralytic', 'Gigolo'), but these poems are hardly ever talked about.[54] 'The Surgeon at 2 a.m.' is not, for instance, discussed by any of the contributors to Linda Wagner's 1984 collection of critical essays, nor by Uroff in her book.[55] Kroll mentions it and dismisses it – interestingly, together with 'Wuthering Heights': 'they did not call forth any private reservoir of associations; nor were they relevant to an organising vision'.[56] The point of drawing attention to these poems is not, however, to suggest that Plath lives the drama she describes any the less intensely as a woman, but that, in a gesture which can be variously described as empathy, pleasure, diagnosis and revenge, she can see, represent – she *cannot avoid* representing – its other (sexual) side. Another way of putting this would be to say that it is because she becomes it (the male 'part') in fantasy that she knows it and can diagnose it so well. But that very insight, in so far as it depends on recognising the place of masculinity in female fantasy, stops us from being able to locate that masculinity in men alone.

What starts to emerge is a set of connections in relation to Plath's poetic writing which touch at multiple points on the question of gender, sexuality and power. Fantasy and identity (linguistic and sexual) belong together both in Plath's writing and in the responses to her work. I would suggest that for one form of criticism the denial of fantasy goes hand in hand with (is in fact the precondition for) a specific image of Plath's femininity – first as passive, and then as a singular and transcendent female selfhood which comes as the eventual, albeit logical, response. Victimisation and transcendence, accusation and apotheosis, are the reverse sides of the same coin, the twin poles of this reading of Plath. And this reading relies in turn on a fixing of her poetic language, specifically at the points where it troubles the forms of identity on which the clarity of that narrative necessarily depends; or else on a view of these moments as transitional, merely, on the journey to the final affirmation of self.[57] The question of sexual difference and the question of poetic language are isomorphic with each other. Plath works over – goes over – the boundaries of both of them at the same time.

Let's look now at 'The Rabbit Catcher', one of the late poems by Plath in which the sexual drama sketched out at the start of this chapter reaches a type of completion. It is a poem whose publishing history can be seen as re-enacting, or testifying to, the sexual confrontation which it represents at the level of theme (it was taken out of the first publication of *Ariel* by Hughes).[58] It is also the poem in which the weight of biographical reference on poetic interpretation operates with the greatest force. Both Linda Wagner-Martin and Anne Stevenson, from their very different positions, read the poem as being about Plath's marriage – identify, therefore, the rabbit catcher with Hughes.[59] This is the first stanza:

> It was a place of force –
> The wind gagging my mouth with my own blown hair,
> Tearing off my voice, and the sea
> Blinding me with its lights, the lives of the dead
> Unreeling in it, spreading like oil.

Nature seems to appear here as unequivocally aggressive, the ambiguity of 'force' in the first line leading forwards to the sexual drama to come. In fact, since we read that 'force' after the title 'The Rabbit Catcher', it can, even at this early stage, be read in two ways – force as in forces of nature, but also forcing, as in violation or rape. Fleetingly, the second line seems to turn this image, turn the violence of nature back on itself, or rather to turn the female speaker on herself, one part of her body against the other, gagging her mouth with her own blown hair. But this does not unsettle the basic, syntactically reinforced, image of her as someone gagged, voice torn off, blinded by the light of the sea. 'Gagging', 'tearing', 'blinding' – the formal repetition drives home the force of the physical constraint, the assault and battery of the natural world. This, then, is the place of force, identified after that suspended declaration of the first line ('It was a place of force –').

The last lines of this stanza, however, seem to confuse this picture. If we read again the line 'Blinding me with its lights, the lives of the dead', 'lives of the dead' can be read in apposition to 'lights', as if one of the things which come at her are these lives of the dead which unreel ('unreeling' picks up the syntactic repetition of 'gagging' 'tearing' and 'blinding') in the sea. The oxymoron ('lives of the dead') shifts the terms of the narrative twice over – the sea has claimed these lives as its victim (its assault is general and in the order of things) and they in turn can be read as part of what assaults her. Unreeling, without motion – no blow to reel from, but also drowned and therefore not wound back to, unclaimed by, the earth – they none the less spread like oil. In what way is this image of dead lives in the ocean, without origin, history, or settled destination, the appropriate image for a narrative of singular – single-aimed – sexual oppression?

In the next stanza the speaker becomes the agent, taking up a place as 'I' at the start of the first line:

> I tasted the malignity of the gorse,
> Its black spikes,
> The extreme unction of its yellow candle-flowers.
> They had an efficiency, a great beauty,
> And were extravagant, like torture.

It is hard not to read this stanza as Plath's own diagnosis, her judgement, wise after the fact, of the dangerous pleasures she has allowed herself to enjoy. What she has put to her mouth is malignant (the image of malignancy is recurrent in Plath's later texts), spiked as in sharp (as in poison?), but efficient, beautiful, extravagant, the contrast of the epithets signalling not the continuing attraction or force of evil, but that it was, all the more effectively, a lure. This stanza would therefore be one of the strongest condemnations of the forms of ambivalence and fantasy I have been reading in Plath, a warning – to women, to feminism – of their dangers.

But for all the strength of this interpretation, the sequence, once again, is less straightforward. This time it is the central line that causes the difficulty: 'The extreme unction of its yellow candle-flowers' – the plant is not just spiked gorse, it also has yellow candle-flowers which offer extreme unction (the two are in fact in a relation of metaphoric substitution) – the rite administered by the priest to the sick in danger of death for the health of both body and soul. The plant that is deadly also contains its own blessing or cure, its own antidote to itself. It is these flowers which are efficient, beautiful, extravagant 'like torture' (the sequence from malignity to healing reverses again). Torture like unction – torture is not just a simile here for the extravagant beauty of the flowers; it also contains a reference to, a condemnation of, a specific religious institution and its history. At the same time, it is impossible not to recognise in that link between torture, efficiency, beauty and extravagance a sexualising and aestheticising of power. The circularity of the stanza – from malignity to torture, with something beautiful (something tortuous) in between – makes it finally impossible to read the relationship between these images in terms of a hierarchy of judgement or control. Plath may therefore be diagnosing such ambivalent, complicit dealings with violence, but she can do so only by repeating them at the same time. She offers no position to her reader from where she or he can, comfortably, look down.

Go back to the beginning of the poem, and those two moments of hesitancy ('lives of the dead' . . . 'the yellow candle-flowers') can be seen not as moments whose uncertainty troubles a basically straightforward sequence or distribution of roles, but as central to the dynamic of the poem. For the sexuality that it writes cannot be held to a single place – it spreads, blinds, unreels like the oil in the sea. Most crudely, that wind blowing, that gagging, calls up the image of oral sex and then immediately turns it around, gagging the speaker with her own blown hair, her hair in her mouth, her tasting the gorse (Whose body – male or female – is this? Who – man or woman – is tasting whom?), even while 'black spikes' and 'candles' work to hold the more obvious distribution of gender roles in their place. For Freud, such fantasies, such points of uncertainty, are the regular unconscious subtexts – for all of us – of the more straightforward reading, the more obvious narratives of stable sexual identity which we write.

If we pass to the next stanza, the uncertainty intensifies as we are given what can only be described as a symbolic geography of (the female) sex:

> There was only one place to get to.
> Simmering, perfumed,
> The paths narrowed into the hollow.

If we read the first line as referring to the rabbit's predicament, lured without option, and if we then read that as the dilemma of the woman, we have to notice too that what lures on the woman, what draws her unfailingly, are nothing other than the most recognisable insignia or clichés of femininity itself (simmering, perfumed, hollow). The reader is raced through these lines. Producing this effect in her poem, Plath writes herself into the place of the rabbit catcher, does to the reader what the poem describes as being done to her. In the middle of the poem, across the next stanza break: 'Zeros, shutting on nothing,// Set close like birth pangs'; the passage to the trap takes on the meaning of a birth canal. We can read this as Plath's (recurrent) image of death as reborning, but there is another meaning, the activity of the mother's body in childbirth as it contracts and opens, ushering the fetus into the world: the activity of the woman, woman at her most active, that activity as its own violence, the woman's body as trap, right in the middle of the poem.

It is in the last two stanzas, however, that the poem brings its story (its message) home:

> I felt a still busyness, an intent.
> I felt hands round a tea mug, dull, blunt,
> Ringing the white china.
> How they awaited him, those little deaths!
> They waited like sweethearts. They excited him.

This is the first moment of gendering, the first moment in which the poem gives the sexual colours of the drama it describes, taking that drama into a domestic setting, where violence closes in on the paraphernalia of everyday life. For Marjorie Perloff, this is hallucinatory – the 'I' feels hands around a tea mug – we read this, we feel this, hallucinating with the speaker, as hands around her neck.[60] If it is virtually impossible not to read this meaning in the poem, impossible not to see concrete reference (together with the more general, but no less concrete, reference to the injustice of marriage), this may, however, be a statement on the institution of reading itself, on the way it is always already implicated in wider institutional and political effects. For it is feminism, as much as a biographic literalism, which centres this reading on the page.

On the other hand, if we reconsider the syntax of these lines, then the confrontation we cannot help but read in this moment is the very confrontation that somehow the poem also seems to refuse. Plath takes out of her first draft of the stanza: 'Those hands muffle me like gloves', just as she takes out of the previous stanza, with reference to the snares: 'I saw the hands of the man behind them.' Look at the way the pronouns then shift across what remains – from that insistent and repeated 'I' ('I felt' 'I felt') to 'they' to 'him'. What she feels is hands round a tea mug, what they feel is him. It is never quite 'I' and 'him'. The 'I' somehow slides through the encounter that is in one sense the climax of the poem.

Once again, the eroticism of this stanza is a crucial part of its meaning (Perloff, comparing the poem with Lawrence's 'Love on the Farm', argues that there is no sexual arousal[61]). 'How they awaited him, those little deaths!/ They waited like sweethearts. They excited him.' How can we not read those 'little deaths' as orgasm as well as death, the death of the rabbits in their trap; how can we not read it, therefore, as saying that sexuality is the trap? This would give to Plath's poem as one of its meanings that complaint against (hetero)sexuality which has been most strongly articulated by Adrienne Rich (Stevenson's choice of Rich as the feminist to whom it would be most 'perverse' to link Plath takes on another meaning in this context[62]).

But this reading should be placed alongside another, equally allowed for by these lines of the poem, which would read them as saying not that sex is (leads to) death, but that death is as desirable, as luring, as sex. And before we pathologise Plath for this association (accuse her of a death-wish or decide she is very bad for girls), we might note that this association has a fully accredited literary tradition that runs from William Shakespeare to the surrealism of Georges Bataille. We would not want to rest Plath's authority on such a parade of male writers, but there is a history of poetic meaning and cultural affiliation present to this poem, running under the surface of her text. It may be that one of the things that is consistently overlooked in the reading of Plath is her link to – her own version *of* – a surrealism not noted for the active participation of the women most famously associated with it.[63] In her early journals, there is a shot-by-shot description of Buñuel's *Un Chien Andalou*, together with a complaint about the absence in America of any serious attention to the avant-garde.[64]

It is in its last stanza, however, that the poem examines, addresses quite specifically, the question of the relationship between the rabbit catcher and the speaker herself:

> And we, too, had a relationship –
> Tight wires between us,
> Pegs too deep to uproot, and a mind like a ring
> Sliding shut on some quick thing,
> The constriction killing me also.

By starting the stanza with 'And' and 'too', the line strangely takes its distance from – places their relationship in addition to – what has come before, suggesting that what is to come cannot in any easy way be simply identified with the setting of the previous verse. It is a connection of similarity (the point of the comparison) but also difference, one which seems to centre on the fact of that 'we' ('And we, too'), on the relationship which it precisely establishes, or recognises, between them. Tight wires between them and pegs too deep to uproot – the suggestion here is all of reciprocal bonding, the danger residing in how far, how deep it has gone (in their lack of differentiation one could say). Pegs too deep to uproot implies that it would be impossible to uproot them *even if* she (or he) had so desired.

And what, finally, is that mind like a ring, the ring of the trap, which – sliding, shutting, constricting – brings the poem to the climax that was given in advance by that first verse? 'Like a ring' – like a hollow? – violence as concentric, as the woman's body, contracting (giving birth), shutting (pleasuring but also retaliating, in the very act of sexual consummation, against the man), the constriction 'killing me also', 'also' meaning that it kills me *as well as him*. Or is this his mind, a reading also invited even though Plath crosses out 'his mind' – amends it to 'a mind' – in the first draft? In which case the poem can be read as an allegory for the destructive powers of the male logos. What constricts, what kills, is the power men exert, not only over women's bodies, but also over their minds. The poem seems remarkable for the way it can offer this political analysis of patriarchal power (violence against nature, violence of the Church, and in the home) at the same time as representing, in terms of sexual pleasure and participation, the competing strains of women's relationship to it. For Plath, the more ambiguous, more troubling, aspects of that pleasure and participation (torture as beautiful, sex as little death) do not work against the analysis, but appear rather as the terms through which it has to pass. Point of view of the woman (of women), we might say – on condition that we open up that concept to both its conscious and unconscious implications. He did it. I did it. Neither or both. Thus Plath sits on the edge of two contrary analyses of women's relationship to patriarchal power.

If we then look again at the first draft of this poem, we find that Plath takes out the most personal of references – 'I aware of my impotence./It might cause him a moment's anger./[I imagined] His body blocked off my vision – stolid and faceless.'[65] The personal, the local accusation, is therefore downplayed or removed, together with the much more direct reference to her lack of power, and the further aggression that it provokes in him. Note too that crossed-out 'I imagined' – she is imagining it, it is really there – followed by the removal of the whole line: the question of inner and outer reality and the question of gender and power tip over into their hallucinatory form. She also takes out this line: 'The pegs were too deep to move, but I buried the prop sticks', takes out her resistance to what appears less equivocally here as his assault on her. In doing so, she removes the very version of the poem (woman's struggle/ man's abuse) which we still find ourselves reading – as if she were almost rewriting it, we could say, against or in anticipation of the readings to come.

A final point about the writing of this poem. Anyone who reads these poems at Smith discovers that Plath wrote most of the *Ariel* poems on the back of a draft of *The Bell Jar*. This has been most fully commented on by Susan Van Dyne, who argues very convincingly that there is more than a casual relationship between what takes place on both sides of these sheets.[66] Some of these poems are also written on the back of drafts of poems by Hughes. The most striking example of this is probably 'Burning the Letters', which is on the back of Hughes's 'The Thought Fox' (Plath directly picks up the theme in the last stanza of her poem, which compares the burning letters with the hunting, the tearing apart of, a fox).[67] On the back of 'The Rabbit Catcher' are three episodes from Plath's novel – the poisoning of the *Mademoiselle* guest editors (the magazine is in fact unnamed in the book) at a *Ladies' Day* banquet; Esther Greenwood's attendance at a childbirth in the company of her boyfriend, who is training to be a doctor; and an episode at the mental hospital where Esther is taken after her breakdown and suicide attempt, when she first responds to the insulin treatment and is then told that she will be moving to the freer hospital environment of Belsize.[68]

It is impossible not to read some of this as leaking directly through the page – especially the second episode, which appears most substantially on the back of the first draft. It is one of Plath's most scathing attacks on the medical profession, a devastating critique of what male doctors do to women giving birth: the woman is lifted on to what looks like 'some awful torture table' and is drugged out of her mind so that she will forget the pain – 'it sounded just like the sort of drug a man would invent'.[69] We can read the poem back into its own textual origins, into the more straightforwardly radical feminist story it tells (make that story the hidden truth of the poem). On the other hand, we can see Plath returning precisely to this narrative, rewriting it, qualifying its sustained, controlled condemnation, putting herself right in it, in both senses of the term.

There is a sense in which the poems in *Ariel* have to be read in relationship to each other – not only in terms of the order Plath proposed for her own collection (which would put 'The Rabbit Catcher' back into *Ariel*, where it belongs), but also in the sense of the way she wrote them – another order emerged only when the *Collected Poems* were published in 1981. Looking at the drafts it is sometimes clear, for example, that the division between poems is almost arbitrary – in the middle of the second draft of 'Brazilia' are the lines which become the first stanza of 'Childless Woman', written on the same day (1 December 1962).[70] Similarly we can read from 'The Rabbit Catcher' across to 'Event', which follows it in the *Collected Poems*, these two poems also having been composed in one day (21 May).[71] The point of doing this is not to establish some Ur-text, to try to recapture the true moment of authorial creativity; interestingly, in relation to *Ariel* we have two competing, equally valid – or invalid – notions of such an originating moment – her order of composition, and the order that she later selected for her work. Rather, the point would be to show the extent to which Plath's poems, and especially the late poems, are in some sense all incomplete, fragments which work as much in dialogue with each other as they do as single texts.

Passing from 'The Rabbit Catcher' to 'Event', for example, we find this at the end of the second poem: 'Who has dismembered us?// The dark is melting. We touch like cripples' – something, someone (the question only partly invites an answer) has maimed them both. The poem rewrites, displaces, the more precisely aimed accusation of 'The Rabbit Catcher', which Plath composes on the same day. In view of this form of dialogism – which mimics, in terms of the process of writing, the forms of ambiguity and hesitancy I have been examining at the level of theme – it seems all the more extraordinary that some critics have argued that all the *Ariel* poems are somehow the same: 'For the life of me [*sic*], I cannot escape the conviction that to experience any five or six of the poems from *Ariel* is to have experienced all forty-three.'[72]

This factor seems to me of particular importance in relation to the concept of an emergent female selfhood which has been so crucial in the reading of these late poems. It is a reading which, as we have already seen, is strangely shared by one form of feminist criticism and by Ted Hughes. What the two have in common is an image of transcendence – poetic, psychological, political – in which Plath finally takes off from, burns herself out of, whatever it was (false self for Hughes, Hughes himself for feminism) that had her in its thrall. This self enters into no dialogue (with others, with other poems) – it simultaneously sheds all others, as well as any otherness in its relation to itself; it sheds the trappings of language and the world. It is the Queen Bee: 'I/have a self to recover, a queen'; it is Lady Lazarus: 'Out of the ash/I rise with my red hair/And I eat men like air'; it is the 'pure acetylene Virgin' of 'Fever 103°': 'Not you, nor him// Not him, nor him/ (My selves dissolving, old whore petticoats) – /To Paradise.'[73]

This reading, as I have already mentioned, tends to be teleological – the rest of Plath's poetry is then read back for the gradual emergence of this selfhood. It also depends on a specific, unitary conception of language as tending, like the subjectivity it embodies, towards the ultimate fulfilment of itself. Anything uncertain in the language, any ambiguity or obscurity, indicates Plath's as yet incomplete knowledge both of her authentic selfhood and of the language she gradually honed to the final perfection of its craft.[74] Thus the taking off of Plath becomes an allegory, not just for female self-emergence but for the flight of poetry and, by implication, for the transcendence of high art.

The arguments against this way of thinking about poetry are now fairly well known, but the issue takes on a very specific significance in relationship to Plath[75] – not because that figure is not there in the poetry, but precisely in so far as it is. By representing it, Plath allows us to examine it, allows us to ask what such a concept of an 'authentic female selfhood' might turn out to be carrying – what, exactly, it might mean. I would suggest that Plath reveals the internal impossibility of this conception of selfhood; that she represents it, while at the same time subjecting it to the most devastating critique. At the most immediate level, how can such a concept work as a model for female (for any) identity, since it involves not the assertion but the sublation of self? Too little or too much of identity, this figure in Plath's late poetry provides no basis for identification, either because it propels itself beyond the (gendered) framework of the world: 'My selves dissolving, old whore petticoats'; or because it can rediscover itself – pure, self-generating ego – only in the place of God: 'I am too pure for you or anyone./Your body/Hurts me as the world hurts God' ('Fever 103°'). As Plath wrote in a letter to Richard Sassoon in 1955: 'god, who masturbates in the infinite void his ego has made about him' (god who masturbates his ego, god who masturbates in the void his ego has made).[76]

We can go straight from here to this famous assertion by Plath:

> I want, I think, to be omniscient . . . I think I would like to call myself 'The girl who wanted to be God.' Yet if I were not in this body, where *would* I be – perhaps I am destined to be classified and qualified. But, oh, I cry out against it. I am I – I am powerful – but to what extent? I am I.

The passage comes from her diary of 1949 and is cited by Aurelia Plath at the end of the introduction to *Letters Home*.[77] That 'I am I' has been taken as the starting point of Plath's search for an authentic selfhood which will reach its completion only with the writing of *Ariel* itself:

> . . . when exploring these limited options, women can and should speak in a style marked by unlimited metaphorical energy, a style of liberated self-analysis that persistently and insistently explores the crucial 'I am I' of female identity.[78]

– this is the lesson of the woman writer that Plath learns from Woolf.

But doesn't this passage already show that such an affirmation wipes out everything other than itself and can speak only from the place of God? The point is not a moral one (the charge of egoism which is the inverse of that celebration of the 'I'),[79] but something about the form of the proposition. Plath is articulating here a problem which we can now see as fundamental for feminism. How can women assert themselves against social oppression ('destined to be classified and qualified') without propelling themselves beyond the bounds of identity, without abolishing identity itself? For there is no such thing as an ego on its own, since the ego exists, comes into being, only as difference from itself. As Plath puts it in her famous 1962 essay on her childhood, 'Ocean 1212-W': 'As from a star I saw, coldly and soberly, the *separateness* of everything. I felt the wall of my skin: I am I. That stone is a stone. My beautiful fusion with the things of this world was over . . . this awful birthday of otherness.'[80] The paragraph which starts immediately after that famous 'I am I' continues: 'Sometimes I try to put myself in another's place, and I am frightened when I find myself almost succeeding.'[81] Or again, at a later point in her *Journals* (none of these is ever quoted): 'there has always furthermore in addition and inescapably and forever got to be a Thou. Otherwise there is no i because i am what other people interpret me as being and am nothing if there were no people.'[82] In this context, 'I am I' is not self-recovery, but disavowal − of life, or the possibility of being a subject, but also of death: 'Tomorrow is another day toward death (which can never happen to me because I am I, which spells invulnerable).'[83] Plath's writing, and commentaries on her writing, illustrate to what extent the category of the ego is subjacent to that of sexuality and power. Like the ego itself, these late poems can be understood only in dialogue with each other.

If we read 'Fever 103°' alongside 'Amnesiac', which was kept out of *Ariel* but was written on the next day (20 and 21 October), then it takes on another set of possible meanings. The first line of 'Fever 103°' asks 'Pure? What does it mean?', with the poem ending on the word 'Paradise'. I am suggesting that in so far as 'Paradise' is the answer to the question 'What does it mean?' it should be taken to imply that this is in fact the only available definition of purity − place of the godhead − as well as in its more utopian meaning as a place free of all distortion where nothing, and nobody, would have any recognisable claims. 'Amnesiac' however, gives the other, male, side of this story.[84] To dissolve for the man is to wipe out his responsibility for the world, to take off like a comet tail, to plunge into Lethe, to abandon, precisely, 'O sister, mother, wife'. In so far as the poem accuses the man, it accuses him therefore of relinquishing − the responsibility is historical, political as well as personal − the woman, the very identities of the woman that Plath dissolves in the poem that precedes it. This is, if you like, the drama, the impasse, of the poet's drive into self-sublation. It involves her own abandonment of all the forms of selfhood whose rejection by the man is pure betrayal.

The relationship between these two poems is not the same as that between 'The Rabbit Catcher' and 'Event' – the first accusing the man (although even this is ambiguous, as we have seen), the second suggesting that this is a misery, a dismembering, in which they are equally implicated or which they share. That tension between accusation and participation may seem the more obvious political narrative for Plath to explore. But the shift from 'Fever 103°' to 'Amnesiac' is no less important – it gives a similar reversal, but this time in relation to the assertion of egos, the taking off of the self. Is Plath suggesting that it is OK for the woman but not for the man? We can see the connection here as causal (he goes off, she takes off; when men get out, the only way for women is up). Or is it that by going from one to the other, Plath is also showing the internal paradox which binds these two moves together?

On the same day that she wrote 'Amnesiac' (21 October) Plath wrote 'Lyonesse', in which she gives the historical dimension of forgetting: 'It never occurred that they had been forgot,/ That the big God/ Had lazily closed one eye and let them slip// Over the English cliff and under so much history!'[85] This God who masturbates (his ego) in the void is neglectful; he closes his eyes on the history of the world, wipes out the memory of its violence: 'He'd had so many wars!/ The white gape of his mind was the real Tabula Rasa.' We will see in relation to 'Daddy' just how central the concept of amnesia is to Plath's analysis of politics, but over and again she returns to this question in those poems that were written at such speed during the October and November of 1962. On November 6 she wrote 'The Night Dances', which rewrites the same problem from the point of view of – or rather in an address to – the child:

> The comets
> Have such a space to cross,
>
> Such coldness, forgetfulness.
> So your gestures flake off –
>
> Warm and human, then their pink light
> Bleeding and peeling

Through the blank amnesias of heaven.[86]

Bleeding, flaking, peeling – this is pure deprivation (there is no celebration or self-discovery here). The child loses itself, sheds its trappings, in the blank spaces of an amnesiac heaven. On the same day Plath writes 'Getting There', one of her clearest indictments of God, man and the logos (the blind thirst for destination of all three).[87] In this poem, the history of the world is a train 'insane for the destination': 'All the gods know is destinations.' A woman drags her body across the terrain of war, attempting at once to repair the ills of history: 'I shall bury the wounded like pupas,/I shall count and bury the dead'; and to get free of patriarchal myth: 'It is Adam's side,/ This earth I rise from, and I in agony./ I cannot undo myself, and the train is steaming.' The last lines of the poem can be read only as a rewriting of the end of 'Fever 103°':

> And I stepping from this skin
> Of old bandages, boredom, old faces
>
> Step to you from the black car of Lethe,
> Pure as a baby.

What this poem seems to be saying is that the drive to undo herself ('I cannot undo myself'), which is more than legitimated by the horrors of the world, is self-defeating, for it can work only by means of the very forgetfulness which allows – which ensures – that those same horrors will be repeated. As Uroff puts it: 'The pure baby who steps from [the black car of Lethe] will perpetrate murder because she has forgotten the world's past history of murderousness.'[88] It seems impossible not to read these lines of Plath as her own diagnosis of the very solution that she herself seems to offer in other poems to the violence of the world. Transcendence appears here not as solution, but as repetition. Read together, these late poems offer one of the most stunning indictments of the very image of transcendence for which Plath has become most renowned. What she seems to be offering is a type of reading in advance of the link between phallocentrism, or phallogocentrism (the phallus as logos), and the feminist assertion of selfhood at that point where they both turn on the isolate ego, where the second finds itself repeating the great 'I am I' of the first – the slide from 'I am I' to 'I did it, I' and its violence, as we have watched it unfolding here. It is a problem that has been central to much recent feminist aesthetic, as well as political, debate – the risk that feminism might find itself reproducing the form of phallocentrism at the very moment when it claims to have detached itself most fully from patriarchal power.[89]

There is no question, therefore, of denying the force of female transcendence, the presence and importance of such a figure in Plath's later work, nor of denying the narratives of vengeance and /or betrayal which this figure expresses or to which she comes as the response. It is also evident, surely, that the monstrous image of a vengeful feminism constantly conjured up by the executors in relation to Plath criticism is nothing other than this figure of Plath's late poetry.[90] Rather the point is to suggest that, by representing this figure, Plath pushes it to its own vanishing point – self-immolation or an ego that knows nothing other than the void of itself (what would be the crudest rendering of self-transcendence if not 'topping yourself'?). Whether intentionally or not, she exposes the conditions of possibility of this figure *even as* she affirms it in her work. We do not in fact have a term for an identity free of the worst forms of social oppression which does not propel us beyond the bounds of identity in any recognisable form. This problem seems to me to be far more important than any discussion of the positive or negative, creative or destructive attributes of this figure of female transcendence in Plath's poetry (these discussions seem to rely on taking the concept of identity in the poems as presupposed). Nor, I think, can it be dealt with by an appeal to the contrary idea of shifting, protean identities which makes lack of identity, rather than its affirmation, the virtue of femininity itself.[91] Neither singular nor protean, this is a tension which resides at the heart of identity – the ego and its other ('identity and its other' or 'the other of identity', to use Julia Kristeva's expression)[92] – in the most specific sense of the term.

The issue here, therefore, is the very form in which (female) transcendence can be thought. Teleology, identity, the ego – Plath's writing, and commentaries on her writing, shows us how this figure of transcendence subordinates all other figures (all other poems) to itself. We read Plath through this figure only by repeating its own ferocious gesture of hierarchisation; only by effacing, therefore, all traces of the sexual and linguistic hesitancy

149

and self-questioning that we have seen running through the body of her work. Awful exigency, which crushes as much as it affirms.

I want to end this chapter by returning to the interaction between Sylvia Plath and Ted Hughes – not in terms of the sexual political drama which I have already discussed, but in terms of the concept of sexual difference which is symbolically mediated between them. For the idea of female transcendence takes on an added, and crucial, set of meanings when we discover it so clearly represented in his own writing, and when we can trace it back to its own fullest articulation in the two main sources (Graves and Jung) on which Hughes, and to some extent also Plath herself, draws. This is one of the sub-texts of Plath's writing – a discourse, which is fully and historically specific, in which transcendence is not a way of being that women seize for themselves but something handed to them with all the weight of male sexual fantasy and demand. It is one of the ironies of this story that, precisely by allowing us to trace the genealogy of the concept, it reveals how far the image of female transcendence can belong inside, rather than being the answer to, patriarchal myth. It also provides one of the most explicit statements of the forms of male fantasy that can attach to (determine?) the concept of poetic transcendence as such. This is Hughes in the Foreword to the *Journals*:

> What did she want? In a different culture, perhaps, she would have been happier. There was something about her reminiscent of what one reads of Islamic fanatic lovers of God – a craving to strip away everything from some ultimate intensity, some communion with spirit, or with reality, or simply with intensity itself. She showed something very violent in this, perhaps very female, a readiness, even a need, to sacrifice everything to the birth.[93]

Without commenting here on this as a description of Plath, we can immediately notice the association between violence and a self-immolating femininity on which it turns, as well as the classic image of woman as enigma (what does a woman want?) to which that association comes in some sense as the reply. Underlying this comment by Hughes is a whole philosophy of culture. Celtic pre-Christian culture celebrated the female principle. It is the loss of this principle, which survived into Catholicism but was finally destroyed or driven underground by the Puritan revolution, that is responsible for the destructiveness of our contemporary world. As Hughes puts it in his famous essay on Shakespeare:

> . . . the Queen of Heaven, who was the goddess of Catholicism, who was the goddess of Medieval and Pre-Christian England, who was the divinity of the throne, who was the goddess of natural law and of love, who was the goddess of all sensation and organic life – this overwhelmingly powerful, multiple, primaeval being, was dragged into court by the young Puritan Jehovah.[94]

Denied, this principle becomes destructive. Above all it turns into an image of terror for the man and provokes his retaliatory violence: 'Then this suppressed Nature goddess erupts, possessing the man who denied her, and creating this king-killing man of chaos' ('killer of the king, or the murderer of women, or both').[95]

Already we can ask what exactly, by way of logic or sequence, is involved. Does this analysis start from an image of female purity, made deadly by the denial of the man, or is it driven by a far more primordial terror of femininity which then creates this narrative, after the fact, to legitimate its own rage? Either way, we can recognise in this threatening, all-devouring female principle the imago of the phallic woman who, because she contains all things, threatens the man at the very core. According to this analysis, the idealisation of the woman is not contrary to the image of her as violent (it does not follow on from it along the lines of a historic or mythic sequence); the idealisation and the aggression are the fully interdependent and reverse sides of the same coin. In relation to Hughes, it certainly seems that this principle is deadly in any of the forms in which it is likely to be encountered today: 'If you refuse the energy, you are living a kind of death. If you accept the energy, it destroys you.'[96]

For Graves, this imago is the figure of poetry, White Goddess and Muse. His account of the experience of reading a true poem could have been lifted straight out of Freud on the Medusa's head:

> The reasons why the hair stands on end, the eyes water, the throat is constricted, the skin crawls and a shiver runs down the spine when one writes or reads a true poem is that a true poem is necessarily an invocation of the White Goddess, or Muse, the Mother of All Living, the ancient power of fright and lust – the female spider or the queen bee whose embrace is death.[97]

In Graves's account, the ambivalence of this figure constantly slides over on to its destructive pole. Note the ambiguity of this sentence: 'though she loves only to destroy, the Goddess destroys only to quicken' (I think the first part is intended to mean 'she loves only then to destroy' – that is, 'having loved, she destroys', but of course it can also be read as saying 'the only thing she really likes to do is destroy').[98] The ambiguity reappears at the centre of her relationship to poetry. She is the Muse – poetry is written only for the rites of she – but her nest is 'littered with the jaw-bones and entrails of poets'.[99] This might be important if we want to think about how this image might be lived out between a man and woman poet (Graves and Laura Riding, Hughes and Plath). Significant, perhaps, too is the fact that the summer goddess, flower goddess, aspect of the female deity in Celtic mythology, is called Olwen.[100]

At two points in her *Journals*, Plath alludes, or refers directly, to Graves. The first is in July 1957, when she is talking about a character in her fiction, Judith Greenwood (this is one of the earliest signs of *The Bell Jar*): 'Make her enigmatic: who is that blond girl: she is a bitch: she is the white goddess.'[101] Plath clearly locates the image of the white goddess in responses to the woman, as one of the answers to the question posed (for men) by femininity. She also historicises the image, suggests that it belongs to a specific moment in time: 'Make her a statement of the generation. Which is you.' Plath therefore grounds this image three times over – places it in quotations, downgrades it ('a bitch') and then, we might say, secularises it. The white goddess is a projection on to the woman and/or it belongs to the fully historical constraints which make her what she is. The concept of transcendence thus shows itself to be as fully historical ('statement of a generation') as the forms of oppression to which it comes as the emancipatory response.

This moment in Plath's *Journals* passes without editorial comment. But when she refers to *The White Goddess* again the following May, describing how she and Hughes were using the book to select names for their future children ('Read a bit . . . of *The White Goddess*, and unearthed a whole series of subtle symbolic names for our children whose souls haunt me'), the title is asterisked and given this comment: 'By Robert Graves: an important influence on Plath's work.'[102] It is the only point in the

*Journals* where the commentary underlines a literary influence in this way. In doing so, it circles back to the allusion to Judith Kroll's book on Plath in the Editor's Note at the beginning of the book: 'the autobiography does not work in Plath as it does in the "confessional" writers, but rather in a mythological sense – as can be seen most clearly in Judith Kroll's critical study *Chapters in a Mythology*'.[103]

Kroll reads Plath entirely through the mythography of Graves. Interpreting her work as a myth of self-emergence, she closes, like the editors, his system around Plath's works. Uroff also comments on this influence: 'it is necessary to remember that Hughes was also heavily influenced by Frazer and Graves, and that through them he directed Plath's attention to the archetypal quality of her experience.'[104] More specifically, she suggests that the 'rising female' of Plath's last poems was 'enlarged through her absorption of *The White Goddess* . . . a figure of power and fecundity – destructive and threatening, but in the end an identity to be celebrated and assumed'.[105] There is no denying that Plath on occasion drew on Graves's mythological scheme. But nowhere have I seen it suggested that there might be a problem in such an inheritance, that it might function as male projection and fantasy ('he directed Plath's attention'), that the archetype might be hellish, might be taken on – for Plath certainly takes it on – at considerable cost. What is involved in the idea that this is an imago that Plath (that a woman) might want – as part of her own self-realisation – to assume?

That the man's unconscious can be experienced as coercion by the woman is the central theme of Plath's short story 'The Wishing Box', in which a husband who boasts of his dreams every morning to his wife, and insists that *she* dream, gradually drives her to suicide (I return to this story in the next chapter).[106] In her poem 'The Shrike', Plath gives the alternative version: the 'envious bride' who cannot follow her husband, beckoned nightly by 'such royal dreams', turns on him in his sleep and drains the blood from his heart.[107] Compare too this entry from her *Journals*: 'we dream: and my dreams get better'.[108] Rather than figuring as 'truth', the unconscious itself has gone into the circuit of (sexual) exchange.

Let's look at what Graves has to say, not about the content of his image of femininity but about women's concrete, lived relationship to it. Despite the idealisation – or rather as its direct effect – this concept of the female principle leaves no place for women. None for the women poet: 'Woman is not a poet: she is either a Muse or she is nothing';[109] and only the most precarious place for any individual woman who might attempt to realise this imago for the man. First the risk for the man:

> ... perhaps he has lost his sense of the White Goddess: the woman whom he took to be a Muse, or who was a Muse, turns into a domestic woman and would have him turn similarly into a domesticated man. Loyalty prevents him from parting company with her, especially if she is the mother of his children and is proud to be reckoned a good housewife; and as the Muse fades out, so does the poet.[110]

Then the risk for the woman:

> The White Goddess is anti-domestic; she is the perpetual 'other woman', and her part is difficult indeed for a woman of sensibility to play for more than a few years, because the temptation to commit suicide in simple domesticity lurks in every maenad and muse's heart.[111]

At its most banal, this reads like the crudest licence to infidelity dressed up as a service to poetry. At a more sinister level, it places the most impossible demand on the woman – that she should be this Muse, that she can be it only for a few years, but that she does so at risk of her own self-inflicted death. Note how domesticity is represented here as something that the woman imposes on the man. The cliché behind the myth is stunning – woman as inspiration, woman as drudge (there are the strongest echoes here of Freud's famous article on the 'Universal Tendency to Debasement in the Sphere of Love').[112]

It is hard not to read in this account – which comes near the end of Graves's book – the most chilling of advance warnings to Plath and Hughes. More important, the image of female transcendence finds itself circling back to – comes to grief on – social reality at its most concrete and oppressive for women ('Make her a statement of the generation', as Plath would say). One could also argue that it is from the felt demands of this reality that the whole mythological system, for the man, is trying to take off. We should notice too how, for all this invocation of mythical beginnings, of sacrifice to the female principle, the male poet must never lose his control: the poet is like the prophet who was 'by the grace of God, the sturdy author and regulator of his own achievement' (god, we might say after Plath, masturbating his ego in the void).[113]

Both Plath's and Hughes's poetry suggest that this conception of femininity was being consciously or unconsciously negotiated between them. At the most immediate, tangible level, Plath lived out the competing demands of domestic life and poetry, for herself as well as in relation to Hughes. Her role as wife, secretary, and mother of his children has received ample commentary; so too has the impossible ideology of domesticity which required nothing short of perfection from the woman.[114] One of the important meanings of 'The Rabbit Catcher' is the violence that it locates inside this very domesticity, at the heart of everyday life.

But Plath and Hughes were also negotiating the concept of femininity more symbolically, as well as the notion of divine or archetypal meaning on which it depends. In an early verse play, 'Dialogue over a Ouija Board', written in 1957 and published in the Notes to the *Collected Poems*,[115] the woman rejects the spirit who seems to direct the glass as a 'mere puppet of our two intuitions', 'a sort of psychic bastard/ Sprung to being on our wedding night'; for the man, the reality of this spirit is less important than the fact of poetic vision which it embodies and can inspire: 'we face/ Obliteration hourly unless our eye/ Can whipcrack the tables into tigers and foist/Castles upon the smug-shaped chairs' (we can reread in this light those early poems on poetic inspiration with which this chapter began). Even more important, however, is the violence that Plath situates quite explicitly inside this male invocation of poetry. Towards the end of the dialogue, the man says:

> I felt drawn
> Deeper within the dark, and as I pitched further
> Into myself and into my conviction
> A rigor seized me: I saw cracks appear,
> Dilating to craters in this living room,
> And you, shackled ashen across the rift, a specter
> Of the one I loved.

Much of Hughes's poetry can be read as the simultaneous acting out and the strongest diagnosis of everything I have been describing so far. There is a sustained critique of masculinity in his writing, of the violence of militarism ('Bayonet Charge', 'Griefs for Dead Soldiers', 'Six Young Men', 'Two Wise Generals' – all from the end of his first collection, *The Hawk in the Rain*) – as well as of the masculine pretension to pure form ('The Perfect Forms', *Lupercal*; 'Logos', *Wodwo*).[116] But there are also all those points, which have been commented on by writers on his poetry, when he seems to venerate or even idealise the same spirit of masculine identity as the celebration and completion of itself.

The most famous example is 'Hawk Roosting' from *Lupercal*. Hughes has described the poem as 'Nature thinking', but it is hard not to read in the hawk who sits at the top of the wood, troubled by no 'inaction, falsifying dream', body without sophistry, mind without argument ('There is no sophistry in my body', 'No arguments assert my rights'), an emblem of pure identity in its fascist mode.[117] Exposure and critique of this pure form of identity (of identity as pure form), the poem has also been seen as partly complicit with what it condemns[118] – especially in the context of those other moments in his poetry when the condemnation seems to falter – the 'bullet and automatic purpose' of Mozart's brain and the shark in 'Thrushes' (*Lupercal*) and, far less ambiguously, right in the middle of his own critique of war: 'The grandeur of their wars humbles my thought' ('The Ancient Heroes and the Bomber Pilot', *The Hawk in the Rain*).[119] Hughes's critique of war is bound into his critique of 'discursive intelligence' (the violence of the logos).[120] But his attempt to detach militarism from something more in the nature of pure spirit might today be seen as a problem, since the elevation of spirit in action can just as easily be identified as one of the key properties, or fantasies, of militarism itself.

Whatever we decide on those early poems (it is probably undecidable), the transition from *The Hawk in the Rain* and *Lupercal* to *Wodwo* seems to chart the collapse of that ethic and its singular purpose:

> But what shall I be called am I the first
> have I an owner what shape am I what
> shape am I am I huge if I go[121]

There is no punctuation in this poem (my break is arbitrary), no points of ending or completion on which that 'I' can alight. Disintegration of (apology for?) what Hughes describes in another poem as the 'world-shouldering monstrous "I"'.[122] In this context, Hughes's poetry can be seen as one of the strongest representations – affirmation/condemnation – of the great male ego at work.

Recent writers have commented on the close link between fascist ideology and the fantasy of an abject femininity.[123] They have argued that it is this feminine-connoted body of liquid, hollows and openings that fascism, at the level of unconscious fantasy, is struggling to control. In her *Journals*, Plath herself gives one of the most graphic accounts of this fantasy:

> Hair blued with oil-slick, nose crusted with hair and green or brown crusts. Eye-whites yellowed, corners crusted, ears a whorl of soft wax. We exude. Spotted bodies. Yet days in a dim or distant light we burn clear of our shackles and stand, burning and speaking like gods.[124]

For Hughes, the abject body is the pagan nature that civilisation has tried to destroy. Suppressed, it becomes deadly, provoking man's ever-renewed assault (this process is enacted most viciously in *Crow*, the emblem, according to Hughes, of 'God's nightmare's attempt to improve on man').[125] This turns Hughes's poetic writing (the activity of writing) into a type of allegory of man's relationship to abjection. In an interview with Hughes, Ekbert Faas – one of Hughes's best-known commentators – points out that Hughes has described the mainstream English poetic tradition against which he writes as a 'terrible, suffocating maternal octopus'.[126] The question constantly sent back to the reader is whether female nature is an object of celebration or repulsion, whether it is that which is disfigured by man, or whether femininity is that which is, radically, primordially, disfigured.

To take just one instance – 'Mayday on Holderness', (*Lupercal*), which describes the speaker's relation to the 'motherly summer' in terms of the bits and pieces, bodily components, of the earth: 'Birth-soils,/ The sea-salts, scoured me, cortex and intestine' . . . 'What a length of gut is growing and breathing –/ This mute eater, biting through the mind's/Nursery floor' (the echoes of Plath's 'Poem for a Birthday' are striking).[127] Like Roethke, however, and in fact even more than him, Hughes seems to represent this realm from a place that is located above: 'I looked down into the decomposition of leaves'; he takes up these remains: 'I had a whole world in my hands', receives them 'like the sun'. At the end of the sequence, the owl 'announces its sanity'. In the penultimate stanza the poem moves into war, where male soldiers call out 'Mother, Mother!' ('The cordite oozings of Gallipoli'). It ends:

> Curded to beastings, broached my palate,
> The expressionless gaze of the leopard,
> The coils of the sleeping anaconda,
> The nightlong frenzy of shrews.

The relations here are complex, difficult to pin down. There is a narrative – the transition from nature to war, their difference, but also their similarity, with war as the image ('cordite oozings') of what goes on inside the earth, as well as constituting a violence against it. But it also seems as if the engagement with the natural world is something which has to be held in check – by the point of view of the speaker, by the sanity of owls, by the invoking of the mother by the soldiers (nostalgia and appeal), and then finally by that frenzy of the shrews, at once the animal and one of the most vicious stereotypes of woman. Diagnosis slides into symptom, which seems to erupt, and close, the text (female sexuality as vicious, woman as shrew). For it is central to the theory on which Hughes explicitly draws that what has been done to nature makes the woman dangerous to others, to herself. Thus Graves on the frenzies of civilised women: 'An English or American woman in a nervous breakdown of sexual origin will often instinctively reproduce in faithful and disgusting detail much of the ancient Dionysiac ritual. I have witnessed it myself in helpless terror.'[128]

More like Roethke, we might say, Hughes situates this realm at a distance, as the object of desire and fear. For desire, read 'Fire-Eater' in *Lupercal*, in which the speaker goes down into, eats out, the earth: 'My skull buries among antennae and fronds'; for fear, read 'Gog' in *Wodwo*: 'I do not look at the rocks and stones I am frightened of what they see'.[129] Gog himself is the dragon from Revelation who 'stood before the woman who was about to bear a child, that he might devour the child when she brought it forth' (12:4).[130]

The clearest articulation of this drama comes in Hughes's radio play 'The Wound' a Gothic rendering of the Tibetan Bardo Thodol, a death, underworld, rebirth, ritual text.[131] It is a play which emerged out of a dream Hughes had during Plath's pregnancy (he has said that he dreamt it twice).[132] Plath refers to it in her late letters to her mother — it was produced for the BBC by Douglas Cleverdon, who was also responsible for her verse drama 'Three Women'.[133] In Plath's play, maternity is not origin, enigma or pure body; it is a dialogue between three voices. The formal division distinguishes at one level between the different experiences of the three women, while also posing the question of maternity's difference from, or sameness to, itself (something which divides the woman's body, differentiates between women, or the constant of women's experience across all differences of personal and historical time). In Hughes's poem, the encounter with femininity takes the form of a terrifying meeting with half-crazed women who lure returning soldiers to an orgy in their castle in the woods. In these Bacchanalia ('lousy old brothel, all tarted up', 'carnivorous pile of garbage if ever there was one'), the women take the soldiers apart — 'one had his leg between her thighs and was trying to twist his foot off. His arms were out of their sockets. What sort of women are they, are they women?'[134] Their violence, however, is mirrored by a no less monstrous violence carried out against the women themselves. In chanting chorus, they describe the first woman's live vivisection:

> They took me with blood dripping off my chin, my mask was blood and went back over my ears and I'd pulled blood up past my elbows and so I was! And they dragged me from the mob and into the Police Station, two constables, my toes slapping the steps.[135]

Here zoologists, bacteriologists, anthropologists, students and attendants take her apart, uncover her facticity (steel skull-plates, jawbone rivets, rubber arteries) until all that is left is 'three gallons of marsh gas and a crust of bread'.[136]

Flood, food and emptiness (all three at once) in the 'mundiform belly' of the woman.[137] If this is a representation of what civilisation and science does *to* women, it also gives to all these epithets, all these contents, the status of hidden truth. Objects of violence at this moment in the narrative, these women are, however, for the most part its source: 'These women are dragging them all into the ground, it's a massacre.'[138] Their own violence is distinct from, but also perpetuates, the horrors of war. From the point of view of feminism, it is impossible not to read this as a narrative that has it both ways — women as the objects of terrible violence for which they finally have only themselves to blame. As Uroff comments:

> The strategy of the poems is to blame the man of iron, the Puritan half-crazed representative, for the perversion of the pagan goddess of fertility; but as the female figure emerges in his own poetry, she comes only as the symbol of death.[139]

The question remains as to how the listener, how Hughes, is situated in relation to this narrative – participator or judge, inside or outside (pathos or anti-pathos, to use David Trotter's terms).[140] As with Plath, we have to allow the coexistence of complicity and critique – the exposure, in Hughes's case, of what one might fairly call the worst of male fantasy which he lays bare, endlessly returns to and repeats. In discussion Hughes situates himself ambivalently, allowing us to read his work simultaneously as the analysis, and the continuing symptom, of what it describes. Responding to a question put by Faas about the presence of violence in his poetry, he states: 'We are dreaming a perpetual massacre' (this is the horror of the contemporary world); but when Faas points out the specific and recurrent association of women and horror in Hughes's writing (the reference is to the ogress in *Crow* and the lady in *Gaudete*), he replies: 'The Tiger, yes. She is the whole works. (Both laughing)'.[141] The editorial intervention is the only moment of its kind in the two interviews – bonding of the men through laughter, horror of femininity a shared joke.

Faas argues in a separate article that Hughes has picked up this violence from Plath: 'her main obsession had entered his imagination through a nightmare'.[142] In their play for French radio on Plath and Hughes, Raymond Bellour and Nancy Huston suggest that if anything it is the other way round, pointing to the clash between Plath's image of female fecundity and the terror of femininity which 'The Wound' (and other moments in Hughes's writing) seems to express.[143] I think this question is unanswerable – it simply repeats that attempt to locate the origins of negativity which we have seen working over and again in responses to Plath, and of which this play by Hughes could be read, symbolically, as another version in itself ('Who – or what – started it?', as we might say). What interests me, however, is the way this image of a violent, terrifying femininity can be seen as the sub-text of that myth of female transcendence which Hughes takes out of Robert Graves. Seen in this context, the myth of female transcendence becomes one half of one of the most classic, and alarming, stereotypes of femininity itself.

Nowhere is this clearer than in the works of Jung, where it reaches its fullest and most articulate theorisation (one could in fact argue that this was one of the crucial issues at stake in the rupture between Jung and Freud). If this is relevant, it is because Hughes also reads Plath through Jung: 'A Jungian might call the whole phase a classic case of the chemical individuation of the self' (the reference is to 'Poem for a Birthday').[144] The link is justified, at least partly, by the fact that Plath herself was reading Jung's *Symbols of Transformation* in 1959.[145] Briefly, in Jung's work individuation passes through the confrontation with the realm of the Terrible Mother. This figure is, again, one half of a dyad. Compare these two descriptions, the first from Jung's *Symbols of Transformation*, the second from 'Fragments of an Antique Tablet', a later poem by Hughes: 'The double being corresponds to the mother-imago: above, the lovely and attractive human half; below, the horrible animal half' . . . 'Above – the well-known lips, delicately downed./ Below – beard between thighs' (the whole poem continues in this form).[146] When Lear produces the same set of alternatives, he is generally considered to have gone mad:

> Down from the waist they are Centaurs,
> Though women all above:
> But to the girdle do the Gods inherit,
> Beneath is all the fiends: there's hell, there's darkness,
> There is the sulphurous pit – burning, scalding,
> Stench, consumption; fie, fie, fie! pah, pah!
> (King Lear IV, vi, 126–31)

In Jung's work, there is the same ambiguity we find in Hughes as to whether this is a projection on to the mother or whether this realm, which draws back the subject, constitutes a real threat.[147] Crucially, however, the battle can be seen as part of an allegory for the libido's passage out of darkness into light. Confrontation with this Terrible Mother is a stage in a narrative whose objective is finally, in an act of violent sacrifice, to leave her – to leave sexuality – behind. In Jung's writing, the Terrible Mother is a fantasy or imago, which becomes the metaphor for the struggle with libido as such:

> This dangerous passion is what confronts us beneath the hazardous mark of incest. It confronts us in the guise of the Terrible Mother, and is indeed the mother of innumerable evils, not the least of which are neurotic disturbances. For out of the miasmus arising from the stagnant pools of libido are born those fatal phantasmagorias which so veil reality that all adaptation becomes impossible.[148]

Jung's *Symbols of Transformation* was the book that confirmed the final split with Freud. Its objective, like the psychic objective it charts for the subject, is nothing less than the repudiation and/or sublimation of sex: 'The sacrifice is the very reverse of regression – it is a successful canalisation of libido into the symbolic equivalent of the mother, and hence a spiritualisation of it.'[149] In reply, Freud reads it as a 'family romance', a version of the story the young child fabricates in fantasy in order to elevate his origins by making himself the child of parents who are royal or divine.[150] In this historic disagreement, femininity, it could be fairly argued, is the stake. Freud's recognition of the importance of pre-Oedipal sexuality for women was to follow this rupture – as if the only possible alternatives in relation to femininity for these key patriarchs of modern psychology were down and back, or up and out.[151] Freud is in fact notorious for the only partial and defensive account that he finally provided for this realm. In the case of Jung, however, the concept of individuation, with all that it implies by way of a finally integrated identity, appears to be a way of repudiating what is most troubling about sexuality and women (the second as the terrifying and abject embodiment or projection of the first).

If I have traced this out in some detail, it is because – as I suggested earlier in this chapter – I think the interaction between Plath and Hughes needs to be understood at least partly in these terms. Following back Plath's figure of female transcendence into its (male) theoretical origins, we find a grotesque fantasy of femininity as its underside and support. If we read Plath's works in terms of the emergence of this identity, if we read it *as* identity, we have to ask what it is that such an image of female transcendence relies on, as well as what, exactly, it requires the woman to leave behind. If Plath takes up, affirms and celebrates this figure (I have suggested that she does, at the same time as she criticises it), is it our task – is it feminism's task – to do so with her? To say that Plath creates her own version of this image, that she turns it back against her male oppressors, or raises it up against them, doesn't work when we see that the vision of a terrible and vengeful femininity is so firmly ensconced inside (is in some sense the origins of) the most stereo-typed and misogynistic versions of the very image she seeks to transform. Once theorised via Jung, the story recounted here gives the strongest measure, or critique, of that concept of transcendence – its image of femininity, its psychical and ethical weight – which has been so central to the goals of one form of feminism. We watch the concept battling itself out between Plath and Hughes (that battle is at least as significant as the other sexual-political battle for which they are most renowned). I am suggesting that the story of Plath and Hughes gives us a unique opportunity to examine the vicissitudes of the stereotype, across the barrier of sexual difference, in action.

On at least one occasion Plath shows herself highly sceptical of Hughes's metaphysical interpretation of his own work. In one of the omitted letters to the mother she tells her not to take 'the metaphysical explanations too seriously' and offers her own politi-cal interpretation of his play ('The Harvesting'): 'which I think reads perfectly as a symbolic invasion of private lives and dreams by mechanical war-law and inhumanity such as is behind the germ-warfare laboratory in Maryland'.[152] Reading Graves, it is clear that his mythic conception of poetry is set quite explicitly against politics and history: 'The White Goddess's Starry Wheel here multiplied into the twelve wheeling signs of the Zodiac . . . are misread as dark, mechanistic images of capitalistic oppression' (the reference is to Blake's 'Satanic Mills').[153] History has a tendency to 'taint the purity of myth'.[154]

In all this there is a very specific politics as well as a no less specific concept of culture. Graves bemoans what he calls our 'cockney civilisation', where the Classics no longer dominate the school curriculum, and then, against democracy ('demogogracy disguised as democracy'),[155] he advocates a non-hereditary aristoc-racy. His contempt for the 'masses' is explicit:

> . . . we are now at the stage where the common people of
> Christendom, spurred on by their demagogues, have grown so
> proud that they are no longer content to be the hands and feet

and trunk of the body politic, but demand to be the intellect as well – or, as much intellect as is needed to satisfy their simple appetites.[156]

We have already seen Hughes's dismissal of anything but the highest of art in relation to Plath. In his discussion with Faas, he gives his vision of what would be possible in a perfect culture: 'In a perfectly cultured society one imagines that jaguar-like elementals would be invoked only by self-disciplinarians of a very advanced grade'[157] (compare Graves on the writer as 'sturdy author and regulator' above). Behind the image of transcendence, a very specific concept of culture. Like women, it must not be low. Let's now look at Plath's writing at those moments when this is what she most wanted to be.

# 5

# SADIE PEREGRINE

... most [of my poems] are in that limbo between experimental art of the poetry little magazines and the sophisticated wit of *The New Yorker*, too much of the other for either.
(*Letters Home*, 25 April 1955)

Either Kafka lit-mag serious or SATEVEPOST aim high [ ... ] Try both styles: do it to your heart's content
(*Journals*, typescript original, 15 July–21 August 1957 p. 4, 20 July, Smith Collection)

There is only one point in Plath's poetry where she explicitly refers to a book from the ambient culture, citing it without giving the name of the author, as if its familiarity to her reader – to any reader – could be safely assumed. The book is *Generation of Vipers* and it appears in the middle of 'The Babysitters', a poem Plath wrote in October 1961, which, on the rare occasions when it is discussed, tends to be dismissed ('a Lowellian exercise'[1]):

> O what has come over us, my sister!
> On that day-off the two of us cried so hard to get
> We lifted a sugared ham and a pineapple from the
>             grownups' icebox
> And rented an old green boat. I rowed. You read
> Aloud, crosslegged on the stern seat, from the
>             *Generation of Vipers*.
> So we bobbed out to the island.

By naming this book, Plath situates herself – or her memory of herself – firmly within the framework of popular culture. The book, written by Philip Wylie, was a massive bestseller, first published during the war in 1942, regularly reprinted, and selected by the American Library Association as one of the major non-fiction books of the twentieth century.[2] *Generation of Vipers* is a tirade against America and its failure – the failure of the peace for not preventing the war: 'You are buying the next peace with this war. Are you trying to purchase a replica of the peace that failed? And if you are not, have you studied why it failed – why America failed – why you failed?'[3] It is most famous, however, for its creation of the concept of 'Momism', the image of a deadly middle-class American female who is ultimately responsible for the collapse of the culture, for sapping the manhood of America from within. This is just one of a number of exemplary quotations:

> I give you mom. I give you the destroying mother. I give you her justice – from which we have never removed the eye bandage. I give you the angel – and point to the sword in her hand. I give you death – the hundred million deaths that are muttered under Yggdrasill's ash. I give you Medusa and Stheno and Euryale. I give you the harpies and the witches and the Fates. I give you the woman in pants, and the new religion: she-popery. I give you Pandora. I give you Proserpine, the Queen of Hell. The five-and-ten-cent-store Lilith, the mother of Cain, the black widow who is poisonous and eats her mate, and I designate at the bottom of your program the grand finale of all the soap operas: the mother of America's Cinderella.[4]

The virulence of this was such that the Voice of America eventually removed the book from its overseas libraries as the 1950s turned the ideology around, or back, into a sanctification of the mother in the home.[5] What is important here, however, is not just the misogyny of the book (more on this later) but the way that misogyny is situated in relation to the concept of popular culture. Look back at that quote and one of the striking things about it is those snide dismissals – the 'five-and-ten-cent-store Lilith', 'the soap operas' at the 'bottom' of the whole program – which set up an association between femininity and those components of the culture that can be designated as cheap. Wylie stakes his right to judgement on his first-hand knowledge of a crucial part of this world: 'Hold your seats, ladies, I have been a *clerk* in a *department store*'.[6] But at a more fundamental level, the destruction of masculinity by Momism is tied into an argument, central to cultural debate of the 1940s and '50s, that the popular, the mass, the consumer, were – like Nazism and then like the Communism to which all of these increasingly became associated – destroying the American mind:

166

The radio is mom's final tool, for it stamps everyone who listens with the matriarchal brand [ . . . ] Just as Goebbels has revealed what can be done with such a mass-stamping of the public psyche in his nation, so our land is a living representation of the same fact worked out in matriarchal sentimentality, goo, slop, hidden cruelty, and the foreshadow of national death.[7]

Plath, I will be arguing in this chapter, belongs crucially within the framework of these debates about the meaning and forms of culture. To detach her from them is to remove a central component of her work. More exactly, it is inadvertently to perpetuate the terms of the debates themselves since the effect, as we have already seen, is to enshrine her unequivocally in the domain of high art. That she belongs in that domain – that she writes herself through her poetry into that place and status – is unequivocal, but it is only one part of the story. As divided as Plath's writing is in relation to identity or subjectivity, so it is in relation to the multiple destinations of the culture for which she writes. She participates in them, she provides her own commentary on them, not just in the discussions that run through her journals and her correspondence about her publications, ambitions, earnings, etc., but *inside* the writing itself. The problem and divisions of culture are a reiterated theme of her prose writing, the point at which her work turns on itself, making the terms of its cultural production into an object of its own representation, commenting in the process on the competing and contested institutions of culture. In relation to these institutions, Plath is a hybrid, crossing over the boundaries of cultural difference with an extraordinary and almost transgressive ease. As Lucas Myers puts it in his Appendix to Anne Stevenson's biography, she was as much at home with Wallace Stevens as she was with *Mademoiselle*.[8]

Given the feminist attention to Plath, it is remarkable to what extent this has been overlooked, or else been relegated to subsidiary status, for feminists have been among the first to point out that the denigration of popular culture carries with it a specific denigration of women. Popular culture has been associated with femininity, not least of all because – along a line that can be traced back to Mary Wollstonecraft's condemnation of the sentimental novel – it has been seen to be predominantly consumed by, if not produced for, women. In her book *Loving with a Vengeance*, Tania Modleski points out how women have inherited this condemnation, adopting, in the attitude of hostility, dismissiveness or flippant mockery that they often strike towards popular writing by and for women, the tone that men often use towards women and popular culture alike.[9]

We can see this in the way Plath's more popular writing has been received by her commentators: 'nastily eager-to-please concoctions', 'the peculiar kind of glossiness that marks fiction in even very good American magazines', or as 'syndrome': 'That the kind of fiction the women's magazine market demanded during the 1950s and early 1960s was at real variance to Plath's best writing is obvious even to the casual reader.'[10] The second of these quotations comes from a review of the collection of her prose writing, *Johnny Panic and the Bible of Dreams*, entitled 'Pass to the Centre', which implies, even before getting to the stories themselves, that they are simply – on the way to the main, that is, serious, artistic business – something to get past. The same cultural deprecation appears with explicit reference to feminism: 'the inappropriateness of calling Plath a feminist . . . with her philosophy of catch your man and be happy, she seems closer to the world of romantic fiction than that of Germaine Greer'.[11] This hostility to popular culture then becomes part of the validation of the rest of Plath's work:

> Today, as language slips away on the one hand into the binary blurps of technology, and on the other into the stereophonic nagging of the mass media (including most works of fiction and nonfiction), it is tougher than ever for a poet to hang on to the battered nucleus of language. [review of *Ariel* in *Newsweek*, 1966][12]

Modleski suggests that women turn against popular women's fiction, see it as shameful, much as the heroines of so many of the stories turn, by the end of the narrative, against any vestiges of a protesting or militant self. Popular fiction, like gossip, becomes an illicit pleasure, something that women – that the culture – indulges on the sly.[13] Plath, however, seems shameless in her desire to write for this market: 'I want to write funny and tender women's stories'; 'I shall write a complete fantasy life of tearful-joyful stories for women – tremulous with all variety of emotion.'[14]

The quotations from Wylie suggest, however, that in this association between the popular and femininity, something more disturbing is at stake. The dangers of femininity and the dangers of mass culture stand in the most intimate and isomorphic relationship to each other. In a 1955 edition, Wylie boasts of the effect of his book ('This chapter has put the word "momism" indelibly in our language'), defends himself against the charge of hating women ('and has typed me apparently forever as a woman hater – indeed, as the all-out, all-time, high-scoring, world champion misogynist'), and then repeats his charge against the middle-class woman, all the more justified now, he implies, by the 'scurrilous, savage, illiterate, vulgar and obscene' letters that he has received.[15] Thus mom reveals herself, not as middle-class, but as vulgar, illiterate and low: 'Today, while decent men struggle for seats in government with the hope of saving our Republic, mom makes a condition of their election the legalising of Bingo.'[16]

Wylie is not alone in this: he has recently been taken as supremely representative of a set of links between politics and culture to which I will return. But the association between femininity and mass culture is by no means exclusive to him. Although there was an important defence of mass culture in the United States (American and democratic as opposed to European and highbrow), critics of different persuasions on the issue were often united by this sexualisation, or feminisation, of the cultural stakes.[17] Thus Dwight MacDonald, one of the most influential writers on mass culture in America in the 1940s and 1950s, ended his 1953 article 'A Theory of Mass Culture': 'staying power is the essential virtue of one who would hold his own against the spreading ooze of Mass Culture' (mass culture as abjection, body and flow; compare 'goo' and 'slop' above);[18] Leslie Fiedler, in his famous article 'The Middle Against Both Ends', at least partly a defence of the popular against the middlebrow, complains: '[Popular culture] is a product of the same impulse which has made available the sort of ready-made clothing which aims at destroying the possibility of knowing a lady by her dress',[19] and Bernard Rosenberg, writing in his introductory article to the 1957 collection *Mass Culture* on the link of that culture to the ethic of success, states: 'Success is still the bitch-goddess of American society'.[20] When Edward Butscher transfers that famous epithet – 'bitch-goddess' – to Plath (it is a term which has been taken up by women writing on her work) he was therefore, amongst other things, turning Plath into an image for the degeneracy of the American culture and mind.[21]

Plath's desire to be part of that mass culture was, however, one of the strongest, reiterated refrains of her journals and correspondence. Her scathing remarks to her mother about the *Ladies' Home Journal* towards the end of her life are famous: 'Don't talk to me about the world needing cheerful stuff [ . . . ] Let the *Ladies' Home Journal* blither about those [happy marriages]'; 'Now stop trying to get me to write about "decent courageous people" – read the *Ladies' Home Journal* for those!'[22] But the pull that this same journal, together with others from the surrounding magazine culture, exerted on Plath tends to be ignored. Some examples:

I'll never get anywhere if I just write one or two stories and never revise them or streamline them for a particular market. I want to hit *The New Yorker* in poetry and the *Ladies' Home Journal* in stories, and so I must just study the magazines the way I did *Seventeen*.

First, pick your market: *Ladies' Home Journal* or *Discovery*? *Seventeen* or *Mlle*? Then pick a topic. Then think.

My supercilious attitude about the people who write Confessions has diminished. It takes a good tight plot and a slick ease that are not picked up overnight like a cheap whore.

I would really like to get something in *The New Yorker* before I die, I do so admire that particular, polished, rich, brilliant style.

Today did the outline for a version of the Matisse-Cathedral which I am going to try in *New Yorker* style first, then perhaps *Ladies' Home Journal* style, and then as a feature article.

I admire the slick market in NYC and find the stories muscular, pragmatic, fine technically and with a good sense of humour.

I am going to write a series of tight, packed, perfect short stories which I shall make into a novel [ . . . ] Ted is with me all the way, and we are rather excited about this. It is 'my own corner' [ . . . ] Will try to sell the stories separately in *The New Yorker* and *Mademoiselle*.

I will slave and slave until I break into those slicks.

I hope to break into the women's slicks this summer. I just haven't had the time to rewrite. The *Ladies' Home Journal* liked my laundromat story and said they'd look at it again if I rewrote the ending – no promises. Well, I sent it to *Good Housekeeping* and when it comes back will rewrite it. I think I should sell it somewhere, the setting is quite 'original'; their motto is: LOVE LOVE LOVE: but not, please, in the same old setting . . . So I put mustard, pepper and curry powder on it.

Sent it off to *The Sat Eve Post*: start at the top. Try *McCall's, Ladies' Home Journal, Good Housekeeping, Women's Day* before getting blue . . . my first good story for five years . . . a slick story but one I consider good.

How irony is the spice of life. My novel will hardly end with love and marriage: it will be a story of the workers and the worked, the exploiters and the exploited, of vanity and cruelty . . . The irony I record here for the novel, but also for *The Ladies' Home Journal*.

I have been writing poems steadily and feel the blessed dawn of a desire to write prose beginning: bought a literary *Mlle* to whet my emulous urge [ . . . ] My next ambition is to get a story in *The New Yorker* – five, ten years' work.

I looked at my sentence notes for stories, much like the notes jotted here on the opposite page. I picked the most 'promising' subject – the secretary returning on the ship from Europe, her dreams tested and shattered. She was not gorgeous, wealthy, but small, almost stodgy, with few good features and a poor temperament. The slicks leaned over me: demanding romance, romance – should she be gorgeous? [ . . . ] I ran through my experience for ready-made 'big' themes: there were none.

When I write my first *Ladies' Home Journal* story I will have made a step forward. I don't have to be a bourgeois mother to do it either.

I only hope I get a women's story or two published in time for her [Mrs Prouty] to see them, as I think that would please her most of all.

I'll have a story in the *LHJournal* or *SatEvePost* yet.

I'm very encouraged by selling my first women's magazine story [ . . . ] I'll get into the *Ladies' Home Journal* yet!

If you happen to think of it, could you pack me off a *Ladies'*
*Home Journal* or two? I get homesick for it; it has an Ameri-
canness which I feel a need to dip into, *now I'm in exile*, and
especially as I'm writing for women's magazines in a small way
now. I shall have fulfilled a very long-time ambition if a story of
mine ever makes the *LHJ*.[23]

Only once does Plath criticise this form of ambition in herself: 'I
must be so overconscious of markets and places to send things that I
can write nothing honest and really satisfying'; and on one other
occasion she suggests that, in comparison with the 'slicks', the
'Literary Market' is 'harder and more aesthetically rewarding' (it is
none the less a market).[24] More often it is the specific pleasures of
this form of writing that she describes: 'The wonderful thing about
these stories is that I can do them by perspiration, not inspiration.'[25] Prose writing can be picked up and put down (women's
work, one might say); it may be 'muscular', 'fine technically', but
the process of producing it evokes a very different body of mess and
of mush: 'Prose sustains me. I can mess it, mush it, rewrite it, pick it
up any time – rhythms are slacker, more variable, it doesn't die so
soon.'[26] And in her 1962 essay 'A Comparison', she describes the
poem as 'concentrated, a closed fist', the novel as an 'open hand':
'Where the fist excludes and stuns, the open hand can touch and
encompass . . . The door of the novel, like the door of the poem,
also shuts. But not so fast, nor with such manic, unanswerable
finality.'[27] This is close to a feminist aesthetics of touch against a
(masculine) brutalism of writing, except that here it is poetic
language that leads to death. In this opposition between poetry and
prose, narrative is not order (the imposition of sequence and linear
control) but mundane clutter (the fragmented bits and pieces of the
world): 'door knobs, airletters, flannel nightgowns, cathedrals, nail
varnish, jet planes, rose arbors and budgerigars . . . rich junk of
life . . . the whole much loved, well-thumbed catalogue of the
miscellaneous'.[28]

As some of these quotations make clear, what is specific to this
type of writing is the collective nature of its form. This is writing to
recipe ('mustard, pepper and curry powder'), to a very specific set of
formulas and demands ('tailored for specifications'[29]) – demands
Plath sometimes seems happy to meet ('I've decided to rewrite the
"In the Mountains" . . . it was an attempt to be understated and

cryptic as Hemingway, which is fine for a lit. course but not for 17'),[30] while at other times they make her hesitate ('no promises') and at yet others are felt as pressures in relation to which she fails ('I ran through my experience for ready-made "big" themes: there were none'). But however Plath situates herself, it is clear that she sees a central component of her identity and ambitions as a writer in terms which are incompatible with – at the opposite pole to – that image of the unique and solitary author which she has come so dramatically to personify. In fact, by occupying both these positions at the same time, Plath demonstrates the extent to which the second – the more familiar idealist conception ('inspiration' versus 'per- spiration') – is not an isolate category but exists only diacritically: that is, in terms of its (lofty) self-differentiation from the first.

Look at the range of Plath's publications – not the forms but the places where she published her work – and it is her simultaneous or alternate occupancy of all the possible sites of cultural production (low and high) which is so dramatic. The list includes *Seventeen* (teenage popular), *The Christian Science Monitor* (religious high didactic), *Mademoiselle* (teenage quality), *Harper's Magazine* (liter- ary sophisticate), *The Atlantic Monthly* (high literary-political), *Gemini* (Oxbridge small-circulation high literary-political), *Granta* (Cambridge small-circulation literary), *London Magazine* (high literary), *The New Yorker* (city sophisticated), *Ladies' Home Journal* (women's quality), *Sewanee Review* (high-prestige literary), *McCall's* (women's popular). Plath may range these hierarchically (the top position seems to be occupied at different moments by *The Atlantic*, the *Saturday Evening Post*, in which she never published, or *The New Yorker*), but she will take, with no hint of snobbery, anything she can get. She is even happy to write the same episode (the Matisse-Cathedral story) three times over in different styles.

Many of these magazines are in themselves hybrid, crossing over a range of different discourses and styles. *The Atlantic*, for example, combines liberal political reportage with high literary writing (Auden's lecture on election to the chair of poetry in Oxford in 1957); the *Ladies' Home Journal* combines recipes with selective quotations from the great (male) thinkers of the world (Emerson, Hazlitt and Goethe, to name three); *The New Yorker* combines high literary writing with the codes and jargon of the city streets. Their own status in relation to the multiple codes of the culture could be described in terms similar to those used by the Danish linguist Louis Hjelmslev to describe the hybrid categories which make up the different forms of ideologically acceptable speech:

> . . . belletristic style – a creative style that is a higher value-style; slang – a creative style that is both a higher and a lower value-style; jargon and code – creative styles that are neither higher nor lower value-styles; colloquial language – a normal style that is neither a higher nor a lower value-style; lecture style – a higher value-style that is speech and common language; pulpit style – a higher value-style that is speech and jargon.[31]

Taken together, these magazines are one of the most important sites in the cultural differentiation of language, active in the production of what Hjelmslev here calls higher and lower value-styles. This might also give another significance to the separation by Hughes of Plath's stories into the 'more successful' and the 'other' stories.[32] Amongst the former, stories published in the *Sewanee Review* and the *London Magazine*; amongst the latter, those published in *Seventeen* and *Mademoiselle*. For Plath, on the other hand, writing fiction is a question of negotiating these disparate linguistic or stylistic forms:

> I need a master, several masters. Lawrence, except in *Women in Love*, is too bare, too journalistic in his style. Henry James, too elaborate, too calm and well-mannered. Joyce Cary I like. I have that fresh, brazen, colloquial voice. Or J. D. Salinger. But that needs an 'I' speaker, which is so limiting.[33]

Plath looks for a male master of fiction, and finds them mostly wanting, sometimes suitable, in what they can offer her (her preference goes to the most popular – 'brazen, colloquial' – of the three).[34] Is this the woman writer searching for an authentic female voice, or is it the woman writer as consumer, appraising, judging, rejecting and selecting from the world's great big literary department store?

If we look now, more closely, at what Plath has to say about popular fiction, we find that it does not escape her own form of critique. This is one instance, addressed to the very women's magazines which somewhere else she so intently aims for and desires:

... the latest women's magazines – *McCall's* and the *Ladies'
Home Journal* irony upon irony: *McCall's* the 'magazine of
togetherness', is running a series of articles on illegitimate babies
and abortions, an article called 'Why Men Desert Their Wives';
three stories and articles considered, seriously here, humorously
there, suicide from boredom, despair, or embarrassment. The
serial story by Sloan (*The Man in the Grey Flannel Suit*) Wilson,
is about a miserable middle-aged woman named, significantly
enough, Sylvia, who commits adultery with the man she should
have married twenty years ago but didn't because she was foolish
and didn't realize when he raped her at the age of sixteen that
they were meant for each other – adultery, love affairs, childless
women, incommunicative and sullen couples – 'Can this Marriage be saved?' the psychologist asks of two selfish, stupid,
incompatible people who were idiots to marry in the first place.[35]

The terms of this critique are important. Plath is not only
reproaching these magazines for reinforcing domestic ideology; she
is also commenting on the extent to which they expose its failure
and its price. For feminism, these magazines have been seen as one
of the chief culprits in the propagation of domestic false consciousness, part of an almost conspiratorial drive to push women, after
the war, back into the home (Wylie's 'Momism' has been seen as
partially fuelled by this anxiety about women's social place). Betty
Friedan, in what is generally recognised as the first book of postwar
feminism, *The Feminine Mystique*, gives women's magazines a
central role in the defeat of a first-generation feminism which she
situates before the war.[36] What the passage from Plath suggests,
however, is that these magazines were only partially able – even
assuming this was their fully conscious intention – to paper over the
cracks, the internal strain, of the very ideology they were attempting
to promote. It is the failure of the ideal (suicide from boredom,
embarrassment and despair) and its violence (rape at the age of
sixteen) which Plath reads in the *Ladies' Home Journal* and
*McCall's*.

The most cursory glance at the *Ladies' Home Journal* will
confirm this sense of ideological ambiguity, the way its famous and
unquestionable promotion of domesticity appears as constantly in
danger *from itself*. In the issues I looked at, which include those
which have been seen as most representative of Plath's '*Ladies'*

*Home Journal* "syndrome"', I find a letter from an unmarried mother about prejudice against single mothers, a feature on cruelty in maternity wards, and a short story told from the point of view of a woman dying of tuberculosis, who traces the breakdown of her marriage and her subsequent elopement as a young woman to her mother's rigid adherence to a morality of sexual innocence ('this, of course, implied that a girl's value lay in one attribute only, and that the value of that attribute was in inverse ratio to its use').[37]

Nor does marriage, for all that it remains the unquestioned framework for women, always produce a passive, compliant image of woman's social role. Following a tradition which places the ideal of a caring femininity in a privileged relation to social welfare (extension of the ideal of domesticity outside the home), the magazine carries features on racial deprivation, on the inadequacy of educational resources, and a critique of the 'cult of masculinity' in Germany which argues that it is women's democratic ethic which is needed to prevent Germany from once again becoming 'a highly centralised and autocratically organised military state' (a classic strand of one feminism that gives to women the privilege of the 'ethical' as such).[38] The magazine also publishes an extract from Margaret Mead's *Male and Female* in the year it was published (Plath referred to it as her 'bible'), which has been seen as the only text raising the issue of sexual difference that was available for women in the 1950s, although they preface it with a qualifying note on its value as background knowledge for mothers educating their children for marriage. Marriage is the constant reference point, it is still somewhere the ideal; but it bears all the weight of that (of any) idealisation, ambivalent as an experience for women as well as in the range of its political and historical effects.

Popular women's magazines cannot, therefore, be understood in terms of a monolithic conception of their own project or of the culture which they serve both to reflect and produce. But this ambivalence is met by another – the reader may be critical of an ideology without necessarily being 'immune' to its effects. Criticism does not rule out identification; protest, as we have seen before, is not incompatible with desire. The passage by Plath continues: 'It came over me with a slow wonder that all these articles and stories are based on the idea that passionate and spiritual love is the only thing on earth worth having', but the rest of the sentence shows her condemning, not this objective, only the difficulty of its being achieved: 'and that it is next to impossible to find and even harder to keep, once caught.'[39] In this next-to-impossible task, Plath has, however, succeeded: 'I turned to Ted . . .'. He is, as she puts it later, 'the man the unsatisfied ladies scan the stories in *The Ladies' Home Journal* for, the man women read romantic women's novels for'.[40]

In the passage that comes immediately after that turn to the ideal man ('next to impossible to find and harder to keep once caught'), Plath records this dream:

> I was lifted up, my stomach and face toward earth, as if hung perpendicular in midair of a room with a pole through my middle and someone twirling me about on it. I looked down at Ted's khaki legs stretched out on a chair, and the bodies of faceless people crowding and the room and my whole equilibrium went off, giddy. As I spun and they spun below I heard surgical, distant, stellar voices, discussing me and my experimental predicament and planning what to do next.[41]

Even if Plath herself does not make the connection, the violence of this (pole through the middle) links straight back to the *McCall's* story of rape that she describes on the previous page; it also links to the theme of medical experimentation on women which runs through Plath's writing and which we also saw in Hughes's radio play 'The Wound'; it sounds not unlike the description of doctors and women in childbirth that appears in *The Bell Jar*, as well as in the short story 'Sweetie-Pie and the Gutter Men' which she wrote in 1959, both of which find their echo in that feature from the *Ladies' Home Journal* 'Journal Mothers Testify to Cruelty in Maternity Wards' (all this is clearly not just a component of the inner phantasmagoria of Plath).[42] More important, the whole sequence here culminates in the desire, and the confidence, to write – and to write, moreover, specifically for the women's magazines. In the next entry in the *Journals*: 'I can write for the women's slicks: More and more this comes over me – as *easily* as I wrote for *Seventeen*, while keeping my art intact.'[43] The process goes in circles – *Ladies' Home Journal* as alternately object of desire, critique and identification – identification not just with its contents, but with its writing. Plath, it seems, will pull off the impossible: engage in popular writing without detriment to – without violating – the purity of her art.

The violence that Plath locates in these women's magazines is, however, a central component of romance fiction for women. It can be read not as the inadvertent slippage of the domestic and sexual ideal, but as a central part of the ideal itself. Both Tania Modleski in *Loving with a Vengeance* and Janice Radway in her book on romance fiction, *Reading the Romance*, write about the 'terrorising effect of [the] exemplary masculinity' that these stories represent.[44] Modleski distinguishes between Harlequin romance, in which 'sexual desire is disguised as the desire to dominate or hurt' (the hero gradually reveals that his offensive behaviour was a cover for the vulnerability beneath), and the Gothic romance, in which the heroine marries only to find that her husband 'may or may not be a lunatic or murderer', 'may be revealed as an insane mass murderer of a whole string of previous wives'.[45] Compare Plath coming across Hughes after running out to look for him in the street: 'if he weren't my husband I would have run from him as a killer'.[46] If we think back to the stories that Hughes sent to Plath at the start of their relationship – in particular the murderer who courts the woman living alone in the woods (Gothic) – as well as to her desire, as she represents it, to repair a violence in him (Harlequin), then we can see Plath and Hughes as lifting their most intimate narratives straight out of the heart of mass culture.

Not surprisingly, it is this form of fiction which, perhaps more than any other, has been used to throw into question the idea of popular culture as always collusive with the dominant ideology in its effect (an argument mounted from the left as well as the right). These stories play out the most troubling underside of the domestic and sexual ideal. Why women might read this fiction, whether they take pleasure in it, and if so why – pleasure in masochism or an attempt to ward off, or take control of, danger by first conjuring it up – is not the issue here (I'm not sure what it means to try and answer a question like this). The point is more simple. Behind Plath's desire for the most mundane cultural signifier of domestic and everyday life (the *Ladies' Home Journal*) we find, not the unequivocal reinforcement of a norm, but its most dramatic points of failure, pleasure and risk.

Hence, perhaps, Sadie Peregrine:

A discovery, a name: SADIE PEREGRINE. I had her being Mrs. Whatsis in the beginnings of my Silver Pie-server story. Suddenly she became the heroine of my novel *Falcon Yard*. Oh, the irony. Oh, the character. In the first place: S.P., my initials. Just thought of this. Then, peregrine falcon. Oh, oh. Let nobody have thought of this. And Sadie: sadistic. La. Wanderer. She is enough, this Sadie Peregrine, to write the novel at Yaddo while I fish for bass.[47]

This Sadie Peregrine erupts at that moment at the end of 1959, always represented as pivotal for Plath's writing, when she writes 'Poem for a Birthday'. Crucially, however, for the argument of this chapter, she is the bearer, not of poetry, but of fiction:

> I have written six stories this year, and the three best of them in the last two weeks! (Order: 'Johnny Panic and the Bible of Dreams,' 'The Fifteen Dollar Eagle,' 'The Shadow,' 'Sweetie-Pie and the Gutter Men,' 'Above the Oxbow,' and 'This Earth Our Hospital') . . . I have done this year what I said I would: overcome my fear of facing a blank page day after day, acknowledging myself, in my deepest emotions, a writer, come what may.[48]

Three years earlier, Plath wrote her short story called 'The Wishing Box', which has become well known for its account of a battle of wills between a husband and a wife over the relative superiority of their dreams (it can be read as an allegory for poetic rivalry between Plath and Hughes). This is not the first time Plath represents sexual difference in her short story writing in terms of a struggle over different forms of imagination, a different register, for the man and for the woman, in the world of signs. One of her earliest publications, 'Sunday at the Mintons', which won the 1952 short story competition in *Mademoiselle* (her only earlier publications were two poems in *Seventeen* and *The Christian Science Monitor*), represented the domestic tension between an elderly brother and sister in terms of his oppressive and fastidious precision ('Always when they were small Henry would be making charts and maps . . . reducing things to scale'), her tendency to drift off, muse and dream ('in her mind . . . pictures coming and going on the misty walls, soft and blurred like impressionist paintings').[49] In the first version of this story, the brother drowns, and the sister floats off into the clouds with a 'high-pitched, triumphant, feminine giggle' (it is all fairly benign as her giggle mingles with the 'deep, gurgling chuckle' of her brother), but Plath amends the text for publication by turning this triumph imagined by the text into a product of the sister's imagination inside the text, which the last lines of the story bring back to earth.[50]

In the later story, it is the man who has the prerogative of the imagination, specifically of the world of dreams; the woman either fails to dream or has nightmares, and her inadequacy eventually leads to her suicide. It is the terms of this opposition, in relation to cultural difference, however, that interest me here. Harold's dreams are all high culture – literature, music and poetry: 'I was just remembering those manuscripts I was discussing with William Blake' . . . 'I was just beginning to play the *Emperor Concerto*' . . . 'I was being introduced to a gathering of American poets in the Library of Congress' (the gathering includes William Carlos Williams, Robinson Jeffers and Robert Frost).[51] Harold's dreams are not only *about* high art, they *are* high art: 'Harold's dreams were nothing if not meticulous works of art.'[52] It is through his dreams that Harold propels himself above his station ('a certified accountant with pronounced literary leanings'), giving a cultural, as opposed to the more common sexual, content to the idea of dreaming as the fulfilment of a wish.[53]

The best Agnes can conjure up, on the other hand, is a childhood dream about Superman (she gives up the idea of trying to fool Harold by stealing examples out of Freud's writings on dreams). Eventually, she deals with the problem by starting, voraciously, to read:

> Seized by a kind of ravenous hysteria, she raced through novels, women's magazines, newspapers, and even the anecdotes in her *Joy of Cooking*; she read travel brochures, home appliance circulars, the *Sears Roebuck Catalogue*, the instructions on soap-flake boxes, the blurbs on the back of record-jackets.[54]

When this fails, she begins going to the movies in the afternoons ('it did not matter if she had seen the feature several times previously; the fluid kaleidoscope of forms before her eyes lulled her into a rhythmic trance'[55]), persuades Harold to buy her a television, starts drinking, and finally kills herself. Harold discovers her like the heroine of a romantic film:

> dressed in her favourite princess-style emerald taffeta evening gown . . . Her tranquil features were set in a slight, secret smile of

triumph, as if, in some far country unattainable to mortal men, she were, at last, waltzing with the dark, red-caped prince of her early dreams.[56]

It is a meaning which is also latent to the name Sadie Peregrine: 'Ann Peregrine was as methodical about committing suicide as she was about cleaning house' (the line ends the entry immediately preceding the one where she chooses the name).[57]

It is left totally ambiguous in this story whether popular culture is what destroys Agnes or whether it provides the very means and forms of her escape. She lacks imagination, but she possesses – she seems finally to rejoin – her own romantic ideal. Furthermore, if popular culture is presented as a drug, in the very terms of passivity and lethargy with which it is most commonly condemned by high art ('lulled her into a rhythmic trance'), this very same culture also gives her a form of power: 'she found, with a certain malicious satisfaction, that his face blurred before her gaze, so she could change his features at will'.[58] To this extent, it is the intoxicating power of vulgarity which breaks her out of the deadening, self-sufficient, unchanging reality of *things*: 'she felt choked, smothered by these objects whose bulky pragmatic existence somehow threatened the deepest, most secret roots of her own ephemeral being'.[59]

Compare those last lines from Plath's story with these remarks by Hughes in the Introduction to *Johnny Panic and the Bible of Dreams* in which this story, first published in *Granta* in 1957, was reprinted:

> Some of them [the weaker stories] demonstrate, even more baldly than the stronger stories, just how much the sheer objective presence of things and happenings immobilised her fantasy and invention . . . The blunt fact killed any power or inclination to rearrange it or see it differently.[60]

Hughes's aesthetic judgement almost repeats the terms of 'The Wishing Box'. It is almost as if, in this story of 1956, Plath was already writing out the script, laying bare the implications for the woman, of what Hughes would eventually come to say about this part of her writing. Except that in her version, what releases the woman's imagination from the killing objectivity of the world is not poetry ('this limitation to actual circumstances, which is the prison of so much of her prose, became part of the solidity and truth of her later poems'[61]) but sherry, cinema, Superman and TV. Popular culture kills, but it also saves. The difficult question of women's relationship to that culture, the fact that women cannot so easily dismiss so-called low art in favour of what the culture sanctifies and regards as high, appears here not as a question about the possible destination of Plath's work (the various sites of its publication) but as the content of the text. This is not the first time we have seen Plath anticipating the terms of more recent feminist engagement with problems of sexuality, culture or writing.

In a passage taken out from her early journals, Plath writes about the relationship between cinema, religion and sex.[62] Cinema is the 'twentieth century god', the 'altar at which more Americans spend their money daily, nightly, than ever before', 'reel after vibrating reel of divine life', 'Bible of the masses', substituting 'sex and slaughter' for the 'sin and sulphur' of the pulpits.[63] It is also the site of heterosexual bonding, offering intimacy without inhibition in the audience ('there is no one to be censorious'), images of the perfect couple on the screen.[64] Plath's account of this aspect of the cinema is pastiche and parody, hovering somewhere between women's magazines and soft porn:

> He wants to see 'Kind Hearts and Coronets' and Somerset Maugham's 'Quartet.' So do you. When he comes, you are fresh and apple-scented in the lovely shimmering silk-tie dress with the lavender design on silvery beige background ... The liquid, gleaming lips of movie actresses quiver in kiss after scintillating kiss; full breasts lift under lace, low scallops: sex incarnate, (and the male worshipper feels his mouth go thick and sweat start and the fire start burning in his loins ... and the female worshipper goes limp, thinking how good it would feel if Johnny got tough, even if it was just playing, now and then ... ).[65]

Cinema is sermon and dream machine; its sexual power comes from its ability to intoxicate, the force of its reality effect: 'you go lifting, speeding into the great moving magic of the silver screen which pulls all into itself', into an 'artificially constructed society' which 'to you, is real', or more than real: 'the most wonderful and temporary reality they could ever hope to know'.[66] The inflated hyper-reality of cinema gives rise to the inflated sex: 'the superterrestrial, supercolossal paeans to the good guy, the good girl, the sex organs of America'.[67]

At one level this can be read as a fairly traditional critique of cinema as cultural illusion. Compare Plath: 'the great moving magic of the silver screen which pulls all into itself, lulling with the magnetic other-worldliness all who sit in adoration before it' with Irving Howe on the cinema's 'soothing and dissolving blackness . . . in a nonreligious age'.[68] But its analysis of sexuality makes all the difference. Cinema is transgressive as well as a site (*the* site) for the production of a norm – good girl and good guy as sex incarnate (lifting breasts and getting tough are not the most obvious connotations for 'good'); religion replaced by, or transmuted into, sex (the passage reads at moments like Joyce's description in *Ulysses* of Gerty McDowell on the beach, a pastiche of romantic fiction in itself). Above all in the passage by Plath, through the play in the writing, the woman appears at once as parodying and desiring the stereotype of herself, at the same time as she identifies with both the male and female parts of the exchange. Cinema is pleasure and illusion, but both of these are represented by Plath as ambiguous in their effects. Cinema draws you into something which is too big – too 'good' – to be true. Later in this chapter we will see how, at a crucial point in her writing, cinema appears as neither pleasure nor illusion, but as the bearer of an unmanageable, historical truth.

This reference to cinema is not restricted to Plath's journals and her fiction. It also appears at the heart of – or rather as a sub-text to – the later poetry. The first draft of 'Medusa', one of the poems from *Ariel*, has:

> I could draw no breath,
> Dead and moneyless,
>
> Overexposed, like a photo
> Pale and freeze like the starry cinema
> An insomniac X-ray.
> Who do you think you are?[69]

The final version edits out the reference to the photo and cinema:

> Overexposed, like an X-ray.
> Who do you think you are?[70]

In the first draft, the medical (constant refrain of Plath's writing) is tied to the cinema via their shared link to the photographic machine. The cultural allusion appears right in the centre of the personal drama of the poem. In this case cinema is not pleasure, but the emptying out of all body and comfort (a very different, even more traditional, rhetoric which stresses the inhumanity of the machine). The point, however, is the presence of image, artefact and institution inside a form of poetic writing whose condition of existence is most often seen to reside in its transcendence of all three. Since Plath herself takes out this reference in the final draft of her poem, we might ask what – by way of commentary on the forms and institutions of culture – does this poetic discourse feel it has to get rid of or repress? That repression is not, however, total. Plath does not wholly succeed in getting rid of the 'popular' or 'vulgar' from the *Ariel* poems. More than one critic has commented on the way they constantly shed the anticipated and literary form of discourse. In the expression 'done for' from 'Death and Co.', Alice Ostriker reads 'contempt for literature alongside dread of death': 'the American language rises gap-toothed from the waves'.[71]

It is the issue which could be seen as centrally posed by *The Bell Jar*, Plath's only published novel, which has been something of a bestseller ever since it first appeared in 1963. Where this novel belongs culturally is ambiguous in itself. Plath published it under a pseudonym, Victoria Lucas, with the intention, it is most frequently assumed, of protecting individuals who might recognise themselves in the book (we have already seen in Chapter 3 the problems, legal and familial, that this eventually gave rise to). The pseudonym has in itself been interpreted: as a reference to one of Hughes's cousins, Victoria (Vicky) Farrar and to one of his oldest Cambridge friends, Lucas Myers, or symbolically – victory to the light, or light will prevail.[72] But there is another way of reading that use of a pseudonym by Plath, and that is to link it to all those other pseudonyms – Sandra Peters, Alison Arnold, Sylvan Hughes, and finally Sadie Peregrine – which she takes on at different points throughout her work.[73] This use of pseudonyms reinforces the divisions and differences of the voices in which, formally or generically, she chose to write. It also underlines – or makes even more explicitly part of her own self-representation – the futility of seeking a singular, monologic reading of Plath. But it has a more obvious meaning here in relation to cultural difference, for the pseudonym is one of the hallmarks of popular fiction. Didn't Plath insist to her mother that the book was a mere 'potboiler' – the term used, by those who aim higher, for low-grade fiction, writing without lofty artistic intention or aim?[74] What happens if we take Plath at her word, instead of reading her remark as the sign of moral evasion or guilt?

Reread *The Bell Jar* with this in mind, and it is hard not to see it as a type of pilgrim's progress (peregrination) for girls through the multiple forms and products of twentieth-century cultural life. We could tell the story something like this: A young college girl from New England, with a bestselling novelist as her benefactress, wins a competition to be guest editor on a New York 'intellectual fashion magazine'.[75] During her time there, she interviews famous novelists, reads piles of manuscripts, talks to the editor (who has lunches with short story writers for *The New Yorker*), and gets picked up with her friend by a famous disc jockey who takes them back to his apartment and gives them a round-up of the week's Top Ten. She then attends a banquet held for the guest editors by another women's magazine, *Ladies' Day* ('the big women's magazine that features lush double-page spreads of technicolor meals, with a different theme and locale each month'), where she, and all the other guest editors, are afflicted with food poisoning.[76] Sitting in the cinema later that afternoon watching the premiere of a technicolor football romance, in which all the girls wear dresses 'like something out of *Gone with the Wind*', she becomes violently, and almost fatally, sick.[77] Horrified at the possibility of adverse publicity, *Ladies' Day* sends, by way of apology, twelve copies, one for each of the guest editors, of *The Thirty Best Short Stories of the Year*. During the rest of her time in New York, she tries and fails to lose her virginity and, on a separate occasion, is almost raped. *The Thirty Best Stories* is the only thing, apart from a plastic sunglasses case and a gift of two dozen avocado pears, that she keeps when, having cast her entire wardrobe to the winds (literally), she leaves New York at the end of her assignment and returns home.

Failing to get a place on a short story summer writing course, she slips into a depression, tries to write a novel and gives up, tries — and fails — to read *Finnegans Wake*. The only thing she can bear to read are the local scandal sheets: 'SUICIDE SAVED FROM SEVEN-STOREY LEDGE' 'STARLET SUCCUMBS AFTER SIXTY-EIGHT-HOUR COMA' (she complains that *The Christian Science Monitor*, which 'treated suicides and sex crimes and aeroplane crashes as if they didn't exist', was the only thing she ever saw in the home).[78] Recovering in hospital after a suicide attempt of her own, she then discovers herself as the subject of this very form of writing in a set of clippings presented to her by an old friend admitted to the same hospital: 'SCHOLARSHIP GIRL MISSING. MOTHER WORRIED' . . . 'GIRL FOUND ALIVE' (the same friend also discovers a picture of her in a fashion magazine which she denies is her).[79] The hospital is a private one, paid for by her benefactress, the bestselling novelist, who drives her there, as if she were something of a film star, in a Cadillac. She is finally helped (saved) by a woman psychiatrist who looks like a cross between her mother and Myrna Loy. The title of the book itself contains an allusion to Hollywood – in the famous 1930s movie *Barbary Coast*, the character played by Miriam Hopkins says to the character played by Joel McCrea: 'I was born in a bell jar.'[80]

From the unnamed women's magazine where she is guest editor, to *Ladies' Day*, *The New Yorker*, *The Christian Science Monitor*, the scandal sheets, cinema (technicolor football romances, *Gone With the Wind*, the Bette Davis movie made out of her benefactress's book), and, in passing, the *Reader's Digest*, *Vogue*, and *Life* and *Time* magazines – it is the range and density of cultural reference in *The Bell Jar* that is so striking. In so far as the book can be read as partial autobiography, it is the autobiography of the coming-into-being of a writer across the fragments of contemporary cultural life. Writing is a passage through all the disparate strata of high and low art (James Joyce to the scandal sheets). Esther Greenwood's development is charted as a negotiation of this multiplicity of cultural forms, of which poetry is only one – it is presented as her long-term desire, but it is the novel itself which is the tangible outcome, or product, of the narrative told by the book.

Far more than the male literary tradition, it is popular writing, and especially popular writing by women, which oppresses – and generates – the woman writer in *The Bell Jar*. Lying in the hospital, Esther Greenwood gets a headache as she muses on all the women who have tried, in one way or another, to adopt her: a famous poet, Philomena Guinea (her benefactress), Jay Cee (her New York editor) and an unnamed Christian Science Lady.[81] They are, so to speak, the nightmare from which she is trying to awaken, the hallucinogenic contents or the component drives of her literary unconscious. *The Bell Jar* recounts a violent initiation rite into the service of art. Its famous allegory of despair and regeneration cannot be detached from the repeatedly cited materials of the culture in which it takes shape.

There is another sense in which *The Bell Jar* can be seen as commenting on the conditions of its own cultural production, and that is not so much at the level of explicit reference, but at the level of its writing. We have already seen how to be published in *The New Yorker* represented one of Plath's most important literary ambitions. Although not part of its original formula, fiction writing had become by the 1950s central to the magazine (Plath owned the *New Yorker* anthology of short stories).[82] Commentators have talked of the predictability of this fiction, and have asked what it was, by way of conformity to set themes, that Plath was desiring by having it so repeatedly in her aim.[83] But less has been said about the form of its language, the unmistakable formula of its tone. This piece of writing by Thurber is selected by Dale Kramer in his 1952 book *Ross and The New Yorker* as emblematic – 'the formula shines' – of the best fiction in the magazine:

> My cleaning woman came the next morning and woke me up. I was still feeling bad. I asked her if she knew where I could get a large box.
>
> 'How big a box you want?' she asked.
>
> 'I want a box big enough for me to get inside of,' I said. She looked at me with big, dim eyes. There's something wrong with her glands. She's awful but she has a big heart, which makes it worse. She's unbearable, her husband is sick and her children are sick and she is sick too. I got to thinking how pleasant it would be if I were in a box now, and didn't have to see her. I would be in a box right there and she wouldn't know.[84]

It is a tone – flip, sarcastic, but also suffering, with a point of view almost scientifically distanced from what it observes (condition of the city or of modern life?) – that occurs over and over again in *The Bell Jar*:

> These girls looked awfully bored to me. I saw them on the sun-roof, yawning and painting their nails and trying to keep up their Bermuda tans, and they seemed bored as hell . . . Girls like that make me sick. I'm so jealous I can't speak . . . I guess one of my troubles was Doreen. I'd never known a girl like Doreen before.
>
> I watched Dodo Conway wheel the youngest Conway up and down. She seemed to be doing it for my benefit. Children made me sick. A floorboard creaked, and I ducked down again, just as

Dodo Conway's face, by instinct, or some gift of supernatural hearing, turned on the little pivot of its neck. I felt her gaze peer through the white clapboard and the pink, wallpaper roses and uncover me, crouching there behind the silver pickets of the radiator. I crawled back into bed and pulled the sheet over my head.

Dr. Gordon's features were so perfect he was almost pretty. I hated him the minute I walked in through the door. I had imagined a kind, ugly, intuitive man looking up and saying 'Ah!' in an encouraging way, as if he could see something I couldn't, and then I would find words to tell him how I was so scared, as if I were being stuffed further and further into a black, airless sack with no way out . . . But Doctor Gordon wasn't like that at all. He was young and good-looking, and I could see right away he was conceited.[85]

This is J. D. Salinger as much as Thurber – the diffusion of this style by the 1950s testified to the extent of its literary effect (Salinger himself wrote for *The New Yorker* in turn).[86] The narrator of *The Bell Jar* is haunted by her female literary ancestors (Philomena Guinea and Jay Cee), but it is in these male writers that she seems to find the model for her own style. Above all, Plath's own version of these forms of writing in *The Bell Jar* says something crucial about the way, in terms of literary ambition, she chose to represent herself. She may have desired above all to be a poet (even that is questionable, as we have seen), but she – or the narrator of this novel at least – finds the most appropriate form of expression for that desire in *The New Yorker* house style. Way beyond the narrator's sights at the level of the content of the story ('The man had just sold six stories to *The New Yorker* and six to Jay Cee . . . I was staggered by the thought of the amount of money six stories would probably bring in'[87]), *The New Yorker* surfaces at the level of the writing as the symptomatic fulfilment of a wish. *The Bell Jar* tells the story of a breakdown after the fact, which is given in advance as resolved, and on almost every other page, by its appropriation of this most recognisable (formulaic) of literary styles.

Look a little more clearly at the multiple components of the culture which Plath negotiates in *The Bell Jar*, and what we then find is that this type of self-consciousness is neither unique nor peculiar to her writing. It is in fact the form in which the culture, from *The New Yorker* to Philomena Guinea, constantly thinks or represents itself. On either side of the imaginary line dividing them as high to low, we find both these types of writing providing a continuous commentary on their own cultural self-placement, as well as on the opposite form of culture which gives to each one its purely differential identity and place. Before returning to Plath's short story writing, I want to look at how this works in two women writers who could be seen as representative of the state (high and low) of the art. Jean Stafford has been characterised as something of a female Proust for the high-art pretension and lofty elaboration of her syntax. Olive Higgins Prouty, the model for Philomena Guinea, was the author of popular fiction (*Stella Dallas* and *Now Voyager*, both of which were made into movies, are the best known).

Both these women writers exerted a crucial influence on Plath, but – unlike Virginia Woolf, for example – they are rarely discussed (Stafford is listed by Plath in 1956 as one of the women writers she most wants to write like[88]). I would suggest that this is because these two women fall outside the high cultural lineage most often established for Plath. They trouble – they *embarrass* – that image of Plath as the glorious, isolate apogee of the woman writer's self-realisation in the domain of high art. But it is not just that they belong on the wrong side of the cultural tracks (the case of Stafford is in fact ambiguous), but rather that they draw attention to the problem of cultural difference in their writing. They make it an issue in their work, underscoring the discriminations of culture and, especially for women, their effects. The fact that Prouty paid for Plath's education and her mental recovery in 1953 makes her dismissal especially significant in this context, as if – the point is in a sense obvious – educational, medical and literary patronage could be detached from the art whose material conditions of possibility (at the start of Plath's career at least) it provides.

Even more than Plath's own, Jean Stafford's life story can be told in terms of the divisions and exclusions of culture. Married for a time to Robert Lowell, but never approved or accepted by the Boston Brahmin society to which he belonged, she then wrote herself into that society in *A Boston Adventure*, her first – and some would argue most successful – novel, which describes a working-class girl's adoption by the exclusive literary Bostonian world.[89]

It is, however, her appearance in the anthology of stories from *The New Yorker* that is most relevant here. 'Children Are Bored on Sundays', first published in *The New Yorker* in 1948, could be seen as another version (as the sub-text) for Plath's 'The Wishing Box'.[90] It tells the story of a woman who finds herself in New York at the Metropolitan Museum on a Sunday afternoon, discovers an ex-lover and then panics as she conjures up the vision of cultural privilege that characterises his world. Frantically, she sees the air populated with the images of composers, painters and writers pronouncing judgement on the artists, thinkers and institutions which control the nation's (the world's) cultural and political life: Hindemith, Ernst, Sartre, Beethoven, Rubens, Baudelaire, Stalin, Freud, Kierkegaard, Toynbee, Thoreau, Frazer, Salazar, Roosevelt, Maimonides, Racine, Wallace, Picasso, Henry Luce, Monsignor Sheen, the Atomic Energy Commission and the movie industry (the narrator's ability to list all these figures is one of the things that distinguishes this story from Plath's 'The Wishing Box').

In Stafford's story, the narrator envies and despises, fears and admires, this world: 'her own childhood had not equipped her to read, or to see, or to listen, as theirs had done'.[91] Her 'pretensions' need 'brushing', her 'ambiguities needed to be cleaned', her 'evasions would have to be completely overhauled'.[92] But lack of education is not so much her problem as its partial or incomplete nature, its piecemeal and spoiling effect: 'her education . . . had painted the poor thing up (the looks of her mind) until it looked a mean, hypocritical, promiscuous malcontent, a craven and apologetic fancy woman'.[93] At the end of the story she triumphs for a moment when she manages to persuade her lover to leave the world of culture for a shared whiskey: 'they scrambled hastily toward this profound and pastoral experience'.[94]

The binaries here are glaringly obvious – nature/culture, outdoors/indoors, woman/man, body/mind. What is interesting, however, is that this story, which shows high culture as part of a fully gendered and class-based set of exclusions and differences, should appear inside *The New Yorker* – should, moreover, be one of the stories it selects in order to represent itself. There is of course a sense in which it is one of the self-defining features of New York sophistication to represent itself in terms of its difference from European culture (Kramer describes how Ross of *The New Yorker* prided himself on his lack of education, Thurber as a 'boy from the sticks'). A fuller cultural history than is possible here would need to look at the extent to which American high culture distinguishes itself from European art (as well as at the story of America's appropriation/depoliticisation of the avant-garde in the late 1940s and 1950s).[95] None the less, Stafford's short story can be seen as going over, or reversing, Plath's move in *The Bell Jar* – as a publication it has reached the 'top', but it turns on the privilege that it at once covets and in itself represents, taking it apart, exposing the cost, in terms of sexual and class power, of its own (of Stafford's own) fully literary pretension.

Exactly the same issue is, however, at the heart of Prouty's *Stella Dallas* (the two texts can be seen as mirror-images of each other), where we find the same association between cultural failing and sexual vulgarity, the same opposition between masculine high culture and a culturally and sexually degraded female world.[96] The fact that this bestselling novel should make the problem of culture into an object of its own representation troubles any easy assigning of the book to the domain of low art. Popular it may be, popular may be the destination which it seeks (and achieves), but the object of desire inside the narrative is the very form of culture from which the book, materially, sunders itself.

*Stella Dallas* tells the story of a woman who rises from the factory world by making a good marriage, only to find the cultural difference between herself and her husband forcing them irrevocably apart. Stella Dallas is in no sense without social pretension (it is the reason for her marriage), but she is unwilling to adapt her manners and culture in the way her husband requires. The narrative takes a form of a struggle for possession of their daughter, Laurel, a struggle which is explicitly represented as a battle between the extremes of high and low art:

Laurel never read 'David Copperfield' when her mother was with her. To-day the book, as usual, would be returned to its hiding-place behind the cushion in the little parlor when she had finished with it . . . On the fly-leaf of Laurel's 'David Copperfield' was written: 'To Laurel, from her father' . . . Laurel knew her mother preferred something more modern, when it came to printed matter – informing literature that kept one up-to-date as to what was going on in the world of clothes, and fashion and society; photo-play magazines, with some theater-talk in them, and a few snappy short stories. The table in the bedroom Laurel shared with her mother was always littered with a dog-eared collection of such periodicals.[97]

Laurel does not only have access to high culture, she *is* high culture. The woman her father finally marries compares her to 'a beautifully bound book, in full leather, and hand-tooled in blue and gold' with 'blank pages' which she once bought in Florence 'to write odd bits of poetry in'.[98]

Stella Dallas is vulgar – culturally (to the glossy periodicals are added movies and musical farce), but also in terms of the form of femininity she represents. The trappings, and masquerade, of her femininity are contrasted throughout the book with the natural, uncosmetic womanhood of Helen Morrison, the woman who becomes her husband's second wife. Laurel's love of high culture is expressed according to the same binary of what is natural and what is false: 'To hear her exclaim that she loved reading – the sort of reading he had described for her . . . Some of his seeds, then, had taken root . . . He must plant and plant and plant, then, while it was still the planting season.'[99] As Stella Dallas's sacrificial maternal instinct gradually emerges during the course of the story (she hands over her daughter to her husband's new world so that she can take advantage of its cultural and social privilege), that instinct is described in almost identical terms: 'the maternal instinct must have been growing underneath the surface, and growing according to Nature's own methods . . . for when it did shoot through into the light, the plant was strong and vigorous'.[100]

The story of Stella Dallas can be compared in many ways with that of Emma Bovary, whose adultery as an adult woman is related directly to the 'garbage' that she reads as a young girl ('Libraries of Choice Fiction'), her education in songs whose 'silly words' and 'shoddy music' could not conceal the 'phantasmagoria' of the 'sentimental substratum' beneath. I lift this account of Flaubert's novel out of Bernard Rosenberg's opening article to the 1957 collection *Mass Culture*.[101] Flaubert's novel represents for Rosenberg a parable of the destructive capacity, especially for women, of low art. For Andreas Huyssen, on the other hand, calling up the same novel in his 1986 essay on mass culture and women, what is interesting about *Madame Bovary* is first, its negative association of popular culture and femininity, and then the status it gave Flaubert as the father of modernism: 'an aesthetic based on the uncompromising repudiation of what Emma Bovary loved to read'.[102]

By representing this antagonism inside her novel, Prouty, as it were, internalises the high-art condemnation of what she herself writes (popular culture diagnoses itself, takes on the voice or values of the elite). But it is not only at this level that Prouty occupies such a crucial position in the debates about popular culture with which this chapter began. Her other famous novel, *Now Voyager*, gives a type of narrative for women of Phillip Wylie's 'Mom'.[103] The character appears in Plath's own work in the shape of Mrs Willard in *The Bell Jar*, who dominates, or mothers, her husband and son. Plath specifically mentions Wylie's book in her *Journals* with reference to Dick Norton's mother, on whom Mrs Willard is based: 'subtle feminine snare', 'insidious female domination', 'a sweet, subtle matriarch, to be sure, but nonetheless, a "Mom"'.[104] 'Momism' is already there, too, in Laurel's anxiety in *Stella Dallas* about her father's new woman friend: 'She dreaded the visit. She was suspicious of women, and especially suspicious of mothers.'[105] But it becomes the overwhelming theme, the central struggle, of Prouty's later novel, published in the same year as Wylie's book.

*Now Voyager* is about a New England woman whose life chances, specifically her sexuality, are effectively destroyed by her powerful and possessive mother. Charlotte Vale's mother is a figure of monstrous fantasy, constructed in the image of the wildest nightmare and/or dreams:

> Charlotte found her mother seated in her high-backed Martha Washington armchair, not in the least suggesting a little red wagon, far more resembling a dowager queen seated in state on her throne. Lavender ostrich plumes covered the top of her body. A gorgeous white robe that looked like bleached caracul fur was spread over her knees. Her transformation, pure white and as glossy as spun glass, rested on her head like a crown, rising high and formidable in rainbow-shaped waves. She wore her pearl and diamond dog-collar around her neck, and in her ears pearl and diamond earrings. On her hands, resting on the short arms of the chair, large diamonds, set in gold, scintillated. In contrast to this brilliance, her skin looked dull. It had a brownish cast, and hung limp and lifeless. But there was

nothing limp or lifeless about her eyes. They were steely blue, bright, keen and piercing.[106]

In all the regalia of fairytale wicked queen and phallic woman, this woman rises up in the middle of Prouty's novel as the diametric opposite of the sacrificial all-giving mother of her earlier book. The daughter finally frees herself from her influence, but at the moment when she confronts her, the mother has a seizure and dies. It is as if in this novel, Prouty was representing one possible narrative for the woman of that hideous and grotesque gendering of high and low culture, whose hierarchical discrimination she had taken on in the earlier book. In *Now Voyager*, the mother is a monster (a 'mom') and she must be destroyed, but the cultural history, the contempt for low culture, attached to and productive of that imaging of the mother as deadly, are less centrally the theme of this book. Traces of the basic distinction, however, remain. In *Now Voyager*, it is the mother who represents all money and finery; the daughter, and the man who assiduously courts her, who share a love of good books. The misogyny of *Now Voyager* is in the service of the daughter's right to self-determination in both her sexual and her cultural life. Inside the prim white bindings of her Jane Austen novels, Charlotte Vale conceals her copies of Boccaccio's *Decameron* and Flaubert's *Madame Bovary*.

At the very least, this novel by Prouty – and the cultural sub-text which supports it – throw a new light on that famous tension between Sylvia Plath and her mother by giving it its fully historical and cultural dimension. Speculatively, and with emphasis on the difference between the two moments, we can also pass from this novel's tale of a daughter's breakdown and final emergence from the hold of her mother to Prouty's involvement of Plath's own mother in the breakdown and treatment of Sylvia Plath in 1953. As we saw in Chapter 3, it was psychoanalytic therapy for the rupture it introduced between the mother and daughter, that was the particular focus of Prouty's critique. All the more extraordinary, then, to find in *Now Voyager* psychoanalysis right at the heart of the battle between mother and daughter. Charlotte: 'Dr Jaquith says independence is freedom from subjection, and reliance on one's own will and judgement'; her mother: 'Dr Jaquith. So he's the snake-in-the-grass! . . . I have no use whatsoever for any of these new-fangled alienists and psychoanalysts.' How can we then read the later correspondence over Plath's medical treatment, if not as a case of Prouty's deferred obedience to the mother, as the return of the (cultural) repressed?

Plath's opening to *The Bell Jar* is famous: 'It was a queer, sultry summer, the summer they electrocuted the Rosenbergs, and I didn't know what I was doing in New York.'[107] Later on the day of the execution, Esther remarks to one of the other girls: 'Isn't it awful about the Rosenbergs?' Apparently in agreement, the girl comments: 'It's awful such people should be alive', and then yawns (this is clearly one of the girls who yawn and stretch on the sun-roof).[108] Plath elaborates on this yawn in the passage on the same episode in the *Journals*: 'The largest emotional reaction over the United States will be a rather large, democratic, infinitely bored and casual and complacent yawn.'[109]

This moment situates Plath's novel historically, making its allegory of the vicissitudes of culture part of another collective narrative. It also situates its narrator, Esther Greenwood, politically by tying her horror of New York City into her revulsion at the execution of these alleged Communist spies. In the passage in her *Journals*, Plath relates to the execution of the Rosenbergs to the Cold War's self-defeating logic and rhetoric of violence:

> They were going to kill people with those atomic secrets. It is good for them to die. So that we can have the priority of killing people with those atomic secrets which are so very jealously and specially and inhumanly ours.[110]

In an earlier passage, taken out of the published *Journals*, she goes from Nagasaki ('The United States did that. Our guilt. My country') straight to the Korean War:

> Why do we electrocute men for murdering an individual and then pin a purple heart on them for mass slaughter of someone arbitrarily labelled 'enemy'? Weren't the Russians Communists when they helped us slap down the Germans? And now. What could we do with the Russian nation if we bombed it to bits . . . How could we control them under our 'democratic' system, we, who even now are losing that precious commodity, freedom of speech?[111]

But the reference to the Rosenbergs has another significance in relation to the politics of culture which have been central to the concerns of this chapter. In his book *No Respect*, Andrew Ross describes how the trial, and especially the letters of the Rosenbergs, published as they awaited the result of their appeal against the sentence, became the focus for the battle over the meaning and limits of culture in postwar America.[112] According to one Cold War logic, the intelligentsia was associated with Communism, as the joint threats to the free and homespun values of American democracy and the American mind (it is this logic which produced the defence of popular culture against the European highbrow). But according to another logic, no less firmly entrenched in the Cold War, the threat of Communism was associated with mass culture, defined as petty-bourgeois Stalinised taste. What was most terrifying about the Rosenbergs, as they became the focus of an increasingly intense and perverse humanising attention, was the 'humdrum petty-bourgeois reality of their lives'.[113] It was their normality – foreignness invisibly infiltrating the fabric of everyday life – that was the greatest threat.

The same ambivalence can be seen at the roots of Wylie's Momism – first the mother is sentimentalised as mainstay against outside infiltration, then she becomes the focus of the most terrifying anxiety that the evil resides not outside, but in the bosom of the family itself. As with the Rosenbergs, so with Momism, this enemy on the inside comes to be linked with mass culture (sometimes vulgar, sometimes middlebrow). In this specific set of equations, Momism, Communism, and the democratisation of culture were all lined up as the united antithesis to American civilisation (fear of Communist infiltration as the displaced focus of fears of mass conformity, or anxiety about mass culture as the problem on to which a more fundamental fear of Communism was displaced).[114] For Communism also read Nazism. When Laurel announces to her mother in *Stella Dallas* that she is going to be a stenographer, Stella could not have been 'more shocked if Laurel had said she was going to be a German spy'.[115]

Placed in this context, that 'large, democratic, infinitely bored and casual and complacent yawn' is ambiguous. Plath condemns the execution of the Rosenbergs and the Cold War rhetoric which both provokes and is attached to that event. We have also seen her allying herself on many occasions with the forms of culture to which the Rosenbergs and Communism together were negatively linked. At the same time she takes on some of the very terms of that associated condemnation of the mass, accusing herself, as a student, of being 'part of the incredulous twentieth century public', while 'rebelling' (her word) at identifying herself with the 'pathetic and lethargic city-dweller', as if she were half accepting, or rather rejecting only as the mark of her individuality, this image of the passive and complacent city mind (she is commenting on Jacques Barzun's *Darwin, Marx and Wagner*, which was published in 1941).[116] And down the margins of Ortega Y Gasset's *The Revolt of the Masses*, generally considered to be one of the most reactionary texts on cultural politics of the 1950s, she voices her enthusiastic agreement with its critique of the 'commonplace' in American culture, although she condemns the 'aristocratic bias' of the book.[117]

In the case of Plath, the critique of conformity, of what often went under the name of cultural democratisation, goes hand in hand with her indictment of the political and cultural limits of democracy itself – it is, for her, *the* American 'myth' ('our "democratic" system'). Her personal library may include Gasset and Randall Jarrell's *Poetry and the Age* ('newspapers and magazines and books and motion pictures and radio stations and television stations have destroyed, in a great many people, even the capacity for understanding real poetry, real art of any kind'[118]), but it also includes the 1947 report of the President's Committee on Civil Rights (*To Secure These Rights*), which she glosses in the margins with even more approval or outrage at the prejudice and discrimination it describes.[119] Her essays for her Government class at Smith are a constant critique of 'America', its racism (the forced confessions of Negro criminal suspects), the myth of American freedom (the 1951 conviction of the leaders of the Communist Party), the compulsory saluting of the American flag.[120] 'It is this sort of bigotry', she writes with reference to the first example 'that the Communists reveal as the seamy side of American democracy.' An early unpublished poem sums up this ambivalence: 'I Am An American' is a pastiche-cum-parody of the myth of American democracy which attacks its discriminatory partiality ('the door marked "Members Only"'), while simultaneously bemoaning the totality of its cultural effect ('the Batting Average' . . .'the easy democracy of mind').[121]

Only at one point, in 1956, does America appear unequivocally positive for Plath, when she represents it, in contrast with insular, inbred England, as the land that is big enough for Hughes ('big enough, free enough for his colossal gestures')[122] and an escape from the horror of Suez ('Britain is dead . . . God bless America!')[123] The desire for America therefore arises simultaneously out of proto-fascist fantasy and political objections to British neo-colonialism in action, momentarily suspending her previous critique of American colonialism. Cut from here to December 1961, to the letter she writes when back in England about her depression at the 'terrifying marriage of big business and the military in America'[124] – the full horror of American militarism returns at the point where that fantasy of Hughes is on the point of its imminent collapse (sex and politics in their most intimate relation).

Plath sits ambiguously in these cultural and political debates. The important point, however, is the extent of her participation in them. Her books on culture and politics, with their underlinings and commentaries, are at least as relevant as those books of literature (Auden, Woolf and Yeats) which have received so much more attention – anxiety of influence as much a cultural-political as a literary effect (the writer's difficult self-situating in relation to the tradition that precedes her).

The link between popular culture and politics took another form – a belief that social and political justice would be meted out in the same way that the hero or heroine of popular narrative always get their revenge. According to this logic, the fate of the Rosenbergs was intimately bound up with the fate of narrative, their execution signalling, for one political imaginary, the end of narrative resolution, the end of ending as such. Writing on popular fiction with reference to *The Thorn Birds*, Cora Kaplan comments on her experience of reading *Gone With the Wind*:

> How could the author refuse a happy resolution? . . . *Gone With the Wind* brought home to me what I already knew at a social and political level, had felt powerfully the day the Rosenbergs were executed that life was, could be, unfair and I met this realisation with howls of rage and pain.[125]

Andrew Ross describes how the Popular Front believed that the release of the Rosenbergs was as 'inevitable as the coming of a people's state': 'All they needed was fortitude and faith, or in their own private motto, "courage, confidence and perspective," an outlook exactly reflected and voiced in the populist songs and literature to which they turned' (this is populist rather than popular, but the rhetoric is close).[126] In Plath's short story 'The Shadow', the narrator, finding herself wronged, relates her conviction that 'justice, sooner or later, would right the balance' to her 'favorite radio programs and comic strips'.[127]

Two stories by Plath can act as type of conclusion to this chapter, since they most clearly bring together culture and politics in this sense, show the extent to which they form part of a mutually related set of concerns. 'Superman and Paula Brown's New Snowsuit' was published in the *Smith Review* in 1955; 'The Shadow', written in 1959, was unpublished until *Johnny Panic and the Bible of Dreams* (it is one of the stories authored by Sadie Peregrine).[128] They are linked by the central place they give popular culture, and then by the association they each set up between that culture and the war. In both these stories, political and historic injustice heralds the end of popular myth.

By naming Superman and The Shadow in their titles, these stories situate themselves predominantly along the axis of what Barthes terms the gnomic or referential code – 'in' references, cultural, historical, or political, which assume that the reader is 'in the know'.[129] In 'Superman and Paula Brown's New Snowsuit', Superman comes crashing into the narrator's dreams (this is the story behind the story of 'The Wishing Box'), object of night-time fantasy – 'In the magic whirring of his cape I could hear the wings of a hundred seagulls, the motors of a thousand planes' – and daytime reverie: 'I was not the only worshipper of Superman in our block ... Before supper every night, we listened to Superman together on the radio, and during the day we made up our own adventures on the way to school.'[130]

Superman signifies escape from a mundane reality, but also from the limiting stereotypes, for both sexes, of gender roles ('boys playing baseball' and 'giggling' girls).[131] It allows the narrator and her male companion to be at once superior and on the other side of the law: 'Our Superman games made us outlaws, yet gave us a sense of windy superiority.'[132] Superman appears again in 'The Shadow', one comic among many on: 'Rack on rack of the latest gaudily-covered comic books – *Superman, Wonder Woman, Tom Mix* and

*Mickey Mouse*',[133] whose colours blur when the narrator, ostra-cised for biting the leg of her friend Leroy Kelly, finds herself cold-shouldered in her local candy store. In this story the chief cultural reference is 'The Shadow', one of those 'favourite radio programs' blaring out the message every Sunday afternoon that justice will be done: '"The weed of crime bears *bitter* fruit. Crime does *not* pay." On his program it never did; at least never for more than twenty-five minutes at a stretch. We had no cause to wonder: *Will* the good people win? Only: *How?*.'[134] In both stories, the narrator is accused of some gross childhood crime – pushing Paula Brown in her 'lovely' new birthday snowsuit into a slick of oil; biting her friend, Kelly, on the leg (she did not push Paula Brown; she did bite Kelly, but was impossibly provoked). In both cases, her failure to vindicate herself signifies the simultaneous collapse of her comic heroes', and of her own, moral world.

Both The Shadow and Superman appear in the contemporary debate about culture. For Fiedler, 'The Shadow' expresses a type of dangerous populism, which leads him to qualify his support of popular culture against the middlebrow: 'beneath the veneer of slogans that "crime doesn't pay" and the superficial praise of law and order, the comics do reflect that dark populist faith which Senator McCarthy has exploited'.[135] This accusation of the masses for being responsible for McCarthyism is, as Andrew Ross points out, the underside of Fiedler's apparent espousal of mass culture and part of his move to the right. Superman, on the other hand, appears on the opposite side of the same argument as part of his critique of middle-class censoriousness towards the 'spontaneity and richness' of popular cultural life: 'One who would be ashamed to lecture his masturbating son on the dangers of insanity, is quite prepared to predict the electric chair for the young scoundrel caught with a bootlegged comic.'[136] 'Superman', he concludes is 'our Sadie Thompson'. Sadie Thompson was the prostitute in Somerset Maugham's short story 'Rain', converted by a missionary in Samoa who then sleeps with her and finally commits suicide.[137] The story was made into no fewer than three Hollywood films (remember Plath's allusion to the film of Somerset Maugham's 'Quartet'). What matters here is that association between popular culture and the socially (and sexually) repressed. In Plath's stories, the heroes fight for justice, but they belong to the order of the illicit or culturally taboo: a 'hard won concession' from the narrator's mother ('The Shadow').[138] But note how that link – again – between popular culture and female sexuality in the figure of Sadie Thompson gives another meaning to Plath's Sadie Peregrine.

In Plath's stories, the personal wrong the narrator suffers, the collapse of justice, is given its fullest meaning in the context of the war. In both stories the significant moment of rupture takes place in the cinema when, without the knowledge or against the advice of her mother, she finds herself watching a film of torture in a Japanese prison camp. The prison camp enters straight into her dream world: 'Night after night, as if my shut eyelids were a private movie screen, I saw the same scene come back', ousting the world of The Shadow and Superman.[139] It is the loss of the happy ending: 'The trouble was, in this dream, my sure sense of eventual justice deserted me: the dream incident had lost its original happy ending', and the ushering in of a new, undecipherable, unmanageable order of truth:

> Prepared as I was for the phenomenon of evil in the world, I was not ready to have it expand in this treacherous fashion, like some uncontrollable fungus, beyond the confines of half-hour radio programs, comic-book covers, and Saturday afternoon double features, to drag out past all confident predictions of a smashing-quick finish. I had an ingrained sense of the powers of good protecting me: my parents, the police, the F.B.I., the President, the American Armed Forces, even those symbolic champions of Good from a cloudier hinterland – The Shadow, Superman, and the rest. Not to mention God himself. Surely, with those ranked round me, circle after concentric circle, reaching to infinity, I had nothing to fear. Yet I was afraid. Clearly, in spite of my assiduous study of the world, there was something I had not been told; some piece to the puzzle I did not have in hand.[140]

Loss of order and of coherent meaning – all the insignia of symbolic paternity (God, the President, Superman and the FBI) collapse, propelling the narrator into a different order of the real: 'That was the year the war began, and the real world, and the difference' – the last lines of 'Superman and Paula Brown's New Snowsuit', when the narrator realises she has failed to convince her uncle of her innocence.[141] In both stories, there is no distinction between the historical and the moral complaint.

Once again these links are in no sense exclusive to Plath. They find expression across a range of contemporary cultural forms. In their book *The Fifties: The Way We Really Were*, Douglas Miller and Marion Novak take as one of the most representative novels William Styron's *Lie Down in Darkness*, which starts with the suicide of the central female character, Peyton Loftis, on Nagasaki day.[142] The book then runs backwards in a series of flashbacks, as if the only movement *could* be backwards, to that initiating event.

To all this, however, 'The Shadow' adds a further meaning, binds injustice into another order of difference, the racial or national difference between the Germans and Americans and, by implication, between the Germans and the Jews. The ultimate affront in this story is not that the narrator, Sadie Shafer, is unfairly ostracised for biting Leroy, but the explanation that is finally offered by way of exoneration by his sister: '"My mother says it's not your fault for biting Leroy," she called out in clear, saccharine tones. "My mother says it's because your father's German."'[143] Although she protests that he is not German but from the Polish Corridor, and that even if he were, it can't be his fault as she is the one who bit Leroy and not him, it is all without effect. The sister's explanation becomes a truth passed around the school in hushed voices, whispered nastily to the narrator during class. Nor can her mother's explanations make good this flaw that has opened up irreparably in the world: her father is not German in the sense Leroy's sister meant it, but he is a German citizen and he has been asked to move, for the duration of the war, to a detention camp. It is the collapse, not just of the father's, but of the mother's order of things: 'For the first time the facts were not slanted mother's way, and she was letting me see it', the end of God's justice as the final court of appeal: '"But you said God . . ." I protested feebly. Mother overrode me. "God will let it happen."' At which point Sadie Shafer understands that her mother 'was trying to give me the piece to the puzzle I had not possessed'.[144]

What strange slippage is going on in this story which leads Plath to give to her narrator, accused of German origin and heritage, such a recognisably Jewish name – the same slip which appears in a moment edited out of her *Journals* when, discussing this story, she substitutes 'concentration' for 'detention' camp: 'Write another *New Yorker* story. Or any story. Look up German concentration, I mean American detention camps.'[145] It is the final meaning of Sadie Peregrine to which I wish to draw attention here. In an article on the representation of minorities in magazine fiction in the 1957 collection *Mass Culture*, edited by Rosenberg and White, the authors describe how

Italian-Americans, Jews and Negroes (as opposed to American hyphenates and foreigners with Anglo-Saxon and Nordic backgrounds) always appeared at the bottom of the pile. On Jews and Italian-Americans in particular, on the trouble they represent for the requisite identifications of magazine fiction, they write:

> An editor or publisher who would eagerly accept another variant of the typical boy-meets-girl story starring Julie Briton and Bill Davis would not consider printing the same story if the leading figures in it were called Sadie Horowitz and Abe Goldstein, or Lorenzina Sereno and Sebastian de Grazia.[146]

Plath, it should be noted, has her own version of the last two, taking up the stereotype in the name Tomollilo, which appears as a figure of ridicule no fewer than three times in her fictional writing – as Mrs Tomollilo in 'The Daughters of Blossom Street' – 'Mrs. Tomollilo walks in on me, furious and wet as a witch' – and in *The Bell Jar*: 'She shoved the bed curtains back and revealed a fat young Italian woman on the next bed . . . a mass of tight black curls, starting at her forehead, that rose in a mountainous pompadour and cascaded down her back'; as Mr Tomollilo, one of the customers of the tattooist in 'The Fifteen-Dollar Eagle': 'an extremely small person wearing a wool jacket that drapes his nonexistent shoulders without any attempt at fit or reformation'.[147]

But on the issue of anti-Semitism Plath positions herself very differently. There is of course a direct link between this issue and the Rosenbergs – between Communist and Jew ('symbols of apostasy', as the father puts it in *Lie Down in Darkness*: 'You become a Communist or marry a Jew'[148]). One of her own favourite stories, 'The Perfect Set-Up', published in *Seventeen*, tells the story of an idyllic summer shattered when the friendship she has built up with another babysitter is ended by her own employer on the grounds that the second family are Jews:

> I have been terribly limited hitherto, and my growing strong concepts of the universe have been excluded from my poetry (coming out, I think, most interestingly in my series of *Seventeen* stories about social problems: Jewish question, sororities, etc., which I still admire!).[149]

Go back from this story to the poem 'The Babysitters', with which I began, and we discover their shared sub-text in the racial prejudice lurking behind, carried by, the American ideal. Or go back to *The Bell Jar*, to that *Ladies' Day* collection of *The Thirty Best Short Stories of the Year*, out of which Esther selects or describes only one – the story of the clandestine meetings under a fig tree between a Jewish man and a Catholic nun: 'It seemed to me Buddy Willard and I were like that Jewish man and that nun.'[150] Much has been made of the story of the fig tree in *The Bell Jar* when it appears later in the story, divested of its racial content, as a plethora of branches and possibilities for women – wife and mother, professor, editor, foreign travel, promiscuity, and Olympic crew champion – between which Esther is unable to choose (the American girl spoiled for choice). But at the point where it is still linked to its cultural origins, it signifies not plurality but difference, and the difference not of the sexes, but of race.

This is, I would suggest, with all the force of its specific historical reference, one of the crucial sub-texts of Plath's fiction writing, and indeed of the whole of her work. The central character of 'Mothers', a short story Plath wrote in 1962, hasn't the heart to tell the rector of the country town she has moved to that 'she had been through all this pious trying ten years before, in Comparative Religion classes at college, and only ended up sorry she was not a Jew'.[151] In 1955, Plath describes herself in a letter to her mother as an 'ethical culturalist': 'not really a Christian in the true sense of the word . . . but I am close to the Jewish belief in many ways'.[152] In her journal entry of September 1959, she records a dream: 'Last night I lived among Jews. Religious service, drinking milk from a gold chalice and repeating a name . . . father, Jewish, at head.'[153] According to an unpublished memoir by one of Plath's friends, Elinor Klein (the memoir is included in Aurelia Plath's notes for the Wellesley College Author's Series Talks), Plath said at the start of her relationship with Hughes that his only flaw was the fact that he was not a Jew (lack of Jewishness the only deficiency in the ideal).[154] From a forced identification with the German aggressor in 'The Shadow', Plath propels herself in fantasy into the opposite side. The question arises finally, as to what happened when she did so in the poems – in *the* poem, it could be argued – on which she, most famously and infamously, made her name.

# 6

## 'DADDY'

Who will forgive me for the things I do . . .
I think it would be better to be a Jew.
(Anne Sexton, 'My Friend, My Friend', 1959)

I am lame in the memory.
(Sylvia Plath, 'Little Fugue', 1962)

For a writer who has so consistently produced outrage in her critics, nothing has produced the outrage generated by Sylvia Plath's allusions to the Holocaust in her poetry, and nothing the outrage occasioned by 'Daddy', which is just one of the poems in which those allusions appear. Here is one such critic, important only for the clarity with which he lays out the terms of such a critique. Leon Wieseltier is reviewing Dorothy Rabinowicz's *New Lives: Survivors of the Holocaust* in an article entitled 'In a Universe of Ghosts', published in *The New York Review of Books*:

> Auschwitz bequeathed to all subsequent art perhaps the most arresting of all possible metaphors for extremity, but its availability has been abused. For many it was Sylvia Plath who broke the ice . . . In perhaps her most famous poem, 'Daddy,' she was explicit . . . There can be no disputing the genuineness of the pain here. But the Jews with whom she identifies were victims of something worse than 'weird luck'. Whatever her father did to her, it could not have been what the Germans did to the Jews. The metaphor is inappropriate . . . I do not mean to lift the Holocaust out of the reach of art. Adorno was wrong – poetry *can* be made after Auschwitz and out of it . . . But it cannot be done without hard work and rare resources of the spirit. Familiarity with the hellish subject must be earned, not presupposed. My own feeling is that Sylvia Plath did not earn it, that she did not respect the real incommensurability to her own experience of what took place.[1]

It is worth looking at the central terms on which this passage turns – the objection to Plath's identification with the Jew: 'the Jews with

whom she identifies'; to the terms of that identification for introducing chance into Jewish history (into history): 'victims of something worse than "weird luck"'; above all, to Plath's failure to
recognise the 'incommensurability to her experience of what took
place'. Wieseltier is not alone in this criticism. Similarly, Joyce
Carol Oates objects to Plath 'snatching [her word] metaphors for
her predicament from newspaper headlines'; Seamus Heaney argues
that in poems like 'Lady Lazarus', Plath harnesses the wider cultural
reference to a 'vehemently self-justifying purpose'; Irving Howe
describes the link as 'monstrous, utterly disproportionate'; and
Marjorie Perloff describes Plath's references to the Nazis as 'empty'
and 'histrionic', 'cheap shots', 'topical trappings', 'devices' which
'camouflage' the true personal meaning of the poems in which they
appear.[2] On a separate occasion, Perloff compares Plath unfavourably to Lowell for the absence of any sense of personal or social
history in her work.[3] The two objections seem to cancel and mirror
each other – history is either dearth or surplus, either something
missing from Plath's writing or something which shouldn't be there.

In all these criticisms, the key concept appears to be metaphor –
either Plath trivialises the Holocaust through that essentially personal (it is argued) reference, or she aggrandises her experience by
stealing the historical event. The Wieseltier passage makes it clear,
however, that if the issue is that of metaphor ('Auschwitz
bequeathed to all subsequent art perhaps the most arresting of all
possible metaphors for extremity') what is at stake finally is a
repudiation of metaphor itself – that is, of the necessary difference
or distance between its two terms: 'Whatever her father did to her it
cannot be what the Germans did to the Jews.' Plath's abuse (his
word) of the Holocaust as metaphor (allowing for a moment that
this is what it is) rests on the demand for commensurability, not to
say identity, between image and experience, between language and
event. In aesthetic terms, what Plath is being criticised for is a lack
of 'objective correlative' (Perloff specifically uses the term[4]). But
behind Wieseltier's objection, there is another demand – that only
those who directly experienced the Holocaust have the right to
speak of it – speak of it in what must be, by implication,
non-metaphorical speech. The allusion to Plath in his article is there
finally only to make this distinction – between the testimony of the
survivors represented in Rabinowicz's book and the poetic metaphorisation (unearned, indirect, incommensurate) of Plath.

Turn the opening proposition of this quotation around, therefore, and we can read in it, not that 'Auschwitz bequeathed the
most *arresting* of all possible metaphors for extremity', but that in
relation to literary representation – or at least this conception of it –
Auschwitz is the place where metaphor is *arrested*, where metaphor
is brought to a halt. In this context, the critique of Plath merely
underlines the fact that the Holocaust is the historical event which
puts under greatest pressure – or is most readily available to put
under such pressure – the concept of linguistic figuration. For it can
be argued (it has recently been argued in relation to the critic Paul
de Man) that, faced with the reality of the Holocaust, the idea that
there is an irreducibly figurative dimension to all language is an
evasion, or denial, of the reality of history itself.[5] But we should
immediately add here that in the case of Plath, the question of
metaphor brings with it – is inextricable from – that of fantasy and
identification in so far as the image most fiercely objected to is the
one which projects the speaker of the poem into the place of a Jew.
The problem would seem to be, therefore, not the *slippage* of
meaning, but its *fixing* – not just the idea of an inherent instability,
or metaphoricity, of language, but the very specific fantasy positions which language can be used to move into place. Criticism of
'Daddy' shows the question of fantasy, which has appeared repeatedly as a difficulty in the responses to Plath's writing, in its fullest
historical and political dimension.

In this final chapter, I want to address these objections by asking
what the representation of the Holocaust might tell us about this
relationship between metaphor, fantasy and identification, and then
ask whether Sylvia Plath's 'Daddy' might not mobilise something
about that relationship itself. The issue then becomes not whether
Plath has the right to represent the Holocaust, but what the
presence of the Holocaust in her poetry unleashes, or obliges us to
focus, about representation as such.


To pursue this question, I want first to take a detour through
psychoanalysis, as the discourse which makes language and fantasy
the direct object of its concern – specifically through the 1985
Hamburg Congress of the International Association of Psycho-
Analysis, as the psychoanalytic event which illustrated most acutely
the shared difficulty of language and fantasy in relation to the

Holocaust itself.[6] To say that the Congress was 'about' Nazism and the Holocaust would, however, be a simplification given the conditions and difficulties in which it took place. It was the first Congress of the Association to be held in Germany since the Congress of Wiesbaden in 1932, and it was held in Hamburg only because an original invitation to Berlin had caused such an outcry that it had had to be withdrawn. Hamburg, then, was the result of a compromise, the first of a series of compromises which continued with the organisational committee's decision that Nazism would not be referred to directly − not as history − but only in terms of clinical practice; that is, in terms of what patients who were survivors, the children of survivors or the children of Nazis brought to the psychoanalytic couch.[7] From the very beginning, therefore, and at every level of organisation, it was the problem of direct address, of direct representation, in relation to this historical moment, that was at stake.

Despite that decision to avoid direct historical reference, history and politics erupted on the fringes of the Congress in the inaugural meeting of 'International Psychoanalysts against Nuclear Weapons'. There is of course a direct connection to the Holocaust in the shared terminology: the term 'holocaust' was used to refer to the nuclear threat in 1949 before being projected back on to the camps. There is also a connection at the level of fantasy, made clearest by Hanna Segal's opening address on nuclear rhetoric, which she analysed in terms of the psychotic mechanisms of splitting and denial − the same mechanisms which were being negotiated and renegotiated in the cases described in the papers of the main event.[8] If all this was a sign of compromise, therefore, like all compromise-formations, it spoke as much as it concealed. Specifically, it spoke the fact that experience is no guarantee of memory since the Congress itself, like the cases it transcribed and in transcribing repeated, was so clearly operating under the dual imperative to remember and to forget. The very title of Hanna Segal's paper, 'Silence is the Real Crime', with all that it implied by way of an injunction, a historical urgency, to speak, was matched by the recognition, endlessly rehearsed in the main Congress, that speech itself is the problem, caught up as it is in the very fantasies she was describing, and nowhere more so than in relation to the Holocaust itself.

To say that the Congress was not addressing Nazism directly is, therefore, misleading inasmuch as the Congress found itself acting out, or repeating, the problem – or impossibility – of direct address in relation to Nazism and the Holocaust as such. At the opening session, Janine Chasseguet-Smirgel quoted these famous words from Freud: 'what has been abolished internally returns from the outside in the form of a delusion'.[9] In the memories of the patients, the Holocaust endlessly recurred in the form of such a delusion, demonstrating with painful clarity the detours which lie, of necessity, between memory and this (any) historical event.

No simple memory, therefore, especially for a second generation shown by analysis as in need of remembering to the precise extent that they did not participate concretely in the event. And no simple identification – not for this second generation but, equally and more crucially perhaps, not for the first generation. For if the experience of this generation was, historically, so unequivocal, their identifications at the level of fantasy constantly dislocated that certainty of historical place. I am referring here not only to what one writer described as the 'sacrilege' or 'disjunct parallelism' involved in juxtaposing the cases of the children of survivors to the children of Nazis (and the reverse)[10] but also, and even more, to the internal vicissitudes of identification revealed in the individual case-histories (two papers had the title 'Identification and its Vicissitudes in the Context of the Nazi Phenomenon').[11] Over and over again these patients found themselves in fantasy occupying either side of the victim/aggressor divide. Like the daughter of a German military family caught in a double role as victor and vanquished, and who thus mirrored, her analyst commented, the children of Jewish survivors who identify with the aggressor and victim alike;[12] or the two sons of the Third Reich fathers oscillating between the 'polar extremes of submission and exertion of power' as the 'defence of experiencing oneself as a victim' gradually met up with the 'repressed experience of harbouring the intentions of the perpetrator';[13] or the daughter of a member of the SS whose analyst comments – and not only in relation to her – on the conflict between the 'partial identities of the shame of the victim and the guilt of the culprit'.[14]

Suspended between these partial identities, these patients lived in a world of fantasy where actuality and memory both did and did not correspond (it would be ridiculous to suggest – even in cases of quasi-psychotic denial – that there was no connection between these fantasies and what they had concretely and historically experienced in the past). But what did emerge from these case-histories was that the question of historical participation in no sense exhausted that of identification and of fantasy – it did not settle the question of from where, and in what form, memory takes place. For being a victim does not stop you from identifying with the aggressor; being an aggressor does not stop you from identifying with the victim. To which we can add a formula only deceptively tautological – that being a victim (or aggressor) does not stop you from identifying with the victim (or aggressor). Identification is something that always has to be constructed. Wherever it is that subjects find themselves historically, this will not produce any one, unequivocal, identification as its logical effect.[15]

Look again at the term 'holocaust' and the ambivalence of identification can be seen to reside inside the very term. What special relationship – Zev Garber and Bruce Zuckerman have asked – does the concept of 'holocaust' set up between Nazi and Jew, what idea of supreme or chosen purpose, carrying as it does the biblical meaning of a sacrifice that is divinely inspired?[16] Track the term through Plath's poetry and the word appears first in this earlier biblical sense: 'Then hurl the bare world like a bluegreen ball/back into the holocaust' ('Song For a Revolutionary Love'), 'till the Announcer's voice is lost/in heresies of holocaust' ('Insolent Storm Strikes at the Skull').[17] This meaning persists throughout Plath's writing – it could be said to be the meaning of *Ariel* itself: 'The meaning of Isaiah 29:1–2 seems to be that Jerusalem, here (prophetically?) called Ariel, is to become like an altar, i.e., a scene of holocaust' . . . 'The altar of holocausts is called the "ariel of God".'[18] This also suggests another interpretation of the passage: 'hoping for houses in a holocaust . . .' discussed in Chapter 2 above.

This is not to deny that the oscillations revealed by these patients can be analysed partly in terms of a logic of the event – the perpetrators experience themselves as victims in order both to deny and to legitimate their role (to be a perpetrator you *have* first to 'be' a victim); the victim identifies with the aggressor out of retaliation in a situation where not only psychic but concrete survival is at stake. Primo Levi made this logic central to what he describes as 'ambiguity fatally provoked by oppression' in his last book, *The Drowned and the Saved*, in which he insists that there must be no historical confusion between the two roles ('precious service rendered (intentionally or not) to the negators of truth').[19]

There is no disagreement with this analysis, therefore, even if one suggests that it leaves a residue unexplained. And that is the very process of alternation – what it is that these partial and transferable identities reveal about the workings of fantasy itself. They show subjects taking up positions in the unconscious which are the opposite of the ones they occupy at the level of their conscious life. The one-sidedness of that conscious identity, even where it corresponds to the concretely lived experience (especially where it does so), is what causes the difficulty. The problem for Mrs B, for example, was not just the violence to which she had been subjected in the camps, but the fact that the extremity of it had made it impossible for her to accept those violent and extreme elements in herself.[20] Her need then was to recognise her own participation in the psychic positions she most desired to exclude. For it is the psychic exclusion or repudiation of those positions which, for psychoanalysis, is most likely to precipitate their projection or acting out. Exclusion turns into unconscious repetition.

For Hanna Segal at least, it is this mechanism which constitutes the political as much as the psychic threat. Thus nuclear rhetoric endlessly reproduces and legitimates a violence which it always locates outside itself, whose cause always, and by definition, belongs somewhere else – a rhetoric of violence which mobilises, not aggression (it denies, projects, splits off aggression) but defence. It is these mechanisms which, it can be argued, were at work in Nazism itself, and were rediscovered here in the fantasies of Nazis and their children, and then (risking that 'sacrilege' of 'disjunct parallelism') in those of the survivors and their children in turn. In *Night and Hope*, one of his collections of short stories about the camps, the Czech author Arnost Lustig writes: 'fear was merely the transformation of one's own thoughts into those of the enemy'.[21]

Projection is not, therefore, something that we can safely locate in the world of the psychotic alone. In his discussion of Schreber, Freud wrote:

> . . . [projection] has a regular share assigned to it in our attitude towards the external world. For when we refer the causes of certain sensations to the external world, instead of looking for

211

them (as we do in the case of others) inside ourselves, this normal proceeding, too, deserves to be called projection.[22]

As if he was suggesting that the way we distribute causality – the way we distinguish – between ourselves and others is something of a paranoid mechanism in itself. Think back to that analysis of Plath as answerable for everything in her life, to the battle that has constantly taken place around her over the location (inner or outer) of the cause, and her story can then be read as a saga of projection, whose fullest historical ramifications can be traced out beneath the surface of responses to, as well as inside, her late texts. Against the entire logic that has so often been brought to bear on Plath as woman and as writer, these cases suggest that psychological innocence is not guaranteed by the historical attribution of guilt (nor the reverse).

Is it going too far to suggest that what is being asked for in the cases described at the Hamburg Congress is a further act of identification, or rather a recognition on the part of these subjects that such an identification has *already* taken place? In the field of sexuality, such a demand has become fairly well known. As Freud puts it with reference to homosexual object-choice: 'By studying sexual excitations other than those that are manifestly displayed, [psychoanalytic research] has found that all human beings are capable of making a homosexual object-choice and *have in fact made one* in their unconscious' (my emphasis).[23] 'Recognise that unconscious desire' has become a commonplace of a recent sexual political version of Freud, meaning: 'Beyond that apparently assumed heterosexual identity in which you think you know yourself so well, know your unconscious participation in its other side.' For it is the homophobic who is most deeply and compulsively involved in the repudiation of homosexuality in him/herself (the social implications of such a general recognition would clearly be vast).

But what happens if we extend that demand beyond the world of neurosis and repression to that of psychosis and projection, where it is not a socially outlawed object of desire but a psychically and ethically unmanageable identification which is at stake? Could it be that the very different encounter between psychoanalysis and politics precipitated here (partially and tardily of necessity) by the Holocaust cannot help but produce this demand as its effect? Note

212

just how far this takes us from those who criticise Plath for putting herself in the wrong place in 'Daddy', for putting herself – the two are, as we will see, inseparable in her poem – in the place of the Nazi as well as in the place of the Jew.

Go back once again to that criticism of Plath, specifically on the issue of metaphor, and it then appears that such a demand, such an identification, relies on the possibility of metaphor: the problem is not the presence of metaphor, but the risk that metaphor, along with the possibility of language itself, may be lost. Loss of metaphor is in itself a form of defence which threatens memory and identification alike. This is the central point of a paper by Ilse Grubrich-Simitis, 'From Concretism to Metaphor: Thoughts on Some Theoretical and Technical Aspects of the Psychoanalytic Work with Children of Holocaust Survivors', a paper not given at the Congress but one to which several of the other papers referred.[24] According to Grubrich-Simitis, the problem for these children of survivors is that the metaphoric function is *impaired*. They reify language into an object world whose blunt and repetitious literality, whose loss of figurality, signals the impossibility for these patients of grasping the nature of the event. They regard what they say as 'thinglike', unable to see it as 'something imagined or remembered', as something having the character of a sign.[25] As one analyst at the Congress put it, with direct reference to the paper: losing metaphor, they have lost that function 'without which the origins of language are unthinkable'.[26] Take metaphor out of language and there is no memory, no history, left.

In the analytic setting, this requires a return to the event, to what Grubrich-Simitis calls a 'non-metaphorical' recognition that it took place (a reversal, as she acknowledges, of that famous and infamous move from actuality to fantasy made by Freud).[27] But this return is made in order to *restore* the function of metaphor, to release the essentially metaphorical work of analysis itself: 'alongside poetry perhaps the metaphorical enterprise *par excellence*'.[28] Only in this way will these patients be freed from the literalness of a language which makes memory impossible – which, paradoxically, is the sign that they have no real knowledge that the Holocaust even took place. Only in this way, too, will they be able to acknowledge the aggressive side of fantasy which the loss of metaphor allows them simultaneously to erase. For metaphor is the recognition and suspension of aggression (the second as the condition of the first),

213

allowing the subject to take up any one of these propositions in turn:

I want X but I do not intend to do it
I want X but I am not doing it
I do X (in fantasy) but I do not (actually) do it
I want X but I do not want to want it

– all mutations of an unspeakable desire, or rather one that can be spoken only to the extent that, as in analysis, as in poetry (the poetry of Plath, for example), it remains within the bounds of speech.

There is a sense here, therefore, in which we can truly say that metaphor was arrested in Auschwitz, in so far as the figural possibilities of language, without which 'the origins of language are unthinkable', are one of the things that the Holocaust put at risk. We can turn that criticism of Plath around again and ask: not whether the Holocaust is 'abused' by metaphor, but rather under what conditions of representation can the fantasies underpinning metaphor itself be spoken?

There is of course an inverse position on the representation of the Holocaust which situates it on the other side of representation itself, and can sometimes take the form of a *privileging* of poetry. According to Hannah Arendt, the judges at the trial of Eichmann rested their right to judge him on the distinction between 'deeds and motives' that belonged in the courtroom, and 'sufferings on so gigantic a scale' as to be '"beyond human understanding"', a matter for the '"great authors and poets"' of the world.[29] When George Steiner praises 'Daddy' as the 'Guernica of modern poetry', he makes the same point: 'perhaps it is only those who had no part in the events who *can* focus on them rationally and imaginatively' (Wieseltier takes issue with Steiner specifically on this).[30] Steiner underlines the metaphoric status of Plath's writing in the poem: 'committing the whole of her poetic and formal authority to metaphor, to the mask of language'; but in doing so seems to attribute the fact of metaphor to poetic language alone. For the Holocaust theologian Emil Fackenheim, the Holocaust is a 'more than poetic truth', a truth that can be measured only by its failure to represent itself: 'each and every explanation is false, if not downright obscene, unless it is accompanied by a sense of utter inadequacy'.[31]

In this case, literature has become the repository for the non-representability of the event. For both positions, however – the rejection of metaphor, the demand for poetic representation alone – the Holocaust seems to be placed outside the domain of language proper, either in the before or beyond of language itself. The question of uniqueness and particularity is latent to the debate about language. The Holocaust can only represent itself, the Holocaust can only fail to be represented. The singularity of the Holocaust is that it is proper only to itself. Without taking sides in the dispute over the uniqueness of the Holocaust, we can notice its implications for – or rather, the extent of its implication *in* – the problem of what can and cannot, what should and should not, be represented in speech. Compare these lines from Karl Kraus, cited in one of the papers at the Hamburg Congress:

> Don't ask me why all this time I never spoke.
> Worldless am I,
> and won't say why . . .
> The word expired when that world awoke.[32]

With these lines from the epigraph to Primo Levi's *If This Is A Man*:

> I commend these words to you . . .
> Repeat them to your children,
>   Or may your house fall apart,
>   May illness impede you,
>   May your children turn their faces from you.[33]

An end to language that can be figured only in words, and an injunction to speech, to bear a witness whose impossibility Levi himself has described: 'I must repeat – we, the survivors, are not the true witnesses'.[34] Compare Paul Celan: 'Niemand/zeugt für den/Zeugen' ('Aschenglorie':'No one/bears witness/for the witness').[35] How can one argue that certain writers do, or do not, have the right to represent the Holocaust, unless one has settled in advance, or suspended, these most fundamental paradoxes that the Holocaust opens up at the heart of language?

One more term, finally, from the criticism of Plath with which this chapter began – the concept of luck ('The Jews with whom she identifies were victims of something worse than "weird luck"'). It can be set against a moment from another representation of the Holocaust by the Ukrainian writer Piotr Rawicz, a survivor of the camps. At the end of his 1961 novel *Le sang du ciel* (translated in 1964 as *Blood From the Sky*), he adds this postscript:

> This book is not a historical record. If the notion of chance (like most other notions) did not strike the author as absurd, he would gladly say that any reference to a particular period, territory or race is purely coincidental. The events that he describes could crop up in any place, at any time, in the minds of any man, planet, mineral . . .[36]

By introducing the element of chance back into the story, Rawicz opens up the issue of who should be able – who should be required – to recognise themselves in what took place. As he himself has argued in debate with Fackenheim, the experience of the Holocaust exceeds concrete participation in the event: 'those who physically lived through the Holocaust are not the only ones who experienced it'.[37] This observation is merely the other side of the recognition that experience and memory do not simply coincide. Note too the date of Rawicz's novel (1961), the historical gap which it signals between event and memory, between memory and writing. Add to this book a list of the other novels of the Holocaust that appeared in the early 1960s – Josef Bor's *Terezin Requiem* (1963), Elie Wiesel's *Night* (1960), Ilse Aichinger's *Herod's Children* (1963) – and we start to get a sense of the general, collective nature of that delay.[38] All these books are discussed in Alvarez's article 'Literature of the Holocaust', first published in *Commentary* in 1964, and reprinted in *Beyond All This Fiddle*, the collection which also includes the article he wrote on Plath at the time of her death.[39] If, therefore, the Holocaust appears as historical reference only in the last years of Plath's writing, the delay is coincident with the memory of the survivors themselves. Her tardiness mimics, or chimes in with, their own.

Forget in order to remember. Somewhere in the trials of this process, Plath's writing – at the most basic level – finds its place. Remember Hughes's statement on his destruction of Plath's last journals: that forgetting, the destruction of memory, was essential in order to survive: 'Two more notebooks *survived* for a while' . . . 'in those days I regarded forgetfulness as essential to *survival*' (my emphasis).[40] The repetition is eloquent of the internal contradiction of this statement (its self-abolition?), which Hughes partly seems to recognise himself: 'in those days'. Annotating T.S. Eliot's *Four*

*Quartets*, Plath writes: 'We live by memory of the past (the dead).'[41]

To all of this must be added another point of instability, and that is the instability of Jewishness itself. In his essay on Paul Celan, Jacques Derrida links this hesitancy of identity, of self-situating in relation to the Jew, to the question of holding, naming, remembering a moment by dating it in time. On 'Conversation in the Mountains' – the line 'July is not July' – he comments:

> This is in the course of a meditation on the Jew, son of a Jew, whose name is 'unpronounceable,' and who has nothing of his own, nothing that is not borrowed, so that, like a date, what is proper to the Jew is to have no property or essence. Jewish is not Jewish.[42]

But that very instability – of Jewishness and of the date – establishes the conditions of a general recognition: 'The Jew is also the other, myself and the other; I am Jewish in saying: the Jew is the other who has no essence, who has nothing of his own or whose essence is not to have one.'[43] Hence both the 'alleged universality of Jewish witness ("All the poets are Jews," says Marina Tsvetayeva, cited in epigraph to "Und mit dem Buch aus Tarussa") and the incommunicable secret of the Judaic idiom, the singularity of its "unpronounceable name"'.[44] What I am focusing on here, however, what I read in Plath, is a related but distinct form of uncertainty – the point at which the abyss at the centre of Jewish identity, for the one who is Jewish and not Jewish, appears in the form of a drama about psychic aggression and guilt.

Most obviously, this is the subject of Anne Sexton's poem 'My Friend, My Friend', on which, it has been argued, Plath's 'Daddy' was based.[45] The poem was written in the year Sexton and Plath attended Lowell's poetry class in Boston together. In this poem, Jewish is an enviable state. It confers origin and divine paternity – the conditions of forgiveness for a crime that is never named:

> Who will forgive me for the things I do?
> With no special legend or God to refer to,
> With my calm white pedigree, my yankee kin.
> I think it would be better to be a Jew.

Victim, without agency, the Jew escapes the burden of historic (of any) guilt:

> I forgive you for what you did not do.
> I am impossibly guilty. Unlike you,
> My friend, I cannot blame my origin
> With no special legend or God to refer to.

For the speaker of this poem, Jewishness offers the possibility of a symbolic deferral of guilt. Blaming one's origin – the poem makes its own diagnosis – is nothing less than the ultimate, divinely sanctioned, attribution, or projection, of the cause. Victimisation becomes an advantage of which its bearer can then be *accused*: 'I forgive you for what you did not do'. The total innocence of the Jew, for the one who is not Jewish, turns into a form of guilt. According to the strictest logic of projection, the Jew becomes culpable for the fact that she cannot be blamed.

As the poem progresses, the guilt comes to centre on the death of the mother, a death experienced as the 'first release' of the speaker of the poem:

> Watching my mother slowly die I knew
> My first release. I wish some ancient bugaboo
> Followed me. But my sin is always my sin.

This is the only content attributed, albeit indirectly, to that impossible burden of guilt, other than the guilt, collective, of simply not being a Jew: 'my calm white pedigree, my yankee kin'. At another level, guilt can remain without content, precisely in so far as it takes the form of a relentless self-accusation, one that the speaker of the poem makes over and again of herself: the repeated refrain 'Who will forgive me for the things I do?', to which the line 'I think it would be better to be a Jew' comes as the repeated reply. In this little-known poem by Anne Sexton, only recently unearthed from the *Antioch Review* of 1959 and published in a selection of her work, Jewishness is offered unequivocally, if not unapologetically, as an object of desire. It is as if Sexton is answering in advance those who criticise Plath on the grounds that her identification with the Jew serves some personal purpose. For what could be an identification *without* purpose? In Sexton's poem, the desire to be Jewish reveals the tendentiousness (and guilt) of identification as such.

In Sexton's poem, the guilt centres on the mother. By transposing the dilemma on to the father, Plath shifts this drama into the realm of symbolic as well as personal law. The father carries the weight, not only of guilt, but of historic memory. In 'Little Fugue', one of the less well known poems from *Ariel* and forerunner of 'Daddy', Plath presents the relation to the father most directly in terms of a language or communication that fails:

> The yew's black fingers wag;
> Cold clouds go over.
> So the deaf and dumb
> Signal the blind, and are ignored.[46]

In fact the poem does not start with failed communication, but with the complete loss of the physical conditions that make communication possible. Deaf and dumb signalling to blind – there are no words here, and what there is in the place of words still goes astray. Likewise, the memory of the speaker's father takes the form of a confusion in the register of signs:

> Deafness is something else.
> Such a dark funnel, my father!
> I see your voice
> Black and leafy, as in my childhood.
>
> A yew hedge of orders,
> Gothic and barbarous, pure German.
> Dead men cry from it.
> I am guilty of nothing.

What does it mean here to 'see a voice'? To be deaf to it? – not in the sense of hearing nothing, but of hearing, of seeing too much. That voice is pure German, a surfeit of orders that is full of the cries of dead men. The poem proposes an impossible alternative at the level of language: signs that are empty because they cannot be heard, either by those who utter or by those who fail to see them, and a language pure only in its powers of destruction, which can speak finally only from the place of the dead. Before the first of these two stanzas, the original draft has: 'The yew is many-footed./ Each foot stops a mouth./ So the yew is a go-between: talks for the dead.' According to Robert Graves, there is a belief in Brittany that churchyard yews spread a root to the mouth of each corpse.[47]

In all this, guilt is not located. Isolated at the end of the verse, the line 'I am guilty of nothing' can be read back retroactively into the cries of the dead men heard in the voice of the father, into – as a consequence – the father's own voice, or into the voice of the speaker herself. The line works at once as denial and as plaint. Doubling over or disappearing into itself as utterance – dead men inside the voice of the father inside the voice of the poet who speaks – it stages a crisis in the historical location of guilt. Plath removes from the first draft at the start of the stanza: 'This dominates me', which offers a more exact, more precisely and directly oppressive, distribution of roles.

In fact, 'Little Fugue' repeatedly unsettles the subjective positions on which such a distribution depends. In the second stanza of the poem, the yew's 'black fingers' meet the 'featurelessness' of a cloud that is 'white as an eye all over!/ The eye of the blind pianist'. Black and white, yew and eye, you and I – in the finger alphabet described by Graves, the letter of the yew tree is the 'I' which is also the death vowel. Death belongs on either side of the binaries – yew/eye: you/I – on which the poem repeatedly puns. It slides from the yew tree to the father, but then, since 'yew' equals 'I', on to the speaker herself. The slippage of the pronouns produces an identity between the speaker and the father she accuses. In 'Little Fugue', therefore, the relationship to the father belongs on the axis of identification, as much as – in this poem to the exclusion of – that of desire (this point will be crucial for 'Daddy').

But if the poem produces such a radical destabilisation, such an unsettling of its enunciative place, it equally offers a more direct sequence, something in the order of a transmission or inheritance passed from the father to the child. The speaker takes on, finds herself forced to utter, words silenced by her father's refusal to speak:

> And you, during the Great War
> In the California delicatessen
>
> Lopping the sausages!
> They color my sleep,
> Red, mottled like cut necks.
> There was a silence!
>
> Great silence of another order.
> I was seven, I knew nothing.

The world occurred.
You had one leg, and a Prussian mind.

Now similar clouds
Are spreading their vacuous sheets.
Do you say nothing?
I am lame in the memory.

The sequence seems to offer a narrative of silence. This silence
ensures that the war can be known only in the sleep of the child who
did not live through it, the same child for whom it also represents
the coming into being of the world: 'I was seven, I knew nothing./
The world occurred.' It cripples the speaker's memory, maims her
like her one-legged father. The identification between them is only
one part of a repetition already guaranteed by the fact that what
happened has still not been spoken in words. As the poem shifts
from the general 'There was a silence!' to the particular 'Do you say
nothing?', the father's silence becomes accountable for the speaker's
inability to write her own history – 'I am lame in the memory' – as
well as for the destiny of the world: 'Now similar clouds/ Are
spreading their vacuous sheets'. In an article published in *Encounter*
in September 1963, 'In Search of a Lost Language', Hans Magnus
Enzensberger describes Germany as 'mute', a 'speechless country' –
hence the linguistic paralysis which afflicted German poets after the
war.[48] The silence figured in this poem thus mimics, as Judith Kroll
has pointed out, a more general postwar silence that was laid on the
German tongue. This silence can therefore be called historical in
two senses – accountable for the future, a product of the trauma of
the past. The tense of 'Little Fugue' then becomes the psychoanalytic tense of the future perfect: 'What I shall have been for what I
am in the process of becoming'.[49] Remembering for the future – the
very formula that has been chosen for returning to the Holocaust
today.[50]

To argue that the personal accusation against the father is part of
a more collective dilemma about memory is not, however, to
substitute a historical for the more common, personal and psychological reading of Plath's work (the alternative that Perloff seems to
propose) but to suggest that Plath is writing from a place where they
are precisely inseparable. As a title, 'Little Fugue' condenses these
different levels in itself – fugue as (historic) flight, fugue as a
technical term for psychological amnesia, a temporary flight from

reality, according to Webster (cause and/or effect of the first), as well as the music of the blind pianist (a little, not gross, fugue). The last lines of the poem are particularly apposite here:

> I survive the while
> Arranging my morning.
> These are my fingers, this my baby.
> The clouds are a marriage dress, of that pallor.

They move the poem into the speaker's personal present – temporary survivor: 'I survive the while'. So easily reduced, after the fact, to the level of personal, biographical premonition (only a while to survive), the line can equally be read as 'this transitional time is the medium in which – or what – I have to survive'. Note too the allusion to the line 'I sing the while' from Blake's 'Infant Joy', an allusion which evokes a poetic and linguistic tradition in which the speaker cannot take her place: she does not sing to her child, she *only* survives (like the Holocaust survivor who, until approximately this moment, survives but does not speak). The dilemma is thus both more and less than the dilemma of the woman writer oppressed by a male tradition in which she cannot find her voice. Likewise, 'Arranging my morning' – the speaker prepares her death (arranging her own mourning), or the speaker completes a mourning that has been historically denied: 'The second generation mourns the denied mourning of their parents' (Hillel Klein and Ilany Kogan, 'Identification Processes and Denial in the Shadow of Nazism').[51]

In 'Little Fugue', the personal present is engendered in its possibility – provisional, precarious – by the drama of a fully historical past. To say, in this context, that Plath uses history as metaphor is to establish a hierarchy of levels – the historic simply signifies the personal drama – and by implication a hierarchy of values between the two levels, which overlooks something presented here more as a sequence, more in the nature of a logic of the event. Inside that sequence, the form of determination between the historic and the psychic instance is impossible to pin down in any easy way. What the poem seems to narrate is at once the historical engendering of personal time and the psychic engendering of history.

'Daddy' is a much more difficult poem to write about.[52] It is of course the poem of the murder of the father which at the very least raises the psychic stakes. It is, quite simply, the more aggressive poem. Hence, no doubt, its founding status in the mythology of Sylvia Plath. Reviewing the American publication of *Ariel* in 1966, *Time* magazine wrote:

> Within a week of her death, intellectual London was hunched over copies of a strange and terrible poem she had written during her last sick slide toward suicide. 'Daddy' was its title; its subject was her morbid love-hatred of her father; its style was as brutal as a truncheon. What is more, 'Daddy' was merely the first jet of flame from a literary dragon who in the last months of her life breathed a burning river of bale across the literary landscape.[53]

Writing on the Holocaust, Jean-François Lyotard suggests that two motifs tend to operate in tension, or to the mutual exclusion of each other – the preservation of memory against forgetfulness and the accomplishment of vengeance.[54] Do 'Little Fugue' and 'Daddy' take up the two motifs one after the other, or do they present something of their mutual relation, the psychic economy that ties them even as it forces them apart? There is a much clearer narrative in 'Daddy' – from victimisation to revenge. In this case it is the form of that sequence which has allowed the poem to be read purely personally as Plath's vindictive assault on Otto Plath and Ted Hughes (the transition from the first to the second mirroring the biographical pattern of her life). Once again, however, it is only that preliminary privileging of the personal which allows the reproach for her evocation of history – more strongly this time, because this is the poem in which Plath identifies with the Jew.

The first thing to notice is the trouble in the time sequence of this poem in relation to the father, the technically impossible temporality which lies at the centre of the story it tells, which echoes that earlier impossibility of language in 'Little Fugue':

### DADDY

You do not do, you do not do
Any more, black shoe
In which I have lived like a foot
For thirty years, poor and white,
Barely daring to breathe, or Achoo.

Daddy, I have had to kill you.
You died before I had time –

223

Marble-heavy, a bag full of God,
Ghastly statue, with one gray toe
Big as a Frisco seal

And a head in the freakish Atlantic
Where it pours bean green over blue
In the waters off beautiful Nauset.
I used to pray to recover you.
Ach, du.

What is the time sequence of these verses? On the one hand, a time of unequivocal resolution, the end of the line, a story that once and for all will be brought to a close: 'You do not do, you do not do/ Any more'. This story is legendary. It is the great emancipatory narrative of liberation which brings, some would argue, all history to an end. In this case, it assimilates, combines into one entity, more than one form of oppression – daughter and father, poor and rich – licensing a reading which makes of the first the meta-narrative of all forms of inequality (patriarchy the cause of all other types of oppression, which it then subordinates to itself). The poem thus presents itself as protest and emancipation from a condition which reduces the one oppressed to the barest minimum of human, but inarticulate, life: 'Barely daring to breathe or Achoo' (it is hard not to read here a reference to Plath's sinusitis). Blocked, hardly daring to breathe or to sneeze, this body suffers because the father has for too long oppressed.

If the poem stopped here then it could fairly be read, as it has often been read, in triumphalist terms – instead of which it suggests that such an ending is only a beginning, or repetition, which immediately finds itself up against a wholly other order of time: 'Daddy, I have had to kill you./ You died before I had time.' In Freudian terms, this is the time of '*Nachtraglichkeit*' or after-effect: a murder which has taken place, but after the fact, because the father who is killed is already dead; a father who was once mourned ('I used to pray to recover you') but whose recovery has already been signalled, by what precedes it in the poem, as the precondition for his death to be repeated. Narrative as repetition – it is a familiar drama in which the father must be killed in so far as he is already dead. This at the very least suggests that, if this is the personal father, it is also what psychoanalysis terms the father of individual prehistory, the father who establishes the very possibility (or

224

impossibility) of history as such.[55] It is through this father that the subject discovers – or fails to discover – her own history, as at once personal and part of a wider symbolic place. The time of historical emancipation immediately finds itself up against the problem of a no less historical, but less certain, psychic time.

This is the father as godhead, as origin of the nation and the word – graphically figured in the image of the paternal body in bits and pieces spreading across the American nation state: bag full of God, head in the Atlantic, big as a Frisco seal. Julia Kristeva terms this father '*Père imaginaire*', which she then abbreviates 'PI'.[56] Say those initials out loud in French and what you get is 'pays' (country or nation) – the concept of the exile. Much has been made of Plath as an exile, as she goes back and forth between England and the United States. But there is another history of migration, another prehistory, which this one overlays – of her father, born in Grabow, the Polish Corridor, and her mother's Austrian descent: 'you are talking to me as a general American. In particular, my background is, may I say, German and Austrian.'[57]

If this poem is in some sense about the death of the father, a death both willed and premature, it is no less about the death of language. Returning to the roots of language, it discovers a personal and political history (the one as indistinguishable from the other) which once again fails to enter into words:

> In the German tongue, in the Polish town
> Scraped flat by the roller
> Of wars, wars, wars.
> But the name of the town is common.
> My Polack friend
>
> Says there are a dozen or two.
> So I never could tell where you
> Put your foot, your root,
> I never could talk to you.
> The tongue stuck in my jaw.
>
> It stuck in a barb wire snare.
> Ich, ich, ich, ich,
> I could hardly speak.
> I thought every German was you.
> And the language obscene

Twice over, the origins of the father, physically and in language, are lost – through the wars which scrape flat German tongue and Polish town, and then through the name of the town itself, which is so common that it fails in its function to identify, fails in fact to name. Compare Claude Lanzmann, the film-maker of *Shoah*, on the Holocaust as 'a crime to forget the name', or Lyotard: 'the destruction of whole worlds of names'.[58] Wars wipe out names, the father cannot be spoken to, and the child cannot talk, except to repeat endlessly, in a destroyed obscene language, the most basic or minimal unit of self-identity in speech: 'ich, ich, ich, ich' (the first draft has 'incestuous' for 'obscene'). The notorious difficulty of the first-person pronoun in relation to identity – its status as shifter, the division or splitting of the subject which it both carries and denies – is merely compounded by its repetition here. In a passage taken out of her journals, Plath comments on this 'I':

> I wouldn't be I. But I am I now; and so many other millions are so irretrievably their own special variety of 'I' that I can hardly bear to think of it. I: how firm a letter; how reassuring the three strokes: one vertical, proud and assertive, and then the two short horizontal lines in quick, smug, succession. The pen scratches on the paper I . . . I . . . I . . . I . . . I . . . I.[59]

The effect, of course, if you read it aloud, is not one of assertion but, as with 'ich, ich, ich, ich', of the word sticking in the throat. Pass from that trauma of the 'I' back to the father as a 'bag full of God', and 'Daddy' becomes strikingly resonant of the case of a woman patient described at Hamburg, suspended between two utterances: 'I am God's daughter' and 'I do not know what I am' (she was the daughter of a member of Himmler's SS).[60]

In the poem, the 'I' moves backwards and forwards between German and English, as does the 'you' ('Ach, du'). The dispersal of identity in language follows the lines of a division or confusion between nations and tongues. In fact language in this part of the poem moves in two directions at once. It appears in the form of translation, and as a series of repetitions and overlappings – 'ich', 'Ach', 'Achoo' – which dissolve the pronoun back into infantile patterns of sound. Note too how the rhyming pattern of the poem sends us back to the first line. 'You do not do, you do not do', and allows us to read it as both English and German: 'You du not du',

'You you not you' – 'you' as 'not you' because 'you' do not exist inside a space where linguistic address would be possible.

I am not suggesting, however, that we apply to Plath's poem the idea of poetry as *écriture* (women's writing as essentially multiple, the other side of normal discourse, fragmented by the passage of the unconscious and the body into words). Instead the poem seems to be outlining the conditions under which that celebrated loss of the symbolic function takes place. Identity and language lose themselves in the place of the father whose absence gives him unlimited powers. Far from presenting this as a form of liberation – language into pure body and play – Plath's poem lays out the high price, at the level of fantasy, that such a psychic process entails. Irruption of the semiotic (Kristeva's term for that other side of normal language), which immediately transposes itself into an alien, paternal tongue.

Plath's passionate desire to learn German and her constant failure to do so, is one of the refrains of both her journals and her letters home: 'Wickedly didn't do German for the last two days, in a spell of perversity and paralysis' . . . 'do German (that I *can* do)' . . . 'German and French would give me self-respect, why don't I act on this?' . . . 'Am very painstakingly studying German two hours a day' . . . 'At least I have begun my German. Painful, as if "part were cut out of my brain"' . . . 'Worked on German for two days, then let up' . . . 'Take hold. Study German today.'[61] In *The Bell Jar*, Esther Greenwood says: 'every time I picked up a German dictionary or a German book, the very sight of those dense, black, barbed wire letters made my mind shut like a clam'.[62]

If we go back to the poem, then I think it becomes clear that it is this crisis of representation in the place of the father which is presented by Plath as engendering – forcing, even – her identification with the Jew. Looking for the father, failing to find him anywhere, the speaker finds him everywhere instead. Above all, she finds him everywhere in the language which she can neither address to him nor barely speak. It is this hallucinatory transference which turns every German into the image of the father, makes for the obscenity of the German tongue, and leads directly to the first reference to the Holocaust:

> And the language obscene

> An engine, an engine
> Chuffing me off like a Jew.

> A Jew to Dachau, Auschwitz, Belsen.
> I began to talk like a Jew.
> I think I may well be a Jew.
>
> The snows of the Tyrol, the clear beer of Vienna
> Are not very pure or true.
> With my gypsy ancestress and my weird luck
> And my Taroc pack and my Taroc pack
> I may be a bit of a Jew.

The only metaphor here is that first one that cuts across the stanza break – 'the language obscene//An engine, an engine' – one of whose halves is language. The metaphor therefore turns on itself, becomes a comment on the (obscene) language which generates the metaphor as such. More important still, metaphor is by no means the dominant trope when the speaker starts to allude to herself as a Jew:

> Chuffing me off *like* a Jew.
> I began to talk *like* a Jew.
> I *think* I may well be a Jew.
> I may be a *bit* of a Jew.

Plath's use of simile and metonymy keeps her at a distance, opening up the space of what is clearly presented as a partial, hesitant, and speculative identification between herself and the Jew. The trope of identification is not substitution but displacement, with all that it implies by way of instability in any identity thereby produced. Only in metaphor proper does the second, substituting term wholly oust the first; in simile, the two terms are co-present, with something more like a slide from one to the next; while metonymy is, in its very definition, only ever partial (the part stands in for the whole).

If the speaker claims to be a Jew, then, this is clearly not a simple claim ('claim' is probably wrong here). For this speaker, Jewishness is the position of the one without history or roots: 'So I never could tell where you/Put your foot, your root'. Above all, it is for her a question, each time suspended or tentatively put, of her participation and implication in the event. What the poem presents us with, therefore, is precisely the problem of trying to claim a relationship to an event in which – the poem makes it quite clear – the speaker did not participate. Given the way Plath stages this as a problem in the poem, presenting it as part of a crisis of language and identity,

228

the argument that she simply uses the Holocaust to aggrandise her personal difficulties seems completely beside the point. Who can say that these were not difficulties which she experienced in her very person?[63]

If this claim is not metaphorical, then, we should perhaps also add that neither is it literal. The point is surely not to try and establish whether Plath was part Jewish or not. The fact of her being Jewish could not *legitimate* the identification – it is, after all, precisely offered as an identification – any more than the image of her father as a Nazi which now follows can be *invalidated* by reference to Otto Plath. One old friend wrote to Plath's mother on publication of the poem in the review of *Ariel* in *Time* in 1966 to insist that Plath's father had been nothing like the image in the poem (the famous accusation of distortion constantly brought to bear on Plath).[64]

Once again these forms of identification are not exclusive to Plath. Something of the same structure appears at the heart of Jean Stafford's most famous novel, *A Boston Adventure*, published in 1946.[65] The novel's heroine, Sonie Marburg, is the daughter of immigrants, a Russian mother and a German father who eventually abandons his wife and child. As a young woman, Sonie finds herself adopted by Boston society in the 1930s. Standing in a drawing-room, listening to the expressions of anti-Semitism, she speculates:

> I did not share Miss Pride's prejudice and while neither did I feel strongly partisan towards Jews, the subject always embarrassed me because, not being able to detect Hebraic blood at once except in a most obvious face, I was afraid that someone's toes were being trod on.[66]

It is only one step from this uncertainty, this ubiquity and invisibility of the Jew, to the idea that she too might be Jewish: 'And even here in Miss Pride's sitting-room where there was no one to be offended (unless I myself were partly Jewish, a not unlikely possibility) . . .'.[67] Parenthetically and partially, therefore, Sonie Marburg sees herself as a Jew. Like Plath, the obverse of this is to see the lost father as a Nazi: 'what occurred to me as [Mrs. Hornblower] was swallowed up by a crowd of people in the doorway was that perhaps my father, if he had gone back to Würzburg, had become a Nazi'[68] – a more concrete possibility in Stafford's novel, but one which turns on the same binary, father/daughter, Nazi/Jew, that we see in Plath.

In Plath's poem, it is clear that these identities are fantasies, not for the banal and obvious reason that they occur inside a text, but because the poem addresses the production of fantasy as such. In this sense, I read 'Daddy' as a poem about its own conditions of linguistic and phantasmic production. Rather than casually produce an identification, it asks a question about identification, laying out one set of intolerable psychic conditions under which such an identification with the Jew might take place.

Furthermore – and this is crucial to the next stage of the poem – these intolerable psychic conditions are also somewhere the condition, or grounding, of paternal law. For there is a trauma or paradox internal to identification in relation to the father, one which is particularly focused by the Holocaust itself. At the Congress, David Rosenfeld described the 'logical-pragmatic paradox' facing the children of survivors: 'to be like me you must go away and not be like me; to be like your father, you must not be like your father'.[69] Lyotard puts the dilemma of the witness in very similar terms: 'if death is there [at Auschwitz], you are not there; if you are there, death is not there. Either way it is impossible to prove that death is there'[70] (compare Levi on the failure of witness). For Freud, such a paradox is structural, Oedipal, an inseparable part of that identification with the father of individual prehistory which is required of the child: '[The relation of the superego] to the ego is not exhausted by the precept: "You *ought to be* like this (like your father)." It also comprises the prohibition: "You *may not be* like this (like your father)".'[71] Paternal law is therefore grounded on an injunction which it is impossible to obey. Its cruelty, and its force, reside in the form of the enunciation itself.

'You stand at the blackboard, Daddy/In the picture I have of you' – it is not the character of Otto Plath, but his symbolic position which is at stake. In her story 'Among the Bumblebees', Plath writes of the father: 'Alice's father feared nothing. Power was good because it was power.'[72] Commenting on what he calls the '*père*-version' of the father, the French psychoanalyst Jacques Lacan writes: 'nothing worse than a father who proffers the law on everything. Above all, spare us any father educators, rather let them be in retreat on any position as master.'[73] The reference is to the father of Schreber, eminent educationalist in pre-Nazi Germany, whose gymnasia have been seen as part of the institutional and ideological prehistory of what was to come.[74] It might then be worth quoting the following lines from Otto Plath's 'Insect Societies' (he was a professor of

entomology, famous for his work *Bumblebees and their Ways*).[75]
Whether or not they tell us anything about what he was like as a
person, they can be cited as one version of such paternal 'perversion', of such an impossible paternal ideal: 'When we see these
intelligent insects dwelling together in orderly communities of many
thousands of individuals, their social instincts developed to a high
degree of perfection, making their marches with the regularity of
disciplined troops . . .', or this citation from another professor, with
which he concludes:

> Social instincts need no machinery of control over antisocial
> instincts. They simply have no antisocial tendencies. These were
> thoroughly eliminated many millions of years ago and the insects
> have progressed along a path of perfect social coordination. They
> have no need for policemen, lawyers, government officials,
> preachers or teachers because they are innately social. They have
> no need of learning the correct social responses. These are
> predetermined by their social constitution at the time of birth.[76]

Loss or absence of the father, but equally symbolic overpresence of
the father (only the first is normally emphasised in relation to Plath)
– it is the father as master who encapsulates the paradox at the
heart of the paternal function, who most forcefully demands an
identification which he also has to withhold or refuse. On more
than one occasion, Plath relates the celebrated violence of her
writing to the violence of that function. In 'Among the Bumblebees',
the father sits marking scripts: 'the vicious little red marks he made
on the papers were the color of the blood that oozed out in a thin
line the day she cut her finger with the bread knife'.[77] And if we go
back for a moment to 'Little Fugue', the same image can be traced
out underneath the repeated 'blackness' of that text. On the back of
the first draft is the passage from *The Bell Jar* in which Esther
Greenwood is almost raped. The typescript has this line – 'In that
light, the blood looked black' – crossed out and replaced with this
one written by hand: 'Blackness, like ink, spread over the handker-
chief'.[78] Underneath the poem to the father, a violence of writing –
the poem's writing (the ink on the page), but equally his own. For
those who would insist that what mattered most for Plath was the
loss of her father, we might add that the only other father who can
stand in for this overmastery of the paternal function is the father
who is dead.

231

One could then argue that it is this paradox of paternal identification that Nazism most visibly inflates and exploits. For doesn't Nazism itself also turn on the image of the father, a father enshrined in the place of the symbolic, all-powerful to the extent that he is so utterly out of reach? (and not only Nazism – Ceauşescu preferred orphans to make up his secret police). By rooting the speaker's identification with the Jew in the issue of paternity, Plath's poem enters into one of the key phantasmic scenarios of Nazism itself. As the poem progresses, the father becomes more and more of a Nazi (note precisely that this identity is not given, but is something which emerges). Instead of being found in every German, what is most frighteningly German is discovered retrospectively in him:

> I have always been scared of *you*
> With your Luftwaffe, your gobbledygoo.
> And your neat moustache,
> And your Aryan eye, bright blue.
> Panzer-man, panzer-man, O You –
>
> Not God but a swastika
> So black no sky could squeak through.

The father turns into the image of the Nazi, a string of clichés and childish nonsense ('your gobbledygoo'), of attributes and symbols (again the dominant trope is metonymy) which accumulate and cover the sky. This is of course a parody – the Nazi as a set of empty signs. The image could be compared with Virginia Woolf's account of the trappings of fascism in *Three Guineas*.[79]

Not that this makes him any the less effective, any the less frightening, any the less desired. In its most notorious statement, the poem suggests that victimisation by this feared and desired father is one of the fantasies at the heart of fascism, one of the universal attractions for women of fascism itself. As much as predicament, victimisation is also *pull*:

> Every woman adores a fascist,
> The boot in the face, the brute
> Brute heart of a brute like you.

For feminism, these are the most problematic lines of the poem – the mark of a desire that should not speak its name, or the shameful insignia of a new licence for women in the field of sexuality which has precisely gone too far: 'In acknowledging that the politically correct positions of the Seventies were oversimplified, we are in danger of simply saying once more that sex is a dark mystery, over which we have no control. "Take me – I'm yours", or "Every woman adores a fascist".'[80] The problem is only compounded by the ambiguity of the lines which follow that general declaration. Who is putting the boot in the face? The fascist certainly (woman as the recipient of a sexual violence she desires). But, since the agency of these lines is not specified, don't they also allow that it might be the woman herself (identification *with* the fascist being what every woman desires)?

There is no question, therefore, of denying the problem of these lines. Indeed, if you allow that second reading, they pose the question of women's implication in the ideology of Nazism more fundamentally than has normally been supposed.[81] But notice how easy it is to start dividing up and sharing out the psychic space of the text. Either Plath's identification with the Jew is the problem, or her desire for/identification with the fascist. Either her total innocence or her total guilt. But if we put these two objections or difficulties together? Then what we can read in the poem is a set of reversals which have meaning only in relation to each other: reversals not unlike those discovered in the fantasies of the patients described at Hamburg, survivors, children of survivors, children of Nazis – disjunct and sacrilegious parallelism which Plath's poem anticipates and repeats.

If the rest of the poem then appears to give a narrative of resolution to this drama, it does so in terms which are no less ambiguous than what has gone before. The more obviously personal narrative of the next stanzas – death of the father, attempted suicide at twenty, recovery of the father in the image of the husband – is represented as return or repetition: 'At twenty I tried to die/ And get back, back, back to you' . . . 'I made a model of you', followed by emancipation: 'So Daddy I'm finally through', and finally 'Daddy, daddy, you bastard, I'm through'. They thus seem to turn into a final, triumphant sequence the two forms of temporality which were offered at the beginning of the poem. Plath only added the last stanza – 'There's a stake in your fat black heart', etc. – in the second draft to drive the point home, as it were (although even 'stake' can be read as signalling a continuing investment).

But for all that triumphalism, the end of the poem is ambiguous.

For that 'through' on which the poem ends is given only two stanzas previously as meaning both ending: 'So daddy, I'm finally through' and the condition, even if failed in this instance, for communication to be possible: 'The voices just can't worm through'. How then should we read that last line – 'Daddy, daddy, you bastard, I'm through'? Communication *as* ending, or dialogue *without end*? Note too how the final vengeance in itself turns on an identification – 'you bastard' – that is, 'you father without father', 'you, whose father, like my own, is in the wrong place'.[82]

A point about the more personal narrative offered in these last stanzas, for it is the reference to the death of the father, the attempted suicide, and the marriage which calls up the more straightforward biographical reading of this text. Note, however, that the general does not conceal – 'camouflage' – the particular or personal meaning. It is, again, the relationship of the two levels which is important (it is that relationship, part sequence, part overdetermination, which the poem transcribes). But even at the most personal level of this poem, there is something more general at stake. For the link that 'Daddy' represents between suicide and a paternity, at once personal and symbolic, is again not exclusive to Plath.

At the end of William Styron's *Lie Down in Darkness*, Peyton, with whose suicide the book opened, is allowed to tell her story; the book has worked backwards from her death to its repetition through her eyes. In one of her last moments, she thinks – encapsulating in her thoughts the title of the book – 'I've sinned only in order to lie down in darkness and find, somewhere in the net of dreams, a new father, a new home.'[83] And then, as if in response to that impossible dream – impossible amongst other things because of the collapse of the myth of America on Nagasaki day, the day Peyton dies – the book ends with a 'Negro' revival baptism, as the servants of the family converge on the mass congregation of 'Daddy Faith'. As if the book was suggesting that the only way forward after the death of Peyton was into a grossly inflated symbolic paternity definitively lost to middle America, available only to those whom that same America exploits.[84] 'Daddy' is not far from this – if it is a suicide poem, it is so only to the extent that it locates a historically actualised vacancy, and excess, at the heart of symbolic, paternal law.

*    *    *

I have said relatively little about the sexual politics of the poem. Although there is nothing to mark its gender identity until fairly late, the poem can none the less be read as offering – after Sherry Ortner – the equation 'as father to daughter' so 'Nazi to Jew' (Ortner's formula was 'as nature to culture' so 'woman to man').[85]. According to this interpretation, the representation of the father as Nazi would reveal something about the violence of patriarchy (patriarchy as violence). The speaker's own violence would then be a legitimate and triumphant retaliation – one feminist reading of the text. Clearly this is one way in which the poem can be read, but, taken on its own, the celebration of this narrative seems as problematic as that other feminist celebration of the breakdown or fragmentation of language to which I have already referred.

Assertion of the ego versus a body and language without identity or form – these are two positions on the poetic language of women which correspond respectively to the political demand for equality and to the demand for difference in the most fundamental psychic sense of the term. But perhaps more than any other poem by Plath, 'Daddy' seems to offer a type of corrective in advance to them both. It demonstrates the psychic and political cost of that desire for fragmentation (both in terms of origin and effects); but it also insists on the speaker's (and reader's) full participation in the most awkward of fantasies, fantasies which the feminist assertion of selfhood can read only as a type of psychic false consciousness, as the internalisation of patriarchy and mimicry of the eternal behaviour of men. It is particularly awkward for this second reading that the father oppresses to the precise extent that he is not there. Once again it is the category of fantasy that these readings have to play down – which also means, perhaps paradoxically, that they have to play down the concrete history in which the poem is set. For fascism must surely be distinguished from patriarchy, even if in some sense it can be seen as its effect. Fantasy and history are both lost in these two readings – in the eternal sameness of patriarchy and of women's singular relationship to it, in the eternal sameness of the femininity which erupts against its law.

Writing on Nazism in their famous book *The Inability to Mourn*, Alexander and Margarete Mitscherlich describe how vengeance as an alternative to failed mourning constitutes one of the unconscious sub-texts of what they call 'a particular German way of loving'.[86] If we add the mourning to the vengeance, then we cannot read

'Daddy' simply in terms of revenge against the oppressor. If we take the revenge and the mourning together, as the poem seems to do, we can reintroduce the concept of fantasy as that which links the motifs of memory and revenge, whose separation in responses to the Holocaust is discussed by Lyotard. More important, if we take their co-presence as a counter-narrative or caution against any straightforward narrative reading of the poem as a whole, then 'Daddy' appears as a poem that represents a set of fantasies which, at a precise historical moment and with devastating consequences, found themselves at the heart of our collective political life. In this context, there seems no point in trying to establish a one-way relation between the personal and the wider political history the poem evokes. The poem offers the implication of the one in the other − implication, rather than determination, precisely because one cannot establish a single, one-track relation between the two.

Whether the poem reproduces these fantasies or exposes them, whether it offers them to the reader for a further identification or critique, is not a question which I think can be answered. Saul Friedlander makes the difficulty of this distinction central to his book *Reflections of Nazism*, which describes the preoccupation with Nazi fantasies in our contemporary cultural life.[87] But the question is not yet historically settled as to whether knowledge of our implication in these fantasies, or the idea that we can and should separate ourselves from them completely, is most likely to prevent their repetition in the world today. Somewhere in the space between the inside and outside of the Hamburg Congress, between the Holocaust and nuclear rhetoric, it was this question that was being posed. In this context, what is most striking about 'Daddy' is its mobility of fantasy, the extent to which it takes up psychic positions which, it is often argued, if they cannot be clearly distinguished, lead to the collapse of morality itself. Plath, on the other hand, moves from one position to the other, implicating them in each other, forcing the reader to enter into something which she or he is often willing to consider only on condition of seeing it as something in which, psychically no less than historically, she or he plays absolutely no part.

Plath was a pacifist. The question then arises of the relation between her politics and these fantasies − between her pacifism and the psychic violence she represents in this poem, and of course not only here. In a much earlier psychoanalytic conference on the

236

psychology of peace and war, held in London in 1934, two years after Wiesbaden, Edward Glover discusses the different relationships between violence in the inner and outer worlds.[88] Pacifism, he suggests, can be as much a repetition of, as a solution to, the problem of inner war. The militarist, on the other hand, is too desperately in search of inner peace to forgo war. But normality, or equilibrium, far from being the ideal scenario, is in many ways the most risky state of all:

> The drawbacks to this state of equilibrium are threefold. First, having no urgent inner problem to solve, the man in the street is likely to ignore the real external urgency of war problems; secondly, the equilibrium will not withstand the panic and excitement of a war crisis; thirdly, it prevents the man in the street ever realising that the problem of war is his own unconscious problem.[89]

I offer Glover's remarks not as an analysis of Plath, nor indeed of pacifism, but in order to suggest something of the reversibility that might hold between pacifism and the commitment to (inner) war. (As Plath puts it in the *Journals*: 'I know it is too simple to wish for war, for open battle.'[90]) In order to suggest too – although Glover does not say it – something of the possible link between knowing the war is in fact one's own unconscious war, and working for peace. More simply, to note how little concepts such as antagonism, illegitimate appropriation, or theft (the terms of that critique of Plath with which this chapter began) can help us to understand the relation of these two concerns, the coexistence of external and inner urgency, in Plath's work.

Finally, I would suggest that 'Daddy' does allow us to ask whether the woman might not have a special relationship to fantasy – the only generalisation in the poem regarding women is, after all, that most awkward of lines: 'Every woman adores a fascist.' It is invariably taken out of context, taken out of the ghastly drama which shows where such a proposition might come from – what, for the woman who makes it, and in the worse sense, it might *mean*. Turning the criticism of Plath around once more, could we not read in that line a suggestion, or even a demonstration, that it is a woman who is most likely to articulate the power – perverse,

237

recalcitrant, persistent – of fantasy as such? Nor would such an insight be in any way incompatible with women's legitimate protest against a patriarchal world. This is for me, finally, the wager of Plath's work.

Marguerite Duras's *La douleur* is her wartime diary. It describes the time when she was waiting for her husband to return from the camps, and her resistance during the war. At the end of this narrative, she introduces two stories:

> Thérèse is me. The person who tortures the informer is me. So also is the one who feels like making love to Ter, the member of the Militia. Me. I give you the torturer along with the rest of the texts. Learn to read them properly: they are sacred.[91]

The psychic terrain that Duras is covering here seems to be not unconnected to that represented in 'Daddy' by Plath – as if the story of the victim (concretely and historically in this instance) had to be followed by the story of herself as torturer, as well as by the story of desire. The last word, however, goes to Sylvia Plath. It is her first outline for the story 'The Shadow', a passage from the unedited journals at Smith, not included in the published text:

> My present theme seems to be the awareness of a complicated guilt system whereby Germans in a Jewish and Catholic community are made to feel, in scapegoat fashion, the pain, psychically, the Jews are made to feel in Germany by the Germans without religion. The child can't understand the wider framework. How does her father come into this? How is she guilty for her father's deportation to a detention camp? [As (*sic*)] this is how I think the story will end. Joanna will come in on her own with the trapeze, Uncle Frank and the fiction of perfect goodness.[92]

# NOTES

## CHAPTER 1 'SHE'

1 In a long letter to the *Guardian* on the subject of the defacement of Plath's grave and the surrounding controversy, Ted Hughes wrote: 'A rational observer might conclude (correctly in my opinion) that the Fantasia about Sylvia Plath is more needed than the facts.' Ted Hughes, 'The place where Sylvia Plath should rest in peace', the *Guardian*, 20 April 1989. For a full discussion of this controversy, see Chapter 3 below.

2 Edward Butscher, 'In Search of Sylvia: An Introduction', in Butscher, ed., *Sylvia Plath: The Woman and the Work*, New York: Dodd, Mead and Company, 1977, p. 5.

3 Richard Howard, 'Sylvia Plath: "And I Have No Face, I Have Wanted To Efface Myself"', in Charles Newman, ed., *The Art of Sylvia Plath*, Bloomington and London: Indiana University Press, 1970, pp. 77–88 (p. 87). The passage is cited by Richard Howard as a 'casual remark that seems to me to be a provocative way into a better understanding of Sylvia Plath's "mythic" structure', in Richard Allen Blessing, 'The Shape of the Psyche: Vision and Technique in the Late Poems of Sylvia Plath', in Gary Lane, ed., *Sylvia Plath: New Views on the Poetry*, Baltimore: Johns Hopkins University Press, 1979, pp. 57–73 (p. 69).

4 Hugh Kenner, 'Sincerity Kills', in Gary Lane, op. cit., pp. 33–44 (p. 35).

5 Shoshona Felman. 'Turning the Screw of Interpretation', in Felman, ed., *Literature and Psychoanalysis: The Question of Reading Otherwise*, New Haven: Yale University Press, 1977, pp. 94–207; also in Felman, *Writing and Madness*, Ithaca: Cornell University Press, 1986.

6 For the critique of Freud, see Marie Balmary, *Psycho-Analysing Psycho-Analysis*, Baltimore: Johns Hopkins University Press, 1982; Marianne Krull, *Freud and His Father*, London: Hutchinson, 1986; Jeffrey Masson, *Freud: The Assault on Truth – Freud's Suppression of the Seduction Theory*, London: Faber, 1984; for replies, see Ann Scott, 'Feminism and the Seductiveness of the Real Event', *Feminist Review*, Special Issue: *Family Secrets: Child Sexual Abuse*, 28, Spring 1988, pp. 88–102; Jean Laplanche, *New Foundations for Psychoanalysis*, Oxford: Blackwell, 1989.

7 Melanie Klein, 'Notes on Some Schizoid Mechanisms', 1946, in Juliet Mitchell, ed., *The Selected Melanie Klein*, Harmondsworth: Penguin, 1986, pp. 176–200 (p. 183).

8 Anne Stevenson, *Bitter Fame: A Life of Sylvia Plath*, Boston: Houghton Mifflin, London: Viking, 1989.

9 David Holbrook, *Sylvia Plath: Poetry and Existence*, London: Athlone, 1976. The only previous full study of Plath was the short book by Eileen M. Aird, *Sylvia Plath*, published by Harper & Row in The United States and by Oliver & Boyd (a branch of Longmans) in Edinburgh in 1973.

10 George MacDonald, *Lilith*, 1895, London: Gollancz 1962, pp. 374–5; H. Rider Haggard, *She*, London: Longmans, Green & Company, 1887. Interestingly, the passage from MacDonald (up to 'divided against itself') also forms one of the two epigraphs to Sandra Gilbert and Susan Gubar's study of the nineteenth-century woman writer, *The Madwoman in the Attic: The Woman Writer and the Nineteenth Century Literary Imagination*, New Haven/London: Yale University Press, 1979. The second epigraph is

this passage from Laura Riding's 'Eve's Side of It': 'It was not at first clear to me exactly what I was, except that I was someone who was being made to do certain things by someone else who was really the same person as myself – I have always called her Lilith. And yet the acts were mine and not Lilith's.' For Gilbert and Gubar the myth of Lilith and women's response to, reappropriation of, it forms in some sense the frame of the nineteenth-century literary imagination.

11 Holbrook, op. cit., p. 7.
12 MacDonald, op. cit., p. 374.
13 Anne Stevenson, *Bitter Fame*, op. cit.
14 Stephen Spender, 'Warnings from the Grave', in Charles Newman, ed., *The Art of Sylvia Plath*, op. cit., pp. 199–203 (p. 203), first published as a review of *Ariel* in *The New Republic*, vol. 154, no. 25, 18 June 1966.
15 D.M. Thomas, *The White Hotel*, London: Gollancz, 1981.
16 Mary Ellman, *Thinking About Women*, 1969, London: Virago, 1979, Chapter 3, 'Feminine Stereotypes', pp. 84–5.
17 Sigmund Freud, 'The Dissolution of the Oedipus Complex', 1924, 'Some Psychical Consequences of the Anatomical Distinction Between the Sexes', 1925, *Standard Edition*, vol. XIX, pp. 171–9, 241–58; Pelican Freud, 7, pp. 313–22, 323–43.
18 Julia Kristeva, *Powers of Horror*, New York: Columbia University Press, 1982.
19 D.W. Winnicott, 'Creativity and its Origins', in *Playing and Reality*, London: Tavistock, 1971, pp. 65–85. The reference to Robert Graves is pointed out by Masud Khan in discussion when the paper was originally presented as 'Split-Off Male and Female Elements Found Clinically in Men and Women: Theoretical Inferences', 1966, in J. Linden, ed., *Psychoanalytic Forum*, vol. 4, New York: International Universities Press, 1972, pp. 362–93 (p. 386). Interestingly, Masud Khan is the analyst Holbrook refers to when describing his book's circulation in analytic circles.
20 See, for example, Murray M. Schwartz and Coppelia Kahn, eds, *Representing Shakespeare: New Psychoanalytic Essays*, Baltimore London: Johns Hopkins University Press, 1980.
21 Holbrook, op. cit., p. 172. Holbrook also refers to R.D Laing, Harry Guntrip and W.R.D. Fairbairn.
22 ibid., p. 180.
23 John Ruskin, *Sesame and Lilies*, first published 1885: London: Allen & Unwin, 1919, pp. 108, 136.
24 Joyce Carol Oates, 'The Death Throes of Romanticism', in Paul Alexander, ed., *Ariel Ascending*, New York: Harper & Row, 1985, pp. 26–45 (pp. 31, 41).
25 Holbrook, op. cit., p. 172.
26 ibid., p. 179; compare also: 'a heroine of women's liberation movements. Her rejection of certain kinds of femininity (and, as I would put it, her hatred of certain aspects of woman)', p. 2.
27 ibid., pp. 20, 5.
28 ibid., p. 2.
29 ibid., pp. 19, 2.
30 ibid., pp. 2, 19 (twice), 20.
31 ibid., p. 2.
32 On *Scrutiny*, see Frances Mulhern, *The Moment of Scrutiny*, London: Verso, 1979; on its prehistory in relation to imperialism, see Chris Baldick, *The Social Mission of English Criticism 1848–1932*, Oxford: Oxford University Press, 1983.
33 *The New Poetry*, selected and edited by A. Alvarez, Harmondsworth: Penguin, 1962.
34 Alvarez, 'The New Poetry, or, Beyond the Gentility Principle', Introduction to *The New Poetry*, p. 27. For a discussion of the ethnocentrism of this cultural use of psychoanalysis, see Alan Sinfield, *Literature, Politics and Culture in Postwar Britain*,

London: Routledge, 1989, Chapter 7, 'Cultural plunder and the savage within', pp. 116–51.

35 The circle is, however, a close one. Holbrook is included as a poet in *The New Poetry*, and Hugh Kenner (see 'Sincerity Kills', above) is one of the two writers to whom Alvarez dedicated his book *The Shaping Spirit* in 1958 (Alvarez, *The Shaping Spirit*, London: Chatto, 1967). Holbrook sees Alvarez's promotion of Plath (and Hughes) as 'menacing' the very 'shaping spirit' he claims to support: see Holbrook, *Lost Bearings in English Poetry*, London: Vision, 1977, p. 239: 'but he does not discuss the essential problem of the loss of the shaping spirit in our time, and indeed in his influence on Sylvia Plath and Ted Hughes menaced it'.

36 Saul Bellow, cited Alvarez, 'Beyond All This Fiddle', *Beyond All this Fiddle,* London: Allen Lane, 1968, pp. 3–21 (p. 6).

37 Holbrook, *Human Hope and the Death Instinct: An Exploration of Psychoanalytic Theories of Human Nature and Their Implications for Culture and Education*, London: Pergamon, 1971, p. 240.

38 Alvarez, 'Beyond All This Fiddle', op. cit., p. 21.

39 Alvarez, 'Sylvia Plath', in *Beyond All This Fiddle*, pp. 45–58 (p. 45). The article was originally transmitted as a radio broadcast in 1963, and was subsequently published in *The Review*, 9, October 1963, pp. 20–26.

40 Alvarez, 'The New Poetry', op. cit., p. 25.

41 'Beyond All This Fiddle', op. cit., p. 17.

42 Holbrook, *Sylvia Plath: Poetry and Existence*, op. cit., p. 3.

43 Alvarez, *The Savage God: A Study of Suicide*, London: Weidenfeld & Nicolson, 1971, p. 216.

44 ibid., p. 33, p. xiii.

45 ibid., p. xi.

46 Alvarez, 'Sylvia Plath', op. cit., p. 57.

47 Alvarez is one of the few critics not to take Plath to task for identification with the Jew in her late poetry. But Jewishness as a concept in his writing is no less caught up in the selection and privileging of distinct classes and cultural forms. Judaism, he writes, is the only religious tone present in the modern arts: 'a force working perennially on the side of sanity'. Jewishness is 'worldliness': 'a precondition of survival'. But 'worldliness' is also a negative value, associated with cinema, which is 'corporate', 'technological', 'commercial' ('since the less we believe in minority culture the more we believe in audience ratings and box office returns as a criterion of excellence'), 'disposable', and 'cynical', and cinema is 'that exclusively twentieth-century and dominantly Jewish art form'. In relation to the argument about cultural value, Jewishness is therefore cause or symptom (a dangerous and cynical materiality) *and* cure (only its worldliness will survive). Alvarez, 'Beyond all This Fiddle', pp. 7, 18.

48 Sinfield, op. cit., p. 226.

49 Alvarez, comment on the back of Sylvia Plath, *The Colossus*, London: Heinemann, 1960: see Sinfield, p. 226.

50 Alvarez, 'Literature of the Holocaust', in *Beyond All This Fiddle*, op. cit., pp. 22–33 (p. 31).

51 Alvarez, 'Beyond All This Fiddle', op. cit., p. 14.

52 Sandra Gilbert and Susan Gubar, *The Madwoman in the Attic*, op. cit. especially Chapter I, 'The Queen's Looking Glass: Female Creativity, Male Images of Women, and the Metaphor of Literary Paternity', pp. 3–44.

53 Joyce Carol Oates, 'The Death Throes of Romanticism', op. cit., p. 26.

54 *CP*, 1960, pp. 149–50, first published in *Crossing the Water*, London: Faber & Faber, 1971.

55 Oates, 'The Death Throes of Romanticism', op. cit., p. 38.

56 Alvarez and Donald Davie, 'A Discussion', *The Review*, 1, April–May 1962, pp. 15–21. Davie comments: 'Of course I refuse the masturbation analogy', p. 18.

57 Holbrook, *English for Maturity: English in the Secondary School*, Cambridge: Cambridge University Press, 1961, p. 45.

58 Holbrook, *Sylvia Plath: Poetry and Existence*, op. cit., pp. 167–73.

59 Spender, 'Warnings from the Grave', op. cit., p. 202.

60 Alvarez, 'Beyond All This Fiddle', op. cit., p. 14.

61 ibid., p. 11.

62 Alvarez, 'The New Poetry, or, Beyond the Gentility Principle', op. cit., p. 32.

63 Alvarez, 'Sylvia Plath', op. cit., p. 52.

64 Gilbert and Gubar, *The Madwoman in the Attic*, op. cit., p. 17; Hélène Cixous, 'The Laugh of the Medusa', *Signs*, 1, Summer 1976, reprinted in Elaine Marks and Isabelle de Courtivron, eds., *New French Feminisms*, Brighton, Harvester, 1981, pp. 245–64. See also Luce Irigaray, *This Sex Which Isn't One*, Ithaca: Cornell University Press, 1985. For a discussion of the two accounts, see Toril Moi, *Sexual/Textual Politics: Feminist Literary Theory*, London/New York: Methuen, 1985; Rachel Bowlby, 'Flight Reservations', *Oxford Literary Review*, vol. 10, 1988, pp. 61–72; on French feminism, Ann Rosalind Jones, 'Writing the Body: Toward an Understanding of l'Ecriture féminine', in Elaine Showalter, ed., *The New Feminist Criticism: Essays on Women, Literature and Theory*, London: Virago: New York: Pantheon, 1985, pp. 361–77.

65 Gilbert and Gubar, op. cit., p. 17.

66 Hélène Cixous, 'The Laugh of the Medusa', op. cit., p. 259.

67 Interestingly, Oates's reading of Plath sits right in the centre of the two. The death throes of Romanticism which she reads in Plath's writing are the death throes of the post-Renaissance 'very masculine, combative, ideal of an "I" set against all the other "I"s', but Oates explicitly sets herself against the aesthetic of the fragment, looking to a future in which the unified and total will be restored: 'Hopefully a world of totality awaits us, not a played-out world of fragments.' Oates, 'The Death Throes of Romanticism', op. cit., pp. 30, 44.

68 See Toril Moi, *Sexual/Textual Politics: Feminist Literary Theory*, op. cit.

69 The first chapter of the first volume of Gilbert and Gubar's three-volume study of twentieth-century women's writing is called 'The Battle of the Sexes', and it opens with a discussion of Plath and Hughes. Gilbert and Gubar, *No Man's Land: The Place of the Woman Writer in the Twentieth Century*, volume 1, *The War of the Words*, New Haven/London: Yale University Press, 1988.

## CHAPTER 2   THE BODY OF THE WRITING

1 *J*, Editor's Note, p. xii. This note is signed by Frances McCullough as Editor of the *Journals*. The expression 'nasty comments' is used by her in a letter about the editing of the *Journals* in the *New York Review of Books* (19 January, 1990). There is, however, considerable disagreement about the editing of this text. In a letter to the *New York Review of Books* (12 December, 1989), Olwyn Hughes states that McCullough edited the journals for publication, Ted Hughes's role, along with that of Aurelia Plath, being restricted to a few cuts requested in the final stages (Olwyn Hughes has subsequently repeated this in correspondence with me). In her reply, McCullough states that she never saw the original journals, but worked on an already typed and apparently edited text. In a conversation with me in September 1990, she explained that she deduced this from the fact that part of the manuscript was typed in a typescript that does not correspond to Plath's known typescript, and that there is barely any mention of Hughes's family about whom she feels it is unlikely that Plath would not have commented. A further communication from the Plath Estate on *The Haunting of Sylvia Plath*, representing the views of Ted Hughes and sent on his behalf (January 1991), states that McCullough was

sent 'a complete typescript transcribed from a variety of originals (mostly handwritten) of Plath's Journals and corresponding to the one still in the Estate's possession'. McCullough agrees that, after receipt of the text, she was responsible for the first round of editing, the manuscript then going through two further rounds of editing, one in which Hughes reinserted certain passages, one in which he requested cuts which she saw as both significant and substantial. In her letter to the *NYRB*, McCullough also points out that it was only at this very last stage of the editing, when she insisted on retaining two parts of the journals against the Estate's wishes, that Hughes became consulting editor only. This came at the end of an attempt to have reinstated sections of the journals which had been taken out of previously agreed text. McCullough further stated to me that she and Ted Hughes discussed the editing on the telephone once at the beginning and several times at the later, more difficult, stages over the last round of cuts; that Hughes went over and agreed all editorial matter, as well as going 'carefully over the text two or three times'. McCullough and Olwyn Hughes agree that final approval of the published text rested with Ted Hughes (conversation with Frances McCullough and Olwyn Hughes, 'Notes on *The Haunting of Sylvia Plath*,' September 1990). The final comments from the Estate, reiterate that Ted Hughes 'had *nothing* to do with the main editing', except for the checking of factual events, although they also state that 'his sole concern in editing the journals [*sic*] was to remove passages damaging or libellous to people and passages about [my] own life, regardless of content'. For a full discussion of the editing, see next chapter.

2 *J*, 25 February 1956, p. 109; 20 January 1958, pp. 185–6.

3 Robert Lowell, 'To Speak of Woe That is in Marriage', *Life Studies*, New York: Random House, 1959, p. 82.

4 Gilbert and Gubar, op. cit., Luce Irigaray, op. cit.

5 *J*, Summer 1951, pp. 32, 33; 7 July 1958, p. 249: 28 February 1958, p. 198.

6 *J*, 20 February 1956, p. 106.

7 *J*, 22 January 1958, p. 188.

8 Nicolas Abraham and Maria Torok, 'Introjection – Incorporation: Mourning or Melancholia', in Serge Lebovici and D. Widlocher, eds, *Psychoanalysis in France*, New York: International Universities Press, 1980, pp. 3–16.

9 *J*, 20 March 1959, p. 299: 21 January 1958, p. 187.

10 *Journals*, Smith, July 1950–July 1953, photocopy original, Autumn 1953, p. 106 (*J*, p. 23).

11 Freud, 'Negation', 1923, *Standard Edition*, vol. XIX, pp. 235–9, (p. 237); Pelican Freud, 11, pp. 435–42, (p. 437).

12 Melanie Klein, 'Early Stages of the Oedipus Conflict', 1929; 'Notes on Some Schizoid Mechanisms', 1946, in Juliet Mitchell, ed., *The Selected Melanie Klein*, op. cit., pp. 69–83, 176–200. For a discussion of Klein's ideas in relation to Freud's paper on 'Negation', see Joan Riviere, Introduction, in Riviere, ed., *Developments in Psycho-Analysis*, London: Hogarth, 1952, pp. 1–36.

13 Freud, *The Interpretation of Dreams*; A.A. Brill, ed., *The Basic Writings of Sigmund Freud*, New York: Random House, 1938, pp. 181–549, Chapter 5, 'The Material and Sources of Dreams', pp. 238–318 (p. 298), Plath's emphasis.

14 *J*, 4 March 1957, p. 157.

15 *J*, 27 September 1958, p. 279.

16 Abraham and Torok, 'Le "crime" de l'introjection', in *L'écorce et le noyau*, Paris: Flammarion, 1987, pp. 123–31.

17 Kristeva, *Powers of Horror*, op. cit., p. 41 (translations slightly modified).

18 ibid., pp. 37–8.

19 ibid., p. 38.

20 Anne Sexton, 'Dancing the Jig', in *New World Writing*, 1960, typescript of first draft,

dated 13 October 1959, Texas Collection, 9 pp., p. 4, 7–8. I am grateful to Diane Middlebrook for letting me see this text by Sexton. Middlebrook discusses the story in her forthcoming biography of Sexton, *Anne Sexton*, Chapter 7, '1959: To Bedlam and Part Way Back', Boston: Houghton Mifflin, typescript pp. 33–4.

21  Sexton, 'Dancing the Jig', op. cit., p. 1.
22  Richard Hamilton, *Robert Lowell: A Biography*, London: Faber, 1983, p. 277: Sexton, 'The barfly ought to sing', in Newman, op. cit., pp. 174–81 (p. 175), both discussed in Middlebrook, op. cit.
23  *J*, 3 November 1952, p. 60: 9 February 1958, p. 192.
24  Kristeva, *Powers of Horror*, op. cit., p. 53.
25  *J*, 3 November 1952, p. 60.
26  *J*, 22 January 1958, p. 188.
27  Freud has become notorious for discussing female sexual development in terms of a transition from clitoral to vaginal sexuality: Freud, 'Some Psychical Consequences of the Anatomical Distinction between the Sexes', op. cit., *Standard Edition*, p. 255; Pelican Freud, p. 339. See Kate Millett, *Sexual Politics*, 1969, London: Virago, 1977. See also Juliet Mitchell for the argument that Freud was not presenting this as a natural sequence for women, but analysing it as one of the edicts of a patriarchal culture: Juliet Mitchell, *Psychoanalysis and Feminism*, London: Allen Lane, 1974.
28  *J*, 4 March 1957, p. 156.
29  *LH*, 14 November 1955, p. 195; *J*, 19 February 1959, p. 295: 13 February 1959, p. 294.
30  Allon White, 'Too Close to the Bone: Fragments of an Autobiography', *London Review of Books*, vol. 11, no. 9, 4 May 1989, pp. 3–9 (pp. 6–7).
31  *J*, 3 November 1952, p. 60.
32  *J*, 28 March 1958, p. 210.
33  Fyodor Dostoyevsky, *The Devils*, Harmondsworth: Penguin, 1953, pp. 586–7, cited Kristeva, op. cit., p. 18.
34  Kristeva, pp. 16–17.
35  'Poem for a Birthday', *CP*, 4 November 1959, pp. 131–7, first published in *The Colossus*, London: Heinemann, 1960, only Parts 5, 'Flute Notes from a Reedy Pond' and 7, 'The Stones', published in the American edition, New York: Knopf, 1962. 'Johnny Panic and the Bible of Dreams', *Johnny Panic*, pp. 17–33, first published in *The Atlantic Monthly*, September 1968.
36  Ted Hughes, 'The Chronological Order of Sylvia Plath's Poems', in Newman, ed., op. cit., pp. 187–95 (p. 192).
37  Marjorie Perloff, '*Angst* and Animism in the Poetry of Sylvia Plath', in Linda W. Wagner, ed., *Critical Essays on Sylvia Plath*, Boston: Hall and Company, 1984, pp. 109–23 (p. 115).
38  *LH*, 1 May 1961, p. 417.
39  *J*, 4 November 1959, p. 325.
40  *J*, 1 November 1959, p. 324.
41  *J*, 19 February 1959, p. 295.
42  Holbrook, *Sylvia Plath: Poetry and Existence*, op. cit., Chapter 2, pp. 23–64.
43  Judith Kroll, *Chapters in a Mythology: The Poetry of Sylvia Plath*, New York: Harper and Row, 1976, pp. 102–6.
44  Hughes, in Newman, op. cit., p. 192.
45  Margaret Dickie Uroff, *Sylvia Plath and Ted Hughes*, Urbana: University of Illinois Press, 1979, p. 122.
46  Anne Stevenson, *Bitter Fame*, op. cit., p. 171.
47  Kroll, op. cit., p. 106.
48  ibid., pp. 102–3.
49  Hughes, 'Notes on Poems 1956–63', *CP*, p. 289. See also 'Ted Hughes and *Gaudete*

(1977)' (an interview with Ted Hughes), in Ekbert Faas, *Ted Hughes: The Unaccommodated Universe*, Santa Barbara: Black Sparrow, 1980, pp. 208–15 (p. 210).

50 *J*, 23 October 1959, p. 323.

51 'Three Women: A Poem for Three Voices', ibid., pp. 176–87, dated March 1962, first published in *Winter Trees*, London: Faber & Faber, 1971.

52 Douglas Cleverdon, 'On "Three Women"', in Newman, op. cit., pp. 227–29 (p. 229). 'Three Women' was transmitted by the BBC on 19 August 1962 and 9 June 1968.

53 'Three Women', BBC: Turret Books, 1968.

54 'Three Women', draft dated December 1962, Smith.

55 Freud, *Beyond the Pleasure Principle*, 1920, *Standard Edition* vol. XVIII, pp. 3–64; Pelican Freud, 11, pp. 269–338.

56 Roman Jakobson, 'Closing Statements: Linguistics and Poetics', in T. Sebeok, *Style in Language*: Cambridge MA,: MIT, 1970.

57 Theodore Roethke, 'The Lost Son', in *The Lost Son and Other Poems*, 1948, *The Collected Poems of Theodore Roethke*, New York: Doubleday, 1975, pp. 50–55.

58 Kristeva, op. cit., p. 54.

59 Robert Graves, *The White Goddess: a Historical Grammar of Poetic Myth*, 1946, London: Faber & Faber, 1961, p. 69.

60 Freud, 'Psycho-Analytic Notes on an Autobiographical Account of a Case of Paranoia (Schreber)', 1911, *Standard Edition*, vol. XII; Pelican Freud, 9.

61 'Tongues of Stone', 1955, in *Johnny Panic*, London: Faber & Faber, 1957, pp. 267–74 (p. 269).

62 'Johnny Panic and the Bible of Dreams', p. 26. Sandra Gilbert discusses this story in relation to D.H. Lawrence in 'In Yeats' House: The Death and Resurrection of Sylvia Plath', in Wagner, ed., *Critical Essays on Sylvia Plath*, op. cit., pp. 204–22.

63 'Johnny Panic and the Bible of Dreams', p. 19.

64 ibid., p. 33.

65 *J*, 27 August 1958, p. 257: 14 October 1958, pp. 262–3.

66 Kristeva, op. cit., p. 5.

67 Shoshona Felman, *Writing and Madness*, op. cit., pp. 12–13.

68 Allon White, op. cit., p. 7.

69 Freud, *Civilization and its Discontents*, 1930, *Standard Edition*, vol. XXI, pp. 57–145 (pp. 64–5); Pelican Freud, 12, pp. 243–340 (pp. 251–2). Rosenfeld makes the point about omnipotence in relation to Winnicott's concept of a primordial feminine state of pure being: Winnicott, in Linden, op. cit., pp. 387–9.

70 For a discussion of the way Plath, and other women writers, draw on and transform the traditional connotations of flower imagery, see Jan Montefiore, *Feminism and Poetry: Language, Experience, Identity in Women's Writing*, London: Pandora, 1987, pp. 17–20. Cora Kaplan ends her discussion of women and patriarchal language with these lines by Plath, 'Language and Gender', *Sea Changes*, London: Verso, 1986, pp. 69–93 (p. 93).

71 Paul Radin, *African Folktales and Sculpture*, Bollingen Series, XXXII, New York: Pantheon, 1952; Hughes, in Newman, op. cit., p. 192. The stories are discussed by Kroll, op. cit., pp. 96–107, and by Ekbert Faas in 'Chapters of a Shared Mythology', in Keith Sagar, ed., *The Achievement of Ted Hughes*, Manchester: Manchester University Press, 1983, pp. 107–24 (p. 110).

72 Radin, op. cit., pp. 93–9.

73 ibid., pp. 250–53.

74 'Mantis the All Devourer', op. cit., p. 93.

75 Claude Lévi-Strauss, 'The Structural Study of Myth', in *Structural Anthropology*, vol. I, London: Allen Lane, 1963, pp. 206–31.

76 Radin, op. cit., Introduction, p. 9.

77 'The Origin of Death II', ibid., pp. 60–61 (p. 60).

78 *Journals*, Smith, July 1950–July 1953; July 1950–April 1953, photocopy of manuscript original, Autumn 1950, p. 54 (*J*, p. 19).

79 In her conversation with me (see note 1 above), Frances McCullough could not recall her reasons for these cuts; Olwyn Hughes suggested in 'Notes on *The Haunting of Sylvia Plath*', that they might have been seen as 'typical youthful material' (this, of course, could be said to apply to everything from this period of the Journals); Ted Hughes comments that he would have considered these passages worth keeping (they were not, however, part of the material reinstated at the late stages of the editing).

## CHAPTER 3   THE ARCHIVE

1 The controversy was prompted by a letter from two students Julia Parnaby and Rachel Wingfield, in the *Guardian*, 7 April 1989. It was supported by a letter of 11 April jointly signed by a group of writers and academics: A. Alvarez, Joseph Brodsky, Helga Graham, Ronald Hayman, Jill Neville, Peter Orr, Peter Porter and John Carey (the text of the letter was written and the signatures collected by Ronald Hayman), with further letters on the 12th, 13th and 15th of April. Joseph Brodsky subsequently wrote dissociating himself from the letter of 11 April explaining that he had not seen the letter and would not have signed it had he done so. Ronald Hayman's article, 'The Poet and the Unquiet Grave' was published in *The Independent* on 19 April. Ted Hughes replied in both the *Guardian*' ('The place where Sylvia Plath should rest in peace') and in *The Independent* 'Sylvia Plath: the facts of her life and the desecration of her grave' on 20 April.

2 Hughes, 'Sylvia Plath: the facts of her life and the desecration of her grave', op. cit.

3 Ronald Hayman, 'The Poet and the Unquiet Grave', op. cit.

4 Letter from Julia Parnaby and Rachel Wingfield, op. cit.

5 'Whatever she may have said to the advisers who were urging her on, she never touched divorce papers, and had no plan to do so', Hughes, 'The place where Sylvia Plath should rest in peace', op. cit.

6 Hughes, 'The place where Sylvia Plath should rest in peace', op. cit.

7 ibid.

8 ibid.

9 Hughes, 'Where research becomes intrusion', *Observer*, 29 October 1989.

10 Julia Parnaby and Rachel Wingfield, letter to the *Guardian*, 26 April 1989.

11 'Mr Hayman tells us that "nobody owns fact". I hope each of us owns the facts of her or his own life.' Hughes, 'Sylvia Plath: the facts of her life and the desecration of her grave', op. cit.

12 ibid.

13 Nicolas Abraham, 'Notes on the Phantom: A Complement to Freud's Metapsychology', in Françoise Meltzer, ed., *The Trial(s) of Psychoanalysis*, Chicago: Chicago University Press, 1988, pp. 75–80. Together with Maria Torok, Abraham has formulated an account of the way patients in analysis reveal themselves to be haunted by a residue of the repressed parental unconscious. This residue often consists of a secret, an unconscious belief, not necessarily based on reality but none the less transmitted down through the generations, that they were guilty of some terrible crime. In the case of Plath, it is as if she has become the guilty secret being passed down through the archive and into our collective literary unconscious. (See Introduction.) On reading this passage, Olwyn Hughes commented: 'I know who I, and everyone who knew Plath well, think are the criminals in this sad unending business. It is not to conduct oneself as "the perpetrator of a crime" to attempt to correct the various changing speculations (for as one is disproved, another appears), incorrect facts, inventions, slanders etc., that various commentators, often ignoring contrary

evidence or proper research, have made.' (Olwyn Hughes, 'Notes on *The Haunting of Sylvia Plath*', September 1990)

14  Hughes, 'Sylvia Plath: the facts of her life and the desecration of her grave', op. cit.

15  Hayman, 'The Poet and the Unquiet Grave', op. cit.

16  Emile Benveniste, 'Subjectivity in Language', 'Correlations of Tense in the French Verb', in *Problems in General Linguistics*, Florida: University of Miami Press, 1971, pp. 223–30, pp. 205–15.

17  Hughes, Introduction to the American edition of *Johnny Panic and the Bible of Dreams*, New York: Harper & Row, 1979, p. 5.

18  Hughes, Foreword, *J*, p. xv.

19  Hughes, Introduction, *CP*, p. 15.

20  Olwyn Hughes, 'Notes on *The Haunting of Sylvia Plath*': Ted Hughes comments that the only American offer to publish the *Ariel* poems (before the Faber publication) was from the US poet Donald Hall to publish 'not more than twenty'. This does not, however, answer the question of the principle of selection involved.

21  No fewer than nine of the poems Hughes chose to omit from *Ariel* had appeared by the end of 1963: 'Thalidomide', 'The Jailor', 'The Other', 'Swarm' (*Encounter*, October 1963), 'Lesbos' (*The Review*, October 1963), 'Magi' (*The New Statesman*, October 1961), 'Stopped Dead' (*London Magazine*, January 1963), 'Purdah' (*Poetry*, August 1963), 'Amnesiac' (*The New Yorker*, August 1963). 'Lesbos' and 'The Swarm' appeared in the American edition of *Ariel*. All the poems have subsequently been made available in *Collected Poems*, which includes the list of Plath's own proposed collection. There were, however, sixteen years between the publication of *Ariel* and the *Collected Poems*; *Ariel* also continues to be Plath's best-known collection of poetry, so many readers will read it without recourse to the *Collected Poems* and with no awareness, therefore, of the selection that was made, which is not indicated in subsequent editions of *Ariel* itself.

22  Marjorie Perloff, 'The Two Ariels: The (Re)making Of The Sylvia Plath Canon', *The American Poetry Review*, November–December 1984, pp. 10–18.

23  'Between these two poles – the pole of "Love" for a man that produces babies and the pole of rebirth as an isolate female self, a rebirth that produces the honey of poetry – the narrative of *Ariel I* unfolds': ibid., p. 12. See also Susan van Dyne, '"More Terrible Than She Ever Was": The Manuscripts of Sylvia Plath's Bee Poems', introductory essay to Sylvia Plath, 'Stings, Original Drafts of the Poem in Facsimile', reproduced from the Sylvia Plath Collection, Smith College, Northampton, 1982, pp. 3–12, reprinted in Linda W. Wagner, *Critical Essays on Sylvia Plath*, Boston: G. K. Hall and Company, 1984, pp. 154–70.

24  See Chapter 2, note 1, for a discussion of the editing of the *Journals*. According to Olwyn Hughes, Aurelia Plath requested the removal of references to Plath's early sexuality; according to Frances McCullough, Aurelia Plath was involved in the editing only in relation to the therapy of 1959 (see p. 85).

25  *Journals*, Smith, 28 August 1957–15 November 1959, typescript. Replying to the charge of censorship by Marianne Nault on a televised discussion of Anne Stevenson's biography, *Bitter Fame* (op. cit.), Hughes wrote:

> Recently on BBC 2's 'Late Show', a Plath scholar, Marianne Nault, bitterly accused the Plath Estate of suppressing vital material about Sylvia Plath by publishing edited sections of her journal rather than the whole thing. She had evidently pored over a photocopy of the publisher's [Harper's] working typescript of the original, and had conjured remarkable revelations from under the deletions of the editor [Frances McCullough] . . . she has only to go to the Smith College Rare Book Room and she can read all the mysteries of the unabridged, original journal, which is deposited there for the use of scholars. (Hughes, 'Where research becomes intrusion', op. cit.)

However, having been to the Smith College Rare Book Room, I can confirm that from 28 August 1957 to 15 November 1959, the only text of the journals that is available for scholars to read is precisely the publisher's typescript to which Hughes refers and which Nault had clearly examined. The originals are unavailable, sections of them under seal until 2013. According to the contract between Smith Library and the Estate, these consist of two envelopes containing references to 'acquaintances in general' from the period 28 August, 1957 to 14 October, 1958 and 'parts of a particular record of Plath's sessions with her analyst' from the period 12 December, 1958 to 15 November, 1959, the latter to be kept sealed during the lifetime of Aurelia and Warren Plath (this information has been provided by the Estate). The main issue here therefore appears to be the protection of friends and colleagues from the time of Plath's return to Smith as a tutor, and of her family. Libellous material accessible to the public in an Archive renders the keepers of the Archive liable to a civil suit for damages. To cover this period, the Estate provided a working transcript typescript used for the Dial Press publications of the *Journals*. It is now being decided whether a fair copy of this text should be typed for future scholars to consult (the heavy censorship marks I comment on here would no longer be visible). On first perusal of my description of this typescript, Olwyn Hughes commented: *'if some parts of the journal are shown only in this form it is neither with the knowledge, the approval, or on the instructions of the Estate'* ('Notes on *The Haunting of Sylvia Plath*', emphasis Hughes). Scholars can read a photocopy of Plath's original manuscript from July 1950 to July 1953, and a typescript original from that date until 28 August 1957. Scholars are granted the right to quote this material by the Estate, as well as the other Plath manuscripts – for example, drafts of *Ariel* poems – on condition of submitting their manuscript to the Estate's literary agent for approval (this condition is occasionally waived if it is a scholar Olwyn Hughes 'respects'). On Frances McCullough's status as the main editor of the *Journals* ('had conjured remarkable revelations from under the deletions of the editor'), see Chapter 2, note 1.

26 *CP*, 1956, pp. 33–4.
27 Hughes, Introduction, *CP*, p. 15.
28 Hughes, 'Notes on the Chronological Order of Sylvia Plath's Poems', in Newman, p. 192, op. cit.
29 Hughes, Notes to *CP*, p. 275.
30 'Winter Landscape, with Rooks', *CP*, p. 21; *J*, 20 February 1956: 'Wrote one Good Poem: "Winter Landscape, with Rooks"', p. 106 (the entry is included in the notes at the end of the *Collected Poems*, p. 275). 'Pursuit', *CP*, pp. 22–3; *J*, 27 February 1956: 'wrote a full-page poem about the dark forces of lust: "Pursuit". It is not bad. It is dedicated to Ted Hughes', pp. 115–16. I have not been able to date the first poem, 'Conversation Among the Ruins', *CP*, p. 21, but its last line appears in a journal entry of 18 April 1956 with specific reference to Hughes, *J*, p. 143.
31 'I am turning out five poems a week, and they get better and better', *LH*, 13 March 1955, p. 164.
32 Hughes, Introduction, *Johnny Panic*, p. 13.
33 Hughes, Foreword, *J*, p. xiv.
34 ibid., p. xiv.
35 In correspondence with Aurelia Plath, Hughes explains that it was others reading the manuscript of the letters and their reactions which prompted him to ask for further cuts; Frances McCullough stated to me in conversation that some of the final cuts from the *Journals* were made at the instigation of other members of Hughes's family; Olwyn Hughes also suggests that the editing of the first encounter between Plath and Hughes was prompted by another person.
36 *Crystal Gazer* and *Lyonesse*, both 1971; see Eric Homberger, 'The Uncollected Plath',

*New Statesman*, September 1972, reprinted in Linda W. Wagner, *Sylvia Plath: The Critical Heritage*, London and New York: Routledge, 1988, pp. 187–91.

37  Aurelia Plath, 'Right to Print: restrictions due to copyright re. letters. Points to Bring Out in Talks and Interviews', Notes for Author's Series Talks, Wellesley College Club, 16 March 1976, Smith.

38  The correspondence over *Letters Home* seems to start in March 1973. In the original agreement, Hughes retained 'right of approval' over the text. On 10 July 1974 he writes very positively to Aurelia Plath on the manuscript, requesting a few personal deletions while suggesting that the whole text is much too long. Aurelia Plath appears to have accepted these recommendations and returns an amended text to him on 28 November. Letters from Hughes to Aurelia Plath (3 and 23 April) indicate that there has been a serious disagreement between them and that Aurelia Plath has consulted a lawyer. Hughes explains that on reflection and with advice from friends, especially in the United States, he has decided that his privacy was damaged by the book. Hughes finally secured an agreement that the book would not be published in England except in a form and at a time he approved; a note from Aurelia Plath suggests that she offered to withdraw the book from English publication, but that Hughes finally withdrew his request, allowing it to be published by Faber. Correspondence, Lilly, August 1962–1977, Box 6.

39  Aurelia Plath, Notes for Author's Series Talks, op. cit., p. 5. The collection was also intended as a corrective to the image of Plath in Nancy Hunter Steiner, *A Closer Look at Ariel: A Memory of Sylvia Plath*, New York: Harper's Magazine Press, 1973.

40  Letter from Aurelia Plath to Ted Hughes, 11 April 1970. Correspondence, Lilly, op. cit.

41  Aurelia Plath, Notes for Author's Series Talks, op. cit., carbon addition, p. 2; 'Letter Written in the Actuality of Spring', in Paul Alexander, ed., *Ariel Ascending: Writings About Sylvia Plath*, New York: Harper and Row, 1985, pp. 214–17. The phrase 'violation of actual circumstances' is taken from Richard Wilbur and is in quotation marks in the text, p. 214.

42  ibid., p. 216. This article is dated April 1983.

43  'Sunday at the Mintons', *Mademoiselle*, August 1952, p. 378. Aurelia Plath gives this quote in her Introduction to *Letters Home*, p. 37, and comments: 'a keynote to be remembered in connection with much of her writing'.

44  Anne Stevenson, *Bitter Fame*, op. cit.

45  Hughes, Introduction, *Johnny Panic*, p. 13.

46  Hughes, 'Sylvia Plath and her Journals', in Alexander, op. cit., pp. 152–64 (p. 152).

47  ibid.

48  Letter from Ted Hughes to Aurelia Plath, 10 July 1974, Correspondence, Lilly, op. cit.

49  *LH*, 28 February 1953, p. 104.

50  Jo Brans, 'The Girl Who Wanted To Be God', *Southwest Review*, 61, Summer 1976, pp. 325–30; Carole Bere, '*Letters Home: Correspondence 1950–1963*', *Ariel*, October 1977, pp. 99–103, both reprinted in Wagner, *Critical Essays on Sylvia Plath*, and in Wagner, *Sylvia Plath: The Critical Heritage*, op. cit.; Erica Jong, 'Letters Focus Exquisite Rage of Sylvia Plath', *Los Angeles Times Book Review*, 23 November 1975, pp. 1, 10, reprinted in Wagner, *Sylvia Plath: The Critical Heritage*.

51  For hostility or disagreements, see 14–15 June 1952 (*LH*, p. 88, dated 15 June in text), 23 February 1953 (*LH*, p. 103), 11 February 1955 (*LH*, pp. 161–3), 25 October 1962 (*LH*, p. 477). For independence, see 10 October 1950 (*LH*, p. 52), 4 December 1950 (*LH*, p. 63), 14 February 1956 (*LH*, p. 216). For illness, see 8, 12, 15 October 1950 (*LH*, p. 52), 6 July 1951 (*LH*, p. 72, dated 7 July in text), 6 January 1955 (*LH*, p, 150), 24 February 1956 (*LH*, p. 217), 31 March 1960 (*LH*, p. 370), 10 January 1961 (*LH*, p. 405). For politics, see 27 June 1952 (*LH*, p. 90), 6 November 1952 (*LH*, p. 96), 26 March 1956 (*LH*, p.231), 1, 6 November 1956 (*LH*,. pp. 282, 284), 6 December 1961 (*LH*, p. 438). Correspondence, Lilly, 1938–77, Boxes 1–6.

52 June 1952, 14 October 1958, *LH*, pp. 90, 188.
53 George Steiner is the only exception I have found: 'It requires no biographical impertinence to realize that Sylvia Plath's life was harried by bouts of physical pain', 'Dying is an Art', review of *Ariel*, *The Reporter*, 7 October 1965, reprinted in Newman, op. cit., pp. 211–18 (p. 215).
54 For one of the best accounts of these connections and their cultural and political effects, see Peter Stallybrass and Allon White, *The Politics and Poetics of Transgression*, London: Methuen, 1986.
55 6 July 1951, *LH*, pp. 71–2 (dated 7 July in text). In the original letter, an account of her illness comes immediately after these lines, which appear in the text: 'My reactions have been primarily blind and emotional – fear, insecurity, uncertainty, and anger at *myself* for making myself so miserable and stupid.'
56 *Journals*, Smith, 26 March–5 April 1956, typescript original, 28 March 1956, p. 11 (*J*, p. 135).
57 27 December 1958, *J*, p. 280.
58 9 March 1956, *LH*, pp. 223–4.
59 ibid., p. 223.
60 Letter from Hughes to Aurelia Plath, 3 April 1975, Correspondence, Lilly, op. cit.
61 Linda Heller, 'Aurelia Plath: a lasting commitment', received by Smith College, 24 February 1976.
62 Aurelia Plath, Introduction, *LH*, pp. 31–2.
63 Letter from Aurelia Plath to Carol and Ted Hughes, 2 July 1972, Correspondence, Lilly, op. cit.
64 15 May 1953, Correspondence, Lilly, February 1953–August 1954, Box 3 (*LH*, p. 114).
65 *Journals*, Smith, July 1950–July 1953, April–July, typescript original, 5 April 1953, p. 114 (*J*, p. 75).
66 Hughes, Foreword, *J*, p. xiii.
67 Postcard, 17 October 1950 (one of three in two days), Correspondence, Lilly, 1938–July 1951, Box 1.
68 Aurelia Plath, Introduction, *LH*, p. 31.
69 The correspondence runs from August to December 1953. The concern about insulin occurs in a letter from Olive Prouty to Dr William H. Terhune, 2 November 1953, Correspondence, Lilly, February 1953–August 1954, Box 3 (*LH*, p. 128). Aurelia Plath, comment, *LH*, p. 128.
70 Olive Prouty to Aurelia Plath, 15 December 1953, ibid.; Walter E. Barton, *The History and Influence of the American Psychiatric Association*, Washington: American Psychiatric Press Inc., 1987, p. 268.
71 Olive Prouty to Dr Terhune, 14 December 1953, ibid. The date of the letter, with its reference to the incipient shock treatment, seems to contradict Aurelia Plath's statement: 'By the fifth of December she seemed to be her normal self', *LH*, p. 128.
72 Olive Prouty to Dr Terhune, 14 December 1953, ibid.
73 Olive Prouty to Dr Terhune, 2 November 1953, *LH*, p. 128.
74 Henry M. Hurd, ed., *The Institutional Care of the Insane in the United States and Canada*, Baltimore: Johns Hopkins, 1916, vol. II, p. 614.
75 Olive Prouty to Aurelia Plath, 22 October 1953, Correspondence, Lilly, op. cit.; Aurelia Plath, Notes for Author's Series Talks, op. cit.
76 Olive Prouty to Aurelia Plath, 15 December 1953, ibid. Olive Prouty writes on separate occasions to Dr Terhune, Dr Ruth Beutscher at McLean, and Dr Lindemann at Massachusetts General Hospital in Boston.
77 Olive Prouty to Aurelia Plath, 22 October 1953, Correspondence, Lilly, op. cit.
78 Olive Prouty to Aurelia Plath, 27 November 1953, ibid. Although Prouty is very critical of the therapy in this letter, in her letter of 15 December she speaks of it more

positively and indicates, by alluding to the concept of transference, that she is familiar with psychoanalytic psychotherapy. See also Chapter 5, pp. 194–5.

79 *J*, p. 265.

80 *LH*, p. 459.

81 *J*, pp. 264–5.

82 Freud, *Studies on Hysteria*, 1893–5, *Standard Edition*, vol. II, Pelican Freud, 3; 'Femininity', 1933, *Standard Edition*, vol. XXII, pp. 112–35 (p. 132); Pelican Freud, 2, pp. 145–69 (pp. 166–7).

83 Aurelia Plath to Olive Prouty, 29 August 1953, Correspondence, Lilly, op. cit.

84 Omissions from letters to Aurelia Plath, 26 September, 9 October, 18 October 1962 (*LH*, pp. 463, 464–5, 470–71); the same point is made to Olive Prouty, 29 September, 15 December 1962; to Warren and Maggie Plath, 16 October 1962 (whole letter omitted although other letters to Warren and Maggie are included).

85 *LH*, p. 461.

86 Stevenson, *Bitter Fame*, op. cit., p. 276. Olwyn Hughes gives Plath's and Hughes's bank statements as the source of this statement ('Notes on *The Haunting of Sylvia Plath*', op. cit.).

87 Stephen Tabor, *Sylvia Plath: An Analytical Bibliography*, London: Mansell, 1987, pp. 22–32. I am grateful to Martin Battey at Bertram Rota for drawing my attention to this publication. Ted Hughes comments that, as the publisher of Turret Books will confirm, he received no money for the Turret publications, nor, he adds, for the Rainbow Press editions. Rainbow Press is owned by Olwyn Hughes.

88 Frances McCullough writes:

> I held out for two single passages, the most important of which was the scene of Ted and Sylvia's meeting, when she bit him on the cheek and drew blood; the other, a wry comment on American virginity and rape ... These two cuts would be reinstated, the remaining cuts would be granted, albeit with clear markings to show omissions, and I would lose the $2000 I was to be paid by the Hugheses for my work on the book. *New York Review of Books*, 18 January 1990.

The money referred to here was the fee arranged by Dial Press with the journal *Grand Street* for part publication of the *Journals* which, according to McCullough, it was agreed should be given to her when she requested payment for her work. According to the Estate, they were never directly involved in any payment to McCullough, who was granted 20 per cent of the first serial rights by Dial Press (in the event, only a version of the Hughes introduction was published, for $2300), which she received. Although McCullough agrees that she received $460, she states that at one point she had been orally promised the whole sum and it was this that was revoked during the final round of cuts (conversation with F. McCullough, February 1991, and 'Comments by the Estate of Sylvia Plath on *The Haunting of Sylvia Plath*').

89 21 October 1962, *LH*, p. 473. Aurelia Plath omits a number of remarks to this effect from the last letters: 'For goodness' sake, stop being so *frightened* of everything, Mother! Almost every other word in your letter is "frightened"! ... It's too bad my poems frighten you', 25 October 1962, Correspondence, Lilly, op. cit. (*LH*, p. 477).

90 Perloff, 'The Two Ariels', op. cit.

91 19 April 1956 (*LH*, p. 234), 3 May 1956 (*LH*, p. 248), Correspondence, Lilly, January 1956–July 1962, Box 5.

92 19 April 1956 (*LH*, p. 234), 23 April 1956 (to Warren) (*LH*, p. 240), 26 May 1956 (*LH*, p. 256), ibid.

92 17 April, 3 May 1956 (*LH*, pp. 233, 248).

94 See, for example, letter to Richard Sassoon, 6 March 1956: 'And then there are the many many times I have given myself to that fury and that death which is loving you' (*J*, p. 121).

95 *Journals*, Smith, 19 February–18 April 1956, typescript original, 26 February 1956, p. 18 (*J*, pp. 111–13).
96 McCullough, Letter to *New York Review of Books*, op. cit.
97 *Journals*, Smith, 26 March–5 April 1956, typescript original, 26 March 1956, p. 1 (*J*, p. 134).
98 For example, 17, 20 July 1957, *Journals*, Smith, 15 July–21 August 1957, typescript original, pp. 2, 4 (*J*, pp. 164, 168); 28 March 1957, *Journals*, Smith, 28 August 1957–14 October 1958, typescript not typed by Plath, excerpts from autograph manuscript of 186 pp. sealed, p. 73 (*J*, p. 214).
99 18 April 1956 (addressed to Richard Sassoon), *J*, pp. 143–4.
100 'Conversation Among the Ruins', *CP*, p. 21.
101 *J*, p. 144.
102 Hughes, 'Sylvia Plath: the facts of her life and the desecration of her grave', op. cit.
103 Frances McCullough, Editor's Note, *J*, p. xii.
104 *J*, pp. 264–5.
105 *J*, p. 227.
106 For example: 'And if I have learned nothing else, it is to listen and to love: *everyone*. A humanitarian faith in man's potential for good', 19 August 1952, *Journals*, Smith, op. cit., p. 312 (*J*, p. 55); 'I am becoming calmer in the core', 10 January 1953, ibid., p. 367 (*J*, p. 69); 'Am dropping, weary, but dogged; more happy for some reason. Am respecting self more', 8 March 1956, *Journals*, 19 February–18 April 1956, Smith, op. cit. p. 33 (*J*, p. 129).
107 Samuel Richardson, *Clarissa, or, The History of a Young Lady*, London: Rivington & Osborne, 1747–8. For a discussion of Richardson's notes, see M. Kinkead-Weakes, '*Clarissa* Restored?', *Review of English Studies*, vol. 10, no. 38, 1959, pp. 156–71.
108 27 December 1958, *J*, p. 278.
109 Hughes, 'Sylvia Plath: the facts of her life and the desecration of her grave'.
110 19 May 1958, *J*, p. 227.
111 19 May 1958, *Journals*, 28 August 1957–14 October 1958, Smith, p. 97 (*J*, p. 277). Olwyn Hughes's comments on this omission: 'this was cut because it was *untrue* and damaging. The remaining statement stands as a *truth* about Sylvia Plath and for that reason was no doubt left in, SP's admissions in this regard not being too frequent.' (emphasis mine) ('Notes on *The Haunting of Sylvia Plath*').
112 Anne Stevenson, *Bitter Fame*, op. cit.
113 Olwyn Hughes, Letter, *The Times Literary Supplement*, June 17–23, 1988.
114 ibid., and Linda Wagner-Martin, *Sylvia Plath: A Biography*, London: Chatto & Windus, 1988.
115 ibid.
116 ibid.; and Ian Thompson, 'Under the bell jar', *The Independent*, 12 March 1988.
117 'In writing this biography, I have received a great deal of help from Olwyn Hughes, literary agent to the Estate of Sylvia Plath. Ms. Hughes's contributions to the text have made it almost a work of dual authorship. I am particularly grateful for the work she did on the last four chapters and on the Ariel poems of the autumn of 1962', Author's Note, Stevenson, *Bitter Fame*, op. cit.
118 Most of the reviews I have found have been critical, ranging from mild to totally condemnatory: Helen Vendler, 'Who Is Sylvia', *The New Republic*, 6 November 1989, pp. 98–106; A. Alvarez, 'A Poet and Her Myths', *New York Review of Books*, 28 September 1989, pp. 34–6; and correspondence (including a letter from Olwyn Hughes), ibid., 26 October 1989; Ronald Hayman, 'Plath: a poet mourned by bongo drums', *The Independent*, 10 November 1989; and correspondence, ibid., 21, 27 November, 5 December 1989; Ian Hamilton, 'Whose Sylvia: the estate's or the biographers'?', *Observer*, 29 October 1989; and correspondence (including letter from

Olwyn Hughes), ibid., 5 November 1989; James Wood, 'Who is Sylvia?', the *Guardian*, 2 November 1989; and correspondence (including letter from Olwyn Hughes), ibid., 9 November 1989; 'Sylvia Cringe', *Private Eye*, 10 November 1989. Needless to say, each of the letters from Olwyn Hughes defended the book against the reviewer's criticisms. For more favourable reviews, see, for example, Anthony Thwaite, 'Meltdown', *London Review of Books*, 29 October 1989; Hilary Spurling, 'Ariel trapped and raging to be free', *Sunday Telegraph*, 5 November 1989; Carol Rumens, 'The sociable self and the poet within', *New Statesman and Society*, 3 November 1989; Diane Middlebrook, 'The Enraged Muse', *The Times Literary Supplement*, 27 October–3 November 1989. Stevenson herself acknowledges the 'vitriolic' character of many of the reviews in 'Sylvia Plath and the Romantic Heritage', *PN Review*, vol. 16, no. 6, 1990, pp. 18–30. See also Lyndall Gordon's review, 'The Burden of a Life', *Poetry Review*, vol. 79, no. 4, Winter 1989–90; Stevenson's reply vol. 80, vol. 1, Spring 1990; and Olwyn Hughes's comments in 'The Plath Myth and the reviewing of *Bitter Fame*' vol. 80, no. 3, Autumn 1990.

119  W. S. Merwin, cited in the Preface, Stevenson, *Bitter Fame*, op. cit., p. xii.

120  ibid., pp. 52, xii. 244.

121  ibid., pp. 32–3.

122  ibid., p. xiv.

123  ibid., pp. 12, 14, 244, xiv.

124  Memoirs by Lucas Myers, Dido Merwin and Richard Murphy are included as separate appendices at the end of the book. As Diane Middlebrook put it in her review in the *Times Literary Supplement*, the effect is 'like emerging from the funeral chapel to find the mourners touching up their hair-dos for the wake', 'The Enraged Muse'.

125  ibid., pp. 257, 267, 283.

126  ibid., pp. 187, 290, 103.

127  Olwyn Hughes, 'Notes on *The Haunting of Sylvia Plath*', op. cit; Ian Thompson, 'Under the bell jar', op. cit.

128  Stevenson, *Bitter Fame*, op. cit., p. 61. Helen Vendler makes the same observation in her review of the book, 'Who Is Sylvia?', op. cit.

129  ibid., p. 101.

130  Olwyn Hughes, 'Notes on *The Haunting of Sylvia Plath*', op. cit.

131  Hughes, *Western Morning News*, 1 November 1989, cited by Ronald Hayman, Letter, *The Independent*, 29 November 1989.

132  Hughes, Letter, *The Independent*, 7 December 1989.

133  Stevenson, *Bitter Fame*, op. cit., pp. 178, 241, 293.

134  For example, letter of 19 April 1956 (*LH*, p. 234) cited in Stevenson, p. 87, excludes the account by Plath of Hughes as both superman and breaker of people and things.

135  cited Stevenson, *Bitter Fame*, p. 71.

136  19 February 1956, *J*, pp. 101–2.

137  Freud, 'Psychogenesis of a Case of Homosexuality in a Woman', 1920, *Standard Edition*, vol. XVIII, pp. 145–72 (p. 162); Pelican Freud, 9, pp. 367–400 (p. 389).

138  Letter to Aurelia Plath, 9 October 1962 (*LH*, pp. 464–5); to Olive Prouty, 29 September, 18 October 1962, Correspondence, Lilly.

139  Stevenson, *Bitter Fame*, op. cit., pp. 256–8.

140  Olwyn Hughes, Letter, the *Guardian*, 29 April 1989.

141  'I have no wish to be the wife, even in name, of a person like Ted', letter to Olive Prouty, 18 October 1962, Correspondence, Lilly, op. cit.

142  Ian Thompson, 'Under the bell jar', op. cit.

143  Anne Stevenson, 'Writing as a Woman', in Mary Jacobus, ed., *Women Writing and Writing About Women*, London: Croom Helm, 1979, pp. 159–76.

144  Marianne Nault, 'Explorer of the underworld within', interview with Anne Stevenson, *Observer*, 15 October 1989.

145 Stevenson, 'Letter To Sylvia Plath', *PN Review*, vol. 15, no. 6, 1989, pp. 28–9. Stevenson gives a much more positive assessment of Plath as writer in the article subsequently written in *PN Review*, 'Sylvia Plath and the Romantic Heritage', op. cit.

146 Stevenson, *Bitter Fame*, op. cit., pp. 304, xiii.

147 Robin Morgan, 'A Conspiracy of Silence against a Feminist Poem', *Monster* (a feminist art journal), New York, 1972. My thanks to Helen Taylor for bringing this to my attention.

148 ibid., [pp. 3–4] pages unnumbered.

149 Virginia Woolf, *A Room of One's Own*, London: Hogarth, 1929.

150 See, for example, Stevenson, *Bitter Fame*, op. cit., p. 238, and the readings of the *Ariel* poems in Chapter 12, 'Getting There', pp. 261–99.

151 ibid., p. 143.

152 James Wood, 'Who is Sylvia?, op. cit.

153 22 October 1959, 27 December 1958, *J*, pp. 322, 278.

154 Introduction, *LH*, p. 35.

155 2 October 1956, *LH*, p. 274.

156 *LH*, pp. 359, 483.

157 Aurelia Plath, Notes for Author's Series Talks, op. cit., p. 9.

158 Editor's Note, *J*, p. xi.

159 Hughes, 'Sylvia Plath and her Journals', op. cit., pp. 156, 159.

160 ibid., p. 162.

161 Hughes, Foreword, *J*, p. xiv.

162 Hughes, 'Sylvia Plath and her Journals', op. cit., pp. 158–9.

163 Hughes, 'Notes on the Chronological Order of Sylvia Plath's Poems', op. cit., p. 195.

164 Editor's Note, *J*, p. xii.

165 Freud, 'Mourning and Melancholia', 1915, *Standard Edition*, vol. XIV, pp. 237–58 (p. 256); Pelican Freud, 11, pp. 245–68 (p. 266).

166 *CP*, pp. 329–31, 6 May 1955, *LH*, pp. 174–5.

167 Hughes, 'Sylvia Plath: the facts of her life and the desecration of her grave', and 'Where research becomes intrusion', op. cit.

168 Herbert Mitgang, 'Suit Based on Portrayal In *Bell Jar* Film Begins', *New York Times*, 20 January 1987; Eleanor Blau, 'Plaintiff Denies *Bell Jar* Film Events', *New York Times*, 28 January 1987; W. J. Weatherby, 'Fact v. Fiction', the *Guardian*, 3 February 1987. I am very grateful to Liliane Weissberg for giving me access to all the documentation cited in this section of the chapter.

169 'Where research becomes intrusion', op. cit. Hughes was held responsible for the consequences of Butscher's identification of Anderson in the novel on the grounds that he should have been aware of it and should have been moved to protect her. Hughes's lawyer questioned whether Hughes should have been involved in the case, but the judge ruled that Hughes could legally have been expected to be aware of Butscher's statement and the case went forward. No charge against Hughes was defined during the course of the trial and the case was finally settled between Anderson and the film companies.

170 ibid.

171 *The Bell Jar*, New York: Harper & Row, 1971.

172 Mark Starr, 'From Book to Film: A Novel Case of Libel, a question of character', *Newsweek*, 2 February 1987; Herbert Mitgang, op. cit.

173 Christopher Hitchens, 'American Notes', *The Times Literary Supplement*, 6 February 1987; Aurelia Plath to Ted Hughes, 9 September 1973, Correspondence, Lilly, op. cit.

174 For a discussion of the irreducible figurative dimension of autobiography (and the reverse) see Paul de Man, 'Autobiography As De-Facement', in *The Rhetoric of Romanticism*, New York: Columbia University Press, 1984. For discussion of a legal case which raises similar issues about the legal status of a fictional character (in this case

Tarzan), see Bernard Edelman, 'The Character And His Double', *Identity*, ICA Documents 6, London: Institute of Contemporary Arts, 1987, pp. 35–8.

175  Hughes, cited in Christopher Hitchens, 'American Notes', op. cit.

176  *The Bell Jar*, London: Heinemann, 1963; Faber & Faber, 1966, p. 231.

177  Carol E. Rinzler, 'Salinger and *The Bell Jar*: What Do They Mean To Publishers?', *Publisher's Weekly*, 24 April 1987. Rinzler is citing this opinion, with which she does not agree; the reference to Salinger in the title of her article is to a concurrent case brought by his estate against Ian Hamilton for use of unpublished materials in his biography.

178  Irving R. Kaufman, 'The Creative Process and Libel', *New York Times Magazine*, 5 April 1987, pp. 28–36.

179  ibid.

180  Weatherby, op. cit.

181  '*Bell Jar* hurt reputation, she says', 'Names and Faces', *The Sun*, Baltimore, 29 January 1987.

182  Cited by Eleanor Blau, '*Bell Jar* Jury Is Told Of Suffering', *New York Times*, 29 January 1987.

183  Alice Walker, *The Color Purple*, London: The Women's Press, 1985.

184  Mitgang, op. cit., John Schidlovsky, 'Defense says woman in *Bell Jar* wasn't based on Anderson', *Sun*, Baltimore, 22 January 1987.

185  Eleanor Blau, 'Plaintiff Denies *Bell Jar* Film Events', op. cit.

186  Schidlovsky, op. cit.

187  Blau, '*Bell Jar* Jury Is Told Of Suffering', op. cit.

188  Blau, 'Plaintiff Denies *Bell Jar* Film Events', op. cit.

189  Kaufman, op. cit.

190  ibid.

191  Government 11, Smith, Smith Memorabilia, Lilly, Box 11.

192  *CP*, 1959, pp. 116–17.

193  Irony that this is the dilemma Stevenson reads as the pathology of Plath: 'Sylvia was trapped in her story, condemned to telling it again and again to whoever would listen', *Bitter Fame*, op. cit., p. 32.

194  4 July 1958, *J*, p. 245, cited in notes to 'Lorelei', *CP*, p. 287. Plath then writes to her mother asking about it the next day: 'What is that lovely song that you used to play to us on the piano and sing to us about the Lorelei?', *LH*, p. 346, in the original letter, Plath quotes the German again: Correspondence, Lilly, op. cit.

195  William Wordsworth, 'Essays upon Epitaphs', in W.J.B. Owen, ed., *Wordsworth's Literary Criticism*, London: Routledge, 1974, Essay III, p. 154. Paul de Man discusses these essays in 'Autobiography as De-Facement', op. cit.

## CHAPTER 4   NO FANTASY WITHOUT PROTEST

1  *CP*, 1957, pp. 65–6. The poem was included in the collection of 43 poems that Plath submitted as Part II of the Cambridge Tripos in 1957.

2  *CP*, 1957, pp. 67–8.

3  *CP*, Juvenilia, pp. 307–8, published in *Poetry*, 2 October 1956.

4  Uroff, op. cit., p. 79.

5  *J*, Autumn 1950, p. 23.

6  *J*, Summer 1951, pp. 29–30.

7  *LH*, p. 33.

8  *J*, Autumn 1950, p. 23.

9  ibid.

10  ibid.

11  Gilbert and Gubar, op. cit., Chapter 1, pp. 3–44.

12  *J*, Summer 1951, p. 30.
13  ibid.
14  *J*, 25 February 1956, p. 151.
15  *J*, Summer 1951, p. 32.
16  *Journals*, Smith, July 1950–July 1953, op. cit., Summer 1950, pp. 189–90 (*J*, p. 33).
17  *Johnny Panic*, back cover of paperback edition, 1977; *J*, 12 July 1958, p. 248.
18  *J*, 25 February 1959, p. 297; 19 February 1959, p. 295; 9 July 1958, p. 247.
19  *J*, 20 May 1959, p. 304
20  *J*, 11 March 1957, p. 157.
21  I am referring here to the tradition of feminist literary criticism represented by Elaine Showalter, *A Literature Of Their Own: British Women Novelists from Brontë to Lessing*, Princeton University Press, 1977, London: Virago, 1978; Ellen Moers, *Literary Women*, Princeton: Princeton University Press, 1977; London: The Women's Press, 1978, Gilbert and Gubar, op. cit. Gilbert and Gubar discuss modern women's writing in terms of a battle of the sexes in *No Man's Land: The Place of the Woman Writer in the Twentieth Century*, op. cit.; see esp. vol. 1, *The War of the Words*. Plath's relation to literary tradition, with specific reference to Woolf and Yeats, is discussed by Sandra Gilbert in 'In Yeats' House: The Death and Resurrection of Sylvia Plath', op. cit.
22  For recent discussion of feminism and fantasy, see Ann Snitow, Christine Stansell and Sharon Thompson, eds, *Desire: The Politics of Sexuality*, New York: Monthly Review Press, 1983; London: Virago, 1984; Carole S. Vance, ed., *Pleasure and Danger: Exploring Female Sexuality*, London and Boston: Routledge & Kegan Paul, 1984.
23  *J*, 26 February 1956, p. 113.
24  *Journals*, Smith, 19 February–18 April 1956, op. cit., p. 18, cited by Nancy Milford, 'The Journals of Sylvia Plath', *New York Times Book Review*, 2 May 1982, pp. 30–32, reprinted in Wagner, *Critical Essays on Sylvia Plath*, op. cit., pp. 77–83 (p. 78).
25  Milford, p. 79, op. cit.
26  Stevenson, *Bitter Fame*, p. 76, op. cit.
27  Gilbert and Gubar, *The War of the Words*, op. cit., pp. 3–5, 61–2, 68. Gilbert and Gubar are discussing Hughes's poem 'Lovesong' (*Crow*, London; Faber & Faber, 1972, pp. 88–9) and Plath's later fictionalised account of their first meeting in the short story 'Stone Boy With Dolphin', 1957/58, *Johnny Panic*, pp. 297–322.
28  ibid., Preface, p. xiv.
29  *Journals*, Smith, 28 August 1957–14 October 1958, op. cit., 14 January 1958, p. 13 (*J*, p. 185).
30  26 February 1956, *J*, p. 113.
31  ibid.
32  *J*, 5 April 1956, p. 142.
33  *J*, 10 March 1956, p. 133.
34  *Journals*, Smith, July 1950–July 1953, op. cit., 20 February 1953, pp. 393–4 (*J*, p. 75).
35  Ted Hughes, *The Hawk in the Rain*, London: Faber & Faber, 1957, 1968 edition, p. 49.
36  19 April, 3 May 1956 (*LH*, pp. 234, 248), Correspondence, Lilly, op. cit.
37  'The Wishing Box', 1956, first published in *Granta*, 1957, *Johnny Panic*, pp. 48–55 (pp. 50–51).
38  Ted Hughes to Sylvia Plath, letters dated October 1956, Correspondence, Lilly (these are one part of the letters from Hughes to Plath which she gave to Aurelia Plath, who then passed them, together with the rest of the correspondence, to the Lilly Library); and 'Comments by the Plath Estate on *The Haunting of Sylvia Plath*'.
39  Juvenilia, *CP*, p. 305.
40  Ted Hughes to Aurelia Plath, August 1958, Correspondence, Lilly, op. cit.
41  19 April, 3 May 1956, ibid.
42  3 November 1952, *J*, p. 60.

43 Kristeva, *Powers of Horror*, op. cit.

44 Hughes, *Lupercal*, London: Faber & Faber, 1960, 1970 edition, pp. 29–30.

45 For the first, see Stevenson: 'irrational rage' transformed 'into qualities attributed to its subject' (citing Helen McNeil), Plath's writing as a set of 'murderous projections' of her inner psychic state (*Bitter Fame*, pp. 265, 270). For the second, see Carole Ferrier: 'a [self-destructive and negative] tendency to which women are prone because of their specific social oppression', Ferrier, 'The beekeeper's apprentice', in Lane, op. cit., pp. 203–17 (p. 207). I see this as a problem in what is otherwise the very strong analysis of fifties domestic ideology offered by Ferrier. See also Sinfield, op. cit., pp. 203–31.

46 'Full Fathom Five', *CP*, 1958, pp. 92–3, first published in *The Colossus*, London: Heinemann, 1960; 'Lorelei', *CP*, 1958, pp. 94–5, first published in *The Colossus*; 'Wuthering Heights', *CP*, September 1961, pp. 167–8, first published in *Crossing the Water*, London: Faber & Faber, 1971; 'The Burnt-Out Spa', *CP*, 11 November 1959, pp. 137–8, first published in *The Colossus*.

47 The clearest version of this reading is given by Uroff, op. cit., pp. 94–6, 112–13. See also Oates, op. cit., p. 36.

48 Holbrook, *Sylvia Plath: Poetry and Existence*, op. cit.

49 Paul de Man is one of the key figures of deconstructive literary analysis. See 'Autobiography as De-Facement', op. cit. and 'The Resistance to Theory', in *The Resistance to Theory*, Minneapolis; University of Minnesota Press, 1986, pp. 3–20. For a brilliant discussion of de Man's own writing in terms of the tension between linguistic and psychic figuration, see Neil Hertz, 'Lurid Figures', in Lindsay Waters and Wlad Godzich, eds, *Reading de Man Reading*, Minneapolis: University of Minnesota Press, 1989, pp. 82–104, and 'More Lurid Figures' *Diacritics*, vol. 21, no. 1, Spring 1991.

50 For a very early instance of this, see 'On Looking into the Eyes of a Demon Lover', Juvenilia, *CP*, p. 325.

51 23 September 1961, *CP*, pp. 168–9.

52 'The Surgeon at 2 a.m.', 29 September 1961, *CP*, pp. 170–1, first published in *Crossing the Water*; 'Lady Lazarus', 23–9 October 1962, *CP*, pp. 244–7, first published in *Encounter*, 21 October 1963, and in *Ariel*, London: Faber & Faber, 1965; 'Fever 103', 20 October 1962, *CP*, pp. 231–2, first published in *Poetry*, 102, August 1963, and in *Ariel*.

53 'Context', 1962, *Johnny Panic*, pp. 92–3 (p. 92), first published in the *London Magazine*, 1962.

54 'Suicide Off Egg Rock', 1959, *CP*, p. 115, first pubished in *The Colossus*; 'The Hanging Man', 27 June 1960, *CP*, pp. 141–2, first published in *Ariel*; 'Insomniac', May 1961, *CP*, pp. 163–4, first published in *Crossing the Water*; 'Leaving Early', 25 September 1960, *CP*, pp. 145–6, first published in *Crossing the Water*; 'Paralytic', 29 January 1963, *CP*, pp. 266–7, first published in *Ariel*; 'Gigolo', 29 January 1963, *CP*, pp. 267–8, first published in *Winter Trees*, London: Faber & Faber, 1971.

55 Wagner, *Critical Essays on Sylvia Plath*, op. cit.; Uroff, op. cit.

56 Kroll, op. cit., p. 223n.

57 Uroff, op. cit., Susan Van Dyne, '"More Terrible Than She Ever Was": The Manuscripts of Sylvia Plath's Bee Poems', in *Sylvia Plath: Stings*, Northampton: Smith College and the Estate of Sylvia Plath, reprinted in Wagner, *Critical Essays on Sylvia Plath*, Gilbert, 'In Yeats' House: The Death and Resurrection of Sylvia Plath', op. cit.

58 'The Rabbit Catcher', 21 May 1962, *CP*, pp. 193–4, included in Plath's own prepared collection of *Ariel* poems as No. 3 (the list is printed in the Notes, *CP*, p. 295). Plath chose a number of titles for this collection *Daddy, A Birthday Present, The Rival, The Rabbit Catcher* – before finally calling the collection *Ariel*. The poem was originally called 'Snares'.

59 Linda Wagner-Martin, *Sylvia Plath: A Biography*, London: Chatto & Windus, 1988, p.

205 (Wagner-Martin stresses how this is much clearer in the first draft of the poem); Stevenson, *Bitter Fame*, op. cit., pp. 244–5; see also Sinfield, op. cit., pp. 218–19, although by using the initials 'TH' throughout his discussion, Sinfield keeps open the distance between Hughes and the 'TH figure' (p. 218).

60 Perloff, 'The Two Ariels', op. cit., p. 12.

61 ibid., p. 12.

62 Stevenson, *Bitter Fame*, op. cit., Preface, p. xiii.

63 See, however, on surrealism and the woman artist, Whitney Chadwick, *Women and the Surrealist Movement*, London: Thames & Hudson, 1985.

64 'Notes on an Experimental Film: Scenario by Dali', *Journals* July 1950–July 1953, Smith, Autumn 1950, p. 109, (*J*, p. 23). On seeing the film *Rêves à Vendre* in Paris in 1956, 'inspired by artists like Max Ernst, Man Ray, Fernand Léger', Plath comments: 'where in America would there be such critical passion? Both fire and flame? I'm sure an American college audience would have gone out like contented cows, feeling comfortably avant-garde without questions.' *Journals*, Smith, 19 February–18 April 1956, op. cit., 28 March 1956, p. 13 (*J*, p. 135).

65 'The Rabbit Catcher', *Ariel* Poems, 10pp., Draft 1, Smith. See Wagner-Martin's discussion of the first draft of the poem, op. cit., p. 205. For extensive discussion of the way Plath gradually refined the personal references out of the *Ariel* poems, see Van Dyne, op. cit., and 'Fuelling the Phoenix Fire: The Manuscripts of Sylvia Plath's "Lady Lazarus"', *Massachusetts Review*, 24, Winter 1983, pp. 395–410.

66 Van Dyne, '"More Terrible Than She Ever Was"', and 'Fuelling the Phoenix Fire', op. cit.

67 'Burning the Letters', *Ariel* Poems, Smith, 10pp., Draft 1, 13 August, 1962, *CP*, pp. 204–5; Hughes, 'The Thought-Fox', *The Hawk in the Rain*, op. cit., p. 15.

68 *The Bell Jar*, Draft A, Chapter 3, p. 1, 'The Rabbit Catcher' Draft 1, p. 1 (*The Bell Jar*, published text, pp. 49–50), Draft A, Chapter 3, pp. 14–15, 'RC', Draft 1, pp. 2–3 (pp. 67–9), Draft A, Chapter 17, pp. 1–2, 'RC', Draft 1, p. 4 (pp. 216–17), Smith.

69 *The Bell Jar*, pp. 67, 68.

70 'Brazilia', 'Childless Woman', *Ariel* Poems, Smith, 7 pp. (each), Drafts 1, 1 December 1962, *CP*, pp. 258–9 (p. 259), both first published in *Winter Trees*.

71 'Event', 21 May 1962, *CP*, pp. 194–5.

72 Robert L. Stilwell, 'The Multiplying of Entities: D.H. Lawrence and Five Other Poets', *Sewanee Review*, 76, July–September 1968, pp. 520–35, section on *Ariel*, reprinted in Wagner, *Critical Essays on Sylvia Plath*, op. cit., pp. 44–5 (p. 45).

73 'Stings', 6 October 1962, *CP*, pp. 214–15; 'Lady Lazarus', 'Fever 103', op. cit.

74 Uroff: 'The lioness unloosed in "Purdah" is the identity for which Plath searched in her bee poems'; 'In this poem ["Elm"], Plath began to explore the creative-destructive female spirit whose identity she was to assume in her late poems', op. cit., pp. 144, 164. Van Dyne: 'Plath's worksheets for the bee poems represent, I believe, Plath's search for an authentic and autonomous self'; 'I read the entire bee sequence as Plath's struggle to bring forth an articulate, intelligible self from the death-box of the hive', '"More Terrible Than She Ever Was"', op. cit., pp. 156, 165. Gilbert: '[she became] most triumphantly, the fierce virgin whose fallen selves peel away from her as she ascends to a heaven of her own invention, shivering all creation with her purified "I am I, I am I"', op. cit., p. 220. Van Dyne discusses the frightening aspects of this persona in her article on 'Lady Lazarus', 'Fuelling the Phoenix Fire', but in terms of an internalisation of outside dangers: 'the wish driving the entire poem, the wish to appropriate the powers that threaten to destroy her', op. cit., p. 409 (see, on this question, note 45 above).

75 See Cora Kaplan, 'Language and Gender', op. cit., and John Barrell, *Poetry, Language and Politics*, Cultural Politics series, Manchester: Manchester University Press, 1988, Introduction, pp. 1–17.

76 Excerpts from a letter to Richard Sassoon, 2 November 1955, *J*, p. 93.

77 Diary, 13 November 1949, cited Introduction, *LH*, p. 40.

78 Gilbert, op. cit., p. 218; see also p. 205. Note how far this concept underpins the feminist aesthetic of Gilbert and Gubar: 'the creative "I AM" cannot be uttered if the "I" knows not what it is', Gilbert and Gubar, *The Madwoman in the Attic*, op. cit., p. 17.

79 Stevenson ends her first chapter with the same passage, which she reads as prophetic, but she takes out the crucial words 'perhaps I am destined to be classified and qualified', which give the social dimension to Plath's lament, *Bitter Fame*, p. 16. Exactly mirroring this reproach of Plath for too grand an ego, Stevenson later suggests that it is 'ego weakness' that is Plath's problem (p. 48).

80 'Ocean 1212-W', *Johnny Panic*, pp. 117–24 (pp. 120–1), first broadcast on the BBC, 1962 and published in *The Listener*, 1963.

81 Cited, Introduction, *LH*, p. 40.

82 10 January 1953, *J*, p. 72.

83 14 May 1953, *J*, p. 80.

84 'Amnesiac', 21 October 1962, *CP*, pp. 232–3, first published in *The New Yorker*, 39, 3 August 1963. The poem is included in Plath's list for *Ariel* as No. 32.

85 'Lyonesse', 21 October 1962, *CP*, pp. 233–4, first published in the *Observer*, 10 May 1970, and in *Winter Trees*.

86 'The Night Dances', 6 November 1962, *CP*, pp. 249–50, first published in *Ariel*.

87 'Getting There', 6 November 1962, *CP*, pp. 247–9, first published in *Encounter*, October 1963, and in *Ariel*.

88 Uroff, op. cit., p. 154.

89 See Toril Moi's discussion of these issues in relation to feminist literary criticism, *Sexual/Textual Politics: Feminist Literary Theory*, op. cit.

90 Interestingly, Plath takes out of her first draft of 'Lady Lazarus' (end of fourth stanza): 'It is I, I is I', although this is the poem most commonly associated with the assertion of selfhood discussed here. See Van Dyne, 'Fuelling the Phoenix Fire', op. cit.

91 Mary Lynn Broe discusses Plath's work in these terms in her book *Protean Poetic: The Poetry of Sylvia Plath*, Columbia: University of Missouri Press, 1980. It is interesting to see the extent to which the fundamental aesthetic here is still ultimately one of encompassment or control: 'And indeed Plath is in control . . . she has found both a critical and emotional vocabulary for *encompassing*'; Broe, '"Enigmatical, Shifting My Clarities"', in Alexander, ed., op. cit., pp. 80–94 (pp 91, 93).

92 Kristeva, 'From One Identity to Another', in *Desire in Language*, Oxford: Blackwell, 1980, pp. 124–47.

93 Hughes, Foreword, *J*, p. xiv.

94 Hughes, Note, *A Choice of Shakespeare's Verse*, selected with an introduction by Ted Hughes, London: Faber & Faber, 1971, pp. 181–200 (p. 187).

95 ibid., pp. 194, 193.

96 'Ted Hughes and *Crow* (1970)', interview with Ted Hughes, in Faas, op. cit., pp. 197–208 (p. 200).

97 Graves, *The White Goddess*, op. cit., p. 24. For Freud on the Medusa, see 'Medusa's Head', 1940 (1922), *Standard Edition*, vol. XVIII, pp. 273–4.

98 Graves, op. cit., p. 434.

99 ibid., p. 26.

100 ibid., pp. 209, 448.

101 20 July 1957, *J*, p. 168.

102 3 May 1958, *J*, p. 221.

103 Editor's Note, *J*, p. xi.

104 Uroff, op. cit., p. 215.

105 ibid., p. 223.
106 'The Wishing Box', op. cit.
107 1957, *CP*, p. 42.
108 20 July 1957, *J*, p. 168.
109 Graves, op. cit., p. 446.
110 ibid., p. 449.
111 ibid.
112 Freud, 'On the Universal Tendency to Debasement in the Sphere of Love', Contributions to the Psychology of Love, II, 1912, *Standard Edition*, vol. XI, pp. 177–90; Pelican Freud, 7, pp. 243–60.
113 Graves, op. cit., p. 441; 22 November 1955, *J*, p. 93.
114 See Ferrier and Sinfield, op. cit.
115 'Dialogue over a Ouija Board: A Verse Dialogue', Notes: 1957, *CP*, pp. 276–86. Plath mentions the poem as her first 'for about six months' in a letter to Aurelia Plath, 6 August 1957, *LH*, p. 324.
116 Hughes, 'Bayonet Charge', 'Griefs for Dead Soldiers', 'Six Young Men', 'Two Wise Generals', *The Hawk in the Rain*, op. cit., pp. 53, 54–5, 56–7, 58; 'The Perfect Forms', *Lupercal*, op. cit., p. 51; 'Logos', *Wodwo*, London: Faber & Faber, 1967, p. 34.
117 'Hawk Roosting', *Lupercal*, op. cit., p. 26.
118 Faas puts this question to Hughes in his 1970 interview, 'Ted Hughes and *Crow*', op. cit., pp. 197–200.
119 'Thrushes', *Lupercal*, op. cit., p. 52; 'The Ancient Heroes and the Bomber Pilot', *The Hawk in the Rain*, op. cit., pp. 59–60.
120 Letter to Aurelia Plath, December 1960, Correspondence, Lilly, op. cit.,
121 'Wodwo', *Wodwo*, p. 183.
122 'The Man Seeking Experience Enquires His Way of a Drop of Water', *The Hawk in the Rain*, op. cit., pp. 39–40. Certainly it is in *Wodwo*, especially in the short stories which make up the second part of the book, that Hughes offers his most powerful representations of the anxiety of masculine identity (persecution by horse in 'Rain', by the spectacle of caged rats fighting to the death in 'Sunday', by tractor in 'Michael').
123 Klaus Theweleit, *Male Fantasies*, volume I, *Women, Floods, Bodies, History*, Cambridge: Polity Press, 1987.
124 4 January 1952, *J*, p. 182.
125 Hughes, *Crow: From the Life and Songs of the Crow*, London: Faber & Faber, 1972; Faas, 'Ted Hughes and *Crow*', op. cit., p. 206.
126 ibid., p. 201.
127 'Mayday on Holderness', *Lupercal*, op. cit., pp. 11–12.
128 Graves, op. cit., p. 458.
129 'Fire-Eater', *Lupercal*, op. cit., p. 33; 'Gog', *Wodwo*, op. cit., pp. 150–53.
130 Cited Uroff, op. cit., p. 176.
131 Hughes, 'The Wound' *Wodwo*, op. cit., pp. 104–46.
132 Hughes cited in Faas, 'Chapters of a Shared Mythology: Sylvia Plath and Ted Hughes', op. cit., p. 115. This article criticises Kroll's mythological reading of Plath: 'to trace this plot from her descent into disintegration towards "Rebirth, and Transcendence", is to add two chapters which Plath herself left unwritten', p. 109.
133 2 February 1961, 7 June 1962, *LH*, pp. 407, 456.
134 Hughes, 'The Wound', op. cit., pp. 124, 126, 131–2.
135 ibid., p. 121.
136 ibid., p. 123.
137 ibid.
138 ibid., p. 143.
139 Uroff, op. cit., p. 198.

140 David Trotter, *The Making of the Reader: Language and Subjectivity in Modern American, English and Irish Poetry*, London: Macmillan, 1984, Chapter 11, 'Playing Havoc: Pathos and Anti-Pathos in the Poetry of Ted Hughes, Geoffrey Hill and J.H. Prynne', pp. 196–230.

141 Faas, 'Ted Hughes and *Crow*', op. cit., p. 198; 'Ted Hughes and *Gaudete*', op. cit., p. 214.

142 Faas, 'Chapters of a shared mythology', op. cit., p. 116.

143 Raymond Bellour and Nancy Huston, *Scènes littéraires/Scènes de ménage*, Episode 5, *La Gémellité Râté: Sylvia Plath et Ted Hughes*, France Culture, 6 June 1986, typescript, p. 26.

144 Hughes, 'Sylvia Plath and her Journals', op. cit., p. 156.

145 4 October 1959, *J*, pp. 317–18.

146 Carl Gustav Jung, *Symbols of Transformation*, The Collected Works of C.G. Jung, vol. II, London: Routledge & Kegan Paul, 1956, p. 182; Hughes, 'Fragment of an Ancient Tablet', *Crow*, op. cit., p. 85.

147 Thus, for example: 'the "mother" is really an imago, a psychic image merely', the unconscious is the '"realm of the Mothers"' beyond which lies the 'prenatal realm of the "Eternal Feminine"', Jung, op. cit., p. 330. Jung is describing a fantasy projection while himself operating entirely in terms of this metaphoric gendering of psychological development.

148 ibid., pp. 174–5. Compare too: 'the "mother-libido" must be sacrificed in order to create the world', p. 421, and: 'Every obstacle that rises in his path and hampers his ascent wears the shadowy features of the Terrible Mother, who saps his strength with the poison of secret doubt and retrospective longing', p. 390.

149 ibid., p. 263.

150 Freud, 'On the History of the Psycho-Analytic Movement', 1914, *Standard Edition*, vol. XIV, pp. 1–66 (pp. 61–6); Pelican Freud, 15, pp. 121–8.

151 Freud, 'Female Sexuality', 1931, *Standard Edition*, vol. XXI, pp. 221–43; Pelican Freud, 7, pp. 367–92; 'Femininity', op. cit. In this context, the language with which the two defend their alternative projects is worth noting. Jung on Freud: 'moral condemnation ... tries by every trick of devaluation to prevent this sacrilegious return to the mother, surreptitiously aided and abetted by the one-sided "biological" orientation of the Freudian school', *Symbols of Transformation*, p. 329; Freud on Jung: 'The rest of us, I hope, will be permitted without hindrance to carry through to their conclusion our labour in the depths', 'On the History of the Psycho-Analytic Movement', p. 66, p. 128.

152 17 December 1961, Correspondence, Lilly, op. cit.

153 Graves, op. cit., p. 461.

154 ibid., p. 101.

155 ibid., p. 479.

156 ibid., p. 476.

157 Faas, 'Ted Hughes and *Crow*', *op. cit.*, p. 199.

## CHAPTER 5   SADIE PEREGRINE

1 Katha Pollit, 'A Note of Triumph', review of *The Collected Poems*, in Wagner, ed., *Critical Essays on Sylvia Plath*, op. cit., p. 70.

2 Philip Wylie, *Generation of Vipers* (1942), New York: Rinehart, 1946.

3 ibid., 'You Bought the War', opening statement to 1942 War edition.

4 ibid., p. 203.

5 See Michael Rogin, '*Kiss Me Deadly*: Communism, Motherhood, and Cold War Movies', in *Ronald Reagan, The Movie, and Other Essays in Political Demonology*, Berkeley: University of California Press, 1987, pp. 236–71.

6 Wylie, op. cit., p. 198.

7  ibid., p. 202.
8  Lucas Myers, Appendix I, in Stevenson, *Bitter Fame*, op. cit., pp. 307–21 (pp. 313, 315).
9  Tania Modleski, *Loving with a Vengeance: Mass-Produced Fantasies for Women*, 1982, New York/London: Methuen, 1984, p. 14.
10  Lorna Sage, 'Death and Marriage', *Times Literary Supplement*, 21 October 1977, review of *Johnny Panic and the Bible of Dreams*, reprinted in Wagner, ed., *Sylvia Plath: The Critical Heritage*, op. cit., pp. 237–43 (p. 238); G.S. Fraser, 'Pass to the Centre', *The Listener*, 27 October 1977, review of *Johnny Panic and the Bible of Dreams*, reprinted in Wagner, pp. 243–5 (p. 243); Linda Wagner-Martin, 'Plath's *Ladies' Home Journal* Syndrome', *Journal of American Culture*, 7 Spring–Summer 1984, pp. 32–8 (p. 32). Linda Wagner writes much more positively about those unpublished short stories by Plath which can be read autobiographically: 'Sylvia Plath's Specialness in Her Short Stories', *Journal of Narrative Technique*, 15, Winter 1985, pp. 1–14.
11  Blake Morrison, 'Book Choice' (discussing Anne Stevenson, *Bitter Fame*), Channel 4, 27 October 1989.
12  'Russian Roulette', review of *Ariel*, *Newsweek*, 20 June 1966.
13  Modleski, op. cit., p. 14.
14  3 August 1959, *J*, p. 253; *Journals*, Smith, 28 August 1957–14 October 1958, op. cit.; 3 August 1959, p. 125 (*J*, p. 254).
15  Wylie, op. cit., 1955 edition, New York: Rinehart, p. 194.
16  ibid., p. 196.
17  For a discussion of the different positions on the broader issue of popular or mass culture, see Andrew Ross, *No Respect: Intellectuals and Popular Culture*, New York and London: Routledge, 1989, pp. 42–64; and Sinfield, op. cit., pp. 106–8.
18  Dwight MacDonald, 'A Theory of Mass Culture', *Diogenes*, 3, Summer 1953, pp. 1–17, reprinted in Bernard Rosenberg and David Manning White, eds, *Mass Culture: The Popular Arts in America*, New York: The Free Press, 1957, pp. 59–73 (p. 73).
19  Leslie Fiedler, 'The Middle Against Both Ends', *Encounter*, 5, 1955, pp. 16–23, reprinted in Rosenberg and White, pp. 537–47 (p. 539).
20  Bernard Rosenberg, 'Mass Culture in America', in Rosenberg and White, pp. 3–12 (p. 10).
21  Butscher offers the concept of 'bitch-goddess' as the frame for his reading of Plath; see *Sylvia Plath: Method and Madness*, New York: Seabury Press, 1976, Preface, pp. xi–xii; it is picked up by Uroff, op. cit., p. 14 and note; and by Carole Ferrier, 'The Beekeeper's Apprentice', op. cit., p. 209.
22  21 October 1962, 25 October 1962, *LH*, pp. 473, 477.
23  14 March 1953, *LH*, p. 107; July 1953, *J*, p. 85; *Journals*, Smith, July 1950–July 1953, op. cit., 5 April 1953, p. 393 (*J*, p. 75); *LH*, 17 January 1956, p. 207; 17 January 1956, p. 208; 18 March 1956, p. 230; 4 May 1956, p. 249; 9 January 1957, p. 290; 7 May 1957, p. 312; *J*, 9 August 1957, pp. 170, 173; 19 May 1958, p. 228; 3 July 1958, pp. 242–3; 12 July 1958, p. 248; 25 February 1959, p. 297; *LH*, undated, *c*, 17 December 1960, p. 402; 24 December 1960, p. 403; undated, end of September 1961, p. 431; 22 October 1961, p. 433.
24  29 September 1959, July 1953, *J*, pp. 315, 83.
25  24 December 1960, *LH*, p. 403.
26  20 January 1957, *J*, p. 186.
27  'A Comparison', 1962, 'The World of Books', BBC Home Service Programme, broadcast July 1962, published in *The Listener*, July 1977; *Johnny Panic*, pp. 56–8 (pp. 57–8).
28  ibid., pp. 56, 58. On femininity and the detail, see Naomi Schor, *Reading in Detail: Aesthetics and the Feminine*, London/New York: Methuen, 1987.

29  29 January 1955, *LH*, p. 155.

30  ibid.

31  Louis Hjelmslev, *Prologomena to a Theory of Language*, Madison: University of Wisconsin Press, 1963, p. 116.

32  Hughes's seeming dismissal of this aspect of Plath's writing is strongly contradicted by a long letter her wrote to Aurelia Plath and Warren Plath in December 1960, in which he discusses Plath's short story writing at length. In this letter he attributes the limitation of her fiction writing to her attempt to conform to the art story preference of periodicals such as *Mademoiselle*. As he saw it, the mistake had been to try to mix art writing with popular narrative which, shorn of its artificial pretensions, became an ideal form for Plath to express herself in. The rest of this part of the letter is then taken up with an analysis of this form of writing (a specific form with a specified audience), and the mechanisms of plot suspense on which it relies (a brilliant account of what the French critic Roland Barthes would call the 'hermeneutic code': 'the various formal terms by which an enigma can be distinguished, formulated, held in suspense, and finally disclosed'; *S/Z*, New York: Hill & Wang, 1974, p. 19). Hughes and Plath produced these plots together, then Plath completed the writing of the story. One could argue that Hughes is still insisting on an absolute division between high and low art, but the letter is still remarkable for the interest it shows in popular fiction as a form. Correspondence, Lilly, January 1956–July 1962, Box 5.

33  4 March 1957, *J*, p. 156.

34  Compare this list of women writers as the models for her craft: 'I am definitely *meant* to be married and have children and a home and write like those women I admire: Mrs Moore [Sarah Elizabeth Rodger], Jean Stafford, Hortense Calisher, Phyllis McGinley.' *LH*, 17 January 1956, p. 208.

35  28 March 1958, *J*, p. 212.

36  Betty Friedan, *The Feminine Mystique*, New York: Norton, 1963; Harmondsworth: Penguin, 1965, Chapter 2, 'The Happy Housewife Heroine', pp. 30–60. Alan Sinfield discusses the extent to which Plath shared the cultural context of Friedan in *Literature, Politics and Culture in Postwar Britain*, op. cit., pp. 210–13. For an excellent discussion of Friedan, see Rachel Bowlby, '"The Problem with no Name": Rereading Friedan's *The Feminine Mystique*', *Feminist Review*, 27, September 1987, pp. 61–73.

37  'Unwed Mother Looks Back', in 'Our Readers Write Us', *Ladies' Home Journal*, November 1950, p. 6; 'Journal Mothers Testify to Cruelty in Maternity Wards', *Ladies' Home Journal*, December 1958, pp. 58–9; Jessamyn West, 'Love', pp. 68–227 *passim*; p. 68, the caption under the story reads: 'What is it that girls today look for in marriage: disappointment and frustration conditioned by a generation of mothers who believe in "the age of innocence"; or love and self-expression encouraged by learning facts and understanding reality?'

38  Ethel Waters, 'His Eye is on the Sparrow' (extract from Charles and Ethel Waters, *His Eye is on the Sparrow*, New York: Doubleday, 1950), *Ladies' Home Journal*, October 1951; the issue also includes an article on slum homes in Miami, p. 23; Dorothy Thompson, 'The Crisis in American Education', *Ladies' Home Journal*, July 1950, pp. 11–12; Dorothy Thompson, 'Never Underestimate the Power of a Woman', *Ladies' Home Journal*, July 1950, pp. 11–12 (p. 11).

39  28 March 1958, *J*, p. 212.

40  1 May 1958, *J*, p. 220.

41  28 March 1958, *J*, p. 213.

42  *The Bell Jar*, pp. 67–9; 'Sweetie-Pie and the Gutter Men', May 1959, *Johnny Panic*, pp. 340–52 (pp. 348–9).

43  13 April 1958, *J*, p. 214.

44  Janice A. Radway, *Reading the Romance: Women, Patriarchy and Popular Literature*, Carolina: University of North Carolina Press, 1984; London: Verso, 1987, p. 128.

45  Modleski, op. cit., pp. 44, 39.
46  22 April 1958, *J*, 219.
47  16 June 1959, *J*, p. 309.
48  31 May 1959, *J*, p. 305–6.
49  'Sunday at the Mintons', prizewinning story, *Mademoiselle*, August 1952, *Johnny Panic* pp. 148–59 (pp. 151, 155).
50  'Sunday at the Mintons', Lilly, Prose Fiction, Box 8, Folder 18a, typescript draft, p. 15.
51  'The Wishing Box', op. cit., pp. 48, 49.
52  ibid., p. 49.
53  ibid. For a discussion of this story in relation to the issue of women's self-situating in high culture, see Gilbert, 'In Yeats' House', op. cit.
54  'The Wishing Box', p. 53.
55  ibid., p. 54.
56  ibid., p. 55.
57  31 May 1959, *J*, p. 309.
58  'The Wishing Box', p. 54.
59  ibid., p. 53.
60  Ted Hughes, Introduction, *Johnny Panic*, p. 12.
61  ibid.
62  *Journals*, Smith, July 1950–July 1953, op. cit., pp. 230–34, 7 July 1953 (*J*, p. 46).
63  ibid., pp. 231, 232.
64  ibid., p. 231.
65  ibid., pp. 230, 232–3.
66  ibid., p. 232.
67  ibid., p. 233.
68  ibid., p. 230; Howe, 'Notes on Mass Culture', in Rosenberg and White, op. cit., p. 497.
69  'Mom: Medusa', handwritten draft, *Ariel* Poems, Smith, 19 pp., Draft I.
70  'Medusa', *CP*, 16 October 1962, pp. 224–6, first published in *Ariel*.
71  Alice Ostriker, 'The Americanisation of Sylvia', in Wagner, ed., *Critical Essays on Sylvia Plath*, op. cit., pp. 97–109 (p. 103).
72  Stevenson, *Bitter Fame*, op. cit., p. 227; Raymond Bellour and Nancy Huston, op. cit., p. 27.
73  Plath signed four early poems, 'Ballade Banale', 'Go Get the Goodly Squab', 'In Passing', 1949, 'Lonely Song', 1949, with the name Sandra Peters (the second is included in the 'Juvenilia' section of the *Collected Poems*, p. 313); she signed 'Doom of Exiles', 1954, with the name Alison Arnold (this was the first poem she wrote after her 1953 breakdown, and she included it in a letter to her mother, 16 April 1954, *LH*, p. 136; it is also included in 'Juvenilia', *CP*, p. 318, Lilly, Poetry Manuscripts, Box 7; Plath chooses the name Sylvan Hughes when she writes of her confidence to break into the 'women's slicks': 'I shall call myself *Sylvan Hughes* – pleasantly woodsy, colorful – yet sexless and close to my own name: a perfectly euphonious magazine name': 13 April 1958, *J*, p. 214.
74  Thanksgiving 1962, *LH*, p. 482.
75  *The Bell Jar*, p. 33.
76  ibid., p. 26.
77  ibid., p. 43.
78  ibid., p. 145.
79  ibid., pp. 210–11, p. 219.
80  Thanks to Val Raworth for telling me about this.
81  *The Bell Jar*, p. 232.
82  *55 Short Stories from* The New Yorker, London: Gollancz, 1952; see also Dale Kramer, *Ross and* The New Yorker, London: Gollancz, 1952, 'The Formula Shines', pp. 185–209.

83  See Sinfield, op. cit., pp. 214–16.

84  Kramer, op. cit., p. 195.

85  *The Bell Jar*, pp. 4, 123, 135–6.

86  For a discussion of Plath and Salinger, see Sinfield, op. cit., p. 225. See also Plath herself on her short story 'Sweetie-Pie and the Gutter Men', *Johnny Panic*, pp. 340–52: 'the backyard tale, with the would-be Salinger child in it', *J*, 20 May 1959, p. 304.

87  *The Bell Jar*, pp. 39–40.

88  17 January 1956, *LH*, p. 208.

89  Jean Stafford, *Boston Adventure*, 1946; London: Hogarth, 1986; Plath reads Stafford during the year when she is in Boston: 'Read Jean Stafford, so much more human than Elizabeth Hardwick' (Hardwick was Lowell's second wife): 31 May 1959, p. 308; later she compares her unfavourably with Eudora Welty ('much more colour and world to her'): 25 September 1959, p. 313.

90  Stafford, 'Children Are Bored on Sundays', *55 Short Stories from* The New Yorker, op. cit., pp. 255–64.

91  ibid., p. 258.

92  ibid., p. 259.

93  ibid., p. 260.

94  ibid., p. 264.

95  Serge Guilbaut, *How New York Stole the Idea of Modern Art*, Chicago: Chicago University Press, 1983.

96  Olive Higgins Prouty, *Stella Dallas*, Boston: Houghton Mifflin, 1923; London: Virago reprint, 1990 (to coincide with the release of a new film version of the book starring Bette Midler).

97  ibid., pp. 5–6.

98  ibid., p. 137.

99  ibid., p. 32.

100  ibid., p. 132.

101  Rosenberg, 'Mass Culture in America', op. cit., pp. 6–7.

102  Andreas Huyssen, 'Mass Culture as Woman: Modernism's Other', in *After The Great Divide: Modernism, Mass Culture, Postmodernism*, Bloomington; Indiana University Press, 1986; London: Macmillan, 1988, pp. 44–62 (p. 45).

103  Olive Higgins Prouty, *Now Voyager*, London: Hodder & Stoughton, 1942.

104  May 1952, *J*, p. 43.

105  Prouty, *Stella Dallas*, op. cit., p. 34.

106  Prouty, *Now Voyager*, op. cit., p. 138.

107  *The Bell Jar*, p. 1.

108  ibid., p. 105.

109  19 June 1953, *J*, p. 81.

110  ibid.

111  *Journals*, Smith, July 1950–July 1953, op. cit., 1950, pp. 84–5 (p. 85) (*J*, p. 23).

112  Andrew Ross, 'Reading the Rosenberg Letters', in *No Respect*, op. cit., pp. 15–41.

113  ibid., p. 20.

114  Rogin, op. cit., p. 266.

115  Prouty, *Stella Dallas*, op. cit., p. 269.

116  Plath, History II, Essay on Jacques Barzun, *Darwin, Marx and Wagner*, Boston: Little, Brown & Co., 1941, Smith College Memorabilia, Lilly, Box 10, Folder 7.

117  Ortega Y Gasset, *The Revolt of the Masses*, London: Allen & Unwin, 1932 (US edition 1950), Plath's copy, comments on pp. 42 and 86, Lilly.

118  Randall Jarrell, *Poetry and the Age*, New York: Vintage, 1953, p. 17.

119  *To Secure These Rights*, The Report of the President's Committee on Civil Rights,

introduction by Charles Wilson, New York: Simon & Schuster, 1947, Plath's copy, Lilly.

120 Government II, Smith College, Chambers *et al*, v. Florida, 1933, Dennis v. United States, 1951, West Virginia State Board of Education v. Barnett, 1943, photocopy original of class exercise, Smith College Memorabilia, Lilly, Box 11, Folder 4.

121 'I Am An American', Poetry, Lilly, Box 7, Folder 12, n.d.

122 19 April 1956, Correspondence, Lilly, op. cit. (*LH*, p. 234). These lines are included in Aurelia Plath's prepared typescript and omitted at a later stage.

123 1 November 1956, *LH*, p. 282.

124 7 December 1961, *LH*, pp. 437–8.

125 Cora Kaplan, '*The Thorn Birds*: Fiction, Fantasy and Femininity', in *Sea Changes*, op. cit., 1986, p. 118.

126 Ross, op. cit., p. 24.

127 'The Shadow', January 1959, first published in *Johnny Panic*, pp. 330–39 (p. 334).

128 'Superman and Paula Brown's New Snowsuit', ibid., pp. 160–66; 'The Shadow', op. cit.

129 Barthes, *S/Z*, op. cit., p. 20.

130 'Superman', op. cit., p. 161.

131 ibid.

132 ibid.

133 'The Shadow', op. cit., p. 334.

134 ibid., p. 335.

135 Fiedler, op. cit., p. 545.

136 ibid., p. 543.

137 Somerset Maugham, 'Rain', *The Complete Short Stories*, vol. 1, London: Heinemann, 1951, pp. 1–38.

138 'The Shadow', op. cit., p. 335.

139 ibid., p. 335.

140 ibid., pp. 335, 336–7.

141 'Superman', op. cit., p. 166.

142 William Styron, *Lie Down in Darkness*, Indianapolis/New York: Bobbs-Merrill, 1951. See also Douglas Miller and Marion Novak, *The Fifties: The Way We Really Were*, New York; Doubleday, 1977.

143 'The Shadow', op. cit., p. 337.

144 ibid., p. 339.

145 *Journals*, Smith, 12 December 1958–15 November 1959, typescript carbon not typed by Plath from her original typescript of 71 pp. sealed, 20 March 1959, p. 51 (*J*, p. 299).

146 Bernard Berelson and Patricia J. Salter, 'Majority and Minority Americans: An Analysis of Magazine Fiction', in Rosenberg and White, op. cit., pp. 235–50 (p. 246).

147 'The Daughters of Blossom Street', 1959, first published in the *London Magazine*, 1960; *Johnny Panic*, pp. 74–91 (p. 88); *The Bell Jar*, pp. 186–7; 'The Fifteen-Dollar Eagle', 1959, first published in the *Sewanee Review*, 1960; *Johnny Panic*, pp. 59–73 (p. 60).

148 Styron, op. cit., p. 74.

149 'The Perfect Set-Up', typescript with holograph corrections and instructor's comments, September 1951, 13 pp., Lilly, Writings, *c.* 1940–75, Prose Writings, Box 8, Folder 16, published in *Seventeen*, 11 August 1952, pp. 100–04; 9 March 1956, *LH*, p. 222. See also Aurelia Plath's discussion of this story, Introduction, *LH*, pp. 36–7.

150 *The Bell Jar*, p. 57.

151 'Mothers', 1962, first published as 'The Mother's Union', *McCall's*, October 1972; *Johnny Panic*, pp. 106–16 (p. 111).

152 10 December 1955, *LH*, p. 201.

153 30 September 1959, *J*, p. 317.

154 Elinor Klein, 'A Friend Recalls Sylvia Plath', included in Aurelia Plath, Notes for Author's Series Talks, op. cit.

## CHAPTER 6 'DADDY'

1 Leon Wieseltier, 'In a Universe of Ghosts', *New York Review of Books*, 25 November 1976, pp. 20–23 (p. 20).

2 Joyce Carol Oates, 'The Death Throes of Romanticism', op. cit., p. 39; Seamus Heaney, 'The indefatigable hoof-taps', *Times Literary Supplement*, 5–11 February 1988, pp. 134–44 (p. 144); Irving Howe, 'The Plath Celebration: A Partial Dissent', in Butscher, *Sylvia Plath: The Woman and the Work*, op. cit., pp. 224–35 (p. 233); Marjorie Perloff, 'The Two Ariels', op. cit., pp. 14–15. For a discussion of similar objections to Marianne Moore's poem 'In Distrust of Merits' and more generally to women's war poetry see Sue Schweik, 'Writing War Poetry Like a Woman,' *Critical Inquiry*, 13, 3, Spring 1987, pp. 532–56, part of her forthcoming study, *A Word No Man Can Say For Us: American Women Poets and the Second World War*.

3 'The sense of history, both personal and social, found in a poem like "For the Union Dead" is conspicuously absent from the *Ariel* poems. This is not mere coincidence: for the oracular poet, past and future are meaningless abstractions . . . For Sylvia Plath, there is only the given moment, only *now*.' Marjorie Perloff, '*Angst* and Animism in the Poetry of Sylvia Plath', op. cit., p. 121. For a much more positive assessment of Plath's relationship to history, see Stan Smith, *Inviolable Voice: History and Twentieth-Century Poetry*, Dublin: Gill & Macmillan, 1982, Chapter 9, 'Waist-Deep in History: Sylvia Plath', pp. 200–25.

4 Perloff, 'The Two Ariels', op. cit., p. 15.

5 The criticism was first directed at Ferdinand de Saussure's *Course in General Linguistics* (1915), London: Fontana, 1974, for what has been seen as an emphasis on the synchronic, at the expense of the diachronic, dimension of language, and on the arbitrary nature of the linguistic sign which, it was argued, made it impossible to theorise the relationship between language and reference. It has become a commonplace to reproach post-Saussurian literary theory with ahistoricism. For discussion of some of these debates, see Derek Attridge, Geoff Bennington and Robert Young, eds., *Post-Structuralism and the Question of History*, Cambridge: Cambridge University Press, 1987, especially Geoff Bennington and Robert Young, 'Introduction: posing the question', pp. 1–11. More specifically, I am referring here to the controversy which has followed the discovery of Paul de Man's wartime writings for the Belgian collaborationist newspaper *Le Soir*. See Werner Hamacher, Neil Hertz and Thomas Keenan, eds, *Responses*, Lincoln, NB/London: University of Nebraska Press, 1989.

6 The conference took place in Hamburg in 1985. The papers were published in a special issue of the *International Journal of Psycho-Analysis*, vol. 67, 1986.

7 I take this account from Janine Chasseguet-Smirgel, '"Time's White Hair We Ruffle", Reflections on the Hamburg Conference', *International Review of Psycho-Analysis*, 14, 1987, pp. 433–44.

8 Hanna Segal, 'Silence is the Real Crime', *International Review of Psycho-Analysis*, 14, 1987, pp. 3–12. For the main Congress, see F.-W. Eickhoff, 'Identification and its Vicissitudes in the Context of the Nazi Phenomenon', *International Journal of Psycho-Analysis*, 67, 1986, pp. 33–44; Hillel Klein and Ilany Kogan, 'Identification Processes and Denial in the Shadow of Nazism', pp. 45–52; David Rosenfeld, 'Identification and its Vicissitudes in Relation to the Nazi Phenomenon', pp. 53–64; Mortimer Ostow, 'The Psychodynamics of Apocalyptic: Discussion of Papers on Identification and the Nazi Phenomenon', pp. 277–85; Dinora Pines, 'Working with Women Survivors of the Holocaust: Affective Experiences in Transference and Counter-Transference', pp 295–307; Ira Brenner and Judith S. Kestenberg, 'Children who Survived the Holocaust: The Role of Rules and Routines in the Development of the Superego', pp. 309–16; Anita Eckstaedt, 'Two Complementary Cases of Identification Involving Third Reich Fathers', pp. 317–27. See also Steven A. Luel and Paul Marcus,

*Psychoanalytic Reflections on the Holocaust: Selected Essays*, Denver: Holocaust Awareness Institute and Center for Judaic Studies/New York: Ktav Publishing, 1984. I am grateful to Nina Farhi and Rachel Sievers for bringing my attention to this book, and to the article by Chasseguet-Smirgel cited above.

9 Freud, 'Psycho-Analytic Notes on an Autobiographical Account of a Case of Paranoia (Schreber)', op. cit., *Standard Edition*, p. 71; Pelican Freud, p. 210, cited by Janine Chasseguet-Smirgel, opening comments, *International Journal of Psycho-Analysis*, vol. 67, 1986, p. 7. Compare also the opening address of Adam Limentani, President of the International Association of Psycho-Analysis: ' . . . we also hope that it will facilitate the mending of old wounds in typically psychoanalytic fashion – through remembering and understanding, rather than denial, rationalisation and forgetting' (p. 5); and of Deiter Olmeier, President of the German Psycho-Analytic Association: 'It is only possible to work through things which are accessible to the conscious, which can again and again and ever more clearly become conscious, which can and must be remembered' (p. 6).

10 Eickhoff, 'Identification and its Vicissitudes in the Context of the Nazi Phenomenon', op. cit., p. 34.

11 ibid., and Rosenfeld, op. cit.

12 The reference here is to an earlier paper by Anita Eckstaedt, one of the contributors to the Hamburg Conference, cited by Henry Krystal in a review of Martin S. Bergmann and Milton E. Jucovy, *Generations of the Holocaust*, New York: Basic Books, 1982, in the *Psycho-Analytic Quarterly*, 53, pp. 466–73 (p. 469).

13 Eckstaedt, op. cit., p. 326.

14 Eickhoff (citing L. Wurmser), op. cit., p. 37.

15 I am aware of the danger of reducing the complexities of these individual case-histories to a formula. Each of them showed a particular set of vicissitudes, not only in relation to the historical position of the patient's parents and their own history in relation to Nazism, but also as regards other details of the patient's personal history (whether or not the parents chose to speak, the death of one or other parent, exile, reinstatement, etc.). Readers are encouraged to refer to the papers, which make an extraordinary historical document in themselves.

16 Zev Garber and Bruce Zuckerman, 'Why Do We Call the Holocaust "The Holocaust"? An Inquiry into the Psychology of Labels', in *Remembering For the Future*, Oxford: Oxford University Press, 1988, vol. 2, *The Impact of the Holocaust on the Contemporary World*, pp. 189–92.

17 Both poems are included in the 'Juvenilia' section of the *Collected Poems*, pp. 320, 325.

18 *Encyclopedia Judaica and Catholic Encyclopedia*, both cited by Judith Kroll, *Chapters in a Mythology*, op. cit., p. 181.

19 Primo Levi, *The Drowned and the Saved*, London: Michael Joseph, 1988, pp. 43, 33. See this whole chapter, Chapter 2, 'The Grey Zone', pp. 22–51.

20 Pines, 'Working with Women Survivors of the Holocaust', op. cit., p. 300.

21 Arnost Lustig, 'Rose Street', in *Night and Hope*, New York: Dutton, 1962, p. 78.

22 Freud, 'Psycho-Analytic Notes on an Autobiographical Account of a Case of Paranoia (Schreber)', op. cit., *Standard Edition*, p. 66; Pelican Freud, p. 204.

23 Freud, *Three Essays on the Theory of Sexuality*, 1905, *Standard Edition*, vol. VII, pp. 123–245 (p. 145n); Pelican Freud, 7 pp. 31–169 (p. 56n).

24 Ilse Grubrich-Simitis, 'From Concretism to Metaphor: Thoughts on Some Theoretical and Technical Aspects of the Psychoanalytic Work with Children of Holocaust Survivors', *Psychoanalytic Study of the Child*, 39, 1984, pp. 301–29.

25 ibid., p. 302.

26 Eickhoff, op. cit., p. 34.

27 Grubrich-Simitis, op. cit., pp. 313, 309n.

28 ibid., p. 316.

29 Hannah Arendt, *Eichmann in Jerusalem: A Report on the Banality of Evil*, New York: Viking, 1963, revised and enlarged edition 1965; Harmondsworth: Penguin, 1977, p. 211.

30 Steiner, 'Dying is an art', op. cit., p. 217.

31 Emil L. Fackenheim, 'From Bergen-Belsen to Jerusalem: Contemporary Implications of the Holocaust', The Cultural Department World Jewish Congress, Jerusalem, Institute of Contemporary Jewry, The Hebrew University of Jerusalem, 1975, pp. 17, 12.

32 Karl Kraus, *Das Karl Kraus Lesebuch*, Zurich: Diogenes, 1980, cited Eickhoff, op. cit., p. 40; Eickhoff discusses these lines in relation to lines from a poem by Brecht – quoted as epigraph to his paper (p. 33) – who had attacked Kraus for raising his voice 'only in complaint that it was insufficient'.

33 Levi, *If This Is A Man*, Oxford; The Bodley Head, 1960, first published in Italian in 1947; Harmondsworth: Penguin, 1979 (with *The Truce*), p. 17.

34 Levi, *The Drowned and the Saved*, op. cit., p. 63.

35 Paul Celan, 'Aschenglorie', *Atemwende*, 1967; *Gedichte*, Frankfurt: Suhrkamp Verlag, 1975, p. 72. The line is discussed by Jacques Derrida, 'Shibboleth' (for Paul Celan), G.H. Hartman and S. Budick, eds, *Midrash and Literature*, New Haven: Yale University Press, 1986, pp. 307–47 (p. 326).

36 Piotr Rawicz, *Le sang du ciel*, Paris: Gallimard, 1961; *Blood From the Sky*, London: Secker & Warburg, 1964. These lines are quoted at the end of Alvarez, 'Literature of the Holocaust', op. cit., p. 33.

37 Fackenheim, op. cit. 'Discussion', p. 26.

38 Josef Bor, *Terezin Requiem*, New York: Knopf, 1963 (original date not given, in translation); Elie Wiesel, *Night*, New York: Hill & Wang, 1960, first published in Yiddish in 1956; Ilse Aichinger, *Herod's Children*, New York: Atheneum, 1963 (Alvarez refers to this work as a recent novel); Arnost Lustig, *Night and Hope*, op. cit., was first published in Prague in 1962.

39 Alvarez, 'Literature of the Holocaust', op. cit. Alvarez comments that the Polish writer, Tadeusz Borowski is one of the few to have written about the camps close to the time. See 'This Way for the Gas – A Story', *Commentary*, vol. 1, no. 34, July 1962, pp. 39–47. See also the Hungarian poet and camp survivor Janos Pilinsky's *Selected Poems*, translated by Ted Hughes, Manchester: Carcanet Press, 1976 (his first collection of poems appeared in 1946); and Levi, *If This Is A Man*, op. cit. The history of the publication of Levi's book is interesting in itself. Levi wrote it as soon as he returned from the camps. It was rejected by several large publishers and then published by a small publishing house run by Franco Antonicelli in 1947; 2500 copies were published. Antonicelli then collapsed and the book was not republished until 1958 by Enaudi. Levi comments: 'in that harsh post-war world, people didn't have much desire to go back in their memories to the painful years that had just finished.' Levi, *Se questo è un uomo*, Turin: Enaudi, 1982, Author's Note, p. 231.

40 Hughes, Foreword, *J*, p. xv.

41 Kroll, p. 243n.

42 Derrida, op. cit., p. 329.

43 ibid., p. 338.

44 ibid., and Paul Celan, op. cit., vol. 1, pp. 287–9.

45 Diane Wood Middlebrook and Diana Hume George, eds, *Selected Poems of Anne Sexton*, Boston: Houghton Mifflin, 1988, p. 5; originally published in *The Antioch Review*, 19, 1959; see Heather Cam, '"Daddy": Sylvia Plath's Debt to Anne Sexton', in Diana Hume George, ed., *Sexton: Selected Criticism*, Urbana/Chicago: University of Illinois Press, 1988, pp. 223–6. I am grateful to Diane Middlebrook for drawing my attention to this poem.

46 *CP*, 2 April 1962, pp. 187–9, first published in *Encounter*, 21 October 1963, and in *Ariel*. The poem was not included in Plath's own list for *Ariel*.

47 Graves, *The White Goddess*, op. cit., p. 194.

48 Hans Magnus Enzensberger, 'In Search of a Lost Language', *Encounter*, September 1963, pp. 44–51. The article is discussed by Judith Kroll in relation to 'Little Fugue'. She compares Plath's poem to a poem by Gunter Eich cited by Enzensberger, but the historical allusion is finally synthesised into the overall mythological schema. Kroll, op. cit., pp. 114–15, 246–7n.

49 The concept comes from Jacques Lacan, who formulates it thus: 'What is realised in my history is not the past definite of what was, since it is no more, or even the present perfect of what has been in what I am, but the future anterior of what I shall have been for what I am in the process of becoming', 'The function and field of speech and language in psychoanalysis', 1953, in *Ecrits: A Selection*, London: Tavistock, 1977, pp. 30–113 (p. 86). See also D.W. Winnicott: 'This search [for a past detail which is not yet experienced] takes the form of looking for this detail in the future', 'Fear of Breakdown', in Gregorio Kohon, ed., *The British School of Psychoanalysis: The Independent Tradition*, London: Free Association Books, 1986, pp. 173–82 (p. 178).

50 *Remembering for the Future*, op. cit.

51 Klein and Kogan, op. cit., p. 48.

52 *CP*, 12 October 1962, pp. 222–4 (strangely, the poem is omitted from the Index), first published in *Encounter*, 21 October 1963, and in *Ariel*.

53 'The Blood Jet is Poetry', review of *Ariel*, *Time*, 10 June 1966, pp. 118–20 (p. 118). The review is copiously illustrated with photographs from Aurelia Plath's personal collection. A letter from her to Ted Hughes suggests that she felt she had been tricked by the reviewer and that this, plus the cover of the issue of *The Atlantic* which published 'Johnny Panic and the Bible of Dreams' ('Sylvia Plath on Going Mad'), had contributed to her reluctance to see *The Bell Jar* published in the United States. Letter from Aurelia Plath to Ted Hughes, 11 April 1970, Correspondence, Lilly, op. cit.

54 Jean-François Lyotard, *The Differend: Phrases in Dispute*, Manchester: Manchester University Press, 1988, p. 27. Lyotard is discussing the issue of Holocaust denial or the Faurisson debate, see p. 3 ff. See also Gill Seidal, *The Holocaust Denial: Antisemitism, Racism and the New Right*, Brighton: Beyond the Pale Collective, 1986.

55 The concept comes from Freud, *The Ego and the Id*, op. cit. *Standard Edition*, pp. 31–2; Pelican Freud, 11, pp. 370–71, and *Group Psychology and the Analysis of the Ego*, 1921, *Standard Edition*, vol. XVIII, pp. 105–6; Pelican Freud, 12, pp. 134–5. It has been most fully theorised recently by Julia Kristeva in *Tales of Love*, New York: Columbia University Press, 1987, pp. 24–9.

56 For Kristeva this father founds the possibility of identification for the subject and is critically linked to – enables the subject to symbolise – the orality, and hence the abjection, which was the focus of discussion of 'Poem for a Birthday', in Chapter 2.

57 'Sylvia Plath', in Peter Orr, ed., *The Poet Speaks*, London: Routledge & Kegan Paul, 1966, pp. 167–72 (p. 169).

58 Claude Lanzmann in discussion of the film *Shoah*, Channel 4 Television, 27 October 1987; see also Lanzmann. *Shoah, An Oral History of the Holocaust: The Complete Text of the Film*, New York: Pantheon, 1985; Lyotard, 'Judiciousness in Dispute, or Kant after Marx', in Murray Krieger, ed., *The Aims of Representation: Subject, Text, History*, New York: Columbia University Press, 1987, pp. 24–67 (p. 64).

59 *Journals*, Smith, July 1950–July 1953, op. cit., September 1950, p. 60 (*J*, p. 20).

60 Eickhoff, op. cit., p. 38.

61 4 July 1958, 7 July 1958, 11 October 1959, *J*, pp. 244, 246, 319; 13 October 1959, *LH*, p. 356; 13 October 1959, 19 October 1959, *J*, pp. 319, p. 321; *Journals*, Smith, 12 December 1958–15 November 1959, op. cit., 7 November 1959, p. 94 (*J*, p. 327).

62 *The Bell Jar*, p. 35.

63 'On one side I am a first generation American, on one side I'm a second generation

American, and so my concern with concentration camps and so on is uniquely intense', Orr, op. cit., p. 169.

64 Letter from Thomas J. Clohesy to Aurelia Plath, 4 September 1966, Smith, Section 5, Biography.

65 Jean Stafford, *A Boston Adventure*, op. cit.

66 ibid., p. 335.

67 ibid.

68 ibid., p. 482.

69 Rosenfeld, op. cit., p. 62.

70 Lyotard, 'Judiciousness in Dispute', op. cit., p. 59. In a reply to Lyotard, Stephen Greenblatt takes issue with him on this specific question: Greenblatt, 'Capitalist Culture and the Circulatory System', in Krieger, op. cit., pp. 257–73 (pp. 260–61).

71 Freud, *The Ego and the Id*, op. cit., *Standard Edition*, p. 34; Pelican Freud, p. 374.

72 'Among the Bumblebees' (early 1950s), *Johnny Panic*, pp. 259–66 (p. 263).

73 Lacan, 'Seminar of 21 January 1975', in Juliet Mitchell and Jacqueline Rose, eds, *Feminine Sexuality: Jacques Lacan and the école freudienne*, London: Macmillan, 1982, pp. 162–71 (p. 167).

74 Freud, 'Psycho-Analytic Notes on an Autobiographical Account of a Case of Paranoia (Schreber)', op. cit.; see also Samuel Weber, Introduction to Daniel Paul Schreber, *Memoirs of My Nervous Illness*, edited by Ida Macalpine and Richard Hunter, 1955, new edition, Cambridge, MA/London: Harvard University Press, 1988, pp. vii–liv.

75 Otto Plath, *Bumblebees and their Ways*, New York: Macmillan, 1934.

76 Otto E. Plath, 'Insect Societies', in Carl Murchison, ed., *A Handbook of Social Psychology*, Massachusetts: Clark University Press; London: Oxford University Press, 1935, pp. 83–141 (p. 83, 136–7). The first quote comes from the epigraph to the chapter and is part of a quotation from Thomas Belt, *The Naturalist in Nicaragua*, 1874; its account of the perfect regiment belongs to a more generally utopian image of community which ends with a quotation from Thomas More.

77 'Among the Bumblebees', op. cit., p. 262.

78 'Little Fugue', Draft 1, page 2, verso, Smith, *Ariel* Poems.

79 Virginia Woolf, *Three Guineas*, London: Hogarth, 1938; Harmondsworth: Penguin, 1977, p. 162.

80 Elizabeth Wilson, 'Coming out for a brand new age', the *Guardian*, 14 March 1989. The same line has also been taken as a slogan to explain German women's involvement in Nazism; see Murray Sayle, 'Adolf and the Women', *The Independent Magazine*, 9 November 1988: '"Every woman adores a Fascist," wrote Sylvia Plath. Is this why so many German women voted for Hitler, despite the male emphasis of the Nazi regime?' (caption under title).

81 For a study of this difficult question, see Claudia Koonz, *Mothers in the Fatherland: Women, the Family and Nazi Politics*, London; Jonathan Cape, 1987.

82 Thanks to Natasha Korda for pointing this out to me.

83 Styron, *Lie Down in Darkness*, op. cit., p. 379.

84 On the question of racism, see John Henrik Clarke, ed., *William Styron's Nat Turner: Ten Black Writers Respond*, Boston: Beacon Press, 1968; and Richard Ohmann, *Politics of Letters*, Chapter 5, 'The Shaping of a Canon: US Fiction, 1960–1975', Middletown: Wesleyan University Press, 1987, p. 68.

85 Sherry Ortner, 'Is Female to Male as Nature Is to Culture?', in Michelle Zimbalist Rosaldo and Louise Lamphere, eds, *Woman, Culture and Society*, California: Stanford University Press, 1974, pp. 67–87. For a critique of this article, see Carol P. MacCormack, 'Nature, culture and gender: a critique', in Carol P. MacCormack and Marilyn Strathern, *Nature, Culture and Gender*, Cambridge: Cambridge University Press, 1980, pp. 1–24.

86 Alexander and Margarete Mitscherlich, *The Inability to Mourn*, London: Grove Press, 1975, Chapter 1 'The Inability to Mourn – With Which Is Associated A German Way of Loving', pp. 3–68.
87 Saul Friedlander, *Reflections of Nazism*, New York: Harper & Row, 1984.
88 Edward Glover and Morris Ginsberg, 'A Symposium on the Psychology of Peace and War', *British Journal of Medical Psychology*, 14, 1934, pp. 274–93.
89 ibid., p. 277.
90 Excerpt from a letter to Richard Sassoon, 15 January 1956, *J*, p. 97.
91 Marguerite Duras, *La douleur*, Paris: POL, 1985; London: Fontana, 1987, introductory statement to 'Albert of the Capitals' and 'Ter of the Militias', p. 115.
92 *Journals*, Smith, 12 December 1958–15 November, 1959, op. cit., 28 December 1958, p. 28 (*J*, p. 283).

# BIBLIOGRAPHY

BY SYLVIA PLATH

*The Colossus and Other Poems*, London: Heinemann, 1960
*The Bell Jar*, London: Heinemann, 1963; Faber & Faber, 1966
*Ariel*, London: Faber & Faber, 1965
*Crossing the Water*, London: Faber & Faber, 1971
*Winter Trees*, London: Faber & Faber, 1971
*Letters Home: Correspondence 1950–1963*, selected and edited with a commentary by Aurelia Schober Plath, London: Faber & Faber, 1975
*Johnny Panic and the Bible of Dreams and Other Prose Writings*, introduction by Ted Hughes, London: Faber & Faber, 1977; revised edition, 1979
*Collected Poems*, edited with an introduction by Ted Hughes, London: Faber & Faber, 1981
*The Journals of Sylvia Plath*, Ted Hughes, Consulting Editor, Frances McCullough, Editor, New York: Random House (Ballantine), 1982
Also unpublished material from The Sylvia Plath Collection, Smith College Library Rare Book Room, Northampton, Massachusetts, and from The Sylvia Plath Collection, Lilly Library, Indiana University, Bloomington, Indiana.

BOOKS AND ARTICLES ON SYLVIA PLATH

Aird, Eileen M., *Sylvia Plath*, New York: Harper & Row/Edinburgh: Oliver & Boyd (Longmans), 1973
Alexander, Paul, ed., *Ariel Ascending*, New York: Harper & Row, 1985
Alvarez, A., 'A Poet and Her Myths', *New York Review of Books*, 28 September 1989
Bellour, Raymond, and Nancy Huston, *Scènes littéraires/Scènes de ménage*, Episode 5, *La Gémellité Râté: Sylvia Plath et Ted Hughes*, France Culture, 6 June 1986
Bere, Carole, '*Letters Home: Correspondence 1950–1963*', *Ariel*, October 1977, in Wagner, ed., *Sylvia Plath: The Critical Heritage*
Blau, Eleanor, 'Plaintiff Denies *Bell Jar* Film Event', *New York Times*, 28 January 1987
—— '*Bell Jar* Jury Is Told Of Suffering', *New York Times*, 29 January 1987
—— '*Bell Jar* Case Ends in Accord', *New York Times*, 30 January 1987
Brans, Jo, 'The Girl Who Wanted To Be God', *Southwest Review*, 61, Summer 1976, in Wagner, ed., *Sylvia Plath: The Critical Heritage*
Broe, Mary Lynn, *Protean Poetic: The Poetry of Sylvia Plath*, Columbia: University of Missouri Press, 1980
—— '"Enigmatical, Shifting My Clarities"', in Alexander, ed., *Ariel Ascending*
Butscher, Edward, ed., *Sylvia Plath: Method and Madness*, New York: Seabury Press, 1976
—— *Sylvia Plath: The Woman and the Work*, New York: Dodd, Mead and Company 1977
Cleverdon, Douglas, 'On *Three Women*', in Newman, ed., *The Art of Sylvia Plath*
Ferrier, Carole, 'The beekeeper's apprentice', in Lane, ed., *Sylvia Plath: New Views on the Poetry*
Fraser, G.S., 'Pass to the Centre', *The Listener*, 27 October 1977, review of *Johnny Panic and the Bible of Dreams*, in Wagner, ed., *Sylvia Plath: The Critical Heritage*
Gilbert, Sandra, 'In Yeats' House: The Death and Resurrection of Sylvia Plath', in Wagner,

ed., *Critical Essays on Sylvia Plath*

Gordon, Lyndall, 'The Burden of a Life', *Poetry Review*, vol. 79, no. 4, Winter 1989–90

Hamilton, Ian, 'Whose Sylvia: the estate's or the biographers'?', *Observer*, 29 October 1989

Hayman, Ronald, 'Plath: a poet mourned by bongo drums', *The Independent*, 10 November 1989

Heaney, Seamus, 'The indefatigable hoof-taps', *The Times Literary Supplement*, 5–11 February 1988

Hitchens, Christopher, 'American Notes', *The Times Literary Supplement*, 6 February 1987

Holbrook, David, *Sylvia Plath: Poetry and Existence*, London: Athlone, 1976

Homberger, Eric, *A Chronological Checklist of the Periodical Publications of Sylvia Plath*, Exeter: University of Exeter (American Arts Pamphlet, 1), 1970

—— 'The Uncollected Plath', *New Statesman*, September 1972, reprinted in Wagner, ed., *Sylvia Plath: The Critical Heritage*, 1988

Howard, Richard, 'Sylvia Plath: "And I Have No Face, I Have Wanted To Efface Myself"', in Newman, ed., *The Art of Sylvia Plath*

Hughes, Olwyn, 'The Plath Myth and the reviewing of *Bitter Fame*', *Poetry Review*, vol. 80, no. 3, Autumn 1990

Hughes, Ted, 'Notes on the Chronological Order of Sylvia Plath's Poems', in Newman, ed., *The Art of Sylvia Plath*

—— 'Sylvia Plath, and her Journals', in Alexander, ed., *Ariel Ascending*

—— 'The place where Sylvia Plath should rest in peace', *Guardian*, 20 April 1989

—— 'Sylvia Plath: the facts of her life and the desecration of her grave', *The Independent*, 20 April 1989

—— 'Where research becomes intrusion', *Observer*, 29 October 1989

Hunter Steiner, Nancy, *A Closer Look at Ariel: A Memory of Sylvia Plath*, New York: Harper's Magazine Press, 1973

Jong, Erica, 'Letters Focus Exquisite Rage of Sylvia Plath', *Los Angeles Times Book Review*, 23 November 1975, in Wagner, ed., *Sylvia Plath: The Critical Heritage*

Kaufmann, Irving R., 'The Creative Process and Libel', *New York Times Magazine*, 5 April 1987

Kenner, Hugh, 'Sincerity Kills', in Lane, ed., *Sylvia Plath: New Views on the Poetry*

Klein, Elinor, 'A Friend Recalls Sylvia Plath', included in Aurelia Plath, Notes for Author's Series Talks, Smith

Kroll, Judith, *Chapters in a Mythology: The Poetry of Sylvia Plath*, New York: Harper & Row, 1976

Lane, Gary, ed., *Sylvia Plath: New Views on the Poetry*, Baltimore: Johns Hopkins University Press, 1979

—— and Maria Stevens, *Sylvia Plath: A Bibliography*, Metuchen, NJ/London: Scarecrow Press, 1978

Middlebrook, Diane, 'The Enraged Muse', *The Times Literary Supplement*, 27 October–2 November 1989

—— *Anne Sexton*, Boston: Houghton Mifflin, 1991

Milford, Nancy, 'The Journals of Sylvia Plath', in Wagner, ed., *Critical Essays on Sylvia Plath*

Mitgang, Herbert, 'Suit Based on Portrayal in *Bell Jar* Film Begins', *New York Times*, 20 January 1987

Morgan, Robin, 'A Conspiracy of Silence against a Feminist Poem', *Monster*, a feminist art journal, New York 1972

Newman, Charles, ed., *The Art of Sylvia Plath*, Bloomington and London: Indiana University Press, 1970

Oates, Joyce Carol, 'The Death Throes of Romanticism', in Alexander, ed., *Ariel Ascending*

Orr, Peter, 'Sylvia Plath', in Orr, ed., *The Poet Speaks*, London: Routledge & Kegan Paul, 1966

Ostriker, Alice, 'The Americanisation of Sylvia', in Wagner, ed., *Critical Essays on Sylvia Plath*

Perloff, Marjorie, '*Angst* and Animism in the Poetry of Sylvia Plath', in Wagner, *Critical Essays on Sylvia Plath*

—— 'The Two Ariels: The (Re)making of the Sylvia Plath Canon', *The American Poetry Review*, November–December 1984

Plath, Aurelia, 'Notes for Author's Series Talks', Wellesley College, 1976, Smith

—— 'Letter Written in the Actuality of Spring', in Alexander, ed., *Ariel Ascending*

Pollit, Katha, 'A Note of Triumph' (review of *The Collected Poems*), in Wagner, ed., *Critical Essays on Sylvia Plath*

Rinzler, Carol E., 'Salinger and *The Bell Jar*: What Do They Mean To Publishers?', *Publisher's Weekly*, 24 April 1987

Rumens, Carol, 'The sociable self and the poet within', *New Statesman and Society*, 3 November 1989

Sage, Lorna, 'Death and Marriage', *The Times Literary Supplement*, 21 October 1977, review of *Johnny Panic and the Bible of Dreams*, in Wagner, ed., *Sylvia Plath: The Critical Heritage*

Schidlovsky, John, 'Defense says woman in *Bell Jar* wasn't based on Anderson', *Sun*, 22 January 1987

Smith, Stan, *Inviolable Voice: History and Twentieth-Century Poetry*, Dublin: Gill & Macmillan, 1982

Spender, Stephen, 'Warnings from the grave', *The New Republic*, 18 June 1966, in Newman, ed., *The Art of Sylvia Plath*

Spurling, Hilary, 'Ariel trapped and raging to be free', *Sunday Telegraph*, 5 November 1989

Starr, Mark, 'From Book to Film: A Novel Case of Libel, a Question of Character', *Newsweek*, 2 February 1987

Steiner, George, 'Dying is an Art', *The Reporter*, 7 October 1975, in Newman, ed., *The Art of Sylvia Plath*

Stevenson, Anne, 'Writing as a Woman', in Mary Jacobus, ed., *Women Writing and Writing About Women*, London: Croom Helm, 1979

—— *Bitter Fame: A Life of Sylvia Plath*, Boston: Houghton Mifflin/London: Viking, 1989

—— 'Letter To Sylvia Plath', *P.N. Review*, vol. 15, no. 6, 1989

—— 'Sylvia Plath and the Romantic Heritage', *P.N. Review*, vol. 16, no. 6, 1990

Stilwell, Robert L., 'The Multiplying of Entities: D.H. Lawrence and Five Other Poets', *Sewanee Review*, 76, July–September 1968, section on *Ariel*, reprinted in Wagner, ed., *Critical Essays on Sylvia Plath*

Thwaite, Anthony, 'Meltdown', *London Review of Books*, 29 October 1989

Uroff, Margaret Dickie, *Sylvia Plath and Ted Hughes*, Urbana: University of Illinois Press, 1979

Van Dyne, Susan, '"More Terrible Than She Ever Was": The Manuscripts of Sylvia Plath's Bee Poems', in *Sylvia Plath: Stings*, Northampton: Smith College and the Estate of Sylvia Plath, reprinted in Wagner, ed., *Critical Essays on Sylvia Plath*

—— 'Fuelling the Phoenix Fire: The Manuscripts of Sylvia Plath's "Lady Lazarus"', *Massachusetts Review*, 24, Winter 1983

Vendler, Helen, 'Who Is Sylvia', *The New Republic*, 6 November 1989, pp. 98–106

Wagner, Linda W. (Wagner-Martin) ed., *Critical Essays on Sylvia Plath*, Boston: Hall and Company, 1984

—— 'Plath's *Ladies' Home Journal* Syndrome', *Journal of American Culture*, 7, Spring–Summer 1984

—— 'Sylvia Plath's Specialness in Her Short Stories', *Journal of Narrative Technique*, 15, Winter 1985, pp. 1–14

—— *Sylvia Plath: A Biography*, London: Chatto & Windus, 1988

—— ed., *Sylvia Plath: The Critical Heritage*, London and New York: Routledge, 1988
Weatherby, W.J., 'Fact v Fiction', *Guardian*, 3 February 1987
Wood, James, 'Who is Sylvia?' *Guardian*, 2 November 1989
'The Blood Jet is Poetry', review of *Ariel, Time*, 10 June 1966
'Russian Roulette', review of *Ariel, Newsweek*, 20 June 1966
'*Bell Jar* hurt reputation, she says', 'Names and Faces', *Sun*, Baltimore, 29 January 1987
'Sylvia Cringe', *Private Eye*, 10 November 1989

## OTHER WORKS CITED

Abraham, Nicolas, 'Notes on the Phantom: A Complement to Freud's Metapsychology', in Françoise Meltzer, ed., *The Trial(s) of Psychoanalysis*, Chicago: Chicago University Press, 1988

—— and Maria Torok, 'Introjection – Incorporation: Mourning or Melancholia', in Serge Lebovici and D. Widlocher, eds, *Psychoanalysis in France*, New York: International Universities Press, 1980

—— 'Le "crime" de l'introjection', in *L'écorce et le noyau*, Paris: Flammarion, 1987

Aichinger, Ilse, *Herod's Children*, New York: Athenaeum, 1963

Alvarez, A., ed., *The New Poetry*, Harmondsworth: Penguin, 1962

—— *The Shaping Spirit*, London: Chatto, 1967

—— *Beyond All This Fiddle*, London: Allen Lane, 1968

—— *The Savage God: A Study of Suicide*, London: Weidenfeld & Nicolson, 1971

—— and Donald Davie, 'A Discussion', *The Review*, 1, April–May 1962

Arendt, Hannah, *Eichmann in Jerusalem: A Report on the Banality of Evil*, New York: Viking, 1963, revised and enlarged edition 1965: Harmondsworth: Penguin, 1977

Attridge, Derek, Geoff Bennington and Robert Young, eds, *Post-Structuralism and the Question of History*, Cambridge: Cambridge University Press, 1987

Baldick, Chris, *The Social Mission of English Criticism 1848–1932*, Oxford: Oxford University Press, 1983

Balmary, Marie, *Psycho-Analysing Psycho-Analysis*, Baltimore: Johns Hopkins University Press, 1982

Barrell, John, *Poetry, Language and Politics*, Cultural Politics, Manchester: Manchester University Press, 1988

Barthes, Roland, *S/Z*, New York: Hill & Wang, 1974

Barton, Walter E., *The History and Influence of the American Psychiatric Association*, Washington: American Psychiatric Press Inc., 1987

Benveniste, Emile, 'Subjectivity in Language', 'Correlations of Tense in the French Verb', in *Problems in General Linguistics*, Florida: University of Miami Press, 1971

Berelson, Bernard and Patricia J. Salter, 'Majority and Minority Americans: An Analysis of Magazine Fiction', in Rosenberg and White, eds, *Mass Culture: The Popular Arts in America*

Bor, Josef, *Terezin Requiem*, New York: Knopf, 1963

Borowski, Tadeusz, 'This Way for the Gas – A Story', *Commentary*, July 1962, vol. 1, no. 34

Bowlby, Rachel, '"The Problem with no Name": Rereading Friedan's *The Feminine Mystique*', *Feminist Review*, 27, September 1987

—— 'Flight Reservations', *Oxford Literary Review*, vol. 10, 1988

Brenner, Ira and Judith S. Kestenberg, 'Children who Survived the Holocaust: The Role of Rules and Routines in the Development of the Superego', *International Journal of Psycho-Analysis*, 67, 1986

Cam, Heather, '"Daddy": Sylvia Plath's Debt to Anne Sexton', in Diana Hume George, ed., *Sexton: Selected Criticism*, Urbana/Chicago: University of Illinois Press, 1988

Celan, Paul, 'Aschenglorie', *Atemwende*, 1967; *Gedichte*, Frankfurt: Suhrkamp Verlag, 1975

Chasseguet-Smirgel, Janine, '"Time's White Hair We Ruffle", Reflections on the Hamburg Conference', *International Review of Psycho-Analysis*, 14, 1987

Chadwick, Whitney, *Women and the Surrealist Movement*, London: Thames and Hudson, 1985

Cixous, Hélène, 'The Laugh of the Medusa', *Signs*, 1, Summer 1976, reprinted in Elaine Marks and Isabelle de Courtivron, eds, *New French Feminisms*, Brighton: Harvester, 1981

Clarke, John Henrik, ed., *William Styron's Nat Turner: Ten Black Writers Respond*, Boston: Beacon Press, 1968

Derrida, Jacques, 'Shibboleth' (for Paul Celan), in G.H. Hartman and S. Budick, eds, *Midrash and Literature*, New Haven: Yale University Press, 1986

Dostoyevsky, Fyodor, *The Devils*, Harmondsworth: Penguin, 1953

Duras, Marguerite, *La douleur*, Paris: POL, 1985; London: Fontana, 1987

Eckstaedt, Anita, 'Two Complementary Cases of Identification Involving Third Reich Fathers', *International Journal of Psycho-Analysis*, 67, 1986

Edelman, Bernard, 'The Character And His Double', *Identity*, ICA Documents, 6, London: Institute of Contemporary Arts, 1987

Eickhoff, F.-W., 'Identification and its Vicissitudes in the Context of the Nazi Phenomenon', *International Journal of Psycho-Analysis*, 67, 1986

Ellman, Mary, *Thinking About Women*, 1969; London: Virago, 1979

Enzensberger, Hans Magnus, 'In Search of a Lost Language', *Encounter*, September 1963

Faas, Ekbert, *Ted Hughes: The Unaccommodated Universe*, Santa Barbara: Black Sparrow, 1980

—— 'Chapters of a Shared Mythology', in Keith Sagar, ed., *The Achievement of Ted Hughes*, Manchester: Manchester University Press, 1983

Fackenheim, Emil L., 'From Bergen-Belsen to Jerusalem: Contemporary Implications of the Holocaust', The Cultural Department World Jewish Congress, Jerusalem, Institute of Contemporary Jewry, The Hebrew University of Jerusalem, 1975

Felman, Shoshona, ed., *Literature and Psychoanalysis: The Question of Reading Otherwise*, New Haven: Yale University Press, 1977

—— *Writing and Madness*, Ithaca: Cornell University Press, 1986

Fiedler, Leslie, 'The Middle Against Both Ends', *Encounter*, 5, 1955, in Rosenberg and White, eds, *Mass Culture: The Popular Arts in America*

*55 Short Stories from* The New Yorker, London: Gollancz, 1952

Freud, Sigmund, and Josef Breuer, *Studies on Hysteria*, 1893–1895, *Standard Edition*, vol. II; Pelican Freud, 3

Freud, Sigmund, *The Interpretation of Dreams*, in A.A. Brill, ed., *The Basic Writings of Sigmund Freud*, New York: Random House, 1938

—— 'Psycho-Analytic Notes on an Autobiographical Account of a Case of Paranoia', 1911, in James Strachey, ed., *The Standard Edition of the Complete Psychological Works of Sigmund Freud*, 24 vols, London: Hogarth, 1953–73, vol. XII; Pelican Freud, 9

—— 'On the Universal Tendency to Debasement in the Sphere of Love', Contributions to the Psychology of Love, II, 1912, *Standard Edition*, vol. XI; Pelican Freud, 7

—— 'On the History of the Psycho-Analytic Movement', 1914, *Standard Edition*, vol. XIV, Pelican Freud, 15

—— 'Mourning and Melancholia', 1915, *Standard Edition*,. vol. XIV; Pelican Freud, 11

—— 'Psychogenesis of a Case of Homosexuality in a Woman', 1920, *Standard Edition*, vol. XVIII; Pelican Freud, 9

—— *Beyond the Pleasure Principle*, 1920, *Standard Edition*, vol. XVIII; Pelican Freud, 11

—— *Group Psychology and the Analysis of the Ego*, 1921, *Standard Edition*, vol. XVIII; Pelican Freud, 12

—— *The Ego and the Id*, 1923, *Standard Edition*, vol. XIX; Pelican Freud, 11

—— 'Negation', 1923, *Standard Edition*, vol. XIX; Pelican Freud, 11

—— 'The Dissolution of the Oedipus Complex', 1924, *Standard Edition*, vol. XIX; Pelican Freud, 7

—— 'Some Psychical Consequences of the Anatomical Distinction Between the Sexes', 1925, *Standard Edition*, vol. XIX; Pelican Freud, 7

—— *Civilisation and its Discontents*, 1930, *Standard Edition*, vol. XXI; Pelican Freud, 12

—— 'Female Sexuality', 1931, *Standard Edition*, vol. XXI; Pelican Freud, 7

—— 'Femininity', 1933, *Standard Edition*, vol. XXII: Pelican Freud, 2

—— 'Medusa's Head', 1940 (1922), *Standard Edition*, vol. XVIII

—— and Josef Breuer, *Studies on Hysteria*, 1893–1895, *Standard Edition*, vol. II; Pelican Freud, 3

Friedan, Betty, *The Feminine Mystique*, New York: Norton, 1963; Harmondsworth: Penguin, 1965

Friedlander, Saul, *Reflections of Nazism*, New York: Harper & Row, 1984

Garber, Zev and Bruce Zuckerman, 'Why Do We Call the Holocaust "The Holocaust"? An Inquiry into the Psychology of Labels', in *Remembering For the Future*, Oxford: Oxford University Press, 1988, vol. 2, *The Impact of the Holocaust on the Contemporary World*

Gasset, Ortega Y, *The Revolt of the Masses*, London: Allen & Unwin, 1932 (1950)

Gilbert, Sandra, and Susan Gubar, *The Madwoman in the Attic: The Woman Writer and the Nineteenth Century Literary Imagination*, New Haven and London: Yale University Press, 1979

Glover, Edward, and Morris Ginsberg, 'A Symposium on the Psychology of Peace and War', *British Journal of Medical Psychology*, 14, 1934

Graves, Robert, *The White Goddess: a historical grammar of poetic myth*, 1946, London: Faber & Faber, 1961

Greenblatt, Stephen, 'Capitalist Culture and the Circulatory System', in Murray Krieger, ed., *The Aims of Representation*

Grubrich-Simitis, Ilse, 'From Concretism to Metaphor: Thoughts on Some Theoretical and Technical Aspects of the Psychoanalytic Work with Children of Holocaust Survivors', *Psychoanalytic Study of the Child*, 39, 1984

Guilbaut, Serge, *How New York Stole the Idea of Modern Art*, Chicago: Chicago University Press, 1983

Haggard, H. Rider, *She*, London: Longmans, Green and Company, 1887

Hamacher, Werner, Neil Hertz and Thomas Keenan, eds, *Responses*, Lincoln, NB/London: University of Nebraska Press, 1989

Hamilton, Richard, *Robert Lowell: A Biography*, London: Faber, 1983

Hertz, Neil, 'Lurid Figures', in Lindsay Waters and Wlad Godzich, eds, *Reading de Man Reading*, Minneapolis: University of Minnesota Press, 1989

—— 'More Lurid Figures' *Diacritics*, vol. 21, no. 1, 1991

Hjelmslev, Louis, *Prologomena to a Theory of Language*, University of Wisconsin Press, 1963

Holbrook, David, *English for Maturity: English in the Secondary School*, Cambridge: Cambridge University Press, 1961

—— *Lost Bearings in English Poetry*, London: Vision, 1977

—— *Human Hope and the Death Instinct: An exploration of psychoanalytic theories of human nature and their implications for culture and education*, London: Pergamon, 1971

Howe, Irving, 'Notes on Mass Culture', in Rosenberg and White, *Mass Culture*

Hughes, Ted, *The Hawk in the Rain*, London: Faber & Faber, 1957, 1968

—— *Lupercal*, London: Faber & Faber, 1960, 1970

—— *Wodwo*, London: Faber & Faber, 1967

—— *A Choice of Shakespeare's Verse*, selected with an introduction by Ted Hughes, London: Faber & Faber, 1971

—— *Crow: From the Life and Songs of the Crow*, London: Faber & Faber, 1972

Hurd, Henry M., ed., *The Institutional Care of the Insane in the United States and Canada*, Baltimore: Johns Hopkins University Press, 1916, vol. II

Huyssen, Andreas, 'Mass Culture as Woman: Modernism's Other', in *After The Great Divide: Modernism, Mass Culture, Postmodernism*, Bloomington: Indiana University Press, 1986; London: Macmillan, 1988

Irigaray, Luce, *This Sex Which Isn't One*, Ithaca: Cornell University Press, 1985

Jakobson, Roman, 'Closing Statements: Linguistics and Poetics', in T. Sebeok, *Style in Language*, Cambridge, MA: MIT, 1970

Jarrell, Randall, *Poetry and the Age*, New York: Vintage, 1953

Jones, Ann Rosalind, 'Writing the Body: Toward an Understanding of *l'Ecriture féminine*', in Elaine Showalter, ed., *The New Feminist Criticism: Essays on Women, Literature and Theory*, London: Virago/New York: Pantheon, 1985

Jung, Carl Gustav, *Symbols of Transformation, The Collected Works of C.G. Jung*, vol. II, London: Routledge & Kegan Paul, 1956

Kaplan, Cora, *Salt and Bitter and Good: Three Centuries of English and American Poets*, London: Paddington Press/Canada: Random House, 1975

—— *Sea Changes: Culture and Feminism*, London: Verso, 1986

Kinkead-Weakes, M., '*Clarissa* Restored?', *Review of English Studies*, vol. 10, no. 38, 1959

Klein, Hillel and Ilany Kogan, 'Identification Processes and Denial in the Shadow of Nazism', *International Journal of Psycho-Analysis*, 67, 1986

Klein, Melanie, 'Early Stages of the Oedipus Conflict', 1929, in Juliet Mitchell, ed., *The Selected Melanie Klein*, Harmondsworth: Penguin, 1986

—— 'Notes on Some Schizoid Mechanisms', 1946, in *The Selected Melanie Klein*

Koonz, Claudia, *Mothers in the Fatherland: Women, the Family and Nazi Politics*, London: Jonathan Cape, 1987

Kramer, Dale, *Ross and The New Yorker*, London: Gollancz, 1952

Krieger, Murray, ed., *The Aims of Representation: Subject, Text, History*, New York: Columbia University Press, 1987

Kristeva, Julia, *Powers of Horror*, New York: Columbia University Press, 1982

—— 'From One Identity to Another', in *Desire in Language*, Oxford: Blackwell, 1980

—— *Tales of Love*, New York: Columbia University Press, 1987

Krull, Marianne, *Freud and His Father*, London: Hutchinson, 1986

Krystal, Henry, Review of Martin S. Bergmann and Milton E. Jucovy, *Generations of the Holocaust*, New York: Basic Books, 1982, in *Psycho-Analytic Quarterly*, 53

Lacan, Jacques, 'The function and field of speech and language in psychoanalysis', 1953, in *Ecrits: A Selection*, London: Tavistock, 1977

Lanzmann, Claude, *Shoah, An Oral History of the Holocaust: The Complete Text of the Film*, New York: Pantheon, 1985

Laplanche, Jean, *New Foundations for Psychoanalysis*, Oxford: Blackwell, 1989

Levi, Primo, *If This Is A Man*, Turin: Antonicelli, 1947; Oxford: The Bodley Head, 1960; Harmondsworth: Penguin, 1979 and Italian edition, *Se questo è un vomo*, Turin: Enaudi, 1982

—— *The Drowned and the Saved*, London: Michael Joseph, 1988

Lévi-Strauss, Claude, 'The Structural Study of Myth', *Structural Anthropology*, vol. I, London: Allen Lane, 1963

Lowell, Robert, *Life Studies*, New York: Random House, 1959

Luel, Steven A. and Paul Marcus, *Psychoanalytic Reflections on the Holocaust: Selected Essays*, Denver: Holocaust Awareness Institute and Center for Judaic Studies/New York: Ktav Publishing, 1984

Lustig, Arnost, *Night and Hope*, New York: Dutton, 1962

Lyotard, Jean-François, *The Differend: Phrases in Dispute*, Manchester: Manchester University Press, 1988

—— 'Judiciousness in Dispute, or Kant after Marx', in Murray Kreiger, ed., *The Aims of Representation*

Macalpine, Ida and Richard Hunter, eds, Daniel Paul Schreber, *Memoirs of My Nervous Illness*, 1955, new edition, Cambridge, MA/London: Harvard University Press, 1988

MacCormack, Carol P. and Marilyn Strathern, *Nature, Culture and Gender*, Cambridge: Cambridge University Press, 1980

MacDonald, Dwight, 'A Theory of Mass Culture', *Diogenes*, 3, Summer 1953, in Rosenberg and White, eds, *Mass Culture: The Popular Arts in America*

MacDonald, George, *Lilith*, 1895; London: Gollancz 1962

Paul de Man, 'Autobiography As De-Facement', in *The Rhetoric of Romanticism*, New York: Columbia University Press, 1984

—— 'The Resistance to Theory', in *The Resistance to Theory*, Minneapolis: University of Minnesota Press, 1986

Masson, Jeffrey, *Freud: The Assault on Truth – Freud's Suppression of the Seduction Theory*, London: Faber, 1984

Maugham, Somerset, 'Rain', *The Complete Short Stories*, vol. 1, London: Heinemann, 1951

Middlebrook, Diane Wood and Diana Hume George, eds, *Selected Poems of Anne Sexton*, Boston: Houghton Mifflin, 1988

Miller, Douglas and Marion Novak, *The Way We Really Were*, New York: Doubleday, 1974

Millett, Kate, *Sexual Politics*, 1969, London: Virago, 1977

Mitchell, Juliet, *Psychoanalysis and Feminism*, London: Allen Lane, 1974

—— and Jacqueline Rose, eds, *Feminine Sexuality: Jacques Lacan and the école freudienne*, London: Macmillan 1982

Mitscherlich, Alexander and Margarete, *The Inability to Mourn*, London: Grove Press, 1975

Modleski, Tania, *Loving with a Vengeance: Mass-Produced Fantasies for Women*, 1982, New York/London: Methuen, 1984

Moers, Ellen, *Literary Women*, Princeton: Princeton University Press, 1977; London: The Women's Press, 1978

Moi, Toril, *Sexual/Textual Politics: Feminist Literary Theory*, London/New York: Methuen, 1985

Montefiore, Jan, *Feminism and Poetry: Language, Experience, Identity in Women's Writing*, London: Pandora, 1987

Mulhern, Frances, *The Moment of Scrutiny*, London: Verso, 1979

Nault, Marianne, 'Explorer of the underworld within', interview with Anne Stevenson, *Observer*, 15 October 1989

Ohmann, Richard, *Politics of Letters*, Middletown: Wesleyan University Press, 1987

Ortner, Sherry, 'Is Female to Male as Nature Is to Culture?', in Michelle Zimbalist Rosaldo and Louise Lamphere, eds, *Woman, Culture and Society*, California: Stanford University Press, 1974

Ostow, Mortimer, 'The Psychodynamics of Apocalyptic: Discussion of Papers on Identification and the Nazi Phenomenon', *International Journal of Psycho-Analysis*, 67, 1986

Pilinsky, Janos, *Selected Poems*, translated by Ted Hughes, Manchester: Carcanet Press, 1976

Pines, Dinora, 'Working with Women Survivors of the Holocaust: Affective Experiences in Transference and Counter-Transference', *International Journal of Psycho-Analysis*, 67, 1986

Plath, Otto, *Bumblebees and their Ways*, New York: Macmillan, 1934

—— 'Insect Societies', in Carl Murchison, ed., *A Handbook of Social Psychology*, Massachusetts: Clark University Press/London: Oxford University Press, 1935

Prouty, Olive Higgins, *Stella Dallas*, Boston: Houghton Mifflin, 1923; London: Virago reprint, 1990

—— *Now Voyager*, London: Hodder & Stoughton, 1942

Radin, Paul, *African Folktales and Sculpture*, Bollingen Series, XXXII, New York: Pantheon, 1952

Radway, Janice A, *Reading the Romance: Women, Patriarchy and Popular Literature*, Carolina: University of North Carolina Press, 1984; London: Verso, 1987

Rawicz, Piotr, *Le sang du ciel*, Paris: Gallimard, 1961; *Blood From the Sky*, London: Secker & Warburg, 1964

Richardson, Samuel, *Clarissa, or, The History of a Young Lady*, London: Rivington & Osborne, 1747–8

Riviere, Joan, ed., *Developments in Psycho-Analysis*, London: Hogarth, 1952

Roethke, Theodore, *The Lost Son and Other Poems*, 1948 in *The Collected Poems of Theodore Roethke*, New York: Doubleday, 1975

Rogin, Michael, *Ronald Reagan, The Movie, and Other Essays in Political Demonology*, Berkeley: University of California Press, 1987

Rosenberg, Bernard, 'Mass Culture in America', in Rosenberg and White, eds, *Mass Culture: The Popular Arts in America*

Rosenberg, Bernard, and White, David Manning, eds, *Mass Culture: The Popular Arts in America*, New York: The Free Press, 1957

Rosenfeld, David, 'Identification and its Vicissitudes in Relation to the Nazi Phenomenon', *International Journal of Psycho-Analysis*, 67, 1986

Ross, Andrew, *No Respect: Intellectuals and Popular Culture*, New York/London: Routledge, 1989

Ruskin, John, *Sesame and Lilies*, 1885; London: Allen & Unwin, 1919

Sagar, Keith, ed., *The Achievement of Ted Hughes*, Manchester: Manchester University Press, 1983

de Saussure, Ferdinand, *Course in General Linguistics*, 1915, London: Fontana, 1974

Sayle, Murray, 'Adolf and the Women', *The Independent Magazine*, 9 November 1988

Schor, Naomi, *Reading in Detail: Aesthetics and the Feminine*, London/New York: Methuen, 1987

Schwartz, Murray M. and Coppelia Kahn, eds, *Representing Shakespeare: New Psychoanalytic Essays*, Baltimore/London, Johns Hopkins University Press, 1980

Schweik, Sue, 'Writing War-Poetry Like a Woman,' *Critical Inquiry*, 13, 3, Spring 1987

Scott, Ann, 'Feminism and the Seductiveness of the Real Event', *Feminist Review*, Special Issue: *Family Secrets: Child Sexual Abuse*, 28, Spring 1988

Segal, Hanna, 'Silence is the Real Crime', *International Review of Psycho-Analysis*, 14, 1987

Seidal, Gill, *The Holocaust Denial: Antisemitism, Racism and the New Right*, Brighton: Beyond the Pale Collective, 1986

Sexton, Anne, 'Dancing the Jig', *New World Writing*, 1960, typescript of first draft, dated 13 October 1959, Texas Collection, 9pp.

Showalter, Elaine, *A Literature Of Their Own: British Women Novelists from Brontë to Lessing*, Princeton University Press, 1977; London: Virago, 1978

Sinfield, Alan, *Literature, Politics and Culture in Postwar Britain*, London: Routledge, 1989

Snitow, Ann, Christine Stansell and Sharon Thompson, eds, *Desire: The Politics of Sexuality*, New York: Monthly Review Press, 1983; London: Virago, 1984

Stafford, Jean, *Boston Adventure*, 1946; London: Hogarth, 1986

—— 'Children Are Bored on Sundays', *55 Short Stories from* The New Yorker

Stallybrass, Peter, and Allon White, *The Politics and Poetics of Transgression*, London: Methuen, 1986

Styron, William, *Lie Down in Darkness*, Indianapolis/New York: Bobbs-Merrill, 1951

Theweleit, Klaus, *Male Fantasies*, vol. I, *Women, Floods, Bodies, History*, Cambridge: Polity Press, 1987

Thomas, D.M., *The White Hotel*, London: Gollancz, 1981

*To Secure These Rights*, The Report of the President's Committee on Civil Rights, introduction by Charles Wilson, New York: Simon & Schuster, 1947

Trotter, David, *The Making of the Reader: Language and Subjectivity in Modern American*

*English and Irish Poetry*, London: Macmillan, 1984

Vance, Carole S., ed., *Pleasure and Danger: Exploring Female Sexuality*, London: Routledge & Kegan Paul, 1984

Walker, Alice, *The Color Purple*, London: The Women's Press, 1985

White, Allon, 'Too Close to the Bone: Fragments of an Autobiography' *London Review of Books*, vol. 11, no. 9, 4 May 1989

Wiesel, Elie, *Night*, New York: Hill & Wang, 1960; Paris, 1960; first published in Yiddish in 1956

Wieseltier, Leon, 'In a Universe of Ghosts', *New York Review of Books*, 25 November 1976

Wilson, Elizabeth, 'Coming out for a brand new age', *Guardian*, 14 March 1989

Winnicott, D.W. 'Creativity and its Origins', in *Playing and Reality*, London: Tavistock, 1971

—— 'Split-Off Male and Female Elements Found Clinically in Men and Women: Theoretical Inferences', 1966, in J. Linden, ed., *Psychoanalytic Forum*, vol. 4, New York: International Universities Press, 1972

—— 'Fear of Breakdown', in Gregorio Kohon, ed., *The British School of Psychoanalysis: The Independent Tradition*, London: Free Association Books, 1986

Woolf, Virginia, *A Room of One's Own*, London: Hogarth, 1929

—— *Three Guineas*, London: Hogarth, 1938; Harmondsworth: Penguin, 1977

Wordsworth, William, 'Essays upon Epitaphs', in W.J.B. Owen, ed., *Wordsworth's Literary Criticism*, London: Routledge, 1974

Wylie, Philip, *Generation of Vipers*, 1942, New York: Rinehart, 1946

# INDEX

Abraham, Nicolas and Maria Torok, 68, 243n, 246n
Aichinger, Ilse, *Herod's Children*, 216, 269n
Aird, Aileen, 239n
Alexander, Paul, 249n, 259n
Alvarez, A., 21–27, 99, 240n, 241n, 246n, 252n; 'Extremism' 21–23; 'Literature of the Holocaust' 24, 216, 241n, 269n; *The New Poetry*, 21, 240n, 241n; *The Savage God*, 22–3, 26
Anderson, Jane, 106–10
Arendt, Hannah, 214, 269n
*Atlantic Monthly, The*, 173
Attridge, Derek, Geoff Bennington and Robert Young, 267n
Auden, W. H., 173, 198

Baldick, Chris, 240n
Balmary, Marie, 239n
Barrell, John, 258n
Barthes, Roland, 263n, 266n
Barzun, Jacques, *Darwin, Marx and Wagner*, 197, 265n
Bataille, Georges, 140
*Bell Jar, The*, suit, 106–11
Bellour, Raymond, and Nancy Huston, 160, 261n, 264n
Bellow, Saul, 21
Benveniste, Emile, 247n
Bere, Carol, 249n
Berelson, Bernard and Patricia J. Salter, 266n
Bergmann, Martin S. and Milton E. Jucovy, 268n
Beutscher, Ruth, 83–5, 250n
Blau, Eleanor, 255n
Bor, Josef, *Terezin Requiem*, 216, 269n
Borowski, Tadeusz, 269n
Bowlby, Rachel, 242n, 263n
Brans, Jo, 249n
Brenner, Ira and Judith S. Kerstenberg, 267n
Brodsky, Joseph, 246n
Broe, Mary Lynn, 259n
Buñuel, Luis, *Un Chien Andalou*, 140
Butscher, Edward, *Sylvia Plath: Method and Madness*, 106, 169, 262n; 'In Search of Sylvia', 11–13, 239n

Cam, Heather, 269n
Carey, John, 246n
Cary, Joyce, 174
Celan, Paul, 215, 216–17, 269n
Chadwick, Whitney, 258n
Chasseguet-Smirgel, Janine, 209, 267n
*Christian Science Monitor, The*, 173, 179, 185–6
Cixous, Hélène 26, 33, 242n
Clarke, John Henrik, 271n
Cleverdon, Douglas, 245n
Coleridge, S.T., 25
Communism, 79, 111, 166, 195–7, 203

Davie, Donald, 24
Davison, Peter, 95
Defoe, Daniel, *Journal of the Plague Year*, 57
Derrida, Jacques, 'Shibboleth', 217
Dostoyevsky, Fyodor, 17, 38, 244n
Duras, Marguerite, *La douleur*, 238, 272n

Eckstaedt, Anita, 267n, 268n
*écriture féminine*, 26, 30, 118–19, 227, 235
Edelman, Bernard, 255n
Eich, Gunter, 270n
Eickhoff, F.–W., 267n, 268n
Eisenhower, 9
Eliot, T.S., 25, 216–17
Ellman, Mary, *Thinking About Women*, 17, 240n
Emerson, R.W., 173
Enzensberger, Hans Magnus, 221, 270n

Faas, Ekbert, 157, 160, 245n, 259n, 260n, 261n
Fackenheim, Emil, 214, 216, 269n
fascism, 7–8, 157, 232–3
Felman, Shoshana, 12, 16, 58, 239n, 245n
feminism, 3, 6, 9–10, 19, 87, 99, 115–18, 123, 163, 167–8
feminist literary criticism, 26–28, 30, 99–100, 118–19, 121–2, 139, 145, 235
Ferrier, Carole, 257n, 260n, 262n
Fiedler, Leslie, 'The Middle Against Both Ends', 169, 200, 262n, 266n
Flaubert, Gustave, *Madame Bovary*, 192–4

Fraser, G.S., 262n
Friedan, Betty, *The Feminine Mystique*, 175, 263n
Friedlander, Saul, *Reflections of Nazism*, 236, 272n
Freud, Sigmund, 4, 5, 9, 13, 17–18, 36, 50, 103–4, 138, 161–2, 224, 230, 240n, 244, 251n, 253n, 257n, 261n, 268n, 271n; *The Basic Writings of Sigmund Freud*, 32; 'Medusa's Head', 151; 'Mourning and Melancolia', 33, 103, 254n; 'Negation', 32, 243n; 'On the History of the Psycho-Analytic Movement', 162, 261n; 'On the Universal Tendency to Debasement in the Sphere of Love', 154; 'Psychoanalytic Notes on an Autobiographical Case of Paranoia (Schreber)', 4, 55, 211–12, 245n, 268n

Garber, Zev and Bruce Zuckerman, 210, 268n
*Gemini*, 173
George, Diana Hume, 269n
Gilbert, Sandra, 245n, 256n, 258n, 259n, 264n
Gilbert, Sandra and Susan Gubar, *The Mad Woman in the Attic*, 24, 26, 30, 117, 145, 239–40n, 241n, 242n, 243n, 259n; *The War of the Words*, 121–2, 256n
Glover, Edward, 237 and Morris Ginsberg, 272n
Goethe, J.W., 173
*Gone With The Wind*, 185–6, 198
*Good Housekeeping*, 170–71
Graham, Helga, 246n
*Grand Street*, 251n
*Granta*, 173, 181
Graves, Robert, 18, 54, 150–4, 160, 163–4, 219, 245n, 260n, 261n, 270n
Greenblatt, Stephen, 271n
Grubrich-Simitis, Ilse, 'From Concretism to Metaphor: Thoughts on Some Theoretical and Technical Aspects of the Psychoanalytic Work with Children of Holocaust Survivors', 213–14, 268n
Guilbaut, Serge, 265n

Haggard, H. Rider, 239n
Hamacher, Werner, Neil Hertz and Thomas Keenan, 267n
Hamilton, Ian, 252n, 255n
Hamilton, Richard, 244n
Hazlitt, William, 173

Hayman, Ronald, 65–9, 246n, 247n, 253n
Heany, Seamus, 206, 267n
Heller, Linda, 250n
Hemingway, Ernest, 172
Hertz, Neil, 257n, 267n
Hitchens, Christopher, 254n, 255n
Hjelmslev, Louis, 174, 263n
Holbrook, David, *Sylvia Plath: Poetry and Existence*, 15–20, 22–25, 41, 131, 239n, 240n, 241n, 242n, 257n
Holocaust, 7–8, 205–17, 221, 227–9
Homberger, Eric, 248n
Howard, Richard, 'Sylvia Plath: "And I Have No Face, I Have Wanted to Efface Myself"', 11–13, 239n
Howe, Irving, 183, 264n, 267n
Hughes, Olwyn, 74, 88, 92–7, 100, 246n, 247n, 251n, 252n, 253n; 'Notes on *The Haunting of Sylvia Plath*' 247n, 252n, 253n; Rainbow Press, 74, 86, 251n
Hughes, Ted, 2, 5, 6, 41–42, 61, 65–74, 76–8, 80, 84–108, 112, 121–9, 136, 144, 150–64, 181, 239n, 241n, 242n, 244n, 245n, 246n, 247n, 248n, 249n, 250n, 251n, 252n, 253n, 254n, 255n, 256n, 257n, 258n, 259n, 260n, 261n, 263n, 264n, 269n, 270n; 'The Ancient Heroes and the Bomber Pilot', 156; 'Bayonet Charge', 156; *A Choice of Shakespeare's Verse*, 150; *Crow*, 157, 160; 'Fragments of an Antique Tablet', 161; 'Fire-Eater', 158; *Gaudete*, 160; 'Gog', 158; 'Griefs for Dead Soldiers', 156; 'The Harvesting', 163; *The Hawk in the Rain*, 156; 'Law in the Country of the Cats', 124; 'Logos', 156; *Lupercal*, 156–8; 'Mayday on Holderness', 157–8; 'The Perfect Forms', 156; 'Six Young Men', 156; 'To Paint A Water Lily', 128; 'Thrushes', 156; 'Two Wise Generals', 156; *Wodwo*, 156–7, 158; 'The Wound', 156–7, 158
Hurd, Henry M., 250n
Huyssen, Andreas, *After The Great Divide*, 192–3, 265n

International Association of Psychoanalysis 207–13
Irigaray, Luce, 30, 33, 242n, 243n

Jakobson, Roman, 50, 245n
James, Henry, 174; *The Turn of the Screw*, 12–15, 125

Jarrell, Randall, *Poetry and the Age*, 197, 265n
Jones, Ann Rosalind, 242n
Jong, Erica, 249n
Joyce, James, 186; *Finnegan's Wake*, 185; *Ulysses*, 120, 183
Jung, Carl Gustav, *Symbols of Transformation*, 161–3, 261n

Kaplan, Cora, *Sea Changes*, 198, 245n, 258n, 266n
Kaufman, Irving, 255n
Kenner, Hugh, 'Sincerity Kills', 11–13, 239n
Klein, Elinor, 204, 266n
Klein, Hillel and Ilany Kogan, 'Identification Process and Denial in the Shadow of Nazism', 222, 267n, 270n
Klein, Melanie, 14, 32, 239n, 243n,
Knopf, 40, 42, 59
Kohon, Gregorio, 270n
Koonz, Claudia, 271n
Kramer, Dale, *Ross and The New Yorker*, 187, 190, 264n, 265n
Kraus, Karl, 215, 269n
Krieger, Murray, 270n, 271n
Kristeva, Julia, 149, 259n; *Powers of Horror*, 18, 25, 33–5, 38–9, 52, 57, 240n, 243n, 244n, 245n, 257n; *Tales of Love*, 225, 270n
Kroll, Judith, *Chapters in a Mythology*, 41, 49, 59, 62, 102, 134–5, 153, 221, 244n, 257n, 268n, 269n
Krull, Marianne, 239n
Krystal, Henry, 268n

Lacan, Jacques, 230, 270n, 271n
*Ladies' Home Journal, The*, 170–2, 175–7, 178
Lane, Gary, *Sylvia Plath: New Views on the Poetry*, 11, 239n
Langdon-Davies, John, *A Short History of Women*, 116–18
Lanzmann, Claude, *Shoah*, 226, 270n
Laplanche, Jean, 239n
Lawrence, D.H., 25, 139, 174
Leavis, F.R., 20, 22 *Scrutiny*, 20
Levi, Primo, 230; *The Drowned and the Saved*, 210–11, 268n, 269n; *If This Is a Man*, 215, 269n
Lévi-Strauss, Claude, 35, 63, 245n
*Life*, 186
Lindemann, Dr. Erich, 83–4, 250n
literary criticism, 1, 11–28 *passim*, 39
*London Magazine, The*, 174
Lowell, Robert, 21, 24–25, 30, 35, 165, 189, 217, 243n, 265n

Luel, Stephen A. and Paul Marcus, 267n
Lustig, Arnost, *Night and Hope*, 211, 268n
Lyotard, Jean-Francois, 223, 226, 230, 236, 270n, 271n

*McCall's*, 171, 173, 175
MacCormack, Carol P. and Marilyn Strathern, 271n
McCullough, Frances, 88, 90, 242n, 246n, 247n, 248n, 251n, 252n
MacDonald, Dwight, 'A Theory of Mass Culture', 169, 262n
MacDonald, George, *Lilith*, 15–16, 239n
McLean Hospital, 83, 110
McNeil, Helen, 257n
*Mademoiselle*, 75, 142, 167, 170, 173–4, 179
de Man, Paul, 132, 207, 254n, 255n, 257n, 267n
Marks, Elaine and Isabelle de Courtivron, 242n
Masson, Jeffrey, 239n
Maugham, Somerset, 'Quartet', 182, 200; 'Rain', 200, 266n
Mead, Margaret, *Male and Female* 176
Meltzer, Françoise, 246n
Merwin, Dido, 253n
Merwin, W.S., 253n
Middlebrook, Diane, 244n, 253n, and Diana Hume George, 269n
Milford, Nancy, 121–2, 256n
Miller, Douglas and Marion Novak, *The Fifties: The Way We Really Were*, 202, 266n
Mitchell, Juliet and Jacqueline Rose, 271n
Mitgang, Herbert, 255n
Mitscherlich, Alexander and Margarete, *The Inability to Mourn*, 235, 272n
Modleski, Tania, *Loving with a Vengeance*, 167–8, 178, 262n, 264n
Moers, Ellen, 256n
Moi, Toril, 242n, 259n
Montefiore, Janet, 245n
Moore, Marianne, 267n
Morgan, Robin, 'The Arraignment', 99–100, 254n
Morrison, Blake, 262n
Mulhern, Frances, 240n
Murphy, Richard, 253n
Myers, Lucas, 167, 253n, 262n

Nault, Marianne, 253n
Nazism, 166, 208–11, 222, 229, 232–3, 235–6
Newman, Charles, ed., *The Art of Sylvia Plath*, 11, 239n, 248n, 250n
*New Statesman*, 3

*New Yorker, The*, 165, 170–73, 185–90, 202
Nixon, Richard, 9

Oates, Joyce Carol, 'The Death Throes of Romanticism', 19, 24, 206, 240n, 241n, 242n, 267n
Oesterrich, Paul, *Possession: Demoniacal and Other*, 57
Ohmann, Richard, 271n
Orr, Peter, 270n, 271n
Ortner, Sherry, 235, 271n
Ostow, Mortimer, 267n
Ostriker, Alice, 184, 264n

Parnaby, Julia and Rachel Wingfield, 246n
*Penthouse*, 108
Perloff, Marjorie, 'The Two Ariels: The (Re)Making of the Ariel Canon', 71, 139, 206, 244n, 247n, 251n, 258n, 267n
Pilinsky, Janos, 269n
Pines, Dinora, 267n, 268n
Plath, Aurelia, 74–87, 89–91, 101–2, 107, 124, 127, 247n, 249n, 250n, 251n, 254n, 260n, 263n, 266n, 271n
Plath, Otto, 229–31; *Bumblebees and Their Ways*, 230, 271n; 'Insect Societies', 230–1, 271n
Plath, Sylvia, works mentioned:
'Above the Oxbow', 179
'All the Dead Dears' (poem), 1
'All the Dead Dears' (story), 1–2
'Amnesiac', 146–7
*Ariel*, 9, 40, 70–3, 75, 76, 102, 133, 135, 142–9, 168, 183–4, 223
'The Babysitters', 165, 203
*The Bell Jar*, 56, 75-6, 82, 104, 106–11, 142, 177, 184–8, 194–6, 203–4, 231
'Blackberrying', 133
'Bluebeard', 126
'Brazilia', 143
'The Burnt-Out Spa', 130, 133–4
'Childless Woman', 143
Collage 1960, 9–10
*Collected Poems*, 72–4, 86, 89–90, 114–15, 143, 155
*The Colossus*, 40, 92, 101, 131
'A Comparison', 172
'Context', 134
'Conversation Among the Ruins', 89–90
*Crossing the Water*, 19
*Crystal Gazer*, 86
'Daddy', 205–7, 213, 220, 222–238
'The Daughters of Blossom Street', 203
'Death and Co.', 24, 184
'Dialogue Over a Ouija Board', 155

'The Disquieting Muses', 75
'Electra on Azalea Path', 111–12
'Event', 143, 147
'Fever 103°', 134, 144–5
'The Fifteen-Dollar Eagle', 179, 203
'Full Fathom Five', 130–3
'Getting There', 148
'Gigolo', 134
'Hanging Man', 134
'I Am An American', 197
'In the Mountains', 172
'Insolent Storm Strikes at the Skull', 210
'Insomniac', 134
'Johnny Panic and the Bible of Dreams', 40, 56, 83, 179
*Johnny Panic and the Bible of Dreams*, 73, 119, 168, 181, 199
*Journals*, 3, 29–31, 33–38, 40, 56, 63–4, 72, 73, 76, 79–80, 81–2, 88–92, 96, 101–3, 116–128, 146, 150, 152, 153, 157, 165, 170–9, 182–3, 195, 202, 204, 226, 227, 238
'The Lady and the Earthenware Head', 2
'Lady Lazarus', 134, 144
'Leaving Early', 134
'Letter in November', 68
*Letters Home*, 36, 40, 74–87, 104, 116–18, 127–8, 145–6, 165, 170–2, 198, 203–204, 227
'Little Fugue', 205, 219–222, 231
'Lorelei', 130
'Lyonesse', 147
*Lyonesse*, 86
'Magi', 19
'Medusa', 183
'Metamorphoses of the Moon', 115
'Mothers', 204
'The Night Dances', 147–8
'Ocean 1212', 146
'On the Difficulty of Conjuring Up a Dryad', 114–15
'On the Plethora of Dryads', 114–16, 123
'Paralytic', 134
'The Perfect Set-Up', 203
'Pursuit', 80
'Poem for a Birthday', 40–63, 83, 85, 103, 157, 161, 179
'The Rabbit Catcher', 135–143, 147, 155
'The Shadow', 179, 199–202, 204, 238
'The Shrike', 153
'Snow Blitz', 73
'Song For A Revolutionary Love', 210
'Superman and Paula Brown's New Snowsuit', 199–201
'Strumpet Song', 72
'Suicide Off Egg Rock', 134

'Sunday at the Mintons', 179
'The Surgeon at 2 a.m.', 134
'Sweetie-Pie and the Gutter Men', 177, 179
'This Earth Our Hospital', 179
'Three Women', 48–49, 102, 159
'Tongues of Stone', 55–6
'The Wishing Box', 124–5, 153, 179–81
'Wuthering Heights', 130, 133, 135
Plath, Sylvia:
– and abjection, 33–34, 37–39, 52–3, 57–8, 127–9
– adulation of, 1, 3, 39
– alias Victoria Lucas, 75, 184, Sadie Peregrine, 178–9, 181, 199, 201–3, Alison Arnold, Sylvan Hughes, Sandra Peters, 184
– culture (high and low), 8–10, 19–23, 81–2, 119, 164, 165–89 passim, 195–204
– and death, 3, 23, 35–37
– diagnosis of, 3–6, 15–19
– editing of her work, 2, 64, 65–105, censorship of, 64, 65–92 passim
– and fantasy, 5, 11, 38, 55–6, 87, 114–164 passim, 205–38 passim; fantasies about, 11–28 passim, 66
– and feminism, feminist readings of, 3, 6, 9–10, 87, 99, 120–1, 130, 133–4, 139, 144–50, 162–3, 167; as term of abuse in relation to Plath, 19, 93, 99
– and ghosts (haunting), 1–3, 6, 8, 10
– her gravestone, 65, 97, 111–12
– and the Holocaust, 7–8, 205–238 passim
– and illness, 36, 78–9, 83–5, 127–9, 224
– and the institution of literary criticism, 11–28 passim, 42, 'psychotic' criticism of, 14–16
– and politics, 7, 63–4, 111, 163, 195–8; Communism, 79, 111, 195, 197; fascism, 7–8, 157
– psychotherapy, 83–85
– writing, the body in relation to, 27–28, 29–64, passim, 117–19, 227, 235; poetry and prose, 119, 172; and sexual difference, 114–20, 172, 227, 235
Plath, Warren, 263n, and Maggie, 251n
Pollit, Katha, 261n
postmodernism, 25, 42
Prouty, Olive Higgins, 83–5, 189, 250n, 251n; Now Voyager, 193–5, 263n, 265n; Stella Dallas, 191–3, 196, 265n

Rabinowicz, Dorothy, New Lives: Survivors of the Holocaust, 205–6

Radin, Paul, African Folktales and Sculpture, 62–63, 245n
Radway, Janice, Reading the Romance, 178, 263n
Rawicz, Piotr, Blood From The Sky, 215–16, 269n
Review, The 22, 24
Rich, Adrienne, 99, 140
Richardson, Samuel, Clarissa, 91, 252n
Riding, Laura, 152, 240n
Rinzler, Carol E., 255n
Rivière, Joan, 243n
Roethke, Theodore, 40, 42, 59, 63; The Lost Son, 29, 50–53, 157, 245n
Rogin, Michael, 261n, 265n
Rosaldo, Michelle and Louise Lamphere, 271n
Rosenberg, Bernard and David Manning White, Mass Culture, 169, 192, 202, 262n, 264n
Rosenberg, Julius and Ethel, 195–9, 203
Rosenfeld, David, 230, 267n, 271n
Ross, Andrew, No Respect, 196, 198–200, 262n, 265n, 266n
Rumens, Carol, 253n
Ruskin, John, 18–19, 240n

Sagar, Keith, 245n
Sage, Lorna, 262n
Salinger, J.D., 174, 188, 255n
Sassoon, Richard, 80, 87, 251n, 259n, 272n
Saturday Evening Post, The, 165, 171, 173
de Saussure, Ferdinand, 267n
Sayle, Murray, 271n
Schidlovsky, John, 255n
Schor, Naomi, 262n
Schreber, Daniel Paul, 4, 55, 211–12
Schwarz, Murray and Coppelia Kahn, 240n
Schweik, Sue, 267n
Scott, Ann, 239n
Segal, Hanna, 'Silence is the Real Crime', 208, 211, 267n
Seidal, Gill, 270n
Sewanee Review, 173–4
Seventeen, 170, 173–4, 179, 203
Sexton, Anne, 35, 36; 'Dancing the Jig', 35, 243n; 'My Friend, My Friend', 217–18, 269n
Shakespeare, William, 140, 151; King Lear 161
Showalter, Elaine, 242n, 256n
Sinfield, Alan, Literature, Politics and Culture in Postwar Britain, 23, 240n, 241n, 257n, 258n, 260n, 262n, 263n, 265n

Smith Library (Rare Book Room), 72, 238, 247n
Smith Review, 199
Smith, Stan, 267n
Snitow, Ann, Christine Stansell and Sharon Thompson, 256n
Spender, Stephen, 'Warnings from the Grave', 17, 24–25, 240n, 242n
Spurling, Hilary, 253n
Stafford, Jean, 263n; A Boston Adventure, 189–91, 229, 265n, 271n; 'Children Are Bored On Sundays', 189–91, 265n
Starr, Mark, 254n
Steiner, George, 214, 250n, 269n
Steiner, Nancy Hunter, 249n
Stevens, Wallace, 167
Stevenson, Anne, 98–9, 253n; Bitter Fame, 14, 17, 41, 66–7, 86, 92–101, 121, 136, 167, 239n, 240n, 244n, 247n, 249n, 252n, 253n, 254n, 255n, 256n, 257n, 258n, 259n, 264n
Stilwell, Robert L., 258n
Stowe, Harriet Beecher, 112
Styron, William, Lie Down in Darkness, 202–3, 234, 266n, 271n
Superman, 180, 182, 199–200

Tabor, Stephen, 251n
Theweleit, Klaus, 260n
Thomas, D.M., The White Hotel, 17, 240n
Thompson, Dorothy, 263n
Thompson, Ian, 252n, 253n
Thwaite, Anthony, 253n,
Time, 186, 223
To Secure These Rights, 197, 265n
Trotter, David, 160, 261n

Uroff, Margaret Dickie, Sylvia Plath and Ted Hughes, 41, 116, 133, 134, 148, 153, 160, 244n, 255n, 257n, 258n, 259n, 260n, 262n

Vance, Carol, 256n
Van Dyne, Susan, 247n, 257n, 258n
Vendler, Helen, 253n

Wagner, Linda (Linda Wagner-Martin), 93, 97, 100, 134, 135, 244n, 247m, 249n, 252n, 257n, 262n
Walker, Alice, The Color Purple, 109–10, 255n
Waters, Ethel, 263n
Weatherby, W.J., 254n, 255n
Weber, Samuel, 271n
Weldon, Fay, Down Among the Women, 1–2
White, Allon, Too Close To The Bone: Fragments of an Autobiography, 37, 60, 244n, 245n; and Peter Stallybrass, 250n
Wiesel, Elie, Night, 216, 269n
Wieseltier, Leon, 205–7, 213–16, 267n
Wilson, Elizabeth, 271n
Wilson, Sloan, The Man in the Gray Flannel Suit, 175
Winnicott, D.W., 270n; 'Creativity and its Origins', 18, 240n
Wollstonecraft, Mary, 167
Women's Day, 171
Wood, James, 253n, 254n
Woodstock, 109
Woolf, Virginia, 120, 145, 189, 198, 256n; A Room of One's Own, 100, 118, 254n; Three Guineas, 232, 271n
Wordsworth, William, 113, 255n
Wright, Richard, Native Son, 107, 110
Wuthering Heights, 112
Wylie, Philip, Generation of Vipers, 165–9, 175, 193, 196, 261n, 262n

Y Gasset, Ortega, The Revolt of the Masses, 197, 265n
Yeats, W.B., 198, 245n, 256n